REGULATING DEVIANCE

The criminal attacks that occurred in the United States on 11 September 2001 have profoundly altered and reshaped the priorities of criminal justice systems around the world. Domestic criminal law has become a vehicle for criminalising 'new' terrorist offences and other transnational forms of criminality. 'Preventative' detention regimes have come to the fore, balancing the scales in favour of security rather than individual liberty. These moves complement already existing shifts in criminal justice policies and ideologies brought about by adjusting to globalisation, economic neo-liberalism and the shift away from the post-war liberal welfare settlement. This collection of essays by leading scholars in the fields of criminal law and procedure, criminology, legal history, law and psychology and the sociology of law, focuses on the future directions for the criminal law in the light of current concerns with state security and regulating 'deviant' behaviour.

Oñati International Series in Law and Society

A SERIES PUBLISHED FOR THE OÑATI INSTITUTE
FOR THE SOCIOLOGY OF LAW

Titles in this Series

Social Dynamics of Crime and Control: New Theories for a World in Transition edited by Susanne Karstedt and Kai Bussmann

Criminal Policy in Transition edited by Andrew Rutherford and Penny Green

Making Law for Families edited by Mavis Maclean

Poverty and the Law edited by Peter Robson and Asbjørn Kjønstad

Adapting Legal Cultures edited by Johannes Feest and David Nelken

Rethinking Law Society and Governance: Foucault's Bequest edited by Gary Wickham and George Pavlich

Rules and Networks edited by Richard Appelbaum, Bill Felstiner and Volkmar Gessner

Women in the World's Legal Professions edited by Ulrike Schultz and Gisela Shaw

Healing the Wounds edited by Marie-Claire Foblets and Trutz von Trotha

Imaginary Boundaries of Justice edited by Ronnie Lippens

Family Law and Family Values edited by Mavis Maclean

Contemporary Issues in the Semiotics of Law edited by Anne Wagner, Tracey Summerfield and Farid Benavides Vanegas

The Geography of Law: Landscapes, Identity and Regulation edited by Bill Taylor

Theory and Method in Socio-Legal Research edited by Reza Banakar and Max Travers

Luhmann on Law and Politics edited by Michael King and Chris Thornhill

Precarious Work, Women and the New Economy: The Challenge to Legal Norms edited by Judy Fudge and Rosemary Owens

Juvenile Law Violators, Human Rights, and the Development of New Juvenile Justice Systems edited by Eric L Jensen and Jørgen Jepsen

The Language Question in Europe and Diverse Societies: Political, Legal and Social Perspectives edited by Dario Castiglione and Chris Longman

European Ways of Law: Towards A European Sociology of Law edited by Volkmar Gessner and David Nelken

Crafting Transnational Policing: Police Capacity-Building and Global Policing Reform edited by Andrew Goldsmith and James Sheptycki

Constitutional Politics in the Middle East: With special reference to Turkey, Iraq, Iran and Afghanistan edited by Saïd Amir Arjomand

Parenting after Partnering: Containing Conflict after Separation edited by Mavis Maclean

Responsible Business: Self-Governance and Law in Transnational Economic Transactions edited by Olaf Dilling, Martin Herberg and Gerd Winter

Rethinking Equality Projects in Law edited by Rosemary Hunter

Regulating Deviance

The Redirection of Criminalisation and the Futures of Criminal Law

Edited by
Bernadette McSherry, Alan Norrie
and Simon Bronitt

Oñati International Series in Law and Society

A SERIES PUBLISHED FOR THE OÑATI INSTITUTE
FOR THE SOCIOLOGY OF LAW

•HART•
PUBLISHING
OXFORD AND PORTLAND OREGON
2009

Published in North America (US and Canada)
by Hart Publishing
c/o International Specialized Book Services
920 NE 58th Avenue, Suite 300
Portland, OR 97213-3786
USA
Tel: +1 503 287 3093 or toll-free: (1) 800 944 6190
Fax: +1 503 280 8832
E-mail: orders@isbs.com
Website: www.isbs.com

Hart Publishing Ltd, 16c Worcester Place, Oxford, OX1 2JW
Telephone: +44 (0)1865 517530 Fax: +44 (0)1865 510710
E-mail: mail@hartpub.co.uk
Website: http://www.hartpub.co.uk

British Library Cataloguing in Publication Data
Data Available

ISBN: 978-1-84113-889-3 (hardback)
ISBN: 978-1-84113-890-9 (paperback)

Typeset by Compuscript, Shannon
Printed and bound in Great Britain by
Lightning Source UK Ltd

Preface

BERNADETTE MCSHERRY, ALAN NORRIE
AND SIMON BRONITT

The essays in this collection were initially presented as papers at a workshop on Regulating Deviance that took place at the International Institute for the Sociology of Law in Onati, Spain in June 2007. The main aim of the workshop was to gather together experts in the fields of criminal law and procedure, criminology, legal history, law and psychology and the sociology of law in order to focus on the future directions for the criminal law in the light of current concerns with state security and regulating 'deviant' behaviour. The papers were subsequently revised and edited to take into account the discussions that took place at the workshop.

The editors would like to thank all those at the International Institute for the Sociology of Law, particularly its Scientific Director, Professor Joxerramon Bengoetxea and administrator, Malen Gordoa Mendizabal for supporting the workshop in June 2007 and José Antonio Azpiazu Elorza for assisting with the publication of this edited collection. The editors also express their gratitude to the contributors for their hard work, dedication and promptness in responding to editorial queries. The other participants in the workshop, Professor Nicola Lacey, Professor Lindsay Farmer and Robert Russo (who delivered a paper co-authored with Professor Wesley Pue) as well as doctoral student Rafael Velandia Montes, all contributed to the development of ideas and the editors thank them for their suggestions.

Thanks also to doctoral students, Danielle Andrewartha and Joanna Kyriakakis for their research assistance, Kathleen Patterson for her administrative and computer skills in putting the collection together and the two reviewers for their helpful comments and suggestions.

Contents

Part IV: The Scope and Justification of Sexual Offences

Part V: Codification and The Liberal Promise

List of Contributors

Kumaralingam Amirthalingam, Professor and Vice Dean (International Programmes), Faculty of Law, National University of Singapore; Director, Asian Law Institute.

Andrew Ashworth, Vinerian Professor of English Law, All Souls College, University of Oxford, UK.

Simon Bronitt, Professor of Law and Director, National Europe Centre, the Australian National University, Australia.

Miriam Gani, Senior Lecturer in Law, The Australian National University, Australia.

Ian Leader-Elliott, Senior Lecturer in Law, University of Adelaide, Australia.

Bernadette McSherry, Professor of Law, Monash University and Australian Research Council Federation Fellow, Australia.

Ngaire Naffine, Professor of Law, University of Adelaide, Australia.

Mark Nolan, Senior Lecturer in Law, The Australian National University, Australia.

Alan Norrie, Edmund-Davies Professor of Criminal Law and Criminal Justice, King's College London, UK.

Peter Ramsay, Lecturer in Law, London School of Economics, UK.

Leslie Sebba, Lawrence D Biele Professor of Law (Emeritus), Institute of Criminology, Hebrew University of Jerusalem, Israel.

Lucia Zedner, Professor of Criminal Justice, Faculty of Law and Corpus Christi College, University of Oxford, UK.

Part I

Introduction

1

Regulating Deviance
The Redirection of Criminalisation and the Futures of Criminal Law

BERNADETTE MCSHERRY, ALAN NORRIE AND SIMON BRONITT

I. INTRODUCTION

THE CRIMINAL ATTACKS that occurred in the United States on 11 September 2001 have profoundly altered and reshaped the priorities of criminal justice systems around the world. Domestic criminal law has become a vehicle for criminalising 'new' terrorist offences and other transnational forms of criminality. 'Preventative' detention regimes have come to the fore, balancing the scales in favour of security rather than individual liberty. These moves complement already existing shifts in criminal justice policies and ideologies brought about by adjusting to globalisation, economic neo-liberalism and the shift away from the post-war liberal welfare settlement. Put together, such developments raise profound questions about the nature of Western criminal justice systems: what have they been and what are they becoming; how do we understand the idea of 'liberal' criminal law and justice; how (and through which general principles) are criminal laws shaped; and what practical and normative resources are at the disposal of criminal justice systems? By examining current changes in the law, and placing them in an overall understanding of what the criminal law is, has been and should be, the chapters presented here together seek to indicate answers to such questions.

The redirection of criminalisation can be described in terms of particular issues such as whether security concerns can be balanced with the traditional rights of the accused; the widening boundaries of the criminal law to include offences of preparation and planning; the scope and justification of offences against the person such as rape, assault and offences of 'indecency'; underlying shifts in penal ideology, including the role of 'victim-driven' criminalisation and their impact on criminal justice practice; the relationships between procedure, substantive criminal law and sentencing; and how a liberal theory of criminal law and justice is to be understood either normatively, critically or historically, or as a combination of all three. The ensuing chapters draw on many of these particular issues.

The inherent plurality of conceptions of the criminal law is caught in this collection's sub-heading: the 'futures' of criminal law. This denotes not just the variety of perspectives that can be adopted in examining the regulation of crime and deviance, but also the differences in terms of place, form and structure that an international and comparative perspective must embrace.

At another level, it is important to recognise that any endorsement of a critical method to understand criminal law and justice must be sympathetic to the variations in historical and cultural experience even in societies that, on the face of it, share common law heritages or trajectories. While many of the chapters are concerned with increased authoritarianism in the law and the neo-liberal state, it is important to see that developments are not all one way. For example, one impact of neo-liberal economic and political globalisation has been a certain liberalisation, in some places at least, in relation to issues of sexuality. The majority of chapters are concerned with the broadening scope of the criminal law, but Singapore's recent debates, discussed in chapter nine, on the possibility of decriminalising homosexual acts as part of broader criminal law reforms provide the opportunity to revisit the delineation of the boundaries of the criminal law from a decriminalisation perspective rather than one that assumes a broadening out of the criminal law.

This collection consists of 12 chapters grouped into five parts: this Introduction; Shifts in Criminal Justice Policies; The Quest for Security; The Scope and Justification of Sexual Offences; and Codification and the Liberal Promise. The following sets out the background to each of these parts.

II. SHIFTS IN CRIMINAL JUSTICE POLICIES

The next chapter, by Alan Norrie, explores different ways of understanding the development of the criminal law in recent years, in terms of changing forms of citizenship and their relationship to law, as well as in terms of changing models of society and how these shape general expectations of the law. Norrie uses these models to explore three broad developments in the criminal law: first, an increasing emphasis on the retributive understanding of criminal behaviour, which is seen in the stress upon the responsibility of individuals for their actions; second, an increasing emphasis on notions of dangerousness for a minority of criminals, for whom exceptional forms of punishment or control are necessary; and third, the development of new forms of criminal justice alongside traditional ideas of crime and punishment. This includes, for example, the development of new forms of control, including preventative detention and control orders for suspected terrorists, and hybrid forms of control and punishment such as the anti-social behaviour order. These developments occur in the context of two linked changes: increased stress on a neo-liberal conception of individual legal subjectivity and increased reliance on the authoritarianism latent in the liberal state and its law.

In chapter three, Lucia Zedner explores the second of Norrie's three developments in the criminal law—dangerousness—by tracing the history of regulating those considered dangerous via models of risk-management through to the current emphasis on the 'precautionary principle' which underpins current pre-emptive measures. These deploy new legal tools and technologies against serious crime and terrorist threats, raising profound questions about the liberal assumptions underpinning most criminal justice thinking.

In chapter four, Leslie Sebba argues that the main thrust of the expansion of criminalisation in traditional areas in the last three decades has been in the area of what may be termed 'victim-driven'—or at least 'victim-oriented'—criminalisation. This type of criminalisation explains the creation of offences such as stalking and sexual harassment, new forms of child abuse, hate crimes, holocaust denial and human trafficking, as well as the expansion of some existing crimes such as rape. His chapter indicates how such developments can be read in different ways—as part of an increasing authoritarianism, but also as an extension of the law's promise to criminalise genuine harm, or perhaps both together. Importantly, the ambiguity of some of the developments that are occurring can be read in the fact that they reflect *both* views. It is this that in part provides authoritarian law with its popular mandate.

From this overview of general shifts in criminal justice policies, the chapters in the next part turn to focus more specifically on measures to regulate crime and deviance in the form of curtailing terrorist activities and anti-social behaviour.

III. THE QUEST FOR SECURITY

Andrew Ashworth in chapter five takes up Norrie's third highlighted development of increasing regulation by examining the spread of 'civil preventative orders'. He argues that the state is rightly concerned with the prevention of harm and reduction of the risk of harm, but that preventative measures involving coercion require justificatory scrutiny. He focuses on rationales for preventative measures in order to evaluate the normative foundations for the various manifestations of the preventative state, and how these might be subjected to control.

Chapter six then focuses more closely on justifications for 'civil preventative orders'. Peter Ramsay points out that such orders have been condemned by liberal criminal law theorists, yet the existence of the power to impose them, and to punish individuals for the breach of them, is not controversial among mainstream politicians, the judiciary, the police and local authorities and it is supported by a large majority of the public. In developing a theory of 'vulnerable autonomy' to help explain the use of civil preventative orders, Ramsay aims to show that in the political world beyond the liberalism of academic criminal law theory, a hugely influential normative argument for such orders already exists, and serves to legitimise this form of penal obligation in practice. Further exemplifying the development of increased regulation, Ramsay indicates the internal malleability of liberal theory, and how it may be pressed against common or traditional understandings towards authoritarian goals. Ramsay picks up Norrie's argument about the shifting historical forms of liberal theory to indicate how liberal law can change under the impact of authoritarian governmental measures. The picture is not always or necessarily clear.

The broad thrust of current developments and their implications do not, of course, leave specific legal forms untouched. Bernadette McSherry in chapter seven turns to the broadening scope of inchoate crimes to include offences of planning and preparation. Concentrating on the case of Faheem Khalid Lodhi, who in 2006 was convicted by the New South Wales Supreme Court of three offences relating to the preparation or planning of a terrorist act, this chapter explores whether such offences should exist at all, whether they can be defined adequately and what punishment they should attract. In the process, it highlights the contours of what liberal criminal lawyers have assumed to be the core understanding of what the law should be, raising questions as to whether such an understanding represents a historical moment that is passing, or something more stable and permanent.

Such concerns do not occur in a vacuum. Decisions to extend legal form and thereby to criminalise in a broader, more authoritarian way occur in the context of public debates that are frequently weighted in favour of particular legal outcomes. This nexus is highlighted in the pairing of McSherry's essay with Mark Nolan's in chapter eight, where he concentrates on what social science can offer the criminal law. Governments often take a tough 'law and order' stance without recourse to contextual material or statistical data. The ways in which public perceptions are shaped by how questions are formulated and asked is highlighted here, and Nolan's chapter provides an overview as to how well-thought-out social science methodology and insights from social psychology can inform public debate on issues of criminalisation. It is apparent that the authoritarian reshaping of the criminal law may be over-determined by political currents, but it is not inevitable, or beyond the reach of responsible policy formation.

IV. THE SCOPE AND JUSTIFICATION OF SEXUAL OFFENCES

The boundaries of the criminal law are tested not only in relation to security issues. They have long been tested in relation to sexual practices. Justice Michael Kirby has summarised this as follows:

> Protecting minors is a proper role of the state. Preventing unwilling [infliction] of violence, injury and loss is a proper role of the state. Protecting the community from gross indecencies in public before unwilling observers, is part of the function of the state, derived from the sovereign's role as keeper of the peace. But intruding into the bedrooms of adults is now considered to be an excess of state power.[1]

In this section are presented two chapters which, focusing on issues of sex, gender and law, cast further light on questions of liberalism and law in the criminal justice field. Kumaralingam Amirthalingam in chapter nine revisits the classic liberal territory of the famous Hart–Devlin debate in assessing Singapore's moves towards the decriminalisation of homosexuality. His analysis provides a timely reminder that the scope of the criminal law may not be forever expanding; from time to time what have been considered offences are no longer thought to be so. Criminal offences will vary across times, across countries.

Amirthalingam's chapter is a worthy reminder that it is by no means clear that social issues should find their resolution through the criminal law. The normative issues of engagement with and openness to other ways of 'being' which lie behind decriminalising homosexuality are also relevant to tackling the often serious threats or harms that recent changes to the criminal law are supposed to address. Whether, to the contrary, the adoption of illiberal methods in the criminal law will help sustain the basic contours of a liberal society is surely open to doubt. However, it would be wrong to think that such issues are simply resolved at the normative level, since, as this collection makes clear, there are deeper historical, social and political forces at work which either sideline traditional liberal ideals and law or push it in new authoritarian directions.

Taking a different tack in chapter ten, Ngaire Naffine focuses on the crime of rape and, arguing from a feminist perspective, considers whether it is in fact the true 'core' crime represented by liberal understanding. While one of the main themes of this book is the broadening of the scope of the criminal law, she argues that such an extension is not always, as often represented, widening from a legitimate core to a more questionable periphery. Rather, the core itself may be questioned.

[1] M Kirby, 'Crime in Australia—Change and Continuity' (1995) 7 *Criminology Australia* 19, 21.

Murder and rape are typically regarded as 'core' crimes, for example in the work of John Gardner who endeavours to explain the true nature of crime and the real basis of criminal responsibility. Naffine argues that Gardner's conceptions of the reasonable person in provocation of 'real rape' assume the quality of a chimera and that this in turn casts doubt on the soundness of the 'core' crime concept within criminal law theory. This is achieved only by standing 'the core' at such a remove from empirical reality and real social concerns as to miss much of the normative truth behind how the law actually works. Naffine's message is an important one: what we understand as a project of criticism of a liberal criminal law must be reflexive as to the meaning of that law, and must not rest on false or simplistic assumptions.

V. CODIFICATION

Concerns about the changing shape of the criminal law often lead to a focus on the potential of codification to control illiberal tendencies. Criminal codes provide a structure for the criminal law in many jurisdictions around the world. While the 19th-century attempts to codify the criminal law failed in the British Isles, the codes drafted in Britain were taken up with enthusiasm by imperial administrators in India and other parts of the British Empire. Indeed, the dominance and influence of codes in common law systems is revealed not only in chapters eleven and twelve, which examine the Australian experience, but also in the key role of the Model Penal Code in the United States. This Penal Code has been the source of judicial inspiration for common law development and the intellectual focus of much American criminal law scholarship.[2] Although the United Kingdom appears stubbornly resistant to the advocacy of codes by law reformers and leading scholars, the liberal aims of codification are nevertheless championed through academic work and, on occasion, receptive appellate courts. This begs the question of whether codification really offers a solution to many of the problems which beset the modern criminal law. A critical consideration of codified systems in chapters eleven and twelve reveals that they too have their own difficulties of interpretation and that the liberal promise of the code is oversold.

In chapter eleven, Simon Bronitt and Miriam Gani point out that the codification of the common law has been presented as the vehicle for delivery of improved accessibility, consistency, comprehensibility and certainty in the criminal law. They examine this liberal promise of codes and codification from both an explanatory and a normative perspective, using

[2] A point made in a recent contribution to the literature on codes by P Robinson and M Dubber, 'The American Model Penal Code: A Brief Overview' (2007) 10 *New Criminal Law Review* 319.

Australia's *Criminal Code* (Cth) as a case study. Codification has always represented the liberal lawyer's promised land, but Bronitt and Gani cast critical light on what a code can deliver, their broad message being that a liberal understanding of law is not necessarily easy to sustain or put into practice, particularly in an illiberal climate of 'law and order' politics. Responses to the reshaping of liberalism may, as many of the chapters in this collection suggest, lie not in law itself but in the broader historical, social, political and policy contexts that law embodies and reflects.

In chapter twelve, Ian Leader-Elliott pursues themes raised by Bronitt and Gani in examining the construction of offences against the person in the Australian *Criminal Code* (Cth). He argues that the Model Criminal Law Officers Committee's original choice of using such offences to help formulate the fault elements set out in Chapter 2 of the *Criminal Code* was unwise. He argues that offences against the person, which are predominantly concerned with the imposition of punishment for causing harm to others, are not typical of the diverse range of offences in a modern criminal code. The Committee's choice to formulate general fault elements based on these offences has therefore caused confusion with the delineation of fault more broadly. This is a more specific engagement than that presented in other essays, but it does illustrate the intrinsic complexity and difficulty in arranging the criminal law in the light of underlying general principles of a liberal normative kind.

VI. CONCLUSION

> A penal code is therefore primarily a product of its time and of the current condition of civil society.[3]

The chapters in this collection reveal the continued durability of liberal ideas in the criminal law, as well as exposing the challenges these ideas face, resulting from their inherent malleability as well as from widespread derogation within current criminal law discourse and practice. The ideas that (re)shape and (re)form the criminal law in each generation are not solely the products of lawyers, far less legal scholars or academics. As George Fletcher points out, the key principles of criminal liability have been 'crystallized primarily in the writing of scholars rather than the opinions of courts'.[4] Yet in the modern law, the scholars' role in constituting the boundaries of criminalisation receives scant attention, whether due to academic self-effacement or the narrow ledge of political legitimacy which legal scholars typically occupy.

[3] GWF Hegel, 'Philosophy of Right' (1821) para 218 in AW Wood (ed) and HB Nisbet (tr), *Elements of the Philosophy of Right* (Cambridge, Cambridge University Press, 1991) 251.

[4] GP Fletcher, *The Grammar of Criminal Law* (Oxford, Oxford University Press, 2007) 91.

This generates a tension in the academic role. On one hand, many legal scholars are not external spectators of the law, but rather play a constitutive role as a caste of (more or less) authoritative legal interpreters engaged in the rationalisation and modernisation of the criminal law. On the other hand, they bear responsibility to interrogate the problems of the law, and to seek to understand its inherent dynamics, its shifts and developments. Legal scholars do not represent a homogenous caste, and the chapters in this collection reflect some of the scholarly diversity of opinion as well as the general concern that criminal law is moving in new and dangerous directions. While there may be many different 'futures' for the criminal law, a focus on present developments gives rise to real concerns as to the present direction of travel. In identifying such changes and by seeking to understand them in the context of deeper social developments, this collection seeks to contribute to debate about how matters will and ought to proceed.

Part II

Shifts in Criminal Justice Policies

2

Citizenship, Authoritarianism and the Changing Shape of the Criminal Law

ALAN NORRIE

I. INTRODUCTION

IN THIS CHAPTER I want to think about the changing forms of the criminal law, and to seek to identify those structural conditions, forces and developments which predicate its shape and development. Many of the chapters in this collection deal with particular issues emerging within the criminal law. In contrast, I plan to sketch some more general elements and to provide some ideas towards a 'structural history of the legal present'.[1] My aim will be to problematise the relationship between 'law' and 'authoritarianism' by suggesting that what is often seen as an opposition in liberal legal theory in fact involves a relation of mutual implication or co-entailment. Liberal law possesses authoritarian dimensions along two axes.

To make my argument, I propose to return to the two ideas underlying my book, *Crime, Reason and History*,[2] concerning the nature of legal individualism and the conflicts which inform it. They were in their original form schematically presented, and I hope to develop them in order to help understand the complex structures that shape recent developments in the modern criminal law. These ideas focus on the 'psychological' and the 'political' aspects of the law's individualist core. It is these two aspects which constitute the axes along which law's authoritarianism can be analysed.

This chapter will take two different directions and then I will try to bring them together in a discussion of the present. One direction is to explore more concretely the historical trajectory of legal individualism canvassed in my previous work to take account of TH Marshall's analysis of three

[1] D Garland, *The Culture of Control: Crime and Social Order in Contemporary Society* (Oxford, Oxford University Press, 2001).

[2] A Norrie, *Crime, Reason and History* 2nd edn (Cambridge, Cambridge University Press, 2001).

different forms of citizenship and rights within modern liberal society: those pertaining to the civil, the political and the social spheres. I will argue that the key to the development of the post-war criminal law was the *fusion* of these three forms of citizenship in the period of consensus that began after 1945 and came to an end in the 1970s. I will then suggest that one way to understand developments over recent years is in terms of the unravelling of the post-war consensus. This involves an unravelling of the three forms of citizenship and a resulting reconfiguration. In their newly *fissile* condition, new possibilities, conflicts and contradictions for criminal law and justice emerged. In the process, the authoritarianism at the core of legal individualism becomes more evident. I deal with this in section II of this chapter.

Thinking about the changing configuration of legal forms also involves thinking in a second direction: that of exploring the relationship between liberal criminal justice and forms of authoritarian government. In section III, my focus will be on Franz Neumann's often neglected essay on the 'Change in the Function of Law in Modern Society', which was originally published in English in 1939 and then in his posthumous volume *The Democratic and Authoritarian State*.[3] I think that if the history of the legal present is to be understood, the nature of state authoritarianism as a structural force in modern law needs to be taken seriously. My overall argument will be that the unravelling of the different forms of rights and the way they are reconfigured owes much to their being placed in the general context of a form of state power that can be characterised as authoritarian and a form of (liberal) law that enables this. However, I want to stress that what comes out of this is a sense not of a single direction or shape to the criminal law, but a set of complexities in which legal forms habitually reveal different aspects, and in which one can talk of hybridity[4] or many-sided inflection within a structural context.

If the major focus of this chapter is the historical structuring of legal forms, I want to anchor the discussion in the particular. In this introductory part, I will outline three broad developments in recent criminal law and justice, which will represent a tentative preliminary focus for the discussion that follows. Then, in the final section, section IV, I will return to these and think specifically about the changing shape of law today.

[3] F Neumann, *The Democratic and the Authoritarian State* (Glencoe, Free Press, 1957); see also his belatedly published doctoral work *The Rule of Law* (Leamington Spa, Berg, 1986). Quotes in the text below are from the 1957 text. For an interesting recent analysis of criminal law with parallel implications, see M Dubber, *The Police Power* (New York, Columbia, 2005).

[4] Compare N Lacey, 'Space, Time and Function: Intersecting Principles of Responsibility Across the Terrain of Criminal Justice' (2007) 1 *Criminal Law and Philosophy* 233 and my accompanying comment 'Historical Differentiation, Moral Judgment and the Modern Criminal Law' (2007) 1 *Criminal Law and Philosophy* 251, on which I draw below.

The three broad developments I have in mind are:

(1) an increasing emphasis on the retributive understanding of criminal behaviour, which is seen in the stress upon the responsibility of individuals for their actions. This involves a decline of rehabilitation as a significant ideology of punishment, an emphasis on notions of moral right and wrong particularly in the recognition of the role of the victim in the system (explored by Leslie Sebba in chapter four), and an increasing reliance on imprisonment as a mode of punishment, even if it does no good. Let us call this a tendency to increased *responsibilisation*, noting, however, that this denotes a different use of the term than that deployed in some recent literature.[5]

(2) an increasing emphasis, in conjunction with, but also in some ways in opposition to, (1), on notions of dangerousness for a minority of criminals, for whom exceptional forms of punishment or control are necessary. This is seen in an increased reliance on mandatory forms of punishment for repeat offences of certain kinds, but also in the development of new categories of offender such as the 'terrorist' (explored by Bernadette McSherry in chapter seven and by Simon Bronitt and Miriam Gani in chapter eleven), for whom new forms of control and surveillance are required alongside severe forms of punishment. Let us call this a tendency to increasing *dangerousness*.

(3) the development of new forms of criminal justice alongside traditional ideas of crime and punishment such as the development of new forms of control, as mentioned in (2). These include control orders for terrorists, but also new hybrid forms of control and punishment such as the anti-social behaviour order (ASBO) and other forms of preventative orders concerning, for example, sexual conduct that have sprung up. Such forms of control are analysed by Lucia Zedner in chapter three, Andrew Ashworth in chapter five and Peter Ramsay in chapter six. These forms of control can be seen as net-spreading activities, but they invoke new forms of criminal justice in the process. Let us call this a tendency to increasing *regulation*.

I will return to these developments in the final section, section IV. With these introductory comments in mind, I now turn to the two ideas from *Crime, Reason and History* that I wish to develop. These concern the conflicts that are contained within the 'psychological' and the 'political' dimension of law's individualism. Considering how these ideas should be

[5] For example, Garland, above n 1, at 124, discusses responsibilisation as involving indirect forms of social control relying on individuals policing themselves and their environment. This reading of responsibilisation in terms of a Foucauldian 'governmentality' thesis is very important, but I want to emphasise the increased reliance on the formal legal invocation of individual responsibility here.

developed helps in thinking about the changing historical character of law and the citizenship contexts in which it operates. Both disclose, though in different ways, liberal law's relationship to authoritarian governance.

II. CITIZENSHIP AND LEGAL FORM

In this section, I begin by outlining the oppositions that pertain to the psychological and political aspects of the form of legal individualism at the core of modern law. I then identify important limits on the way I addressed those forms in earlier work. One problem concerns the historically differentiated nature of modern legal forms and the need to periodise more adequately their development. These matters are considered in the context of an engagement with Marshall's three forms of citizenship. A second problem identified in this section concerns the co-existence of oppositional elements of freedom and political power within the modern law. The first problem relates to what I have called the law's 'psychological' individualism, the second to its 'political' individualism, though it should be noted that these are dialectically connected aspects of the same thing: the modern form of law. I will now outline these two aspects of modern individualist law and then contextualise the idea of the responsible subject in terms of Marshall's threefold conception of citizenship.

A. Psychological and Political Individualism in Criminal Law

One way of understanding criminal law, I have argued,[6] is to see its doctrine as structured around the liberal idea of the juridical individual, which emphasises individual responsibility as the basis for punishment through central categories of physical and fault elements and the defences. However, law is essentially a relational phenomenon, mediating underlying social conditions, structures and relations, and these make the juridical individual the site of two basic oppositions which play out as contradictions within the law. Legal individualism can be seen to possess both a 'psychological' and a 'political' dimension. The first of these emphasises the importance of human agency through 'psychologistic' ideas of intention, voluntariness of acts, and reason for finding that an individual is responsible for his or her actions. This was, in historical terms, as Adorno puts it, an 'assist to freedom' under modern conditions,[7] but its morally progressive and expressive quality was immediately limited by the fact that the universal attributes of human freedom recognised in law excluded contextual and motivational

[6] Norrie, above n 2, at chs 2 and 11.
[7] T Adorno, *Negative Dialectics* (London, Routledge, 1973) 238.

conditions for action. As a result, the model of the juridical individual finessed substantive moral and political justifications and differences as well as the deep-rooted social conflicts that predicated them.

The psychological individual, I argued, 'is a political and ideological construction which operates to seal off the question of individual culpability from issues concerning the relationship between individual agency and social context'.[8] If it operates in a morally *expressive* way, that is, by way of valuing individual freedom, as liberal theory tells us, it also possesses an important *repressive* function, albeit one that is articulated in a seeming paradox in the language of human freedom. This combination of expressivity and repression gives law its double-edged quality, and can be regarded as the 'cunning of legality': it is at the same time legitimating and co-ordinative.[9]

The nature, the significance and the value of this claim have been debated,[10] and I have sought to defend and develop its relevance for criminal law in different ways.[11] I do not intend to pursue that ground here. What I want to do instead is to note the limits the argument has for thinking about the history of modern criminal justice. It is too schematic to pick up properly two issues.[12]

The first issue is the growth and impact of forms of regulative or welfare-oriented criminal law from the second half of the 19th century, which became the basis for those many strict liability offences which make up the bulk of the criminal law today.[13] Psychological individualism is relevant primarily to those offences which are regarded, mostly, but not always, appropriately, as the most serious offences in the criminal calendar: those which 'count down' from murder. How can an argument which sees psychological individualism as core to the development of the modern criminal law account for the existence of strict liability offences?

A second related issue concerns historical 'periodisation'. *Crime, Reason and History* sees the foundations of the modern criminal law in the first

[8] Norrie, above n 2, at 223.

[9] By the latter, I mean the way in which law forces and canalises action through power. There is a difference in the way the German and the Anglo–American traditions think of 'co-ordination': in the latter, it can be presented in anodyne terms as facilitating the smooth running of society, for example, through 'rules of the road'. In the former, it can be understood as involving the exercise of authoritarian force, of forcing people to conform their conduct to norms they might otherwise resist.

[10] See A Duff, 'Principle and Contradiction in the Criminal Law: Motives and Criminal Liability' in A Duff (ed), *Philosophy and the Criminal Law* (New York, Cambridge University Press, 1998); J Horder, 'On the Irrelevance of Motive in Criminal Law' in J Horder (ed), *Oxford Essays in Jurisprudence: 4th Series* (Oxford, Oxford University Press, 2000).

[11] A Norrie, *Punishment, Responsibility and Justice* (Oxford, Oxford University Press, 2000); *Law and the Beautiful Soul* (London, Routledge-Cavendish, 2005).

[12] P Ramsay, 'The Responsible Subject as Citizen: Criminal Law, Democracy and the Authoritarian State' (2006) 64 *MLR* 29.

[13] L Farmer, *Criminal Law, Tradition and Legal Order* (Cambridge, Cambridge University Press, 1997).

half of the 19th century, in particular in the Bentham-inspired work of the Victorian Criminal Law Commissioners. It has, however, been pointed out that, while they may be the forerunners of the modern orthodox subjectivist approach which dominated English criminal law in the 1960s and 1970s, and to some extent to this day, it was not until the post-war period that orthodox subjectivism became dominant.[14] For most of the 19th century and the first half of the 20th, the law was a mixture of different forms of objectivist as well as subjectivist elements.[15] It was only with the eminence of Glanville Williams, Sir John Smith and HLA Hart, and the impact of reform documents concerning capital punishment, homosexuality and prostitution in the 1950s and 1960s, that a recognisably liberal project with the responsible psychological individual at its core came into its own. The question is, then: why should there be this time lag? What else was going on, and what held things back? Why the fruition of orthodox subjectivism only one hundred and more years after it was first thought of? Attempting to answer these questions indicates a better way of understanding the structural history of our present, and I will develop it below.

Just before doing so, however, let me say something about the limitations of my previous position on the law's *political* individualism. Turning from the psychological to the political dimension of the legal individual, here the original argument is also truncated. Essentially, what it does is to observe that legal individualism claims the freedom of the individual as its starting point, but individual legal freedom is organised within a political system and with regard to a need for social control that limits its possibilities. Criminal law is not just about the moral relations between individuals; it is also the basis for a system of state control over individuals, and as such there is a constant possibility that arguments based upon state necessity will kick in to negate ideas of individual right and responsibility. This is seen in the criminal law in the frequent resort to 'policy' concerns over those of 'principle', and this, I argued, is a structuring opposition *inside* law that flows from the conflict between individual freedom and political power it embodies. Again, however, this is a rather limited view of the matter and further thought needs to be given to precisely what is the nature of this overriding political power. Plainly the idea of such a power intervening against individual rights suggests an authoritarian element within the law, but how does it work, and does it have different effects in different periods? Are communities more or less prone to authoritarian interventions today, and if so how does authoritarianism shape legal forms and responses? In section III, I will consider this question in discussing Neumann's work.

[14] N Lacey, 'Contingency, Coherence and Conceptualism' in A Duff (ed), *Philosophy and the Criminal Law* (New York, Cambridge University Press, 1998).

[15] J Horder, 'Two Histories and Four Hidden Principles of *Mens Rea*' (1997) 113 *LQR* 95.

My overall aim is to argue that developing a sense of the contexts in which legal individualism is embedded, in both its psychological and political aspects, provides a better understanding of the structural forces that give us our legal present. In particular this will involve relating the idea of subjective right contained in the law's psychological individualism to the development of citizenship forms in modern society, and this is discussed immediately below (see section B). Thereafter, it will involve thinking about subjective right as a liberal political argument in the context of what it means to call modern societies authoritarian (see section C). The goal is to reflect on where modern Western societies are in terms of how they deploy ideas of subjective right in legal practice today.

B. Three Forms of Citizenship and Their Dynamic

An effective way of dealing with the problems I have identified in a psychological individualist account of criminal law is provided by Peter Ramsay's recent work.[16] This focuses on the differential impact of three conceptions of citizenship identified by TH Marshall as emerging from the 19th century onwards.

The earliest form of modern individual citizenship for Marshall is the *civil* form, which involves rights necessary for individual, primarily economic, freedom. This is particularly linked with individual property rights, and came into existence in England in the 18th century. While this form of citizenship is associated with the rights and interests of the property-owning citizen, it provides a foundation for thinking about political freedoms more generally and therefore about criminal justice and the rights and responsibilities of citizens as a universal category. Such a conception of civil citizenship is a necessary, but not a sufficient, condition for criminal law to be based upon the idea of the free individual subject. For this to happen, the second form of what Marshall calls *political* citizenship[17] is also necessary.

Political citizenship involves a further commitment not just to individual rights and liberties but also to a universal order in which every individual has the right to participate in political decision-making. Once that is introduced, the basic form of the responsible individual introduced by a civil conception of citizenship can be generalised politically to all relevant areas of social life, including criminal law. Of course, the introduction of the rights of political citizenship took many years to be introduced for both

[16] Ramsay, above n 12.

[17] Note that Marshall's use of the term 'political' to denote the move to public and universal notions of citizenship is distinct from my use of the term to denote one contradiction—that between individual freedom and state power—within the law's individualist core.

men and (particularly) women, but the British utilitarians, in conceiving of society in universal terms as based upon the pursuit of individual interest, took a first step in that direction. In so doing, they laid the groundwork for a subjectivist account of criminal law and responsibility, and it was this that was introduced in law reform documents in the first half of the 19th century by the Victorian Criminal Law Commissioners.

What, however, of the time lag noted above? As stated, this model only came to practical fruition in the second half of the 20th century, while political citizenship rights date from the end of the 19th and early 20th centuries. This was after a government had come to power committed to a radical opening up of channels of political citizenship in the wake of the Second World War and resulting social expectations. But the advent of civil and political citizenship rights per se was insufficient by itself to determine the modern development of the criminal law. Something else was needed to push this through.

Marshall's third form of citizenship—*social* citizenship—was introduced from the late 19th century onwards and had the effect among others of introducing standards of social and economic welfare into penal measures across a range of aspects of life. One effect of social citizenship was to produce those forms of regulation that generate alternatives to subjectivist, capacity-based approaches to individual responsibility, and which focus more on the control of outcomes than on fault and blame. The growth of regulatory offences from the late 19th century can be explained according to the rise of this third form of citizenship, which, slotted in alongside the first two, provides for the juxtaposition of two rather different forms of criminal law regulation in modern society, one outcome/strict liability based, the other capacity, fault and responsibility based.

Marshall's account of the three forms of citizenship is helpful in terms of explaining the gaps in my previous analysis. It helps explain, as I have just noted, the first problem identified above, the co-existence of strict liability alongside forms of individual responsibility in the modern criminal law. If civil/political citizenship generates the conception of the responsible individual, social citizenship generates the conception of strict liability. How, though, does it help explain the problem of time lag, that it was only the period from the 1950s to the 1970s that represented the fruition of the capacity-based, orthodox subjectivist, liberal project based on the psychologically free, responsible individual? Why was *this* in particular the time of these ideas' dominance, when universal political citizenship had been around for a much longer time? Was it just the political radicalism of the post-war government?

My suggestion is that this was the period in which the three ideas of citizenship—civil, political and social—came together, and that the historical fusion of a social conception of citizenship rights with an already existing civil/political conception gave real impetus to the civil/political conception.

The dominant liberal conception of the criminal law is shaped by the civil commitment to personal freedom and the political commitment that this should be universalised and generalised. What the new post-war social welfare commitment did was, in combining with the civil and the political commitments, to add a drive to 'perfect' the existing commitments to civil and political freedoms, to insist that they should be actualised in practice. While earlier individualistic freedoms of a civil and political form were not sufficient for the social welfarist vision, they were nonetheless a necessary component of the good society that would be completed by the introduction of social welfare measures. For example, the poor not only required welfare benefits, they also needed rights and access to legal services to achieve those benefits and to emancipate themselves before the law and the state. The universalisation of legal freedoms invoked by political citizenship would have to be actualised fully in any world in which social citizenship also played a significant part. Pushing beyond the civil and political, social citizenship of necessity included implementation of these other, in a sense 'lesser', forms of citizenship, and the legal freedoms they embodied.

To be sure, this historical fusion of different purposes also resulted in tensions between civil and political conceptions of citizenship and the newer social conceptions, as seen, for example, in conflicts between lawyers, social scientists and proponents of the 'psy-disciplines' of the period,[18] but the drive beyond civil and political citizenship notions still gave a new thrust to their development and actualisation. If the post-war Welfare State were not also a state committed to civil and political liberties, it would not have been true to the underlying, though complex and conflicted, inter-relation between the different forms of citizenship.[19] Under the aegis of a commitment to social citizenship, there was a joint thrust of the different kinds of citizenship rights, and the criminal law model of the responsible individual flourished as one deduction from the form of political citizenship within an overall liberal-welfarist, social democratic project. The time lag was, then, due to the fact that it was only after the Second World War that this fusion of rights-based purposes occurred.

I have elaborated the place of a liberal theory of responsibility in modern society because I think it helps to understand what is happening to the law today. If the post-war period involved a coming together of civil, political and social forms of citizenship so that the growth of the political was encouraged under the aegis of the social, the relationship between these forms has proved more problematic from the 1970s onwards. What

[18] See HLA Hart, *Punishment, Responsibility and Justice* (London, Oxford University Press, 1963) ch 2; compare Lacey, above n 14.

[19] This is why the Western welfare-liberal polities of the 1960s were also engaged in struggles for basic democratic rights, in the southern states of the USA and in Northern Ireland. The broader liberating dimension pulled the narrower, more basic one along in its wake.

has occurred over the last 25 years or so has been a series of attacks on the idea of social citizenship in its post-war welfarist form in the name of neo-liberal economic, social and political policies. This has tended to set the different strands of citizenship in Marshall's vision against each other so that conflicts between forms of rights, which had been less apparent previously, have surfaced. The underlying dynamic has been an attack on social citizenship in the name of civil citizenship, with political citizenship caught in the middle. By this, I mean that the core idea of the economically self-interested individual, *homo economicus*, which originally animated the idea of civil citizenship, has become the core idea legitimating the stripping back of welfare measures, and therefore an attack on social citizenship. A neo-liberal polity sets civil (individualist, economic) citizenship against social citizenship, challenging the latter in the name of the former.

What of political citizenship in this context? In the process of the civil attack on social citizenship, political citizenship comes to play a dual, complex and contradictory role. On the one hand, since the political individual is seen as reflecting the interests of the ('private') economic individual in the ('public') sphere of state activity, the political rights and freedoms of the individual are portrayed as an important element in the neo-liberal economy and polity. 'Freedom from state intervention' and 'under the rule of law' become legitimating slogans associated with the critique of the Welfare State. To be a libertarian in civil or economic terms is also to be one in political terms. In the sphere of criminal justice, this is observed in the increased weight placed upon libertarian ideas of decriminalisation, the idea of 'doing justice' through the criminal process, and on a retributive philosophy of punishment based upon the responsibility of the individual. The increased responsibilisation strategy referred to in the Introduction is rooted in this development. Until the 1980s, something of a balance was sought between individual and social conceptions of responsibility and justice. Thereafter, more weight was placed on individual responsibility, in opposition to demands based upon a social conception.

On the other hand, political liberty comes under attack in a neo-liberal polity as the drive to restore economic or civil liberty, or the 'discipline of the market', encounters social opposition. As a result, conservative and authoritarian modes of governance are deployed to secure the market order against the demands of political citizenship for more freedom. In the neo-liberal world, civil citizenship tends also to split off from its fractious bed-fellow political citizenship, and the latter is placed in question. Without the protective cover social citizenship gave to it, political citizenship operates both as a legitimating rhetoric for change and practice and, contradictorily, as a barrier to be overcome where necessary. In sum, where the sense that the state should support and protect the individual in socially substantive or welfarist ways is lost, political citizenship is both held up as crucial to individual liberty and seen as a threat to it.

To summarise this broad history of the present, my argument is that the overall political and historical dynamic from social democracy and welfare to neo-liberalism has reconfigured the relation between civil, political and social forms of citizenship. Fusion of purpose is replaced by fission in a way that brings out more clearly the latent conflicts between these forms, and sets them against each other. This is seen in a conflict in the treatment of political citizenship under modern conditions. This is the form of citizenship most relevant to the classic form of the responsible legal individual within the criminal law, and it means that the present period treats that law in an ambivalent way. On the one hand, it prioritises law and responsibility as a primary legitimating device for the neo-liberal polity; on the other, it looks askance at its claims on behalf of individual freedom where social order appears, or is presented as being, under threat. I will return to this issue of the evolving relation between different citizenship forms and their impact on the changing shape of the criminal law in section IV. For now, I want to move to a discussion of law and authoritarianism, for neo-liberal strategies on citizenship are closely aligned with authoritarian state responses to opposition to change. So doing, we move from considering the nature of the law's psychological to its political individualism.

III. LAW AND AUTHORITARIANISM: THE WORK OF FRANZ NEUMANN

Turning now to the second, 'political', conflict of legal individualism, between individual right and social power, I want to consider this in the context of what it means to talk about an authoritarian state. Such a concept may in recent years have seemed surpassed in light of the depiction of authoritarianism present in everyday life inspired by Foucault's work on 'discipline' and 'governmentality'.[20] Developments of new capabilities and technologies, including technologies of the self, have focused attention away from the state and onto the ways in which power operates through a variety of individual, informal, non-state (but also state-sponsored) media.[21]

Notwithstanding these important arguments, I think it is still helpful to return to a discussion of state authoritarianism, for two reasons. The first is that recent developments, which are the subject of discussion in this book, indicate clearly the ways in which the state remains at the core of significant developments of an authoritarian kind. The second is that, while it is of course true that the life of the law is lived and experienced

[20] M Foucault, *Discipline and Punish* (Harmondsworth, Allen Lane, 1977); 'Governmentality' in G Burchell *et al*, *The Foucault Effect* (Hemel Hempstead, Harvester Wheatsheaf, 1991).

[21] See Garland, n 1, at 124–7.

across a society, it nonetheless has a crucially significant formative locus in the institutions of the state. In thinking about authoritarian law, it is hard to avoid considering state authoritarianism. For these reasons, I have gone back to Franz Neumann's work[22] on the changing functions of law and the state in modern society. Neumann in fact wrote this essay just before the Second World War, as a refugee from German fascism. It considers how law changed from classic 19th-century forms concerning the *Rechtsstaat* to those interventionist forms associated first with the Weimar Republic, and then, on an increased scale, with fascism, totalitarianism and authoritarianism in Nazi Germany. Because of its specific historical context, and the fact that Neumann associates the authoritarian state with fascism, his analysis needs to be treated with some caution. It would take a fair imagination to describe—other than rhetorically—a society such as Britain today as 'fascist'. Nonetheless, there are components of the authoritarian state that are generic. If Neumann is taken to be describing the extreme case, his analysis can be used to see how things work in an intermediate case such as is provided by the fading, authoritarian democracies of the West today.

A. Between Liberal–Legal Right and the '*Arcanum Dominationis*'

The starting point in understanding Neumann's work is his account of the liberal–legal polity, and its *intrinsic* linkage to authoritarianism, before getting to the idea of the authoritarian state per se. Thinking of the classic liberal state generally brings to mind the 'negative state' or the Lockeian 'night-watchman state': a state with limited functions and forms of power. However, Neumann notes that there is a serious mistake in associating 'negativeness' with 'weakness'. The liberal state, to the contrary,

> has always been as strong as the political and social situation and the interests of society demanded. It has conducted warfare and crushed strikes; with the help of strong navies it has protected its investments, with the help of strong armies it has defended and extended its boundaries, with the help of the police it has restored 'peace and order'.[23]

In short, the liberal state has 'been a strong state precisely in those spheres in which it had to be strong and in which it wanted to be strong'.[24] Accordingly, the image of the liberal state as one resting on 'right' as opposed to 'might' is from the beginning a false one. The liberal state—and its law—work *through* oppositions they embody, between law and force, freedom and sovereignty,

[22] Neumann, above n 3.
[23] Neumann, above n 3, at 22.
[24] *Ibid.*

ratio (the articulation of freedoms) and *voluntas* (the expression of power), between 'subjective right' and 'objective right' (the last in the German legal context). Intrinsic opposition is reflected from the very beginning of liberalism in Locke's philosophy, for whom the state rests upon the rights of the people, but who also recognises state prerogative powers reflecting sovereign necessity. To these constitutive oppositions, I would add the one that informs *Crime, Reason and History*—individual right versus state power—to argue that liberal criminal law contains *both* individualist legal form *and* a power that over-reaches or surpasses it: what one might call an 'extra-legal power'. This formulation is not, however, quite right, because what is constitutive of law must be already within it. That law embodies 'extra-legal power' already indicates that what is described as 'extra-legal' is no such thing. The vision that liberal lawyers endorse of the possibility of regulating or taming power through law is a false one, for liberal law already entails, indeed is 'contaminated' by, that which it would control. Modern liberal law *combines* in its form individualist right and political necessity.

If the authoritarian dimension *within* liberal law is recognised, is it nonetheless possible to think of a development *beyond* liberal law, to a more authoritarian form of rule? The answer for Neumann lay in the way in which the axis constructed by the polar oppositions of liberal law moves increasingly towards one pole as a liberal society becomes more authoritarian. Law comes increasingly to support force over law, sovereign power over individual freedom, will over reason, and objective over subjective right. Under the extreme case of fascism, law becomes 'nothing but a technical instrument for the execution of certain political objectives; it is nothing but the command of the ruler'.[25] Accordingly the legal theory of the achieved authoritarian state is 'decisionism and law is nothing but an *arcanum dominationis*, i.e. a means serving the stabilisation of power',[26] and this occurs through a progressive shifting towards one pole in an oppositional form.

It is important to pursue Neumann's analysis a little further into his account of the distinctions between a liberal and an authoritarian legal order. In order to get to law as *arcanum dominationis*, those features of liberal law associated with freedom, reason and subjective right have to be discarded. What are these? Neumann suggests three special features of liberal legal form: that law must be formulated in general terms, and not be specifically addressed to individuals; it must at the same time be formulated with a high degree of specificity so that discretion in its application is removed; and it must not be retroactive. One could, I think, add more: a fourth feature would be that law must to a significant extent respect the

[25] Neumann, above n 3, at 61.
[26] *Ibid.*

freedom of individuals in ways associated with Marshall's account of civil and political rights. Liberal legality operates where these elements are held in balance or tension alongside matters of sovereign power and will.

Despite the emphasis on oppositions, this seems a fairly positive account of liberal law, but Neumann is no wide-eyed supporter of the liberal state and its law. This comes out when he discusses the different functions of liberal law, of which he identifies three:

> All three functions of the generality of laws—obscuring the domination of the bourgeoisie, rendering the economic system calculable, and guaranteeing a minimum of liberty and equality—are of decisive importance.[27]

The first of these gives Neumann's account its most critical quality. He argues that liberal law obscures domination in a conflicted and exploitative society. Second, it provides calculability for the economic system and therefore protects its functioning. Third, it guarantees minimum levels of liberty and equality across the board. In the second and third of these functions, Neumann's analysis aligns with Marshall's account of the significance of civil and political rights under capitalism. In the first, however, his position is more critical, and is aligned with the argument I sketched in section II concerning the distinct yet conjoined 'legitimative' and 'co-ordinative' ideological qualities of modern law. To speak of the domination achieved through law in a conflicted and exploitative society refers back to the repressive function of modern law with regard to the law's psychological individualism. It is important, I will argue, to hold on to this function in order to grasp fully what is significant in modern law.

Despite this inherently repressive, exploitation-masking function of modern law, the fact that it also guarantees calculability and minimal liberty and equality entails that a contrast must still be drawn between a liberal and an authoritarian system, where the functions and the form of law both change. Neumann associated the rise of fascism in Germany with the onset of the period of monopoly capitalism, in which cartels and big business dominated social life. In such a society, the economic function of calculability was less important because business wielded power through its size rather than through law, and the general guarantee of liberty and equality was also rendered otiose.

Domination also assumed different forms, through the emphasis on the role of 'the Leader' and the construction of 'the enemy' either within or without, or both.[28] In this situation, 'new auxiliary institutions' arose to promulgate and enforce the direct commands of the sovereign, or, as it was called, 'Leader' (*Führer*), state as administrative acts 'which directly protect the

[27] Neumann, above n 3, at 42.
[28] Neumann, above n 3, at 193.

interests of the monopolist and restrict or abolish the old guaranties'.[29] Law itself undergoes a radical change in which flexible 'general principles' concerning 'good conscience', the 'will of the people', or the general values of the fascist polity take over from general rules. These lack specificity, becoming a broad licence to interpret actions according to a Leadership principle. Under this approach, generality of rule and the specificity required for individual liberties are lost, and retroactivity becomes possible. As a result, in the authoritarian state 'all restraints are abolished which parliamentary democracy, even when functioning badly, had erected against the unlimited execution of the requirements of monopolies'.[30] Law, which should involve *voluntas* and *ratio*, ceases eventually to be law as it becomes associated purely with *voluntas*, an *arcanum dominationis*. This, then, is Neumann's sophisticated analysis of the changing functions and forms of law as they evolved from the Weimar Republic to Nazi Germany. The next section explores its significance for thinking about legal authoritarianism today.

B. Authoritarianism and Legitimation Pre- and Post-War

Does Neumann's analysis translate to the post-war, post-fascist world? Neumann's account is bound up with a particular historical experience, but he did return to these themes in work produced after the Second World War.[31] Here he maintained the relevance of his discussion for contrasting democratic and authoritarian modes of government in the new socio–political context, but modified his position in one crucial aspect. In the post-war world, he identified the importance of the citizen's alienation from government in an 'I-don't-care' attitude, the shrinking from political matters, and the failure to offer alternatives as factors which 'play into the hands of demagogues, and ... may lead to caesarism'.[32] Underlying factors included the growing complexity of government, the growth of public and private bureaucracies, the concentration of power in private hands, and the hardening of political parties into machines. This is plainly a set of descriptions that differs from, though perhaps in some ways overlaps with, the earlier 'monopoly capitalist' thesis. The growth of collective power and the marginalisation of law are both present, but their nature and circumstances are described differently.

One important change, however, is that Neumann became less hard on liberal law than previously. Where earlier he had viewed such law as rooted

[29] Neumann, above n 3, at 58.
[30] Neumann, above n 3, at 59.
[31] 'The Concept of Political Freedom', published in Neumann, above n 3, was written in 1953.
[32] Neumann, above n 3, at 190.

in the vectors of social and economic power, after the war, his position became more ambivalent. In his essay 'The Concept of Political Power', he maintained the view that 'within the scope of the juristic concept of liberty, escape clauses like the clear and present danger formula permit political power to prevail over individual rights',[33] but he also wrote of law's 'traditional guarantees' and minimal liberties as being undermined not from within but from without by new socio-economic developments. He depicted law as involved in a democratic process whose aim is 'maximising the freedom of man', and whose integrating element 'is a moral one, whether it be freedom or justice'. To this liberal conception of the embedding of law in a dynamic of justice and democracy, and involving traditional minimal guarantees of freedom, Neumann now straightforwardly opposed the authoritarian (fascist) integrating principle that fear of an enemy, either within or without, is the key to legitimation.[34] Liberal law in this view becomes the locus of freedom and justice in opposition to power rather than itself the locus of their opposition. It is seen as on the side of right *against* authoritarianism, rather than as imbued with authoritarianism itself. In terms of analysing the relationship between freedom and power, freedom is regarded as inside law, whereas power is outside it.

In order to make this argument, Neumann also changed his view of the functions of law. It will be recalled that in his earlier essay he wrote of liberal law's different and conflicting functions of ensuring domination, calculability and freedom/equality. In this post-war work, the first of these functions becomes invisible when law's freedom is aligned with democratic process and the broadening of justice. I would argue against this that it is necessary to continue to think of the place of authoritarianism in modern law in terms of the more complex picture Neumann presented in his pre-war essay. There, his account of the dominatory aspect of modern law plus his account of law as containing both freedom- and power-related oppositions seems to me to be more profound and more helpful in terms of understanding law and authoritarianism today.

IV. SHAPING THE CRIMINAL LAW

In this final part, I want to bring together the discussion of the two previous sections around the 'psychological' and 'political' aspects of legal individualism, the dynamic of citizenship forms, and Neumann's account of authoritarianism in law. I will argue that the contradictory repressive/expressive quality of the law's psychological individualism, also caught in Neumann's analysis of the dominatory/freedom enhancing nature of law, is

[33] Neumann, above n 3, at 178.
[34] Neumann, above n 3, at 193.

relevant to an understanding of the tendency to increased *responsibilisation* in modern criminal justice. As for the way that modern law contains as its two poles *ratio* and *voluntas*, freedom and sovereignty, the conflict between individual right and political power is relevant to the understanding of increased *dangerousness* and *regulation* more generally in recent times. These three tendencies are rooted in the law's conflicts of psychological and political individualism and are enabled at the level of the dynamic of citizenship forms by the fission where previously there was fusion between the civil/political and the social forms (in Marshall's terms) since the 1970s.

A. Increased Responsibilisation

If one way of understanding authoritarianism through law leads to the opposition within law between *ratio* and *voluntas*, a second way looks at the ideologically dominatory or repressive nature of individualist legal form per se. That is, it considers how law as *ratio* or as freedom is itself authoritarian in its effects. Here, I want to argue that criminal justice provides an authoritarian mode of legitimation through its emphasis on punishment as a morally proper social response to individual criminal acts. It establishes through the classical retributive discourse a sense of the justice or moral propriety of acting in an authoritarian manner. In this it provides a classical political legitimation of domination that is based on *ratio*, not *voluntas*, and is all the more powerful as a result.

This returns us to the discussion of increased responsibilisation in the context of the shifting relationship between the different forms of Marshallian citizenship under modern conditions. Increased responsibilisation arises out of the renewed emphasis on political citizenship as a mode of legitimation in an increasingly authoritarian neo-liberal polity. I argued in section II that aligning political and social citizenship in the 1960s and early 1970s meant that the classic 19th-century model of the criminal law was supported in its actualisation in the context of a socially progressive, welfare-oriented polity. In that context, the criminal law was seen as part of a generally liberal, social democratic project in which matters of individual and social justice were linked.

However, the model of political citizenship is subject to two contradictory pressures once the supportive overlay of principles of social citizenship is withdrawn. On the one hand, it retains its importance as a political legitimating device to stand alongside the demands of civil (economic) citizenship; on the other, it comes under attack as an unnecessary appendage and threat to economic efficiency, that is, to economic policies pursued in the name of civil citizenship. Responsibilisation in criminal law draws on the first of these two contradictory alternatives, for the classical, decontextualised, individual, psychological model of responsibility provides an alternative legitimation to social intervention. Responsibility and justice in the model of political citizenship rest upon individualist rather than social premises: it is up to individuals to act responsibly within the law, and where they do not do so, they may be appropriately punished under classical retributive principles of justice. Removing the contextualising manifold of principles of social citizenship, welfare and justice places renewed emphasis on individual responsibility as a primary legitimating and dominatory ideological device. Legal responsibilisation comes to the fore.

This fall back to principles of individual as opposed to social justice promotes the idea that individuals are criminally responsible for their action and helps divide society along class lines into the 'haves' and the 'have nots'. It does so, however, indirectly, through the mechanism of a strongly *universalising* sense of moral justice for punishment. That is its special power. This helps explain the emphasis on increased punishment as the state relies more for its sense of moral vindication on its retributive, rather than its redistributive, function. Increased punitiveness follows increased responsibilisation and is one reason for the increasing numbers of people being sent to prison. The return to legitimation through the decontextualised and remoralised psychological individual of the criminal law, without the tempering cover of social citizenship principles, presses remorselessly on the punishment button. In so doing, authoritarian legitimation relies upon the dominatory or repressive nature of legal individualism in its psychological aspect. Such legitimation takes place not because of a shift between the poles of freedom and sovereignty *but by virtue of the concept of legal freedom itself*.

Increased responsibilisation is also linked, I think, to the increasing role of victims in the system. The latter is explored by Leslie Sebba in this volume, chapter four. At the same time as the neo-liberal state invokes punishment with greater regularity, it loses some of its own moral standing in the matter of redressing wrongs. Under the older welfare-liberal model of the state, a clear line was drawn between the role of the state and the role of the public, and in particular the victim, with regard to crime. Crime was the infraction of a public norm and it was the state, as the representative of the general will, which was effectively the injured party. Punishment should therefore be both its right and its responsibility. The current emphasis on the victim in the criminal process arises out of the sense that it is a moral relationship between individual citizens that punishment addresses, and that it is the private person who is centrally the wronged party. As social interventionist provisioning decreases, the moral role of the state also decreases, and it becomes less able to absorb the moral passions invoked by crime. As it re-presents itself as a formalistic 'night watchman', its substantive moral authority is reduced. As the state takes less of a moral stance, moral passions find their home among victims and their families in a reallocation of the moral economy. Increasing the role of victims accompanies increased responsibilisation of perpetrators just because the repressive side of law's psychological individualism is relied upon for legitimation purposes.

B. Increasing Dangerousness

Turning now to the second tendency, that of increasing dangerousness, it is necessary to distinguish the 'politically' and the 'pathologically' dangerous offender. As regards the latter, penal policies of bifurcation into 'normal' and 'abnormal' or dangerous offenders have a long history, and reflect different underlying structural elements. This history is explored by Lucia Zedner in this volume, chapter three. The idea of a dangerous offender who lacks qualities of civil and political citizenship can be traced to the turn of the 19th century when, under the influence of doctrines of social intervention, certain groups of people were subjected to special measures of control because of their residual deficiencies.

Whereas I have heretofore focused on the progressive qualities of a model of social citizenship, it should be noted, and this is part of the overall complexity of thinking about the criminal justice system, that such citizenship itself involves its own distinct undertow of authoritarian intervention. Ways of treating the mentally ill, inebriates, habitual prostitutes and persistent offenders reveal what can happen to those in whom it is thought that 'the essentials of citizenship' do not reside, as the turn of the (last) century philosopher Bernard Bosanquet put it.[35] For such people, the promise of social citizenship in recompense for their own failings as civil and political citizens was always a hollow one. For them, law was already an *arcanum dominationis* before the concept was generalised under totalitarian rule.

Such people may be said to experience psychological conditions that make it hard for them to conform their behaviour to law. In a social world that relies increasingly on an authoritarian sense that the state should be in control of everything, ever greater emphasis is placed on identifying groups of persons who must be controlled by law where their conduct is in some way threatening. Sexual offenders convicted of committing offences of an 'abnormal' kind are an obvious case in point, but the general rise of punishments of an indeterminate kind is also relevant here. A general sense of the pathological or abnormal dangerous offender comes to the fore as a special class to be treated according to rules tailored to their dangerousness. In this move, authoritarian state intervention does not affirm a juridical model of the responsible citizen (as in increased responsibilisation) but rather cuts against it, seeing political citizenship as an obstruction to the demand for control and the legitimation benefits that control brings. Control becomes a

[35] B Bosanquet, *The Philosophical Theory of the Modern State* (London, Macmillan, 3rd edn, 1919) 210.

matter of state will and bureaucratic determination rather than the juridical allocation of rights and responsibilities.

Alongside the increased targeting for control of those who are seen as dangerous in the sense that they are pathologically unable to conform their conduct to law, there are those who are seen as at war with society in general. Here, the idea of a split between 'them' and 'us', foe and friend, in more classically authoritarian terms emerges, where being one of 'them' involves being treated as outside the law and denied rights associated with political citizenship, for example to normal criminal justice or due process requirements. To the extent that the state ceases to treat certain crimes of violence as part of the normal criminal calendar and recategorises them as part of a 'war against terror', it legitimates the denial of legal rights to those involved, and itself as a strong state.

In considering the logic of this development, it is important to note the shift away from the aspect of domination through legal freedom to the moving between poles enabled by the law's political individualism, for here the form of law is pushed towards political power, sovereignty and *voluntas* and away from individual right, freedom and *ratio*. The pathologically abnormal offender and the political offender, constructed as a terrorist, are both cast beyond the citizenship pale, and submitted to a general regime of control that resembles Neumann's *arcanum dominationis*. Here it can be noted that increased dangerousness can also align—rhetorically at least—with increased responsibilisation, for the person who undertakes dreadful acts of violence either as a pathological or a political offender becomes precisely the most heinous kind of criminal, for whom increased punishment is justified. Dangerousness and culpability both point in the same direction in practice, towards the likelihood of increasing prison populations. But the main thrust of increased dangerousness stems from the reshaping of legal form towards authoritarian interventions and away from principles of individual right. Where dangerousness is in issue, it is that conflict in legal form that is brought to the fore.

C. Increasing Regulation

Finally, there are the legal phenomena associated with increasing, and new forms of, regulation. Many could be mentioned here, including special laws governing terrorists, drug dealers, and sex offenders. I will, however, only briefly consider the United Kingdom's anti-social behaviour order (ASBO), and here I am beholden to Peter Ramsay's previous work[36] and his further exploration of the topic in chapter six. The key to understanding the ASBO

[36] P Ramsay, 'What is Anti-Social Behaviour?' (2004) *Crim LR* 908; Ramsay, above n 12.

is the way in which it reflects many of the different issues canvassed in the above discussion.

First, it involves pursuing a dangerousness strategy, and therefore undermining the juridical model of the political citizen in favour of authoritarian ordering principles. As Neumann points out, the classic political citizenship doctrine of the rule of law involves both generality of law and specificity in its application.[37] An instrument such as the ASBO undermines legal generality since it represents in effect a criminal law specifically tailored to particular individuals with regard to forms of conduct that would not be criminal were anyone else to do them. An order on X, for example, not to meet with Y at a particular place where it would be otherwise lawful to do so because this elicits a sense of fear in the bystander, leads by another route to Neumann's idea of law as *arcanum dominationis* within the authoritarian state.

Second, the idea of the ASBO also reflects the idea of state intervention as a means of achieving moral legitimacy and consensus by deploying authoritarian measures, for it is in essence a way of dealing with the bad behaviour of problem families on council estates, of controlling the 'rough poor' for (what are presented as) morally valid reasons. Third, the idea of the ASBO plays around with the concept of citizenship to establish moral legitimation in terms of the individual in that it stresses the duties owed by the citizen to the community as well as the rights and privileges he or she enjoys. In a way, it represents a new form of social interventionism after the demise of welfare-oriented forms of social citizenship, and one that bases itself on a revised (communitarian) vision of the political model of citizenship. But it uses that model as a means of denying the core idea of citizenship *rights* that the political model itself implied.

V. CONCLUSION

In conclusion, even from this brief and preliminary discussion of how the dynamic of citizenship forms interacts with a ratcheting up of state authoritarianism to favour increased responsibilisation, dangerousness and regulation, it will be appreciated that what is at stake here is not an easy one-to-one matching of underlying developments with particular forms of law and justice. Many variables are at play, so that a fuller identification of structural forms would have to be aligned with a more finely grained understanding of particular forms of criminal justice to achieve a satisfactory analysis. My comments above are only a beginning in a complex task. Alongside this pluralism, it is necessary to understand how individual developments can display different facets, feed into and off each other, and

[37] Neumann, above n 3, at 28.

satisfy different agendas at one and the same time. For example, although the ASBO can be seen as a form of attack on the basic ideas of liberal political citizenship, that is, the idea of the individual as an abstract, general member of a liberal polity, it at the same time can be presented, as my third point above makes clear, as a way of getting individuals to measure up to the responsibilities of being a member of such a polity, that is, as a way of renovating political citizenship for more legitimating work in authoritarian times. It seems to me that it is often the case that an 'idea whose time has come' is just the kind of idea which can serve a number of different and conflicting agendas just because of its multi-faceted quality. What needs to be aimed for is a sense of how legal measures or forms are shaped by their structural contexts, but are not reducible to them. Herein lies what might be called their 'relative autonomy'.

More broadly, what I have sought to develop is a sense of the *implication* of liberal law in the evolution of authoritarianism within criminal justice. It is too tempting to seek to oppose authoritarian developments in the criminal law by resorting simply to a liberal conception of justice. If that conception is itself imbued with authoritarianism, it is necessary to be reflexive about the nature and limits of legal freedom. Law is too complex a phenomenon, embodying moments of partial freedom within a socio–economic matrix that shapes and conditions its overall possibilities, to be the source of easy answers to problems posed by an authoritarian state. At the same time, it would be foolish to throw the baby out with the bathwater, as Neumann's contrast between liberal legality and the *arcanum dominationis* makes clear. By analysing liberal criminal law as co-constituted by elements of individual right and authoritarian power in its political individualist moment, and by depicting its model of the responsible individual as entailing both repressive (freedom-denying) and expressive (freedom-enabling) elements in its psychological individualist moment, I have argued that its own contribution to authoritarianism in terms of increased responsibilisation, dangerousness and regulation must be acknowledged. If we are aware of these implications of liberal law, we may be more alert to the complexities involved in identifying legal solutions to the problems of authoritarianism today.

3

Fixing the Future? The Pre-emptive Turn in Criminal Justice

LUCIA ZEDNER*

I. INTRODUCTION

ALTHOUGH THE FOUNDATIONS of the criminal process rest on the ascription of responsibility and sanction for wrongs done, the prediction of dangerousness and the attempt to pre-empt future harm through deterrence, rehabilitation and incapacitation are well-established pillars of punishment. The rise of risk has brought about a more marked temporal shift toward trying to calculate, anticipate and forestall harms before they occur. The logic of risk licenses future-oriented preventative and incapacitative measures justified by the claim that it is possible to determine in advance who poses a risk and in what degree. A fundamental problem with this claim is that predicting human behaviour is necessarily an uncertain business. As earlier attempts to define and detect dangerousness made abundantly clear, determining who poses a risk and who does not tests the limits of predictive capacity. Despite the growing sophistication of actuarial tools, surveillance and intelligence gathering, and despite the growing political confidence invested in these diverse technologies, future human activity can rarely be foretold with certainty. Notwithstanding our aspiration to calculate, assess and manage risk, it is our ability to act in the face of uncertainty that poses the greater challenge. The larger the scale of the potential threat, the less defensible is it to do nothing. It follows that, as perceived threats grow, dealing with uncertainty marginalises risk as the dominant problem for governments and policy makers. Uncertainty ushers in an era of precaution that has significant and worrisome implications for the criminal law.

* I would like to thank colleagues at the University of Oslo; the International Institute for the Sociology of Law, Oñati; the Law and Society Association Meeting, Humboldt University, Berlin; the University of New South Wales Law Faculty, Sydney and Regnet, the Australian National University, Canberra, for their comments. Special thanks to Andrew Ashworth, Benjamin Goold, Bernard Harcourt and Myles Leslie for their criticisms of earlier drafts. This chapter was inspired by the work of Richard Ericson, a former colleague and good friend. I dedicate this piece to his memory.

The need to act despite a lack of full scientific certainty is well established in respect of the catastrophic risks posed by environmental damage, nuclear power and other hazardous industries. Post-9/11, policy makers have similarly been beset by the quandary of how to maximise security against terrorism in the face of considerable uncertainty. The former US Defense Secretary Donald Rumsfeld infamously observed of terrorist threats:

> There are known knowns. These are things we know that we know. There are known unknowns. That is to say, there are things that we know we don't know. But there are also unknown unknowns. These are things we don't know we don't know.[1]

Although his speech was widely derided at the time, it is arguable that it articulates the important place occupied by uncertainty in the security field. Whereas the risk paradigm promised, but could not deliver, reliable calculations about the likelihood and severity of future threats, advertence to uncertainty acknowledges that the future is unknowable. This acknowledgement imposes upon politicians and policy makers the burden of deciding what measures to take and what policies to develop in respect of the 'known unknowns' and the 'unknown unknowns'.

Attempts to pre-empt grave harms and to articulate an accompanying rationale and jurisprudence are not new endeavours. This chapter begins by examining how thinking about pre-emption has changed over time and with what implications for security. This historical examination renders transparent what might otherwise be opaque, namely the complex of factors that underpins present policy-making. By tracing the genealogy of precautionary thinking, it will reveal the interdependent relationships that exist between changes in the threats faced by modern societies; prevailing political concerns; new forms of expert knowledge; changing rationales; and emergent legal structures. The chapter examines the history of preemptive endeavour from dangerousness, through risk, to precaution as successive dominant modes of analysis in policymaking.

If one aim of the chapter is to show that precaution has historical antecedents, a second is to explore its novel and distinctive implications for legal developments in the fields of crime and security. The third and chief purpose is to show how a precautionary approach to the threats posed by serious organised crime and contemporary terrorism has led to a raft of new measures that depart radically from established legal principles to criminalise in the face of uncertainty. Security was once predicated upon

[1] D Rumsfeld, United States Department of Defense, *News Briefing*, 12 February 2002 <http://www.defenselink.mil/transcript/transcript.aspx?transcriptid=2636>.

knowledge 'in the sense that security functions as knowledge, relies on knowledge, produces knowledge, and uses its claim to knowledge as license to render all aspects of life transparent to the state'.[2] All this is changing. The drive to precaution recognises that attempts to fix the future necessarily take place under conditions of imperfect information. Precaution thus places uncertainty—not knowledge—centre stage.

II. FROM DANGEROUSNESS TO RISK

This section examines the genealogy of pre-emptive endeavour. One of the principal precursors to current thinking about risk and security is the notion of dangerousness. Dangerousness itself is not a static concept. It underwent significant transmutations over the course of the hundred years or so in which it dominated thinking about crime control. In the early 19th century it was, above all, the articulation of political fear about the threat supposedly posed by the 'dangerous classes'.[3] The dangerous classes were those political agitators, working men, unemployed and also (but not necessarily) criminals who collectively appeared to pose a significant threat to the interests of the propertied classes who had most to lose by the disruption posed to the social order of the time. Dangerousness in the first part of the 19th century thus had an explicitly political quality and associations with the rumblings of proto-revolutionary struggle that characterised many European countries from time to time throughout this period.

Only in the later 19th century was this early political conception of dangerousness overlaid by a more recognisably modern formulation aimed at identifying particular groups of individuals whose habitual criminality marked them out as posing a continuing threat to society. Central to this reformulation was the rise of social statistics and the bureaucratic processes of record keeping that accompanied the emergence of the modern state that made possible for the first time the collection of data on large classes of offenders. Systematic collation of criminal statistics began in many continental European countries in the 18th century but was not begun in England until 1810.[4] It made possible the identification of that class of

[2] M Neocleous, 'Theoretical Foundations of the "New Police Science"' in MD Dubber and M Valverde (eds), *The New Police Science: The Police Power in Domestic and International Governance* (Stanford, Stanford University Press, 2007) 37.

[3] J Pratt, 'Dangerousness and Modern Society' in M Brown and J Pratt (eds), *Dangerous Offenders: Punishment and Social Order* (London, Routledge, 2000); M Ignatieff, *A Just Measure of Pain: The Penitentiary in the Industrial Revolution 1750–1850* (London, Macmillan, 1978).

[4] L Radzinowicz and R Hood, *The Emergence of Penal Policy in Victorian and Edwardian England* (Oxford, Oxford University Press, 1986) 92.

individuals 'whose very manner of living seemed a challenge to ordered society and the tissue of laws, moralities, and taboos holding it together'.[5]

In the late 19th and early 20th centuries concern shifted again, away from the idea of dangerous classes to a growing obsession with the threat posed by identifiable individuals. The rise of the modern 'psy-' professions was central to the identification of those whose mental, psychological and physiological inadequacies were said to mark them out as 'incorrigibles', 'feeble-minded' or 'habitual inebriates'. Their frailties, being endogenous, licensed the development of a now well-documented carceral archipelago of prisons, asylums and other institutions designed for the long-term and often indefinite incapacitation of those deemed incapable of law-abiding behaviour.[6] In much of continental Europe the influence of eugenics focused attention on the detection of 'born' criminals whose physical traits, interpreted through the new science of phrenology, marked them out as atavistic. In Britain the influence of psychiatry focused attention instead on mental degeneracy which, although it permitted no great optimism, furnished grounds for reformatory endeavour. Hence the development of reformatories for juveniles, inebriates and mental defectives in late 19th- and early 20th-century Britain. The legal recognition of mental incapacity in *M'Naghten's* case[7] and of feeblemindedness in the Mental Deficiency Act 1913 tended, however to replace reformatory endeavour with provision for the indefinite detention of those deemed mentally defective.

Later in the 20th century, debate around the concept of dangerousness was revived. In Britain this debate was prompted in large part by the concern of legal scholars to set out the principles according to which the risk of grave harm should be tackled and to establish the grounds upon which 'protective sentencing' could be imposed.[8] The debate centred upon whether and in what degree it was justifiable to impose incapacitative sentences proportional not to the wrong done but to the gravity of anticipated harm. Significantly, incapacitative or protective sentences were contemplated only where an offender had 'done, attempted, risked, threatened or conspired to do *grave harm* and has committed an act of a similar kind on a previous occasion to the instant offence'.[9] Claims to predict the future were thus based upon evidence drawn from the past. No surprise, then, that the ability of the criminal justice system to predict dangerousness was

[5] K Chesney, *The Victorian Underworld* (London, Maurice Temple Smith, 1971) 38.

[6] D Rothman, *The Discovery of the Asylum: Social Order and Disorder in the New Republic* (Boston, Little, Brown & Co, 1971); M Foucault, *Discipline and Punish: The Birth of the Prison* (Harmondsworth, Middlesex, Peregrine, 1979).

[7] *M'Naghten's* case (1843) 8 ER 718, 722.

[8] J Floud and W Young, *Dangerousness and Criminal Justice* (London, Heinemann, 1981).

[9] Floud and Young, above n 8, at 155–7.

a matter of profound controversy. The philosophical, moral and political bases of pre-emptive decision-making and in particular the legitimacy of taking action against individuals in advance of wrongdoing were likewise a matter of dispute.[10] Concern centred on the high rate of false positives and the insistence that incapacitation could not be justified unless there was a sufficiently high level of certainty that harm would otherwise eventuate. The point is worth emphasising here because, as will become clear, the certainty principle has since proven to be far from sacrosanct.

Today, while 'dangerousness' remains an important term of art, it has come to be used in respect of a more narrowly defined class of offenders. This class now has its own label: they are said to suffer from 'Dangerous and Severe Personality Disorder' (DSPD). Dangerousness has in many quarters been discredited as a pseudoscientific construct amounting to little more than the claim that past harms predict future behaviour[11] and as being reliant upon a questionable medicalisation of human behaviour. Defining dangerousness has come to be seen to suffer from multiple difficulties: that it seeks to impose a rigid legal classification upon what are often fluid or contested clinically based judgments; it forces a binary distinction between dangerous and non-dangerous that cannot take into account gradations or marginal cases; and, as a static designation, it categorises people as fixed members of stable dangerous or non-dangerous populations.

III. THE RISE OF RISK

In the discrediting of dangerousness, the rise of a more subtle and malleable categorical tool—risk—played no small part.[12] Risk relies not upon the legal designation of the individual but upon administrative techniques; it relies not upon binary distinctions but graduated assessments upon a continuum; and risk tools are not static but capable of assessing and re-assessing dynamic risk factors over time.[13] The rise of risk was promoted

[10] AE Bottoms and R Brownsword, 'The Dangerousness Debate after the Floud Report' (1982) *British Journal of Criminology* 229; T Honderich, 'On Justifying Protective Punishment' (1982) *British Journal of Criminology* 268; L Radzinowicz and R Hood, 'Dangerousness and Criminal Justice' (1981) *Crim LR* 756.

[11] N Rose, 'At the Risk of Madness' in T Baker and J Simon (eds), *Embracing Risk: The Changing Culture of Insurance and Responsibility* (Chicago, University of Chicago Press, 2002).

[12] R Castel, 'From Dangerousness to Risk' in G Burchell, C Gordon and P Miller (eds), *The Foucault Effect: Studies in Governmentality* (London, Harvester Wheatsheaf, 1991); D Garland, 'The Rise of Risk' in R Ericson and A Doyle (eds), *Risk and Morality* (Toronto, University of Toronto Press, 2003); M Power, *The Risk Management of Everything* (London, Demos, 2004).

[13] Rose, above n 11, at 211.

upon the grounds that actuarial assessments were more reliable than clinical judgements of dangerousness[14] and more conservative in their estimates than those proffered by clinicians.[15] Whereas one might have expected a backlash by psychiatrists anxious to defend their professional expertise, the usurpation of their clinical judgements by actuarial tools appears to have occurred with remarkably little controversy. Part of the explanation may be that whereas in the post-war period the most debated failure of psychiatry was the plight of individuals whose lives had been blighted by inadequate treatment, increasingly criticism focused on failures to identify and manage those deemed to pose a serious risk to the public. Uncomfortable in their role as adjuncts to a penal system that sought to forestall risk by incarcerating people upon the basis of questionable diagnoses, forensic psychiatrists seemed almost relieved to see their judgments sidelined by the purportedly scientific apparatus of statistical tools.[16]

The rise of risk can also be attributed to two developments. First, over the same period the increasing sophistication of statistical processing in the neighbouring hard sciences of engineering, materials, medicine and environmental science found new applications in the crime control and security industries. Of course, statistical calculation of criminality was not new. The history of criminal statistics can be traced back to sociological and criminological studies of offending behaviour begun in the late 19th and early 20th centuries but developed in their most sophisticated form in the post-war Chicago School.[17] The striking difference here is that criminal statistics came to be used not only as a way of documenting past and present levels of criminality but as a basis for making predictive statements about future harms. It is arguable that the extension of these tools to human activity stretched their predictive capacity beyond safe reliance.

The second is the influence of actuarialism.[18] Actuarial models were developed first by the insurance industry to predict mortality rates so as to set individual premiums at levels appropriate to the risk and later also by

[14] E Janus and R Prentky, 'Forensic Use of Actuarial Risk Assessment: How a Developing Science can Enhance Accuracy and Accountability' (2004) 3 *Federal Sentencing Reporter* 176; J Monahan, 'A Jurisprudence of Risk Assessment: Forecasting Harm Among Prisoners, Predators, and Patients' (2006) 3 *Virginia Law Review* 391.

[15] R Hood and S Shute, *The Parole System at Work: Home Office Research Study No. 202* (London, HMSO, 2000) 46–7.

[16] N Eastman, 'Public Health Psychiatry or Crime Prevention' (1999) *British Medical Journal* 549, 550.

[17] B Harcourt, *Against Prediction: Punishing and Policing in an Actuarial Age* (Chicago, University of Chicago Press, 2006) ch 2.

[18] M Feeley, 'Actuarial Justice and the Modern State' in G Bruinsma, H Elffers and J de Keijser (eds), *Punishment, Places, and Perpetrators: Developments in Criminology and Criminal Justice Research* (Devon, Cullompton, Willan Publishing, 2004); M Feeley and J Simon, 'Actuarial Justice: The Emerging New Criminal Law' in D Nelken (ed), *The Futures of Criminology* (London, Sage, 1994).

marketing organisations to categorise consumers into identifiable 'prospect' groups. In origin, therefore, actuarial calculation is an economic affair determining levels of payments required to secure a profit on likely losses payable.[19] Again the transfer of actuarial techniques to the legal domain, and more particularly their deployment as a technique for determining preventative and incapacitative measures, raises questions about the appropriateness of their use as instruments of justice.[20] Central to the growing dominance of actuarialism was its claim to furnish more reliable data about likelihood of future offending than the subjective professional judgements previously relied upon. Despite their claim to objectivity it is questionable whether actuarial tools generate substantively different categorisations from those yielded by psychiatric experts. The indicia of risk which form the basis for actuarial modelling are the product of cumulative individual human judgements.[21] Risk assessment of human behaviour is better understood not as the impartial application of technology, therefore, but as the institutionalisation of subjective opinions, prior political leanings, and prejudices. While technology itself is neutral, it is shot through with social meaning, it is politicised and filtered through the cultural lens of those applying it in ways that technological determinist accounts belie.[22]

Claimed improvements in the sophistication and resultant accuracy of actuarial tools have led to the assertion that they have attained a level of reliability comparable to that required by the standard of proof in the criminal trial.[23] As Slobogin has observed:

> [t]he final assertion underlying the jurisprudence of dangerousness ... is that we can predict danger adequately for legal purposes. That assertion is based in part on improvements in prediction science, but stems mostly from the belief that we cannot justifiably demand more accuracy in the preventive detention setting than we do in the criminal law.[24]

While this view is now widely defended, it is arguable that to deploy actuarial data pre-emptively, particularly as a ground for preventative detention,

[19] R Ericson and A Doyle, *Uncertain Business: Risk, Insurance and the Limits of Knowledge* (Toronto, University of Toronto Press, 2004); P O'Malley, *Risk, Uncertainty and Government* (London, The Glasshouse Press, 2004) ch 6.

[20] B Harcourt, 'The Shaping of Chance: Actuarial Models and Criminal Profiling at the Turn of the Twenty-First Century' (2003) 70 *University of Chicago Law Review* 105; L Zedner, 'Seeking Security By Eroding Rights: The Side-Stepping of Due Process ' in B Goold and L Lazarus (eds), *Security and Human Rights* (Oxford, Hart Publishing, 2007).

[21] P O'Malley, 'Risk, Power, and Crime Prevention' (1992) 3 *Economy and Society* 252.

[22] BJ Goold, *CCTV and Policing: Public Area Surveillance and Police Practices in Britain* (Oxford, Oxford University Press, 2004) ch 8.

[23] Monahan, above n 14.

[24] C Slobogin, 'A Jurisprudence of Dangerousness' (2003) 1 *Northwestern University Law Review* 1, 62.

ought to require a higher standard of accuracy than that required in respect of post-hoc punishment since it imposes deprivation of liberty without the prior justifying fact of wrong doing.

It follows that a larger normative debate about the role and deployment of actuarial tools is needed. Is actuarialism merely an exogenous technical intervention into the domain of just law? Note that the very label 'actuarial justice', although used critically by its originators, Feeley and Simon, nonetheless speaks not only of technological innovation but of a new conception of justice.[25] The substantive consequences of actuarialism have been much explored in the wake of Feeley and Simon's seminal writing. With a few notable exceptions[26] the normative ramifications of actuarialism for existing conceptions of just punishment have been subject to little debate. Yet as Harcourt has observed,

> the use of predictive methods has begun to distort our carceral imagination, to mold our notions of justice, without our full acquiescence, without deliberation, almost subconsciously or subliminally. Today we have an intuitive but deep sense that it is just to determine punishment largely on the basis of an actuarial risk assessment.[27]

This silent incursion of actuarial thinking is all the more surprising if one recalls the sophisticated and often heated deliberation that was held over the ethics of dangerousness. By contrast, and with little comparable controversy, actuarialism has challenged the dominance of desert as the central rationale in penal theory and has insinuated itself into policing, sentencing and parole decision-making.

How has this occurred? Harcourt suggests that this actuarial takeover arose not from a deliberate determination by policy makers. Rather, he claims:

> it chose us ... *the production of technical knowledge*: our progress in techniques of predicting criminality is what fuelled our jurisprudential conception of just punishment ... It is deeply troubling because it demonstrates the influence of technical knowledge on our sense of justice. We have become slaves of our technical advances.[28]

The proposition is an intriguing one but is Harcourt right to suggest that it is simply 'this quest for technical knowledge that has helped shape our

[25] Feeley and Simon, above n 18.

[26] For example, B Hudson, *Justice in the Risk Society* (London, Sage, 2003); C Shearing and L Johnston, 'Justice in the Risk Society' (2005) 1 *Australian and New Zealand Journal of Criminology* 25.

[27] Harcourt, above n 17, at 31.

[28] Harcourt, above n 17, at 32.

contemporary notions of justice'?[29] By his account actuarialism is a technological takeover as a consequence of which established principles of retributive justice are forgone simply because we have the capacity to make predictive statements about the future. How plausible is this determinist account? Granted, the mere fact of technological possibility is not unimportant. Without fingerprints and DNA, forensic science would not have its present place in police investigations; without electronic tagging, curfew orders might not have credibility; and without CCTV cameras and satellite tracking, opportunities for surveillance would be much diminished. But to ascribe major shifts in penal policy solely to technological possibility may be to place the proverbial cart before the horse. The causal relationship between the technology of profiling and predicting and the political demand for public protection is surely more complex than the simple assertion that actuarialism 'chose us'.

Claims of technological takeover rely upon a curious denial of human agency, attention to which requires us to consider other causal factors. First, the growing dominance of actuarial techniques over proportionate punishment may be seen as symptomatic of a larger shift in political allegiance from classical conceptions of retributive justice to the consequentialist orientations of deterrence and incapacitation.[30] Second, the demand to avert risk stems from the growth of penal populism, with its attendant calls for public protection, bolstered by media-fed perceptions of the risks of sexual predation, violent crime and terrorist threat. These contribute to a growing sense that the presumption of innocence, proof beyond reasonable doubt and the requirement of proportionality in punishment are legal luxuries ill-suited to present perils.[31] Finally, averting disaster has become a political imperative for governments anxious to safeguard their reputation against the adverse fallout that inevitably occurs if harms eventuate. As the role of the state retrenches in many Western neo-liberal polities, security has become a last bastion of legitimate state activity.[32] There is consequently much more at stake in the prospect of failure in this limited domain of the state as night watchman. Together these factors feed recourse to actuarial technologies, providing their justifying rationale and the political environment in which they flourish. As a consequence, profiling software, risk schedules and classification of offenders by risk category furnish the basis for preventative detention, indefinite detention of high-risk offenders and

[29] Harcourt, above n 17, at 33.

[30] C Steiker, 'Civil and Criminal Divide' in J Dressler (ed), *Encyclopedia of Crime and Justice* (New York, Macmillan Reference, 2002).

[31] A Ashworth, 'Four Threats to the Presumption of Innocence' (2006) *South African Law Journal* 62; M Ignatieff, *The Lesser Evil: Political Ethics in an Age of Terror* (Edinburgh, Edinburgh University Press, 2004).

[32] R Nozick, *Anarchy, State and Utopia* (Oxford, Blackwell, 1974).

risk management in policing, imprisonment and parole. Here again, a complex web of relations between changing expertise, new technology, underlying rationales and overarching political imperatives results in legal frameworks that both justify and make possible proactive responses to 'fix' future harm and wrongdoing before it occurs.

IV. FROM RISK TO UNCERTAINTY

More recently, the dominance of risk has been challenged by a newer logic imported from the environmental sciences: the logic of precaution in the face of uncertainty.[33] Of course, risk and uncertainty are not entirely discrete concepts. As Ericson has observed: 'risk assessment is rarely based on perfect knowledge, and typically frays into uncertainty'.[34] Notwithstanding the growing sophistication of risk assessment technologies, none claims infallibility and all acknowledge a margin of error that admits to uncertainty. It follows that even where claims as to the reliability of risk assessment dominate, uncertainty stands as the unacknowledged companion to risk. O'Malley captures this relationship well: 'making the distinction between risk and uncertainty cannot be regarded as setting up a rigid binary. It may be better to regard them as related along multiple axes, with the effect that no single continuum (such as one running from statistical probability to vague hunches) will adequately represent the relationships between them'.[35]

In the sphere of crime control, risk is better thought of less as an actuality than a social fact by which states construct the world they seek to govern. Understood as a technique of government rather than an objectively observable reality, the vulnerability of risk to changing political priorities is unsurprising. Whereas it may be politically instrumental to assert confidence in the reliability of tools designed to assess the risk of severe personality disorder, propensity to violence or sexual predation, other sources of grave threat remain less readily amenable to such claims. The difficulties of intelligence gathering render risk assessment an altogether less plausible tool in respect of serious organised crime, drug and people trafficking, and terrorist networks about which information is scarce and less easily reduced to categorical risk profiles. It is not only in the sphere of terrorism, therefore, that the acknowledged inescapability of 'unknown unknowns' makes it impossible to base policies on risk assessment alone. Little surprise that risk

[33] K Haggerty, 'From Risk to Precaution: The Rationalities of Personal Crime Prevention' in R Ericson and A Doyle (eds), *Risk and Morality* (Toronto, University of Toronto Press, 2003); O'Malley, above n 21.

[34] R Ericson, 'Governing Through Risk and Uncertainty' (2005) 4 *Economy and Society* 659.

[35] O'Malley, above n 19.

assessment and management have given way to a larger and more pressing preoccupation with uncertainty.[36]

Uncertainty can productively be understood as resulting from two distinct sources: first, actual uncertainty as to the nature, likelihood, scope or target of a particular threat; and, second, fabricated uncertainty caused by the unwillingness or inability of states to adduce evidence. In respect of security, uncertainty may arise both from the unknown nature of the terrorist threat and from the secrecy that, it is said, necessarily attends the operations of intelligence services. Live to the difficulty of adducing sufficient evidence for prosecution, the need to protect service operatives and their informants from the dangers attendant on disclosure, and to ensure the continuing efficacy of their operations, intelligence services are often loathe to reveal what they know and still less willing to put it to test in open court. Uncertainty here is in an important sense manufactured by the privileging of security and the protection of covert operations. Whereas agents of criminal justice are required to satisfy tests as to the sufficiency of evidence before they seek to prosecute, the logic of precaution licenses action even when evidence is not available or, if available, where it cannot or will not be disclosed.

Uncertainty is thus no more real than risk and quite as much a means by which to conjecture about possible futures. Yet whereas risk permits calculation which in turn provides the basis for decision-making, the acknowledgement that the future is uncertain suggests incalculability, that the future cannot be reduced to statistical probabilities, which could translate into fatalism warranting inaction.[37] It is precisely to overcome this tendency to fatalism, particularly in the case of catastrophic threats, that uncertainty has been crafted as a ground not merely for action but for robust pre-emptive measures and the enactment of emergency powers in the face of the unknown.[38] Whereas risk-thinking stimulated the development of profiling, targeted surveillance, categorisation of suspect populations and other actuarial techniques for managing high-risk populations, uncertainty promotes a different set of techniques geared at requiring public officials to act preemptively to avert potentially grave harms using undifferentiated measures that target everyone. Risk does not disappear since it remains a tool by which officials target their resources. It is, in Power's terms, the basis of 'a new risk management in which the imperative is to make visible and manageable essentially unknowable and incalculable risks'.[39] The important

[36] C Aradau and R van Munster, 'Governing Terrorism through Risk: Taking Precautions, (un)Knowing the Future' (2007) *European Journal of International Relations* 89, 93.

[37] O'Malley, above n 19, at ch 1.

[38] J McCulloch and B Carlton, 'Preempting Justice: Suppression of Financing of Terrorism and the "War on Terror"' (2006) 3 *Current Issues in Criminal Justice* 397.

[39] Power, above n 12, at 30.

difference is that whereas risk made claims as to the possibility of calculating future harms and required therefore that officials assess the likelihood and degree of threat posed before taking preventative measures, uncertainty warrants pre-emptive action even where it is impossible to know what precise threat is posed. Seen one way, uncertainty is simply a more honest acknowledgement as to the limits of our knowledge; seen another way, it ushers in the logic of precaution.

The precautionary principle seeks to fix the future not by attempting to calculate risk but by providing a framework for decision-making in the absence of scientific knowledge. The precautionary principle takes many forms but at its core is a legal principle that imposes upon public actors a duty to act to avert serious or irreversible damage.[40] It states that in the face of serious harm, lack of full scientific certainty shall not be used as a reason for inaction or postponement of cost-effective measures to prevent such harms.[41]

The effect of the precautionary principle is partially to displace risk and its attendant claim that it is possible through risk assessment tools to know the future. By explicitly acknowledging the impossibility of knowing when, where or how grievous harms will occur and yet denying public bodies the luxury of inaction in the absence of that knowledge, the precautionary principle places uncertainty centre stage. While the precautionary principle is most developed in respect of grave environmental harms, its enormous power as a standard for public decision-making has led to its export beyond its originally intended domain. Although the principle is applicable in law only in respect of grave and irreversible harms, the culture of precaution is spreading downwards to provide a warrant for decision-making in situations of uncertainty even where the anticipated harms are of a considerably lesser gravity. What began life as a legal principle narrowly applicable within administrative law has come to inform a larger and altogether less principled precautionary approach that serves less as a constraint upon public officials than as a licence.

In this broader sense, precaution has clear resonances with the concept of pre-emption which is well developed in the field of international relations.[42] Pre-emption tackles the problem of uncertainty by licensing action in conditions of threatened but unpredictable grave harms.[43]

[40] SM Gardiner, 'A Core Precautionary Principle' (2006) 1 *Journal of Political Philosophy* 33.

[41] E Fisher, 'Risk and Environmental Law: A Beginner's Guide' in B Richardson and S Wood (eds), *Environmental Law for Sustainability: A Critical Reader* (Oxford, Hart Publishing, 2005).

[42] AD Sofaer, 'On the Necessity of Pre-emption' (2003) 2 *European Journal of International Law* 209.

[43] M Bothe, 'Terrorism and the Legality of Pre-emptive Force' (2003) 2 *European Journal of International Law* 227; A Dershowitz, *Preemption: A Knife That Cuts Both Ways* (New York, WW Norton, 2006).

One consequence of the 'war on terror' has been to erode the distinction between seeking security on the international stage and the pursuit of domestic security as a task of national government. Serious crime, trans-national and organised crime, and terrorist activity are said to interconnect and are seen by the new security specialists to blur into one another, posing an increasingly undifferentiated threat. It should come as no surprise, therefore, that the technologies of international relations and their accompanying discourse of 'anticipatory self-defence', 'pre-emptive strikes', 'rapid-fire justice' and 'deterrence' have come to be deployed in relation to crime control quite as readily as to military intervention.[44]

At the same time, international relations has undergone a significant shift wrought in no small part by the fact of 9/11, an event so unanticipated and so catastrophic that it has had the effect of making the future appear a much less readily predictable place than was once the case.[45] 'Incalculability' and 'radical contingency' are central currency of what Aradau and van Munster term governing 'at the limit of knowledge'.[46] This imperative to govern at the limit of knowledge displaces risk calculation to place uncertainty as the dominant driver of current trends in crime control and anti-terrorism policy.

V. APPLICATIONS OF UNCERTAINTY

In what follows, four recent United Kingdom examples of the application of uncertainty will be examined, borrowing for analytical convenience from Rumsfeld, the categories of 'known unknowns' and 'unknown unknowns'. The first of these, the known unknowns, comprise threats thought to be posed by those 'who are suspected of involvement in', who seek 'to encourage or otherwise induce' or engage in 'acts preparatory to' or 'likely to facilitate' serious harms.[47] The second category, the unknown unknowns, are those 'things we don't know, we don't know' which, by virtue of this dual ignorance, are said to necessitate pre-emptive action even before possible suspects are in the frame. This latter category, as we shall see, abandons targeted measures against known individuals for indiscriminate strategies that treat all as potential suspects or 'persons of interest'—a more uncertain designation that nevertheless licenses law enforcement surveillance and monitoring.

[44] J Braithwaite, 'Pre-empting Terrorism' (2006) 1 *Current Issues in Criminal Justice* 96.

[45] The role of such events is well captured by the notion of a 'black swan': a highly improbable event that is unpredictable, carries massive impact and causes us to concoct explanations that make it appear less random, more predictable than it was: NN Taleb, *The Black Swan: The Impact of the Highly Improbable* (New York, Random House, 2007).

[46] Aradau and van Munster, above n 36, at 91.

[47] All these terms are lifted from legislative instruments discussed in detail below. For an analysis of preparatory terrorism offences, see Bernadette McSherry, this volume, ch 7.

First, the known unknowns. In Britain, one of the most controversial anti-terrorist measures is the control order under the Prevention of Terrorism Act 2005 (UK).[48] The control order can be made against terrorist suspects by executive *fiat* without the need to present evidence in open court: the court's role is reduced to post-hoc ratification, which may be in closed session, of an executive decision. Notwithstanding the fact that control orders impose quasi-house arrest and almost unlimited restrictions upon their subjects (for 12-month periods renewable indefinitely), the Home Secretary need have no more than 'reasonable grounds for suspecting that the individual is or has been involved in terrorism-related activity'.[49] This legal requirement that the state need merely suspect (rather than believe on reasonable grounds) is entirely consistent with Ericson's observation that '[p]recautionary logic fuels suspicion'.[50] It is commonly claimed that there is a significant difference between belief and suspicion in this context. However, it is only a matter of difference in degree: the issue is not so much the level of knowledge required but the *reasonableness* of that mental state (whether it is a belief or suspicion) and how that assessment is being made (that is, what evidence/data can be used to generate that belief or suspicion). Precautionary logic bears as much on the issue of reasonableness as it does on the decision maker's level of knowledge. Facing uncertainty and potential catastrophes, we are prepared to admit a much wider range of material to determine the reasonableness of those beliefs/suspicions. Further, the control order empowers the state to impose such obligations as are necessary 'for purposes connected with protecting members of the public from a risk of terrorism'.[51] Those subject to control orders may be electronically tagged at all times; be required to abide by curfews (by remaining at home or in a specified place between specified times); and suffer restrictions on association with other people, on communication, movement and residence.

The control order is thus an extraordinary measure that does serious damage to basic presumptions of criminal procedure.[52] It lays waste to the right to a fair trial, including the presumption of innocence;[53] to adversarial justice; to transparency (not least in its use of closed session and special advocates); and to proportionality. It imposes burdensome restrictions

[48] M Nellis, 'Electronic Monitoring and the Creation of Control Orders for Terrorist Suspects in Britain' in T Abbas (ed), *Islamic Political Radicalism* (Edinburgh, Edinburgh University Press, 2007); L Zedner, 'Preventive Justice or Pre-Punishment? The Case of Control Orders' (2007) 59 *Current Legal Problems* 174. See further Peter Ramsay, this volume, ch 6.

[49] Prevention of Terrorism Act 2005 (UK), s 2(1)(a).

[50] R Ericson, *Crime in an Insecure World* (Cambridge, Polity, 2007) 23.

[51] Prevention of Terrorism Act 2005 (UK), s 1(1).

[52] D Bonner, 'Checking the Executive? Detention without Trial, Control Orders, Due Process and Human Rights' (2006) 1 *European Public Law* 45.

[53] Ashworth, above n 31.

without furnishing an adequate basis for challenge or access to the information necessary to test the evidence or rebut the grounds upon which these restrictions were deemed necessary. Breach of these conditions is a criminal offence punishable by imprisonment for up to 5 years.[54] The control order thus institutionalises uncertainty by enabling the state to impose restrictions upon suspects without exposing intelligence to the public scrutiny attendant upon prosecution. It also perpetuates uncertainty in a number of important ways: the key definitions of 'terrorism'[55] and 'related activity' are vague and potentially expansive; the conditions imposed are imprecisely set out; and the distinction between restriction of liberty and its deprivation under Art 5 of the European Convention on Human Rights (which provides that everyone has the right to liberty and security of person) is nowhere articulated. Further, no precise line between non-derogating and derogating control orders is specified in the Act. As Ericson has observed, whereas in law 'uncertainty has conventionally spelled innocence, within precautionary logic uncertainty is a reason for extreme pre-emptive measures for which designated agents are held responsible, and monitored and sanctioned accordingly'.[56]

The control order is just one in a raft of anti-terrorist measures that derive from the precautionary approach increasingly adopted by governments around the world in respect of terrorism. In Britain this precautionary logic is nowhere better evidenced than in recent anti-terror legislation. Here, the impulse to govern at the limit of knowledge results in two worrisome tendencies.

First, offences are defined in broad, imprecisely defined terms that have the potential to criminalise an extraordinarily wide range of activities remote from the actual preparation or planning of any specific terrorist act. Section 1 of the Terrorism Act 2006 (UK), for example, prohibits the making of 'a statement that is likely to be understood by some or all of the members of the public to whom it is published as a direct or indirect encouragement or other inducement to them to the commission, preparation or instigation of acts of terrorism or Convention offences'. 'Indirect encouragement' includes statements that glorify the commission or preparation (whether in the past, in the future or generally) of such acts or offences; and from which members of the public could reasonably be expected to infer that what is being glorified is conduct that should be emulated by them. Provided that the perpetrator is aware of the risk that the public may perceive it to be encouragement, he or she is liable, under s 1, to a penalty of up to 7 years' imprisonment.

[54] Prevention of Terrorism Act 2005 (UK), s 9(4)(a).
[55] Prevention of Terrorism Act 2005 (UK), s 1(9).
[56] Ericson, above n 50, at 23; McCulloch and Carlton, above n 38.

Second, inchoate offences are targeted at earlier points in time, remote from commission of the substantive offence or the actual infliction of harm.[57] Section 5 of the Terrorism Act 2006 (UK) criminalises for the first time 'any conduct in preparation' of the commission of acts of terrorism or assisting another to commit such acts and attaches a maximum penalty of life imprisonment. Sections 6 and 8 make criminal the giving or receiving of training in terrorist activities, and being at a place where training is going on (both of which carry a 10-year sentence of imprisonment). They are also made the subject of extraterritorial jurisdiction, so that they can be tried in the courts in the United Kingdom even if committed abroad. These new offences extend even further the range of inchoate crimes established by the Terrorism Act 2000 (UK) which include widely drafted offences of possession; of providing financial support to a terrorist organisation; of omission; and of supporting, belonging to, or wearing the uniform of proscribed organisations.[58] The combined effect of this anti-terrorism legislation is significantly to extend the ambit of inchoate offences within the criminal law.[59] Criminalisation of activities remote from the actual commission of an act of terrorism is justified by the need to furnish the legal grounds for action against individuals at the very earliest stages of preparation.

Attempts to develop legal categories upon which to legitimate pre-emptive action come at a cost. The definition of these offences is broad and, at least in the case of terms like 'indirect encouragement' or 'conduct in preparation', extremely vague. The long-established principles of English criminal law that offences be clearly defined and that inchoate offences can be the subject of sanction only if they amount to attempts 'more than merely preparatory' to a criminal offence is here overridden in favour of the unabashed criminalisation of indistinctly defined and merely preparatory actions.[60] The 'principle of maximum certainty',[61] namely that an offence should be clearly defined in law such that an individual can know from the wording of the relevant provision what acts and omissions will make him or her liable—the requirement of 'no punishment without law',[62]—is

[57] See Bernadette McSherry, this volume, ch 7.

[58] An excellent analysis of these offences is provided in V Tadros, 'Disciplining Terrorism' (2007) 10 *New Criminal Law Review* 658.

[59] A Hunt, 'Criminal Prohibitions on Direct and Indirect Encouragement of Terrorism' [2007] *Crim LR* 441. See also Bernadette McSherry, this volume, ch 7.

[60] The tendency toward criminalisation on the ground of probabilistic rather than actual harm has generated fierce debate. In its defence see F Schauer and R Zeckhauser, 'Regulation by Generalization' (2007) *Regulation and Governance* 1. For robust criticism of this approach, see D Husak, 'Guns and Drugs: Case Studies on the Principled Limits of the Criminal Sanction' (2004) *Law and Philosophy* 23.

[61] Ashworth, above n 31, at 74.

[62] European Convention on Human Rights 1950, Art 7.

likewise a fatal casualty of the precautionary approach.[63] Ashworth makes a powerful two-fold defence of the requirements of 'certainty, predictability, and "fair warning"'.[64] First, that 'respect for the citizen as a rational autonomous individual and as a person with social and political duties requires fair warning of the criminal law's provision and no undue difficulty in ascertaining them' and, second, that: 'if rules are vaguely drafted, they bestow considerable power on the agents of law enforcement ... creating the very kind of arbitrariness that rule-of law values should safeguard.'[65] In a striking inversion of these maxims, where precaution reigns, legal precision is no longer deemed a virtue but a hindrance. The criminalisation of uncertainty in the field of counter-terrorism thus exemplifies what Ericson has dubbed 'counter-law' or the proliferation of 'laws against law'.[66]

Further evidence of the way in which uncertainty now provides the grounds for action against individuals who are believed, but not known, to be involved in harmful behaviours can be found in new measures against serious and organised crime. Under s 1 of the Serious Crime Act 2007 (hereafter 'SCA') the British Government has introduced serious crime prevention orders, modelled on the control order, but applicable to those who have been 'involved in' serious crime, where 'involvement' is given a very wide meaning. It suffices under s 2(1)(b) SCA that the individual 'committed a serious offence', 'facilitated the commission by another person of a serious offence' or, most germane to our discussion, 'conducted himself in a way that was *likely to facilitate* the commission by himself or another person of a serious offence' [emphasis added]. This formulation recalls the earlier and controversial basis for the anti-social behaviour order (ASBO), namely that anti-social behaviour is any 'conduct which caused or was likely to cause alarm, harassment, or distress to one or more persons not of the same household as him or herself' and where an ASBO is seen as 'necessary to protect relevant persons from further anti-social acts by the Defendant'.[67]

The inclusion of the word 'likely to' in the conditions precedent to this order further evidences the attenuated requirement of certainty before the state permits itself to intrude into the liberties of its subjects. Although the formulation 'likely to' suggests that the risk of harm is calculable, the

63 There is a strong argument that the ordinary criminal law of attempts (with its amorphous test of 'more than merely preparatory') does not meet this test either and provides little meaningful guidance to citizens, tribunals or the courts. Peter Glazebrook has argued for the abolition of the law of attempts in favour of a range of offence-specific preparatory inchoate crimes precisely to address these liberal concerns: P Glazebrook, 'Should We Have a Law of Attempted Crime?' (1969) 85 *LQR* 28.

64 Ashworth, above n 31.

65 Ashworth, above n 31, at 76.

66 Ericson, above n 50, at 24.

67 Crime and Disorder Act 1998 (UK), s 1(1). See also Peter Ramsay, this volume, ch 6.

lack of any clearly articulated basis for calculation or any developed jurisprudence has in practice admitted a worrying degree of uncertainty as to which conduct is or is not liable to be caught by this provision. There is no requirement to demonstrate a causal relationship between the individual's action and any resulting crime, nor indeed that any crime in fact resulted: it must be merely 'likely to' facilitate serious crime. The definition of 'serious' is extremely wide and extends to any offence set out in sch 1 to the Act[68] or which 'in the particular circumstances of the case, the court considers to be sufficiently serious to be treated for the purposes of the application or matter as if it were so specified'.[69]

There is no requirement to meet the criminal standard of proof beyond reasonable doubt in making such an order; the court need only have 'reasonable grounds to believe that the order would protect the public by preventing, restricting or disrupting involvement by the person in serious crime'.[70] Nor does the court need to prove criminal intent on the part of the suspect. Indeed, s 4(2)(b) SCA expressly requires the court to ignore intention or any other aspect of his or her mental state. Moreover, s 4(2)(a) requires that in deciding whether a person has facilitated the commission of a serious offence by another, the court must ignore 'any act that the respondent can show to be reasonable in the circumstance'—thus severely limiting the availability of a defence of reasonable excuse.

As in the case of control orders, the range of conditions set is very wide. Section 1(3) SCA states that the order may contain: '(a) such prohibitions, restrictions or requirements; and (b) such other terms; as the court considers appropriate for the purpose of protecting the public by preventing, restricting or disrupting involvement by the person concerned in serious crime'.

The types of restrictions are not limited within the SCA, but a list of possible examples includes prohibitions, restrictions and requirements relating to an individual's financial, property or business dealings or holdings; working arrangements; and the means by which an individual communicates or associates with others, the provision of goods or services by such persons and the premises to which such persons have access or the use to which premises may be put.[71] Any breach of these conditions is again a criminal offence punishable by imprisonment for up to 5 years.

[68] As one legal commentator has observed: 'The Schedule 1 list is nothing if not comic. Murder, rape, arson, manslaughter, kidnapping, ... theft are not thought to constitute serious crimes. Fishing for salmon in breach of the Salmon and Freshwater Fisheries Act 1975 is': G Campbell, 'Serious Crime Prevention Orders: Unleashed!' (2007) *Counsel* 21.

[69] SCA, s 2(2)(b).

[70] SCA, s (1)(b).

[71] House of Lords, *The Serious Crime Bill: Library Note* (London, House of Lords Library, 2007). See also briefings provided at <www.liberty-human-rights.org.uk/>.

The poorly defined and extensive scope of the offence, together with the low standard of proof required, and the far-reaching restrictions imposed constitutes a considerable expansion of legal powers and a concomitant erosion of existing legal norms and procedural protections. Justified as a necessary measure against those 'who believe they are beyond the law and untouchable',[72] these orders are intended to disable criminal masterminds or underworld bosses whose remoteness from the actual commission of offences have hitherto made them particularly difficult to police. Serious crime orders may indeed prove applicable to the 30 or so 'Mr Bigs' that the Home Office anticipate subjecting to these orders per annum. Whether the requirement that conduct be 'likely to facilitate' serious crime is a sufficiently certain basis for criminalisation and whether the imposition of the multiple restrictions that constitute the order is justified ought to be a matter for vigorous debate.

The second categorisation of uncertainty—that of the unknown unknowns—gives rise to a further set of measures which, by definition, can have no target but instead treat all as possible sources of suspicion. These measures move from acknowledging uncertainty to imagining the worst. As Ewald, drawing on Descartes, observes, they make doubt active:

> Before any action, I must not only ask myself what I need to know and what I need to master, but also what I do not know, what I dread or suspect. I must, out of precaution, imagine the worst possible, the consequence that an infinitely deceptive malicious demon could have slipped into the folds of an apparently innocent enterprise.[73]

In the field of security this rationality (if it is such) stands behind proposals for mass surveillance, mass data collection and mass data retention. It is driven by an increasing 'demand for governance of the unknowable'[74] or desire to 'collect data on anything that is possible regardless of its relevance to the real risks the organisation is supposed to be addressing'.[75] One such example is the proposal by the British Government to permit data sharing across public and private sectors in order to combat fraud by disrupting the operations of organised criminals. Current proposals overturn an existing principle in English law that personal information provided to a government department for one purpose should not in general be used for another.[76]

[72] Home Office Minister Vernon Croaker quoted in *The Times* (London 18 January 2007): 'Super-ASBOs to Tackle the Bosses of the "Untouchable" Underworld'.

[73] F Ewald, 'The Return of Descartes's Malicious Demon: An Outline of a Philosophy of Precaution' in T Baker and J Simon (eds), *Embracing Risk: The Changing Culture of Insurance and Responsibility* (Chicago, University of Chicago Press, 2002).

[74] Power, above n 12, at 40–41.

[75] Ericson, above n 50, at 13.

[76] Data Protection Act 1998 (UK).

The Serious Crime Act 2007 reverses this principle so that 'information will normally be shared in the public sector, provided it is in the public interest'.[77] By so doing, the Act makes possible large-scale data-matching exercises using software designed to search databases to identify suspicious patterns of activity not discernible when data is viewed in isolation.

The fear, articulated by human rights organisations such as Liberty in Britain, is that mass data sharing will permit so-called 'fishing expeditions' against private bodies and companies without any prior requirement of suspicion of fraud.[78] This data mining goes well beyond data matching in that it uses specialist software to profile mass data in order to identify patterns or characteristics that might indicate unusual behaviour or impropriety. Requirements of proportionality are overridden by the need to mine huge quantities of data, based on no suspicion or intelligence that a particular person or company has done anything wrong. Further, the 'national fraud initiative' which involves 1,300 public bodies has the potential to gather data well beyond that relating to fraud and may be used to collect intelligence in pursuit of other crimes, or conceivably for other purposes altogether (enforcement of immigration laws being one such example).

This move toward large-scale data collection and mining in Britain is mirrored by similar developments elsewhere. The European Data Retention Directive (2006) permits all Member States to retain data pertaining to the communications traffic between individuals and organisations. Although the retention of such data had long been resisted as being incompatible with human rights protections,[79] it has been adopted as an essential tool in the fight against the ill-defined and amorphous threat posed by international terrorism.

The diffuse organisational structure and lack of hierarchical command that characterise contemporary terrorist activity combine to render conventional intelligence targeting of known terrorist leaders inadequate to the task. Recognition that Al-Qaeda is less an organisation than an ideology inspiring emulation makes it all but impossible to predict who poses a risk and who does not. As Power observes: 'the management of uncertainty is inherently paradoxical, an effort to know the unknowable'.[80] This is seen to justify entirely new intelligence-gathering tactics that not only focus on known risk categories, profiling and targeting but employ mass surveillance mechanisms, such as communications data retention, passenger name

[77] 'Ministers Overturn Data Protection Rules in Fight Against Organized Crime': *The Guardian* (London 19 January 2007).

[78] Liberty, *Liberty's Response to the Home Office Consultation—New Powers against Organised and Financial Crimes* (London, Liberty, 2006) 6.

[79] Not least the right to privacy under Art 8 of the European Convention on Human Rights 1950.

[80] Power, above n 12, at 59.

record data collection and biometric ID—all designed to observe everyone everywhere.[81] Where once such mass surveillance was resisted and considered unjustified, the impact of the Madrid, Bali and London bombings has secured its place as an essential plank in the armoury of the war on terror. The goal of 'total information awareness' (as it is called in the United States) is a chimera but in the face of uncertainty it is central to the logic of precaution.[82]

In sum, whereas uncertainty once spoke of incalculability, of an unknown future impossible therefore to control or of a lack evidence sufficient for prosecution for criminal offences, it has now become a developed set of discourses and techniques through which state action is both warranted and required. And though it may be the most serious threats of serious organised crime, sexual depredation or terrorist activity or attack that are invoked to justify pre-emptive measures, it should not surprise that precautionary logic is rapidly percolating its way down the tariff to less serious harms. The bid to 'gain access to a seamless web of information on citizens and non-citizens drawing on all potential sources'[83] is precisely the logical counter to the impasse that the conundrum of the unknown unknowns would otherwise pose. Ericson is surely right to suggest therefore that: 'A future direction for analysis regarding criminal law is the "criminalization of uncertainty": how, in face of limited knowledge about threats, criminalization—more legislation, intensified surveillance, lower due process standards, and greater punishment—is too often the preferred response.'[84]

One might expect that the cavalier fashion with which established principles of the criminal law and entrenched protections of the criminal process are presently being discarded would prompt legal academics to rally to their defence. Instead, quite the opposite appears to be occurring. A growing cast of legal luminaries have shown themselves content not merely to defend but to embrace the logic of precaution.[85] Willingness to envisage and endorse pre-emptive endeavour is, perhaps predictably, highest where the potential threat is greatest. In respect of terrorism, the perceived imperative to 'fix the future' before catastrophic threats are realised has seen even left-leaning and formerly rights-regarding scholars abandon their principles to think the previously unthinkable.

[81] MH Maras, 'From Targeted to Mass Surveillance: Is the Data Retention Directive a Justified Measure?' (DPhil thesis, University of Oxford forthcoming).

[82] J Stern and JB Wiener, 'Precaution Against Terrorism' (2006) 4 *Journal of Risk Research* 393.

[83] R Whitaker, 'A Faustian Bargain? America and the Dream of Total Information Awareness' in KD Haggerty and RV Ericson (eds), *New Politics of Surveillance and Visibility* (Toronto, University of Toronto Press, 2006).

[84] Ericson, above n 50, at 669.

[85] In varying degrees Ignatieff, above n 31; R Posner, *Catastrophe: Risk and Response* (Oxford, Oxford University Press, 2004); Dershowitz, above n 43.

For others, precautionary techniques, uncoupled as they are from the reactive post-hoc activities of blame and punishment, open the door, theoretically at least, to non-punitive forms of intervention. Shearing and Johnston ask '[i]s it possible to widen justice within the context of governance of security in ways that uncouple it from punishment?'[86] Yet the distinction drawn in law between precautionary measures and punishment has not resulted in retreat from hard treatment and there is little ground for confidence that preventative measures can operate non-punitively. If we consider the examples of preventative detention, of control orders, and of serious crime prevention orders, it is clear that neither a lack of proven culpability on the part of the individual nor a lack of punitive intent on the part of the state results in measures that are any less burdensome or punitive.[87] If intrusions into civil liberties and the burdens of hard treatment are the common accompaniment to purportedly precautionary, preventative measures then our attachment to the principles of criminal law and protections of the criminal process should be stronger than many academics currently allow. As yet, but lone voices speak out against the logic of precaution.[88]

VI. CONCLUSION

This chapter has sought to trace the changing rationales underpinning recent developments which seek to fix the future. The shifting logics of dangerousness, risk and uncertainty underpin changing discourses, direct distinct policy developments and have been deployed as successive governmental techniques to define problems and direct solutions.[89] Dangerousness was the purview of expert clinicians and risk the purview of expert statistical analysts, while uncertainty is arguably the child of expert politicians. Seen another way, dangerousness may be viewed as the product of classical liberalism, risk the product of social liberalism and the drive to redistribute exposure to the hazards of life, whereas uncertainty is the hallmark of neo-liberalism.[90]

There are two dangers, however, with this account. First, these shifting rationales may be understood as sequential changing fashions, whereas in practice they accumulate, layering upon one another to become ever more burdensome. Second, these rationales come to be seen as determinative of

86 Shearing and Johnston, above n 26, at 33.

87 Zedner, above n 48.

88 C Sunstein, *Laws of Fear: Beyond the Precautionary Principle* (Cambridge, Cambridge University Press, 2005).

89 Ericson, above n 34, at 668.

90 O'Malley, above n 19.

technological and legal change: as if the diagnostic tool for determining dangerousness is the product of faith in psychiatric expertise; the offender assessment tool results from the logic of risk; and the pre-emptive strike against a suspected terrorist cell is the child of precaution. As O'Malley observes, 'retrospectively it might appear that rationalities simply bring technologies into being'.[91] A more nuanced, more accurate reading might be rather that these rationalities cause existing techniques to be deployed and repackaged in different ways. Precaution alters the ways in which they are deployed by intelligence and police forces and licenses their more extensive use at earlier points in time and in respect of more remote harms than was hitherto the case.

The rise of risk[92] has commonly been represented as 'the taming of chance';[93] the assertion of technological and scientific endeavour over the vagaries of life to anticipate, reduce and even to eliminate harm. Actuarial calculation made it appear possible to know the future by reducing it to the statistical data of probabilities. In the spheres of policing, crime control and surveillance, the possibility of deploying risk-based technologies was eagerly grasped as a means of managing threats to security. Where the resultant strategies impinged on personal freedoms this was justified by asserting the high level of confidence that could be placed in statistical calculation. Officials were able to assert 'We are X% certain that if not detained he will reoffend' where X was a high figure sufficiently proximate to the known vagaries of proof within the criminal process to satisfy liberal qualms about locking up those yet to offend.[94]

More recently, claims as to the accuracy of risk prediction techniques have been substantially sidelined by an embracing of uncertainty that makes no claim to know the future but insists that, in the face of grave harm, uncertainty is no ground for inaction. Precaution overrides the criminal law requirement on public officials to establish proof beyond all reasonable doubt and leads to the introduction of measures that permit them to act on the basis of a prima facie case alone. In part this shift derives from the scale and seriousness of threats now faced. The prospect of catastrophic terrorist attacks does not invite cautious deliberation or calculation of the risks faced; such threats appear to call for *pre*-cautious, pre-emptive measures taken even in the face of uncertainty. But it is not only the scale, or the *feared* scale, of terrorist threats, that drives pre-emption. It is that precaution, the basis of a legal principle designed to frame administrative

[91] O'Malley, above n 19, at 173.
[92] Garland, above n 12.
[93] I Hacking, *The Taming of Chance* (Cambridge, Cambridge University Press, 1990).
[94] Monahan, above n 14.

decision-making in other fields (notably environmental catastrophes and industrial disasters), has become so dominant a mentality for public officials that it has seeped into spheres well beyond those for which it was originally intended. The mentality of precaution feeds on existing insecurities and gives sway to the exercise of fevered bureaucratic imagination. The consequence is that the old 'certainties' of risk have in significant measure been usurped by uncertainty as justification for governmental action. In a curious inversion of the well-rehearsed Foucauldian maxim that knowledge is power, here instead lack of knowledge is power. It is now our not knowing, our inability to know or unwillingness to prove what we think we know that provides the reason to act before that unknown threat makes itself known.

4

'Victim-Driven' Criminalisation? Some Recent Trends in the Expansion of the Criminal Law

LESLIE SEBBA*

I. INTRODUCTION

IN QUANTITATIVE TERMS the expansion of the criminal law in recent times is, as noted by Andrew Ashworth, primarily the product of new areas of regulation such as those relating to the use of computers or the protection of the environment.[1] Indeed, it is logical that additions to the criminal law will be focused mainly on such new areas, since traditional areas of criminalisation which protect fundamental interests such as physical integrity, property rights and personal autonomy are by definition already covered by the criminal law. Interest in these traditional areas tends to focus not so much on their substantive content but rather on the extent and manner of their enforcement—and in particular the sanctions imposed on the perpetrators when convicted.

However, the substantive content of these traditional areas, too, is constantly undergoing modification. This occurs as a result of codification, judicial interpretation (or, some would say, creativity), and reforms or modifications inspired by the prevailing concerns on the part of pressure-groups, of the general public and of policy makers—including populist politicians.[2] These concerns may in turn be a product of moral panics

* Thanks are due to the participants in the workshop on the topic of this volume held in Oñati in June 2007 and in particular to the editors for their comments on an earlier draft; to my assistant Efrat Zoe Kedem and to Ely Aharonson for bibliographical suggestions; and to the British Friends of the Hebrew University in memory of Lord Taylor for the facilities provided to the Jerusalem Criminal Justice Group.

[1] A Ashworth, 'Is the Criminal Law a Lost Cause?' (2000) 116 *LQR* 225; I Loveland (ed), *Frontiers of Criminality* (London, Sweet & Maxwell, 1995).

[2] On the dynamics of legislative processes, see WJ Chambliss and MS Zatz (eds), *Making Law: The State, The Law and Structural Considerations* (Bloomington, Indiana University Press, 1993); and R Tomasic, 'The Sociology of Legislation' in R Tomasic (ed), *Legislation and Society in Australia* (Sydney, Allen and Unwin, 1980).

on the one hand or, on the other, of considered reflection on the part of professional bodies (including public committees) of academic commentaries, or of international norm-setting. The variation in the modes whereby the modification of the substantive law occurs, as well as the inevitable variations in the patterns of such modifications in geographical terms, render these patterns difficult to identify.

From among the traditional areas of the common law, there is clearly a strong argument for identifying public order as the focal area in which the expansion of criminalisation has taken place in recent times with, on the one hand, the plethora of terror-related legislation which many Western countries have adopted in the wake of anxieties in this sphere and, on the other hand, concern at the 'soft end' for incivilities and other forms of pre-delinquent or quasi-delinquent behaviour.[3] Dubber argues that Herbert Packer's Crime Control Model 'has given way to the Police Power Model, as the War on Crime of the past three decades has shifted the focus of the American criminal process from the control of interpersonal crime to the affirmation of state authority',[4] that this model has shifted the focus 'from protecting individual interests or rights to public interests', and that the current process is concerned neither with offenders' nor victims' rights: 'the victim of criminal law is not the person, but the state'.[5]

Nevertheless, this chapter will argue that the main thrust (or at least a competing thrust) of the expansion of criminalisation in traditional areas in the last three decades has been in the area of what may be termed 'victim-driven'—or at least 'victim-oriented'—criminalisation. The types of criminal offence which I suggest may qualify for inclusion in this category include a number of new offences such as stalking and sexual harassment, new forms of child abuse, hate crimes and holocaust denial, and human trafficking.[6] Also included would be the expansion of some existing crimes, notably rape. Nor is the 'general part' of the criminal law entirely immune from victim-oriented reforms—particularly in the context of the defences of self-defence or provocation.[7]

[3] AP Simester and A von Hirsch (eds), *Incivilities* (Oxford, Hart Publishing, 2006); and Peter Ramsay, this volume, ch 6.

[4] MD Dubber, 'The Possession Paradigm: The Special Part and the Police Power Model of the Criminal Process' in RA Duff and SP Green (eds), *Defining Crimes* (Oxford, Oxford University Press, 2005).

[5] Dubber, above n 4, at 93. It should be noted that this last assertion is not intended to be a restatement of classical criminal law theory, but an empirical account of current developments.

[6] The extent to which all the offences in this list can be defined as 'new' will be considered below.

[7] For comparison, see L Sebba, 'Victims' Rights and Legal Strategies: Israel as a Case Study' (2000) 11 *Criminal Law Forum* 47. A broadening of *mens rea* concepts would also operate in favour of the victim. For the most part, however, the trend in criminal law doctrine in recent times has been to limit and 'subjectivise' principles of culpability.

The suggestion that trends in criminalisation during a particular period may be characterised as victim driven or victim oriented must surely provoke, at the least, a raising of eyebrows. For, except in the case of so-called 'victimless crimes'—itself a contested categorisation[8]—all offences have victims, whether personal or otherwise. Thus, one of the challenges in arguing that recent trends in criminalisation are victim driven will inevitably be *definitional*.

A casual observer of the criminal justice system, or even a consumer of the media, might assume that the enhanced importance of the victim in the criminal law is clearly evidenced by the not infrequent references to victim support organisations as well as a constant rhetoric on victims' rights. Section II of this chapter will therefore consider the possible impact on the scope of the criminal law of the rise of victimology, and in particular the extent to which expansions of the criminal law may be attributed to the victims' rights movement, which has developed during the period with which this chapter is concerned. The establishment of such a causal link would clearly provide a justification for the identification of the criminalisation process as 'victim driven'. Surprisingly, the conclusion will be reached that there is little direct link between the victims' rights movement and the developments alluded to here, although alternative meanings of the term 'criminalisation', of greater relevance in the context of procedural rights, might lead to a different conclusion.

The view that criminal law reforms are victim oriented, however, does not depend exclusively on proving that their adoption has been the result of victim advocacy,[9] and section III will consider alternative methodologies for validating my hypothesis. The focus here will be upon the characteristics of the penal provisions themselves and the manner and extent to which these differ from traditional norms of criminalisation, rather than the political processes leading to their adoption. (Some reference will be made, however, to the arguments for their enactment.)

Section IV will focus on a case study: the recent measures adopted to criminalise the administration of physical punishment on the part of parents, as well as other educators, against their children—including the practice of smacking. While two alternative rationales may be proffered by way of explanation for this development (in itself a dramatic *volte-face*, when placed in historical perspective), it will be argued here that both rationales lend support to the view that this reform has a strong victim orientation.

A notable feature of the diffusion of the anti-smacking norm is that it has emerged from the institutions of international law, and thus involves

[8] EM Schur and HA Bedau, *Victimless Crimes—Two Sides of a Controversy*, (Englewood Cliffs, NJ, Prentice Hall, 1974).

[9] Some reference, however, will be made in this chapter to the role of other advocacy groups which appear to have been more significant than the victims' rights movement in their contribution to the reform of the substantive criminal law.

an imposition from above. Section V will elaborate other ways in which a duty of active intervention to prevent or to respond to victimisation has been imposed either upon states, notably by dint of the 'doctrine of positive obligation', or upon individuals, by means of a duty to report or a duty of rescue.

Should my account of these developments provide a basis for the argument that criminal law reform has in recent years assumed a victim orientation, it remains to consider to what extent this has become 'the new paradigm',[10] or whether it is in competition for this title with Dubber's Police Power model or similar. However, it is also possible that beyond mere co-existence the two developments are in fact politically or conceptually related—a claim which would be analogous to the one sometimes made in respect of Packer's presumed dichotomy between the Due Process and Crime Control models.[11] Indeed, other chapters in this volume—notably Ramsay's and Norrie's—lend some support to the existence of such a connection between measures ostensibly designed to enhance the protection of victims and the expansion of state power, a theme also supported by some other recent writing on justice and social control.

From a very different perspective, a recent monograph by Kirchengast[12] employs a Foucauldian analysis based upon the ubiquity of governmentality to conclude that the wide powers wielded by the victim in the Middle Ages have continued to underlie the state's authority in the area of criminal justice, and the recent revival of the victim is merely an expression of this. He specifically claims that 'the victim has always played a fundamental role in the formation of criminal law and justice on both a procedural and substantive level' and that 'the genealogy of the victim is a vital aspect of the genesis of modern criminal law and procedure in common law systems'.[13]

The concluding section (section VI) will endeavour to link the material covered by the chapter with the above literature, as well as with some of the recent theoretical work on criminalisation.

II. THE RISE OF VICTIMOLOGY AND THE VICTIMS' RIGHTS MOVEMENT

The early developments of victimology from around the middle of the 20th century focused on the identity of victims, their psychopathologies

[10] Compare Alan Norrie, this volume, ch 2.

[11] Thus it has been argued that due process may serve to enhance or legitimate crime control: see the sources cited in KK Roach, 'Four Models of the Criminal Process' (1999) 89 *Journal of Criminal Law & Criminology* 671, 688.

[12] T Kirchengast, *The Victim in Criminal Law and Justice* (Basingstoke, Palgrave Macmillan, 2006).

[13] Kirchengast, above n 12, at 3 and 7.

and their relationship with 'their' offenders.[14] While this literature could have been invoked to draw attention to the need to protect vulnerable victims, it was rather seen as inviting a shift of responsibility from the offender to the victim.[15] Indeed, the sophisticated empirical research undertaken by criminologist Marvin Wolfgang led not only to his establishing a socio–cultural link between offender and victim populations,[16] but also to his coining the term 'victim-precipitation', a phenomenon which, according to Wolfgang's research findings, characterised a substantial proportion of homicides—a finding with clear implications for criminal law defence doctrine.[17]

During the 1970s the focus of criminology (or at least penology) moved away from positivist behavioural research and an adherence to determinist philosophy with a treatment orientation to concerns of justice and 'desert sentencing'. Wolfgang became involved with techniques for the measurement of victim harm as an indication of offence seriousness and thus as a basis for tariff sentencing.[18] The reorientation of corrections towards victim harm was strengthened by the development at this time of victim surveys, which drew attention to the dimensions and characteristics of victimisation.[19] These developments in turn set the scene for the rise of the victims' rights movement[20] which, by virtue of its role as an instrument for policy change and its potential appeal to a wider public, has

[14] For an account of the early developments of victimology, see S Schafer, 'The Beginning of Victimology' in I Drapkin and E Viano (eds), *Victimology* (Lexington, Lexington Books, 1974) 17 and S Schafer, *The Victim and his Criminal* (New York, Random House, 1964).

[15] W Ryan, *Blaming the Victim* (New York, Vintage Books, 1976). For a recent discussion of this concept, see AM Cole, *The Cult of True Victimhood* (Stanford, Stanford University Press, 2007) ch 5.

[16] ME Wolfgang and F Ferracuti, *The Subculture of Violence* (London, Social Science Paperbacks, 1967).

[17] J Gobert, 'Victim Precipitation' (1967) 77 *Columbia Law Review* 511. Similar issues have been raised in recent times in relation to battered women who kill their partners and by the Tony Martin case in Britain: see L Farmer, 'Tony Martin and the Nightbreakers: Criminal Law, Victims, and the Power to Punish' in A Armstrong and L McAra (eds), *Perpectives on Punishment* (Oxford, Oxford University Press, 2006) .

[18] Wolfgang's interest in the 'measurement of delinquency' was originally conceived as a method of improving the nature of crime statistics: T Sellin and ME Wolfgang, *The Measurement of Delinquency* (Montclair, NJ, Patterson Smith, 1964/1978), but the methodology was later adapted as a tool for sentencing: ME Wolfgang, 'Seriousness of Crime and A Policy for Juvenile Justice' in JF Short (ed), *Delinquency, Crime and Society* (Chicago, University of Chicago Press, 1978). See also n 32 below.

[19] Victimisation surveys were originally conceived not as a source of information about victims but simply to improve our knowledge as to the true dimensions of crime and as an alternative source to police-based statistics.

[20] I use this as a term of convenience to refer to the organisations seeking to draw attention to the neglect of crime victims by both the criminal justice system and the social services. However, it has been argued that the 'victim movement' differs from the 'new social movements' in that it does not comprise a single identifiable disadvantaged social group and it reflects very disparate political ideologies: J Goodey, *Victims and Victimology: Research, Policy and Practice* (Edinburgh, Pearson/Longman, 2005) ch 4.

tended to overshadow the more narrowly based 'academic' victimology of the previous generation.[21]

The victims' rights movement came into its own in the 1980s. Its main objectives have been to improve the treatment of crime victims on the part of the criminal justice system and other social agencies and, increasingly, the enhancement of the role of the victim in the criminal justice system. Filling the vacuum created by the decline in interest in the personality of the offender, the victims' rights movement drew attention to the negative experiences of victims deriving both from the initial act of victimisation itself and from the subsequent criminal justice processes which were dubbed 'secondary victimisation'.[22] These negative experiences were in turn attributed to the failure of the criminal justice system to grant the victim any recognised status other than that of witness to the crime and to the absence of social services for the provision of treatment and compensation. While the proposals emanating from victim advocates and their organisations have been varied,[23] they have focused mainly on enhancing victims' procedural rights before, during and following the trial process, and the provision of victim services both as part of the criminal justice system and in the community. More controversially, some victim advocates have sought modifications to the sentencing structure, including harsher or mandatory penalties.[24]

In the United States of America, a leading player in this area of reform, the above-mentioned objectives have sometimes been achieved by means of 'Victims' Bills of Rights', a rhetorical device intended as a 'response' to the historic amendments to Constitution designed to protect the rights of suspects and defendants; and indeed a large number of states have entrenched victims' rights in their constitutions. (A campaign to amend the federal constitution has not yet come to fruition.) While the extent to which victim-related reforms have radically altered the experiences of the average victim in the criminal justice system (or in the community) may be unclear,[25] the

[21] While there are many national and local victim support associations—most focusing on victim assistance, some on policy—the few academic organisations such as the World Society of Victimology also tend to lean towards advocacy, in addition to their academic activities. Much of the academic research in the field remains under the aegis of the institutions of mainstream criminology. See also Goodey, above n 20.

[22] Goodey, above n 20, at 157.

[23] L Sebba, *Third Parties: Victims and the Criminal Justice System* (Columbus, Ohio State University Press, 1996). On the question as to whether the victims' movement is a 'social' movement, see V Poliny, *A Public Policy Analysis of the Emerging Victims' Rights Movement* (San Francisco, Austin & Winfield, 1994) ch 4.

[24] See generally: WG Doerner and SP Lab, *Victimology*, (Cincinnati, Ohio, LexisNexis, 4th edn, 2005).

[25] R Elias, *Victims Still: The Political Manipulation of Crime Victims* (Newbury Park, Sage, 1993). See also the critical appraisal of the services provided in Britain on the part of Victim Support (the main victim assistance organisation), reported in Goodey, above n 20, at 107.

transformation of the formal role of the victim in many criminal justice systems cannot be doubted.

Moreover, in one sense (and perhaps two) the victim movement has almost certainly resulted in the expansion of criminalisation. Police have been educated or instructed to be more sympathetic to victims in order to encourage them to report the victimisation, and the victim's encounter with victim support personnel may operate in the same direction. These developments have been more salient in areas where victims were reluctant to report, such as in the wake of sexual assaults or domestic violence. The recognition of victims' rights, including both the right to receive information regarding the criminal justice processes and the right to provide information to the courts in respect of their injuries—in some systems accompanied also by the right to express their views at the various stages of the system—are also calculated to enhance their motivation to co-operate. It is probable that these developments have resulted in increased rates of reported crime, particularly in the sensitive areas referred to, and in more convictions.[26] Moreover, victim-sensitive reforms of both rules of evidence and the modes of giving testimony are also calculated to increase the probability of conviction. I refer, for example, to the restrictions on the cross-examination of rape victims with regard to their moral character, and the special provisions protecting victims of sexual assault, and especially child victims, from exposure to traumatic cross-examination.[27] The extent of criminalisation, in the sense of the numbers of persons successfully prosecuted, is likely to have been enhanced by such victim-sponsored reforms.[28] Reference may also be made here to the expansion of the courts' trial jurisdiction as the result of extensions to the statutes of limitations to enable child victims of sex offences to file complaints after reaching the age of majority.

Further, if increasing the severity of sentencing may also be considered a form of 'expanding criminalisation', here too victims' rights organisations may have made an impact. Some victim advocacy organisations believe that victims should *not* become involved in sentencing decisions,[29] and much research shows that victims are not necessarily punitive,

[26] In terms of absolute numbers, owing to the increase in reporting rates, but perhaps also higher conviction rates (see following).

[27] CH Hoyano and C Keenan, *Child Abuse Law and Policy: Across Boundaries* (Oxford, Oxford University Press, 2007) pt IV. Such provisions are intended to enable victims to present more cohesive testimonies, as well as encouraging prosecutors to proceed with the trial rather than staying the proceedings out of consideration for the trauma inflicted upon the victims—as well as out of concern for their possibly problematic testimony.

[28] But compare the view expressed by Ngaire Naffine, this volume, ch 10, regarding the failure to process rape as a crime.

[29] Compare *Victims in Criminal Justice: Report of the JUSTICE Committee on the Role of the Victim in Criminal Justice* (London, JUSTICE, 1998); see also Goodey, above n 20, on the stand adopted by Victim Support.

in particular if the procedures are perceived as fair and satisfactory. Nevertheless in some jurisdictions, notably the United States[30] and New Zealand,[31] tougher sentencing has been a part of the agenda of victim groups, and their influence appears to have been significant. Mention again may be made here of the views of the academic victimologist Marvin Wolfgang who advocated a greater orientation towards victim categories in sentencing tariffs,[32] as indeed occurred with the adoption of sentencing guidelines.[33]

If, however, by the expansion (or redirection) of criminalisation we are referring exclusively to the formal ambit of the criminal law as reflected in the manner in which offences are defined and in which criminal responsibility is determined (whether in the relevant legislative provisions or in their judicial interpretation)—the victims' rights movement has been surprisingly reticent. The manifestos and policy documents of the victims' rights organisations such as the National Organisation of Victims' Assistance in the United States, or Victim Support in the United Kingdom, have rarely, if ever, referred to the need for any modification of the provisions of the substantive criminal law; and the same is true for such seminal documents as the President's Task Force on Victims of Crime in the United States of America and the Victim's Charter or the Justice report in the United Kingdom.[34] Nor do Paul Rock's searching analyses of the development of victim-related policies in Britain and Canada indicate any interest in the substantive criminal law. Indeed, his recent comprehensive monograph on the development

[30] C McCoy, *Politics and Plea Bargaining* (Philadelphia, University of Pennsylvania Press, 1993); SA Scheingold, T Olson and J Pershing, 'Sexual Violence, Victim Advocacy and Republican Criminology: Washington State's Community Protection Act' (1994) 28 *Law and Society Review* 729.

[31] J Pratt and M Clark, 'Penal Populism in New Zealand' (2005) 7 *Punishment and Society* 303.

[32] ME Wolfgang, 'Basic Concepts in Victimology Theory: Individualisation of the Victim' in H-J Schneider (ed), *The Victim in International Perspective* (Berlin, de Gruyter, 1982). See above, n 18 and accompanying text.

[33] Sebba, L, 'Sentencing and the Victim: The Aftermath of Payne' (1994) *International Review of Victimology* 141 at 148. The historical theme of Wolfgang's seminal 1982 article was 'from the individualisation of the offender to the individualisation of the victim'. Compare Erez, E and Sebba, L, 'From Individualization of the Offender to Individualization of the Victim' (1999) 8 *Advances in Criminological Theory* 171 which is concerned with *categories* of victim as well as individuals—and normative structures such as sentencing guidelines inevitably focus on categories. Other more recent developments, however, such as victim impact statements, have led to the possibility of sentences becoming tailored to *individual* victim characteristics. For a more detailed analysis of this issue and a comparison with early conceptualisations of the individualisation of the offender, see Sebba, L, 'The Individualisation of the Victim: From Positivism to Postmodernism' in A Crawford and J Goodey (eds), *Integrating a Victim Perspective in the Criminal Justice System* (Dartmouth, Aldershot, 2000) 55.

[34] See *Victims in Criminal Justice*, above n 29, and Goodey, above n 20. It seems that the German victim support organisation, the Weisse Ring, made an exception from their policy of non-intervention in issues relating to the substantive law in advocating the criminalisation of stalking (personal communication from Prof Christian Pfeiffer).

of victim policies under the British Labour Government makes almost no reference to this area of the law.[35]

It could, of course, be argued that the reason victims' rights organisations have not been concerned with the substantive criminal law is that for the purposes of their mission to improve the rights of victims in the criminal justice system they inevitably limit their concern to persons who have been identified as victims by this system, that is, those who are affected by the *prevailing* criminal law; and they are not concerned with persons who might have been regarded as victims were the criminal law to be expanded.

In one notable case, however, victims of abuses which were not formally criminalised in certain parts of the world were recognised as victims by an official international body at the behest of victim advocates from the areas in question—and the relevant states were exhorted to ensure the criminalisation of these abuses. I refer to the abuses of human rights which were rampant in Central and South American cultures during the heyday of the dictatorships prevailing in those areas, and the special chapter which was included in the United Nations Declaration of Basic Principles of Justice for Victims of Crime and Abuse of Power (1985) recognising victims of such abuses even if they did not constitute criminal conduct in the particular jurisdiction.[36] A somewhat similar approach has been adopted by proponents of international legislation directed against other forms of human rights abuse such as torture and trafficking in persons. International Conventions adopted in these areas specifically require the criminalisation of such abuses on the part of the international community.[37] Such measures, however, are not generally identified with the victim movement as such.

In her recent text on victims and victimhood, Spalek has noted that alongside the 'official' movement represented by the larger national organisations, 'unofficial' victim movements have been established, consisting of small organisations focusing on particular areas of victimisation.[38] Unlike the former category, some such groups have on occasion been concerned with reform of the substantive law, an illustration of this being the pressure

[35] PE Rock, *Constructing Victims' Rights: The Home Office, New Labour and Victims* (Oxford, Oxford University Press, 2004).

[36] Under s 19 of the Declaration: 'States should consider incorporating into the national law norms proscribing abuses of power and providing remedies to victims of such abuses. In particular, such remedies should include restitution and/or compensation, and necessary material, medical, psychological and social assistance and support.'

[37] See Convention against Torture and other Cruel, Inhuman or Degrading Treatment or Punishment 1984, and the Protocol to Prevent, Suppress and Punish Trafficking in Persons, Especially Women and Children, supplementing the United Nations Convention against Transnational Organised Crime, 2000.

[38] B Spalek, *Crime Victims: Theory, Policy and Practice* (Basingstoke, Palgrave Macmillan, 2007). Compare the category of 'single-issue groups' discussed by Goodey, above n 20, at 107.

exerted by Mothers against Drunk Drivers (MADD) in the United States for the reform of the laws relating to drinking and driving.[39]

The list of victim movements having an impact on criminalisation processes can be expanded if, with Spalek, we also designate as victims' movements the numerous action groups 'that have been formed around identities in relation to race, gender, sexuality, disability and so forth'.[40] In particular, hate crime legislation is shown to be an area that has been influenced by the activity of such groups. Moreover, a wide range of feminist organisations, many of which have been instrumental in the criminalisation of sexual harassment and stalking and in the expansion of the definition of rape, could also be included. However, unlike such 'unofficial' single-issue groups such as those of bereaved parents,[41] most of the groups identified by Spalek in this context would not generally be considered victim organisations.[42]

Why was this approach not adopted by mainstream victims' rights organisations? Why did they not propose extensions of the criminal law with a view to increasing the ambit of victim protection? The failure to adopt a more flexible approach (beyond the focus on procedural rights and social services) is even more surprising given that the victims' rights movement developed out of victimology, and victimology has been characterised by an ongoing debate as to whether its contours should be determined exclusively by criminal law definitions or broadened out to incorporate other types of victimisation.[43] Moreover, the contemporary discourse on the desirability or otherwise of the status of 'victimhood',[44] with its potential implications for both substantial and procedural criminal law policies, also seems to have bypassed the 'official' victims' rights and advocacy groups.

In an earlier publication I suggested that a number of alternative legal strategies were available for the promotion of victim interests—including the reform of the substantive criminal law, both general and special parts.[45]

[39] Kirchengast, above n 12, at 178; compare Goodey, above n 20, at 109.

[40] Spalek, above n 38, at 144.

[41] Compare Goodey, above n 20, at 107, citing the research of Paul Rock in this area.

[42] While Spalek's list includes a Holocaust survivors' organisation, it also includes the National Gay and Lesbian Task Force, the Organisation of Chinese Americans and the Japanese American Citizens League—all groups referred to as being active on the issue of hate crimes in the study by Jacobs and Potter in the United States: Spalek, above n 38. On the difference between the victim movement and the 'new social movements', see Goodey, above n 20.

[43] The latter view is identified with the later writings of Beniamin Mendelsohn, one of the founders of victimology. The issues have recently been reviewed in S Garkawe, *'Revisiting the Scope of Victimology—How Broad a Discipline Should it Be?'* (2004) 11 *International Review of Victimology* 275.

[44] M Minow, 'Surviving Victim Talk' (1993) 40 *UCLA Law Review* 1411; A Leisenring, 'Confronting 'Victim' Discourses: The Identity Work of Battered Women' (2006) 29 *Symbolic Interaction* 307; S Walklate, *Imagining the Victim of Crime* (Maidenhead, Open University Press, 2007) ch 1. See also Cole, above n 15.

[45] Sebba, above n 7.

The fact is, however, that the victims' rights movement has all but ignored this potential. That being the case, the recent expansions of the substantive criminal law considered in this chapter cannot be regarded as 'victim driven' by virtue of their roots in this movement and its advocates.

So how can it be argued that criminal law reforms are 'victim driven', or even 'victim oriented', if the community of victims' rights advocates cannot be identified with these reforms? One possible rationale is that alluded to in the preceding discussion, namely that the reforms have been promoted not by victims' rights advocates as such, but by the various groups upon which the reforms have focused (such as those identified by Spalek) which have perceived themselves as insufficiently protected by the pre-existing law—notably women, children and minorities. Arguably, such groups have been laying claim to their victim status, and insofar as they have been influential in bringing about the criminal law reforms under consideration here (and there is certainly some evidence for this[46]), this analysis could be used to support the argument that such expansions of the criminal law were victim driven. On this analysis, it is not the victims who have already (by definition) attained such recognition who have sought expansion of the law but rather the groups not yet protected, or inadequately protected, by criminal law definitions who are now claiming recognition of their victim status. According to this conceptualisation, which can be subsumed under the heading of 'identity politics', claims on the part of such groups derive from their perceived victim status, and the resulting criminalisation may therefore be described as 'victim driven'. A detailed analysis of this hypothesis, however, which in the context of hate crimes has been considered in the work of Jacobs and Potter and of Jenness and Grattet,[47] would require a close examination of the functioning of a variety of advocacy groups and would be beyond the scope of this chapter.

Alternatively, it may be that recent developments in the expansion of criminalisation can only be accounted for in terms of broader theories pertaining to the social policies of late modernism in the neo-liberal state, such as those of David Garland, Jonathan Simon[48] and, in the context of this volume, Peter Ramsay. Even under these theories, however, the expansion of criminalisation is not entirely unconnected with the status of victims and the perceptions of potential victims.

[46] On the role of advocacy groups in the process of the enactment of hate crime laws in the United States, see V Jenness and R Grattet, *Making Hate a Crime: From Social Movement to Law Enforcement* (New York, Russell Sage Foundation, 2001).

[47] JB Jacobs, and K Potter, *Hate Crimes: Criminal Law and Identity Politics* (New York, Oxford University Press, 1998); Jenness and Grattet, above n 46.

[48] D Garland, *The Culture of Control* (Oxford, Oxford University Press, 2001); J Simon, 'Megan's Law: Crime and Democracy in Late Modern America' (2000) 25 *Law and Social Inquiry* 1111; and now J Simon, *Governing Through Crime* (Oxford, Oxford University Press, 2007).

I will return to these themes in my concluding section. However, rather than try to examine the explanations for the processes of criminalisation implicit in these analyses in greater depth with a view to establishing their victim orientation, I will attempt to approach this topic from another angle.

III. ALTERNATIVE METHODOLOGIES FOR THE DESIGNATION OF OFFENCES AS 'VICTIM DRIVEN'

If the expansions of criminalisation cannot be attributed to the influence of victim advocacy groups (and related explanations have still to be tested), what alternative rationales can be invoked as a basis for describing the developments referred to here as 'victim driven'? Two alternative approaches might be adopted. One approach would be to consider the nature of the offences in question in order to determine whether they possess some characteristic or characteristics which link them in some conceptual way to victims, either in a manner or to a degree which differentiates them from pre-existing types of offences. This approach may be termed *analytic*. The second approach would be to focus on the *language* employed in the offence definitions or, alternatively, in the debates preceding their enactment. This approach could be called *rhetorical* (or *discursive*).[49]

The following discussion will draw upon both these approaches somewhat indiscriminately. One reason for this is that the scope of the present chapter is exploratory in character, raising tentative hypotheses rather than rigorously testing them. Another reason is that the two approaches may overlap. The use of unequivocally victim-related language under the rhetorical approach may itself constitute a special characteristic under the analytical approach.

The primary indicator that the enactment or expansion of an offence is victim oriented is, inevitably, some reference to the victim in the offence description. Historically, offence definitions were concerned almost exclusively with the offender, or rather with his or her conduct. References to victims and their characteristics were rare, examples being the age of a rape victim, or a fatal outcome in the case of result offences. In recent years, however, there has been a proliferation of such references in offence definitions, particularly in the context of the offences referred to above, which are intended to bestow special protection upon spouses, children, the elderly and other vulnerable persons, or persons implicitly identified

[49] A third approach, considered in the previous part, where the possible influence of victim advocacy groups on the criminalisation process was examined, might be termed *empirical*.

by ethnic or other affiliation (hate crimes and holocaust denial). Gender, too, plays a prominent part, as is implicit in the offences of sexual harassment and stalking. Vulnerability of the victim, however, is the paradigmatic feature[50]: the common characteristic of the new offences is that they derive from the recognition that the vulnerability of certain categories of victim was not adequately acknowledged in the pre-existing offence categories.

Designation of vulnerable victim categories is also prominent in the framework of international norm-setting. Attached to the United Nations Convention against Transnational Organised Crime is a Protocol on human trafficking (Annex II to the Convention).[51] The aim of the protocol, as evidenced by its title, is to 'Prevent, Suppress and Punish Trafficking in Persons, *Especially Women and Children*' (emphasis added).

While the expression 'victim' does not generally appear in the offence definition, such offences are often intended to protect particular categories of victims who are designated therein. The term 'victim' will be salient in the course of the legislative processes, while in cases in which the criminalisation process follows from international norm-setting, concern for the welfare and rights of the victims may be as much or more of a focal concern than the prosecution of the offenders. This, again, is illustrated by the provisions of the United Nations Protocol on Trafficking in Persons.[52]

Arguably, however, it is not only the designation of the type of victim which should lead to the identification of the offence as victim driven; a focus in the offence definition on the nature of the harm inflicted may sometimes serve as a proxy for the designation of the victim. Thus, one of the offences specified in Israel's new chapter of the Penal Law on 'Injury to Minors and Vulnerable Persons' is 'physical, psychological or sexual abuse'.[53] The epithets qualifying the type of abuse with which the provision is concerned is additional to the specification of the victim categories to which it applies—namely, minors and (other) vulnerable persons.

Concern with the infliction of harm in itself is hardly indicative of a novel victim-oriented approach. The infliction of harm is almost inseparable from the notion of *actus reus*—and absolutely so in the case of 'result offences'. Under liberal theory, harm is the *sine qua non* for the invocation of the criminal law[54] and has more recently been the dominant principle behind desert

[50] In 1989 a new chapter was added to Israel's Penal Code, entitled 'Injury to Minors and Vulnerable Persons'.

[51] Compare n 37.

[52] Thus the Preamble notes that international measures are required 'to prevent such trafficking, to punish the traffickers and to protect the victims of such trafficking, including by protecting their internationally recognised human rights'.

[53] Penal Law 1977, s 368C (as amended).

[54] J Feinberg, *The Moral Limits of the Law* (New York, Oxford University Press, 1984).

sentencing,[55] where it has been developed as one of the main parameters for measuring the seriousness of the offence. Indeed, the focus on the harmfulness of the conduct seems increasingly to be acquiring a significance independent of the offender's culpability, as illustrated by the admissibility of victim-impact statements.[56] The trauma of the victimisation may be factored in as a measure of the offence seriousness without undue attention to the offender's mental attitude.[57]

Indeed in many cases it is this new victim-oriented perspective which serves as the main justification for the adoption of the new offence, rather than any major *lacuna* in the coverage of the criminal law. This point is made by Duff and Green in their consideration of the 'Moralistic Approach' to offence definitions, wherein the purpose of the definition is to draw attention to the moral character of the prohibited conduct rather than its precise content.[58] (This is contrasted with the 'Descriptivist Approach' which emphasises the latter.) In accordance with the Moralistic Approach, the moral context of the offensive conduct may give rise to pressure to adopt a new offence, even when the actual conduct prohibited is substantially covered by an existing offence. In this context Duff and Green allude to an article by Tadros in support of a separate offence of domestic abuse even though the prohibited conduct is largely covered by the existing offence of assault[59]—the purpose being to 'recognize the distinctive, even unique, effects such abuse has on its victims' sense of self-worth'.[60] In the same context Duff and Green point to the symbolic role played by the creation of a new offence which 'marks out the failure of an earlier regime to recognize such behaviour as significantly wrong'.[61] While I agree with this analysis, in my view it is the formulation adopted in the first of the two quotations, recognising the centrality of the victim's role, that is the more

[55] A von Hirsch, *Doing Justice: The Choice of Punishments* (New York, Hill and Wang, 1976).

[56] This is, of course, problematic from the point of view of criminal law doctrine. Indeed, it seems odd that the emphasis on victim harm as the primary measure of offence seriousness has been developing during a period when criminal law doctrine has tended to emphasise the subjective element in culpability. This has been particularly problematic at the sentencing stage (see following note), where the extent of victim harm plays a focal role under the desert approach, but where historically culpability requirements in relation to the harm inflicted have been treated as less relevant: see Sebba, 'Sentencing ... ', above n 33.

[57] Sebba, 'Sentencing ... ', above n 33. The incorporation of degrees of victimisation is of course more common in sentencing tariffs than in offence definitions. However, Ian Elliott-Leader, this volume, ch 12, argues (in the context of Duff's communication theory) that *mens rea* gradations are also victim oriented and should be considered at the sentencing stage.

[58] RA Duff and SP Green, 'Introduction: The Special Part and its Problems' in Duff and Green, above n 4, at 1 and 10ff.

[59] There is a similarity here with the Israeli legislature's enactment of the chapter on vulnerable victims referred to above.

[60] Duff and Green, above n 4, at 15.

[61] Duff and Green, above n 4, at 16.

significant: the main thrust of these offences is directed less at hitherto ignored offenders than it is at hitherto neglected victims.[62]

IV. THE SPECIAL CASE OF CHILD-SMACKING

In some respects prohibitions on child-smacking provide the quintessential illustration of my claim that recent developments in the extension of criminalisation are victim driven. In the first place, this is conduct which was universally permitted until around 30 years ago, the steps towards criminalisation coinciding in time precisely with the period of my focus in this chapter. Second, the pressure to introduce a prohibition on child-smacking may be attributed at least in part to the focus of victimologists and child welfare personnel on child abuse during this period.[63] In addition to the harm inflicted directly upon the child was the concern that there was a high probability that child victims would subsequently become delinquent—and later still hit their own children.[64] Finally, in the context of the broad prohibition on the use of any physical punishment against children (rather than restricting the prohibition to cases of violent abuse), the focus of concern seems to have been almost exclusively the victim and not the perpetrator, if only because the parental conduct in question was not widely seen as deviant.

At the same time, the manner in which such criminalisation has been achieved (insofar as this is so) is far from typical. There do not seem to be any jurisdictions in which a provision has been introduced in a penal code which explicitly prohibits child-smacking and attaches a sanction thereto.[65] However in at least two cases the functional equivalent has been achieved

[62] I may add that this analysis does not depend on the adoption of Duff and Green's 'Moralistic Approach' to the definition of the offences. It may be that some offences employ the Descriptive Approach in order clearly to articulate the parameters of a new prohibition but, again, the emphasis will be less on clarifying to the offender the nature of the prohibited conduct (compare Duff and Green, above n 4, at 10), but rather on specifying with greater precision the prohibited forms of victimisation, or the characteristics of the victim to be protected by the particular offence. (In the latter respect this trend seems to challenge the view of Bronitt and McSherry that allusions to the status of the victim belong to an era of misplaced paternalism: S Bronitt and B McSherry, *Principles of Criminal Law* (Sydney, LBC, 2nd edn, 2005) 513.

[63] A vast amount of literature on this topic has emerged during this period, to some extent pioneered by the 'discovery' by Helfer and Kempe of the 'battered child': RE Helfer and CH Kempe (eds), *The Battered Child* (Chicago, University of Chicago Press, 1968). The topic was the subject of at least one of the papers presented at the First International Symposium of Victimology in 1973. (One may recall the controversial procedures of this period whereby suspicions of widespread parental abuse led to the removal of children into care, and the subsequent view that a moral panic had lead to injustices: J Fortin, *Children's Rights and the Developing Law* (United Kingdom, LexisNexis, 2nd edn, 2003).

[64] See, generally, ET Gershoff, 'Corporal Punishment by Parents and Associated Child Behaviors and Experiences: A Meta-Analytic and Theoretical Review' (2000) 128 *Psychological Bulletin* 539.

[65] R Boyson, *Equal Protection for Children* (London, NSPCC, 2002); <www.endcorporalpunishment.org/>.

by abolishing the traditional defence of reasonable chastisement which was available in common law countries—with the result that parents (or educators) would become liable for common assault if they touched their children without consent.[66] In most of the jurisdictions which have reportedly criminalised child-smacking the process has been somewhat opaque. The reviews of this legislation cite mainly welfare legislation or civil code provisions as the source of the prohibition.[67] It is not entirely clear from the reviews whether the penal element here is provided by the attachment of a penal sanction (which is, of course, common in regulatory legislation) or by the implicit removal of a defence to criminal charges, where this defence was itself based on civil law provisions which have now been amended.

Further, while the total number of jurisdictions included in this list number only around 20, a continuing impetus for the growth of this number derives from what resembles a concerted campaign[68] of international standard-setting. First and foremost, the Children's Rights Committee, operating under the Children's Rights Convention which has been ratified by almost all nations, has, since 1993, adopted a critical approach when reviewing the periodic reports submitted by states when these do not indicate that the use of physical punishment against children is prohibited;[69] and this despite the lack of clarity of the Convention itself on this point.[70] Similarly, the Human Rights Committee, which monitors compliance with the International Covenant on Civil and Political Rights, and the equivalent committee under the International Covenant on Economic, Social and Cultural Rights, both issued General Comments (in 1992 and 1999 respectively) holding the physical punishment of minors to be unacceptable under the terms of the respective covenants. (The latter was concerned with the use of corporal punishment in education.) In a purely European context, not only did the European Court of Human Rights find the scope of the English defence of reasonable chastisement to be unacceptable, but the European Committee of Social Rights (which operates under the European Social Charter) issued an opinion in 2001 requiring Member States to prohibit 'any form of violence against children ... in their home or elsewhere' and this applied to 'any other

[66] This was the route followed in Israel, except that the abolition of the defence—the origin of which was common law precedent—was achieved by virtue of a Supreme Court decision.

[67] Boyson, above n 65.

[68] I add the qualification 'what resembles' since it is not clear to me that the 'campaign' is in fact orchestrated.

[69] L Sebba, 'Child Protection or Child Liberation? Reflections on the Movement to Ban Physical Punishment by Parents and Educators' (2005) 12 *International Review of Victimology* 159, 171.

[70] Art 19 of the Convention requires states to 'protect the child from all forms of physical and mental violence, injury or abuse, neglect or negligent treatment, maltreatment or exploitation, including sexual abuse, while in the care of parent(s) ... ' etc. It seems that the lack of a formula that would have clearly prohibited smacking was deliberate: G Van Bueren, *The International Law on the Rights of the Child* (Dordrecht, Nijhoff, 1995) 89.

form of degrading punishment or treatment'. In the wake of these broadly formulated normative declarations, the Children's Rights Committee has now issued its own comprehensive General Comment asserting the child's unequivocal right to protection from corporal punishment.[71]

In the light of such normative declarations emanating from a variety of international agencies, and with pressure exerted from both international and domestic non-governmental organisations,[72] it seems inevitable that additional countries will follow suit in criminalising such conduct. Indeed, recent developments in the field as described by the website of the Global Initiative to End Corporal Punishment suggests that this is the case, with legislation enacted during the last months in New Zealand, and currently proceeding in the Dutch Parliament. This process, whereby a 'softish' universal prohibition[73] is penetrating national domestic jurisdictions mainly via their welfare laws, appears to be a kind of criminalisation by osmosis.

My concern here, however, is not the manner of the criminalisation but its content, character and origins. As noted in my earlier article on these developments,[74] the prohibition on child-smacking can be linked historically to the child protection movement which has its roots in the 19th century, and became part of international law (albeit, again, soft law) in the form of the Declaration of the Rights of the Child dating from 1924 and later documents, including the 1959 Declaration. The concern at that time was not exposure of children to dangers in the home or school, but rather in the workplace. However, its subsequent extension to these new areas with the 'invention' of child abuse (referred to above) may be seen as a continuation of the child protection philosophy—now linked to the discourse of victimisation. As noted, these were the developments which provided the social underpinnings for a criminal prohibition on the physical punishment of children.

This, however, is only one half of the story. For, almost in parallel to the development of the victims' rights movement in the last decades has been the development of a more general human rights discourse—it, too, having

[71] Committee on the Rights of the Child, *The Right of the Child to Protection from Corporal Punishment and Other Cruel or Degrading Forms of Punishment* (Arts 19; 28, para 2; and 37, inter alia), General Comment No 8 (42nd Sess), UN Doc CRC/C/GC/8, 15 May–2 June 2006 (re-issued for technical reasons 2 March 2007). By way of justification for the strictness of the prohibition as elaborated in the General Comment as compared with the vaguer wording of Art 19 of the Convention on the Rights of the Child, para. 20 of the Comment states that 'the Convention, like all human rights instruments, must be regarded as a living instrument, whose interpretation develops over time'.

[72] In Israel strong pressure for a ban was exercised by the National Council for the Child.

[73] International conventions are, of course, formally binding on the ratifying states—although in most cases not on their courts, without specific legislation. However, in this case, as noted, the norm was not unequivocally incorporated in the conventions, but is rather emerging via a number of international institutions. Arguably, if widely accepted it may eventually in this way become part of international customary law, and thus binding even in the absence of an international legislative provision.

[74] Sebba, above n 69.

an international basis. (The development of international human rights law in fact began soon after the Second World War, inspired by the Universal Declaration of Human Rights—but became significant for children only with the adoption of the Convention on the Rights of the Child in 1989.[75]) This raises the question as to whether the move to criminalise child-smacking, rather than emanating from a concern for the welfare of abused children, in fact derives from recognition of their dignity and autonomy rights.[76] If an unwanted touching of an adult is an assault, why not of children?

One of the main purposes of my earlier article on this topic was to determine which of these two philosophies, paternalist protectionism or autonomy rights, was the more critical in bringing about the prohibitions on child-smacking. My conclusion was that the protectionist philosophy was the more influential. The grounds for this conclusion were (a) the language and reasoning employed for the most part by the prohibition agencies, such as concern for the mental suffering of the victim in the General Comment of the Human Rights Committee;[77] (b) the identity of the agencies and the provisions most instrumental in supporting the prohibition—in particular the provision under the European Committee of Social Rights, in reliance on its provision for 'the Right of Mothers and Children to Social and Economic Protection';[78] and (c) the fact that in some cases (for example, under New South Wales and Scottish law) a compromise was reached whereby the imposition of physical punishment on children was restricted, for example, by age and/or method of punishment. This is also true of the case law of the European Court of Human Rights, which focused on the extent of the injury inflicted in the particular case, rather than the principle. In these cases the focus was clearly welfare-protectionist. Had the rationale been to equalise children's rights with those of adults, no such compromises would have been considered.

While the above conclusion adds strength to my argument that the prohibition on the physical punishment of children, being motivated primarily by welfare considerations, is victim driven, it seems to me that the children's

[75] Interestingly, Van Bueren, above n 70, regards the 1924 Declaration of the Rights of the Child as the first human rights instrument to have been adopted by the international community, although of course it was limited in scope and legal force.

[76] It should be noted in this context that the Convention on the Rights of the Child represented a major turning point. While earlier documents on children's rights focused on children's needs and 'best interests' (as determined by adults), the Convention recognises children's autonomy rights such as the right to participate and to express their views in matters affecting their future. Welfare considerations, however, are not excluded, the respective weight attributed to each type of consideration being influenced by the age of the child.

[77] It is interesting to note that the General Comment of the Committee on Social, Economic and Cultural Rights, which might have been expected to place less emphasis on autonomy rights, actually relied primarily on an autonomy/equality/dignity rationale: Sebba, above n 69, at 67.

[78] It seems strange that the Committee chose to make use of this provision (Art 17) rather than the provision for 'the Right of Children and Young Persons to Protection' (Art 7).

autonomy argument (which has undoubtedly *contributed* to the prohibition movement[79]) is also not inconsistent with my hypothesis. While this approach is not concerned with the vulnerability of the child victim, it nevertheless focuses on the child and his or her right to autonomy, that is, his or her right not to be victimised.[80] The movement is thus pro-child rather than anti-adult. The call is to end the smacking *of children*, rather then smacking *by parents*.

V. A UNIVERSAL DUTY TO PREVENT VICTIMISATION?

The foregoing discussion related to a phenomenon whereby a number of international normative bodies have been developing a policy for the imposition of a new criminal norm (in the instant case, against child-smacking). This development has its echo in other areas in which norms are being developed to require other agencies to take action to ensure that crime victims, or potential crime victims, enjoy maximum protection. The common element in these situations is the use of a hierarchical power structure to ensure the protection of victims, invoking the criminal law and its sanctions for this purpose.

I refer to cases (a) in which the international community or its representative agencies call upon individual states to take action in order to ensure the safety of its citizens (examples of which we have seen in the previous section), or (b) in which the state requires its citizens to take such action. In the first case the action required on the part of the state may be criminalisation of the harmful conduct. In the second case the omissions of the individuals who fail to act may be deemed to constitute an offence.[81]

The requirement that citizens take action to prevent the infliction of harm upon victims (or intended victims) may be expressed normatively in a variety of ways, and the availability of the various solutions differs remarkably among different jurisdictions. One expression of such a norm is the duty to warn of an impending crime. In Israel this rarely invoked provision of the penal code was resurrected in connection with the assassination of Premier Rabin.[82] This type of provision is, analytically, strongly victim related: often there will be a specific individual in danger who may be warned. However, this 'victim remedy' does not seem to have been incorporated into the contemporary discourse on victims' rights. Nor does it seem to be prominent in the context of criminal law debates, but rather in the context of psychiatric

[79] See <www.endcorporalpunishment.org/>.

[80] For an integration of these terms, see Peter Ramsay's concept of 'vulnerable autonomy', this volume, ch 6.

[81] An intermediary case is where a local authority or police force is called to task for its failure to protect victims.

[82] M Gur-Arye, 'A Failure to Prevent Crime—Should it be Criminal?' (2001) 20 *Journal of Criminal Justice Ethics* 3.

ethics—such as in discussions as to whether or not there should be a 'duty to protect' third parties outside of the therapeutic relationship.[83]

A different issue is that of the duty to report an offence which has been—or is in the course of being—committed. Traditionally this has been seen as a law enforcement issue rather than a victim issue. Indeed, the primary 'offenders' in this context have been the victims themselves, a majority of whom, as revealed by victim surveys, do not report their victimisation. In the case of vulnerable victims, however, who may lack the power or resources to report their victimisation, victim-related discourses have given rise in some jurisdictions to a 'duty to report' being imposed upon neighbours or professionals who have a basis for suspecting such victimisation.[84] The failure to report in such cases will be punishable by a penal sanction. Such provisions were part of the vulnerable offenders 'package' adopted in Israel in 1989. The duty to report was primarily intended to deal with 'ongoing' victimisations, but is not so limited; moreover, it is not conditional on any pre-existing duty of care relationship. This offence, identified in particular with the child abuse literature, may be said to be victim driven in the causal-empirical, rhetorical and analytic senses.[85]

Conceptually very similar are the 'duty to rescue' or 'Good Samaritan' laws, requiring passers-by to assist a person in distress if not involving a substantial risk to themselves. The failure to do so will attract either tortious or criminal responsibility (or both). Historically such laws or provisions have been more common in civil law countries than in common law jurisdictions,[86] where they were thought to be inconsistent with the spirit of liberal philosophy. While such laws have become more acceptable in common law jurisdictions than in the past (notably in the United States), it is unclear that this trend has been influenced by a concern for victims as such rather than by a revival of communitarian philosophies. In the latter case, the emphasis when legislating such norms would be on the duty imposed upon the bystander[87] rather than the needs of the victim for whose benefit the bystander is obligated to intervene.

[83] P Appelbaum, G Kapen, B Walters, C Lidz and L Roth, 'Confidentiality: An Empirical Test of the Utilitarian Perspective' (1984) 12 *Bulletin of the American Academy of Psychiatry and Law* 109; B McSherry, 'Confidential Communications Between Clients and Mental Health Care Professionals: The Public Interest Exception' (2002) 37 *The Irish Jurist (ns)* 269; A McCall Smith, 'The Duty to Rescue and the Common Law' in MA Menlowe and A McCall Smith (eds), *The Duty to Rescue: The Jurisprudence of Aid* (Dartmouth, Aldershot, 1993).

[84] Under Israeli law the scope and duration of the duty differs somewhat as between these two categories.

[85] See n 49 and accompanying text.

[86] Compare Menlowe and McCall Smith, above n 83.

[87] The Good Samaritan principle has its counterpart in the Old Testament—Leviticus 19: xvi, which in 1998 inspired Israel's Knesset to enact the Thou Shall not Stand Aside when Mischief Befalls thy Neighbour Law, originally proposed as an amendment to the penal code, but enacted as an independent statute. The penalty for infringement is a fine.

The other normative category under consideration in this section is where international agencies require a state to penalise a particular type of conduct. Examples of this were noted in the previous section in the context of child-smacking: human rights bodies, invested with a monitoring role in the framework of various international conventions, have interpreted their mandate as requiring, or at least justifying, the imposition of a ban on such conduct. Furthermore, human rights conventions increasingly incorporate explicit requirements that states parties penalise forms of conduct to which the conventions relate—examples being torture and human trafficking.[88] In recent years, however, a more general 'doctrine of positive obligation' has been developed by the European Court of Human Rights. During the last two decades, the Court has faulted states which fail to provide comprehensive fulfilment of the guarantees incorporated under the provisions of the European Convention on Human Rights, including the failure to provide criminal penalties for the infringement of personal rights on the part of a fellow citizen. As with the provisions relating to abuse of power under the United Nations Declaration of the Rights of the Child referred to earlier, we have here the recognition by an international agency of offending conduct which has not yet been criminalised in the jurisdiction in question, and—unlike the (more recent) conventions on torture and human trafficking referred to above—without the relevant Convention having specified any obligation to criminalise.[89]

The scope of this doctrine is analysed by Emmerson *et al* in their *Human Rights and Criminal Justice*.[90] Suffice it here to refer to the pioneering case *X and Y v The Netherlands*,[91] in which the Court held that Dutch criminal law was inadequate in its failure to criminalise a sexual assault committed against a handicapped minor, to the cases on the adequacy of the corporal punishment provisions in the United Kingdom, to *MC v Bulgaria*,[92] in which the need to prove physical resistance in order to secure a conviction in a rape case was held to be a breach of the applicant's rights, and most recently to *Siliadin v France*,[93] in which French justice was found wanting in providing only civil compensation as a remedy for an African girl employed in domestic service—in effect in servitude, in breach of Art 4 of

[88] See nn 37, 51 and accompanying text.

[89] This also raises the question considered in section II as to the extent to which constitutional and human rights documents are intended to protect individuals from fellow citizens, as opposed to governments. See also the debate in the United Kingdom on the relationship between the Human Rights Act and the substantive criminal law: J Rogers, 'Applying the Doctrine of Positive Obligations to the European Convention of Human Rights to Domestic Substantive Criminal Law in Domestic Proceedings' (2003) *CLR* 690, 691.

[90] B Emmerson, A Ashworth and A McDonald, *Human Rights and Criminal Justice*, (Oxford, Oxford University Press, 2nd edn, 2007).

[91] 8978/80 [1985] ECHR 4 (26 March 1985).

[92] 39272/98 [2003] ECHR 651 (4 December 2003).

[93] 73316/01 [2005] ECHR 545 (26 July 2005).

the Convention. Cullen[94] notes the rationale of the Court in this last case to the effect that 'the criminal law legislation in force at the material time did not afford the applicant, a minor, practical and effective protection against the actions of which she was a victim'. Again, the need for criminalisation derives not from the moral opprobrium with regard to the conduct of the perpetrators, but because of the need to protect victims.

In the previous section I argued that the scope of certain international human rights principles was being expanded—in the instant case, for the purpose of securing a prohibition on the use of physical punishment against children—on the basis of victim-oriented considerations. In addition to that *quantitative* expansion, I have in this section considered a *qualitative* one: the upgrading of the need for victim protection to a quasi-constitutional status, whereby human rights principles which have traditionally served to protect individuals from the all-powerful state are now invoked to protect potential victims from fellow citizens by means of the criminal law.[95] This parallels the trend noted earlier towards the constitutionalisation of victims' procedural rights.

An additional phenomenon implicit in the above-mentioned developments is a trend to provide enhanced protection to particularly vulnerable victims. This is reflected not only in increased severity tariffs but also in enhanced procedural rights for such victims,[96] and now also in the higher-order norms of the substantive criminal law discussed in the present section, whereby the norm of prohibition may, on the one hand, be internationalised or, on the other, be enforced by means of the penalisation of innocent bystanders who fail to take preventative action. This wide-ranging concern for victims in all branches of criminal justice policy, and their differentiation according to their degree of vulnerability, is conceptually reminiscent of the focus on offenders in the early stages of positivism.[97]

VI. CONCLUSION

While it is widely recognised that, at least on the normative level, crime victims have recently assumed an enhanced role in the criminal justice system, this

[94] H Cullen, '*Siliadin v France*: Positive Obligations under Article 4 of the European Convention on Human Rights' (2006) 6 *Human Rights Law Review* 585.

[95] See the comments of Chief Justice Barak on the application of one of Israel's Basic Laws to victims in Sebba, above n 7.

[96] In Israel many of the rights guaranteed to victims under the Victims' Rights Law, especially the right to be heard at various stages of the proceedings, are limited to victims of sex and violence offences. Mention may also be made here to the special modes for giving testimony available to women and children in sexual assault cases: Sebba, above n 7; compare Hoyano and Keenan, above n 27.

[97] I refer to the special provisions for dangerous or recidivist offenders. For an expansion of this analogy, see Sebba, 'The Individualisation ... ', above n 33.

development has almost exclusively been identified with reforms in criminal procedure and, more controversially, sentencing. The 'victim revolution' has not generally been associated with the substantive criminal law. This chapter set out to show that much of the recent expansion of the substantive criminal law has also been 'victim driven' or at least 'victim oriented', and that the victim connection in these instances is somehow qualitatively different from its previous role in the development of criminal law. I believe I have succeeded in showing, on the basis of selected and possibly non-representative examples, that at least some such change is evident in this respect, and that victims play a larger rhetorical and conceptual role today in the criminalisation process than previously. The main arguments in support of this conclusion were (a) the focus in the formulation of crime definitions on victim characteristics and on particular categories of victim, and (b) the new hierarchical dynamic whereby new offences are created for the purposes of enhancing the protection for victims from harmful conduct the prevention of which has hitherto been insufficiently guaranteed—whether because of the lack of recognition of its criminality in the jurisdiction in question[98] or because of inadequate law enforcement on the part of the local community.[99]

If my conclusion is correct, it would be of interest to identify the factors giving rise to this change of emphasis in the criminalisation process. As elaborated in section II, the change cannot be attributed to the activities of the mainstream victim advocacy organisations, which have focused on procedural rather than substantive rights. On the other hand, NGOs representing sectorial groups such as women and children (and perhaps also 'single-issue' and 'unofficial' victim advocacy groups) have undoubtedly been influential in many of the victim-related reforms, including some of those involving the substantive criminal law, such as reforms of the definition of rape, and the prohibition on the physical punishment of children.

Adopting a broader sociological perspective, an increasing focus in the criminal law on victim interests may be linked to various contemporary discourses which seek to explain current trends in penality in terms of political economy and the nature of contemporary governance. Elsewhere in this volume Peter Ramsay has developed a theory of 'vulnerable autonomy' in order to explain the recent popularity in Britain of quasi-penal protective measures, such as control orders for use against suspected terrorists and anti-social behaviour orders for perceived nuisances and incivilities. According to Ramsay's analysis, the state has taken advantage of the average citizen's fear of crime ('constructing the ordinary citizen as vulnerable') to assume wide powers of penal control.

98 This refers to the cases falling within the doctrine of positive obligation.

99 This refers to the cases in which domestic law has mandated reporting, notification or assistance.

There are two important implications here for my own analysis. In the first place, according to Ramsay's thesis, vulnerability to victimisation is not a phenomenon restricted to certain minority groups fighting for recognition of their special sensibilities but is universally experienced; for Ramsay emphasises its subjective character—it is the perception of vulnerability which is prevalent. Consequently, legislative norms such as ASBOs which, unlike my own examples, are not intended to protect any specified and particularly vulnerable population, are nevertheless also consistent with his vulnerability theory. In the second place, the dichotomy raised by Dubber between criminal law norms focusing on victim interests and those asserting the prioritisation of state interests becomes irrelevant as the two paradigms merge, and a focus on the victim in Ramsay's theory is seen to be a part of the assertion of state power. (There is a parallel here with the historical analysis of Kirchengast referred to in the introduction, in which he argues that much of the power exercised by the state is in effect a reflection, or an expression, of the victim's historic powers.)

Insofar as Ramsay links his analysis to the characteristics of neo-liberal economies, it bears strong similarities with the work of other contemporary writers on social control, such as David Garland (on the culture of control),[100] Barbara Hudson (on crime control in the risk society)[101] and Jonathan Simon (on the centrality of crime in contemporary governance in these economies).[102] While all these writers emphasise the relationship between the fears and uncertainties of the middle classes in these societies and the trend to punitiveness, Simon emphasises the centrality of victims, as illustrated by the naming of new extensions of penality after victims who were the centre of media attention, such as 'Megan's Law'.[103] On the other hand, Garland's concept of 'responsibilisation',[104] whereby the government has largely given up on any systematic attempt to pursue meaningful criminal justice policies, transferring responsibility for this to the community at large (a theme somewhat in conflict with Ramsay's and Dubber's thesis of enhanced police power), might be consistent with my suggested or implicit analysis of various minority constituencies seeking legitimation for their perceived victim status by promoting criminal law norms which provide enhanced protection for their own community or sector. This approach—supported by the literature on the enactment of 'hate crimes'—might in turn be linked

[100] Garland, above n 48.

[101] B Hudson, *Justice in the Risk Society* (London, Sage Publications, 2003).

[102] Simon, '*Governing* ...' above n 48.

[103] Simon argues that the legislation only takes into account the concerns of white, middle-class victims: Simon, '*Governing* ...', above n 48, at 77.

[104] D Garland, 'The Limits of the Sovereign State: Strategies of Crime Control in Contemporary Society' (1996) 36 *British Journal of Criminology* 445; see also Garland, above n 48, at 124–7. Garland's use of this term differs from the way it is used by Alan Norrie, this volume, ch 2, who is referring to the responsibilisation of the *offender*.

to such postmodern themes as the role of emotions and group identities, and the growing literature on the social construction of victimhood.

Such themes, however, appear to be in strong conflict with an alternative narrative underlying much of the preceding chapter, which suggested—at least in the context of the developing norm prohibiting the use of physical punishment for disciplinary or educational purposes—that the new norms are emerging in the framework of international human rights law, and thus represent 'universal truths' as they come to be recognised by the established international agencies and its bureaucracies. The emergence of a victim orientation in the criminal law may thus also be consistent with an entirely modernist and positivist narrative, whereby empirical evidence of the neglect and abuse of vulnerable populations as well as the importance attributed to universal values such as autonomy and dignity, have led to the formulation of new norms for the protection of these populations.

It might be possible to test the relative validity of the alternative narratives by means of in-depth case studies of the manner in which various victim-oriented reforms are achieved and of their potential for enhancing the protection provided to the vulnerable populations whom the norms are intended to protect. In Israel, the legislative power assumed by individual Knesset members[105] may be indicative of the fragmentation of authority and of the relevance of the late- or post-modern analyses. Prima facie such critical perspectives are less applicable to the norm-creation processes which originate in international institutions where supposed 'expertise' is a byword; but, even there, political correctness and the assertion of power on the part of the international institution, and the desire to impose its norms on recalcitrant Member States, may be no less important than any genuine expectation—in the case of the prohibition on child-smacking—that recognition of the norm will in fact protect small children from parental abuse.[106] It is possible that Gusfield's analysis of the symbolic (rather than practical) effects of legislation[107] applies to international norms also.

Finally, whether the victim-oriented reforms and policies under consideration in this article are based upon 'evidence-based' rationales, or whether they derive from less rational socio–political pressures related to the power structure in liberal late modern neo-liberal societies, it would be appropriate

[105] In recent years, since the adoption of political primaries and the need for personal popularity, more than one half of successful Knesset Bills have been 'private' rather than government sponsored.

[106] Some (disputed) empirical Swedish research, however, claims that the ban in that country had a positive effect: JE Durrant and S Janson, 'Law Reform, Corporal Punishment and Child Abuse in Sweden' (2005) *International Review of Victimology* 12.

[107] Gusfield was primarily concerned with the ideological struggle in relation to Prohibition in the United States: JR Gusfield, *Symbolic Crusade: Status Politics and the American Temperance Movement* (Urbana, University of Illinois Press, 1963).

in the context of a volume devoted to current trends in criminalisation to consider whether the developments described are consistent with the various theories relating to the proper scope of the criminal law[108]—or whether they reinforce the perception that the criminal law is 'a lost cause'.[109] Some of the offences which were referred to in section V are clearly consistent with communitarian theory;[110] but this approach does not seem to capture the thrust of many of the victim-focused developments which, on the contrary, tend to have a sectorial emphasis. Another possibility is that we have here a new, victim-based, paradigm of criminalisation, in the same way as some writers see the integration of the victim in criminal procedure as giving rise to a new procedural model.[111] On the other hand, the developments described may also be quite consistent with liberal theory, since the new or expanded offences are all contingent on the infliction of some form of harm. Indeed, a victim-oriented theory might supply the missing element in Feinberg's approach which, as Ashworth points out, while it insists on the infliction of harm as a requirement for criminalisation, fails to inform us what is the character of the harm which is such that criminalisation is *required*.[112]

These questions cannot be comprehensively addressed here, if only because there has been no discussion of many significant aspects of the victim-driven criminalisation considered in this chapter, including the mental element required for culpability. Nor has the nature of the harm been systematically analysed. Indeed, the more problematic aspects of the harm issue arise in the context of offences such as hate crimes,[113] described here as 'victim driven' but not considered further. Perhaps of even greater interest in the present context is the issue of prostitution, which was removed from the penal codes of most liberal societies as it was perceived to be a victimless offence, the criminality of which could be supported only on the ground of immorality—or perhaps Feinberg's principle of causing offence to others.[114] Recently, however, there has been a move in some 'western' societies to recriminalise, based precisely upon victimisation-related arguments. The processes of criminalisation in these societies should provide a basis for the examination of current discourses on the construction of victimisation and harm, and the extent to which they are consistent with traditional liberal theories of criminalisation.

[108] Bronitt and McSherry, above n 62; A Ashworth, *Principles of Criminal Law*, (Oxford, Oxford University Press, 5th edn, 2006).

[109] Ashworth, above n 1.

[110] Compare J Braithwaite and P Pettit, *Not Just Desert: A Republican Theory of Justice* (Oxford, Clarendon Press, 1990).

[111] DE Beloof, 'The Third Model of Criminal Process; The Victim Participation Model', (1999) *Utah Law Review* 289; Roach, above n 11.

[112] Bronitt and McSherry, above n 62, at 53.

[113] Feinberg's concept of 'offence to others' will be relevant here: Feinberg, above n 54, vol 2.

[114] Feinberg, above n 54, vol 2; see also Ashworth, above n 108, at 43.

Part III

The Quest for Security

5

Criminal Law, Human Rights and Preventative Justice

ANDREW ASHWORTH

I. INTRODUCTION

THE PURPOSES OF this chapter are twofold: first, to identify and to re-assess certain coercive measures which have been introduced in the name of prevention; and, second, to explore the normative frameworks that might be appropriate for determining whether such measures are justified and to what constraints they might properly be subjected. The legislative features that are the focus here are often regarded as part of a major shift in political emphasis. Some have characterised this in terms of the growth of actuarial justice and the rise of a new penology.[1] Others have pointed to the rise of what is often termed 'the risk society': a state of affairs in which governments, organisations and individuals are increasingly concerned about the risk presented by certain people or situations and so organise their arrangements in order to minimise the risk.[2] More recently it has been argued that the problems of risk and its management have now been superseded by the problem of uncertainty, often magnified by science and provoking forceful responses from governments and others who argue that it is necessary to take protective action even though the precise nature and magnitude of the perceived threats are unknown and unknowable.[3] In section IV below, several developments along these lines will be noted, some within the criminal justice system and many outside criminal justice. It is not contended that these developments are new and unprecedented—only that they are prevalent and raise questions about the proper limits of state

[1] M Feeley and J Simon, 'Actuarial Justice: the Emerging New Criminal Law' in D Nelken (ed), *The Futures of Criminology* (London, Sage, 1994).

[2] See, for example, R Ericson and K Haggerty, *Policing the Risk Society* (Oxford, Oxford University Press, 1997) and B Hudson, *Justice in the Risk Society* (London, Sage, 2003).

[3] See, for example, P O'Malley, *Risk, Uncertainty and Government* (London, Glass House, 2004) and R Ericson, *Crime in an Insecure World* (Cambridge, Polity, 2007). Compare the re-assessment by Lucia Zedner, this volume, ch 3.

authority. They are characterised here as manifestations of 'the preventative state', a term designed to point to the preventative, protective, precautionary or pre-emptive terms in which the first line of justification for the various measures is usually phrased.[4] Nor is it contended here that these manifestations of the preventative state are supplanting or replacing the criminal justice model[5]: that is being employed as much as ever, although in section II below it will be suggested that preventative rationales are being adapted in order to extend the boundaries of the criminal justice system.

It will be argued that the state is rightly concerned with the prevention of harm and reduction of the risk of harm, but that preventative measures involving coercion require justificatory scrutiny, no less than powers taken through the criminal justice system. The focus of this chapter is on rationales for preventative measures and on limiting principles to which they should be subject, recognising (as O'Malley has urged) that governmental responses to risk involve a choice and that their moral foundations require scrutiny.[6] Any such examination must be grounded in concrete examples of the features being studied. Thus, in section II it will be shown that the criminal justice model is still being used enthusiastically by the state, at least in the United Kingdom, and indeed that it is being expanded and extended in ways that ought to be challenged. Section IV identifies some different, non-criminal legal forms that are being used ostensibly in the furtherance of prevention. However, the core of the chapter is not in the descriptive sections, II and IV, but rather in the exploration of normative frameworks that takes place in section III (relating to the criminal justice model) and in section V (evaluating the normative foundations for the various manifestations of the preventative state).

II. EXPANDING AND EXTENDING THE CRIMINAL JUSTICE MODEL

The criminal justice model or paradigm consists of criminal offences, investigated and prosecuted according to criminal procedure, and followed by the imposition of a sentence. Some evidence that governments are continuing to make great use of this model—if that were thought to be a controversial proposition—is provided by two recent English surveys. One survey focused on the period between the election of the Labour Government in 1997 and the end of 2005, and counted some 3,000 criminal offences that

[4] Although distinctions can be drawn between protective, precautionary and pre-emptive measures, they are taken together here under the general rubric of 'prevention', unless otherwise stated, on the basis that all of them can be said to involve measures to prevent certain events from occurring.

[5] As suggested in the final chapter of Ericson, above n 3.

[6] O'Malley, above n 3.

were created.[7] It cannot be claimed that all of these were new offences, because legislatures often re-enact or revise offences that were in previous enactments, but the overall numbers are so high that they suggest a fairly ready resort by government to the criminal justice model. The second survey analysed all 165 criminal offences created by primary legislation in the calendar year 2005: 40 per cent were strict liability offences, and a further 26 per cent were offences of strict liability leavened by the clause 'without reasonable excuse'. Some 31 per cent of offences required some form of subjective fault, chiefly intention or knowledge. Two other features of these new crimes are worthy of note: some 26 per cent were offences of omission, and burdens of proof were distributed between prosecution and defence inconsistently, even within the same statute.[8]

The criminal justice paradigm remains a central part of government strategy, therefore, and references to the coming of the 'risk society' or to the management of uncertainty must not be allowed to obscure that. However, there is evidence that the criminal justice model is being stretched and, possibly, over-extended by the invocation of preventative rationales. In order to substantiate this point without overloading the chapter with details, three examples each will be given from criminal procedure, criminal law and sentencing in England and Wales.

A. Criminal Procedure

First, recent legislation 'for the prevention of terrorism' extends the power of the police to stop and search people. No longer do the police need to have 'reasonable suspicion' before stopping and searching a person.[9] According to ss 44–45 of the Terrorism Act 2000, where the police have designated an area on the ground that it is 'expedient' for the prevention of terrorism to have extra investigative powers (and the whole of London has been continuously designated for several years), the police may stop and search any person, even though there is no particular reason for suspicion.[10] This

[7] These figures come from a survey organised by the Liberal Democrat spokesman on Home Affairs, Nick Clegg MP. The bulk of these new offences were created by secondary legislation under powers granted by primary legislation (1,854), but some 1,169 were created by primary legislation. For further reference, see A Ashworth, 'A Change of Normative Position: Determining the Contours of Culpability in Criminal Law' (2008) 11(2) *New Criminal Law Review* 232.

[8] Ashworth, above n 7.

[9] For empirically based doubts about whether this requirement is or has ever been effective, see D Dixon, AK Bottomley, CA Coleman, M Gill and D Wall, 'Reality and Rules in the Construction and Regulation of Police Suspicion' (1989) 17 *International Journal of the Sociology of Law* 185 and B Bowling and C Phillips, 'Disproportionate and Discriminatory: Reviewing the Evidence on Stop and Search' (2007) *MLR* 70.

[10] See *R (on the application of Gillan) v Commissioner of Police for the Metropolis* [2006] UKHL 12.

power goes much further than the general law, and the alleged justification is found in the 'fight against terrorism' even though some of the steps seem to have little to do with that objective.[11]

Second, the Terrorism Act 2006 provides for detention of a terrorist suspect for up to 28 days before charge: rather than the normal maximum of 96 hours, the police have been given this much longer period before they must either charge or release a suspect. Importantly, there are provisions for periodic judicial review. But nonetheless, this is a considerable extension of normal powers, again allegedly justified by the special difficulties and importance of investigating terrorist cases.[12]

Third, as already mentioned, many of the new offences allow defences only to the extent that the defendant can prove them. For example, s 128 of the Serious Organised Crime and Police Act 2005 creates an offence of trespassing on a designated site, and then provides that 'it is a defence for a person ... to prove that he did not know, and had no reasonable cause to suspect, that the site ... was a designated site'—a tough reverse burden of proof for an offence carrying a possible prison sentence.

B. Criminal Law

First, offences are being created that stretch back even further than the traditional inchoate offences. Under the Criminal Attempts Act 1981 (UK) a person is not guilty of attempting a crime unless he or she has done an act that is 'more than mere preparatory' to the full offence, with the required intention. Under the Terrorism Act 2006 (UK), it is an offence, with intent to commit an act of terrorism or to assist another to do so, to 'engage in any conduct in preparation for giving effect to' that intention. This might be termed a 'pre-inchoate' offence, since any act seems to suffice as the *actus reus*: all the arguments against criminalising mere thoughts are brought into play by such a wide provision, but the alleged justification lies in the prevention of terrorism.

Second, there is an expansion of possession offences, often without any requirement of intent and sometimes supported by reverse onus provisions.[13] And third, the Proceeds of Crime Act 2002 introduced widely drafted offences of money laundering which, even after a decision of the House of Lords that considerably tightened the *mens rea* requirement

[11] See the facts of *R (on the application of Gillan) v Commissioner of Police for the Metropolis* [2006] UKHL 12. For an analysis of these issues in an Australian context, see G Carne, 'Reconstituting "Human Security" in a New Security Environment: One Australian, Two Canadians and Article 3 of the Universal Declaration of Human Rights' (2006) 26 *Australian Yearbook of International Law* 1.

[12] The police had asked for 96 days and the Government began by supporting this. But, after defeats in the upper chamber, the Government settled for 28 days: Terrorism Act 2006 (UK), s 23.

[13] See V Tadros, 'Justice and Terrorism' (2007) 10(4) *New Criminal Law Review* 658.

where conspiracy is charged,[14] remain broad in their effect and indeed broader than international conventions demand.

C. Sentencing

First, recent years have seen a relentless escalation of maximum penalties. Apart from the reduction of the maximum for theft from 10 to 7 years in 1991, there is hardly any other example of a reduction, and widespread examples of increases (causing death by dangerous driving, from 5 to 10 to 14 years' imprisonment; various offences in the Sexual Offences Act 2003); some more supportable than others.

Second, there is the increasing prominence of confiscation orders, now under the Proceeds of Crime Act 2002 (UK). This statute requires a court to follow a given procedure in order to ensure that assets of a convicted offender are confiscated, and certain assumptions about property possessed by an offender are to be made if the court forms the view that the offender has had a 'criminal lifestyle'. The details are complex, and the outcome may be draconian.[15]

Third, numerically the most significant development is the introduction of the imprisonment for public protection (IPP) sentence by the Criminal Justice Act 2003. Any person convicted of a second 'scheduled' offence is liable to be sentenced to imprisonment for public protection—indeed, in many circumstances there is a presumption of dangerousness to which the judge must respond[16]—and the result is indeterminate detention until it is thought safe to release the offender. The rationale is said to be public protection, but the net is cast extremely wide and large numbers of offenders have been imprisoned for longer under these provisions. More will be said about the IPP sentence below.

The purpose of these examples is to illustrate some of the ways in which the traditional boundaries of the criminal justice paradigm are being extended by recent English legislation, mostly for preventative reasons. In the present enquiry, a pressing question is whether such extensions can be challenged in any way. Does the legislature have a free hand in these matters, or are there limits? If there are, what is their origin, and how substantial are they? These are the topics to which we must now turn.

III. NORMATIVE FRAMEWORKS FOR CRIMINAL JUSTICE

The justifications for the institution of criminal justice raise fundamental questions of political philosophy. For present purposes, suffice it to say that

[14] *Montilla* [2004] UKHL 50.

[15] For analysis and critique, see P Alldridge, *Money Laundering Law* (Oxford, Hart Publishing, 2003).

[16] The IPP sentence has now been narrowed by the Criminal Justice and Immigration Act 2008.

it is regarded as axiomatic, in 'Western' countries at least, that it is necessary (and, for many people, right and just) for the state to have a formal system of censure and sanctions. The next set of questions concerns the constraints that ought to be placed on such a system. What limits should be set to the criminal law, and to the investigative and sentencing powers that go with it? To answer the question of limits, we will look first at the constraints set by European human rights law, on the basis that in Europe there is a shared commitment to this set of norms[17]; and then we will look beyond, to certain aspects of liberal theory.

The European Convention on Human Rights contains a range of safeguards against the excessive and arbitrary use of state power in criminal justice. Article 5 declares the right to liberty and security of person, but allows (in Art 5(1)(c)) an exception for 'lawful arrest or detention of a person effected for the purpose of bringing him [or her] before the competent legal authority on reasonable suspicion of having committed an offence.' Whether the power to stop and search people without reasonable suspicion (described in section I above) violates that provision remains to be determined.[18] Similarly, Art 5(3) declares the right of everyone who is duly arrested 'to be brought promptly before a judge', and Art 6(2) declares the presumption of innocence. These are designed to set limits to the forms of criminal procedure, although they are more or less vigorously applied.[19] More broadly, Art 6 declares the right to a fair trial, and Art 6(3) sets out five distinct rights that should be safeguarded when a person is 'charged with a criminal offence'. For example, the right to confront witnesses places constraints on the use of hearsay evidence.[20]

When it comes to the criminal law itself, European human rights law imposes few constraints. The content of criminal laws must not interfere unjustifiably with a person's Convention rights—for example, the right to respect for private life (Art 8), the right to freedom of thought and religion (Art 9), the right to freedom of expression (Art 10) and the right to freedom of association (Art 11).[21] The doctrine of positive obligations requires states to have in place laws that protect the Convention rights of individuals,

[17] Note also that many of the human rights here discussed are recognised in international human rights documents, notably the International Covenant on Civil and Political Rights.

[18] The House of Lords in *R (on the application of Gillan) v Commissioner of Police for the Metropolis* [2006] UKHL 12 held that there is no violation of Art 5, but it is not clear what view would be taken by the Strasbourg Court.

[19] The Strasbourg Court has been more indulgent towards reverse burdens of proof than the British courts. For discussion, see A Ashworth, 'Four Threats to the Presumption of Innocence' (2006) 10 *Evidence and Proof* 241.

[20] For discussion of the impact of the Convention on English criminal procedure and evidence, see specialist works such as B Emmerson, A Ashworth and A Macdonald (eds), *Human Rights and Criminal Practice* (London, Sweet & Maxwell, 2007), particularly chs 14 and 15, or more general texts such as A Choo, *Evidence* (Oxford, Oxford University Press, 2006).

[21] Further discussed in Emmerson, Ashworth and Macdonald, above n 20, ch 8.

including the right not to be subjected to unwanted sexual contact and also the right of a child not to be subjected to non-minor physical chastisement.[22] Beyond that, however, there is little in the Convention to constrain the form and scope of criminal offences.

So far as sentencing is concerned, there are some definite constraints. Article 7 prohibits the imposition of a heavier penalty than was applicable at the time the offence was committed. There is some support in the Strasbourg case law for the proposition that a wholly disproportionate sentence may be held to violate Art 3 (inhuman punishment) or Art 5 (right to liberty and security of the person),[23] but that in turn depends on whether the sentence is punitive or preventative. The proposition applies to punitive sentences only, including the punitive portion of a preventative sentence.[24] The Strasbourg jurisprudence establishes that, where a sentence is preventative (or, so far as concerns the preventative portion of a sentence), the principal constraint is only that in Art 5(4) of the Convention—which requires periodic review by a court of the need for continued detention. In other words, a sentence such as IPP (discussed in section II above) would be viewed under the Convention as consisting of two parts: the punitive part (or minimum term) would be subject to a disproportionality restriction, which would be unlikely to 'bite' since the punitive portion should be set by reference to the offence(s) committed; and the preventative part may continue indefinitely, so long as there is a periodic judicial re-assessment. The latter part of the sentence is the more important one, but the constraint is procedural rather than substantive.

From this brief survey it will be evident that the constraints imposed by the European Convention on Human Rights are significant in relation to criminal procedure, slightly less significant in matters of sentencing and not extensive at all in the criminal law itself. We must leave for other occasions the fascinating issues of how these came to be the contours of European human rights law, and whether principles of criminal law ought to be regarded as no less deep and worthy of high protection than procedural safeguards. The fact is that the Convention leaves large gaps in its normative coverage, having nothing to say on many major issues. The next question, therefore, is whether there are any strands of liberal criminal justice theory that might cover this ground and yield constraining principles to which we might subscribe.

[22] *A v United Kingdom* (1998) 27 EHRR 611; and Emmerson, Ashworth and Macdonald, above n 20, ch 18.

[23] Compare *Weeks v United Kingdom* (1988) 10 EHRR 293 and *V and T v United Kingdom* (2000) 30 EHRR 121 with the English decision in *Offen (No 2)* [2001] 1 Cr App R 372. For a broader review, see D van Zyl Smit and A Ashworth, 'Disproportionate Sentences as Human Rights Violations' (2004) 67 *MLR* 541.

[24] No such limitation appears on the face of Art 49(3) of the Charter of Fundamental Rights of the European Union, which declares that 'the severity of penalties must not be disproportionate to the criminal offence.' See further van Zyl Smit and Ashworth, above n 23.

The analysis might start with sentencing, and with proportionality theory—the principle that the punishment for an offence ought to be proportionate to the seriousness of the offence, taking account of the harm, wrongdoing and culpability involved. In principle, respect for individuals as autonomous citizens requires that sentences express the degree of wrongdoing and a commensurate degree of censure. This ought to be contingent on a judgment that the conduct was rightly criminalised, on account of the elements of wrongdoing and harm: the need here is for a liberal theory of criminalisation, on which productive work has only just started.[25] Even if we are satisfied that the conduct was rightly criminalised, conviction should be possible only if the appropriate procedural safeguards have been respected (this is where the European Convention is at its strongest). Moreover, conviction should be possible only if the defendant has been proved to be at fault, at least (and this is a weaker alternative) where the offence carries a possible sanction of imprisonment. It is plain that the propositions in this paragraph require a great deal of supporting argument if they are to yield robust principles, and it is not the function of this chapter to supply them. The purpose of setting out these tenets of a liberal theory of criminal law is to demonstrate in what ways a liberal theory might establish constraints on the substantive criminal law, and thereby fill some of the major gaps left by European human rights law.[26] In the present context these general tenets are simply a staging post on the way to section V below, where the argument will be taken up again.

IV. DEVELOPING THE PREVENTATIVE MODEL

The use of preventative measures by the state is not new. Thus, for example, the European Convention on Human Rights provides that the right to liberty and security of person is subject to an exception for 'the lawful detention of persons for the prevention of the spreading of infectious diseases, of persons of unsound mind, alcoholics or drug addicts or vagrants'. There is also a longstanding exception for the detention pending trial of persons charged with a criminal offence, subject to various limits and safeguards.[27]

[25] See D Husak, '*Overcriminalization*' (New York, Oxford University Press, 2007); and Ashworth, above n 19.

[26] For significant developments of liberal theories of criminal law, see RA Duff (ed), *Philosophy and the Criminal Law: Principle and Critique* (Cambridge, Cambridge University Press, 1998); AP Simester and GR Sullivan, *Criminal Law: Theory and Doctrine* (Oxford, Hart Publishing, 3rd edn, 2007); J Gardner, *Offences and Defences: Selected Essays in the Philosophy of Criminal Law* (Oxford, Oxford University Press, 2007).

[27] A Ashworth and M Redmayne, *The Criminal Process* (Oxford, Oxford University Press, 3rd edn, 2005) ch 8.

What is of growing concern, however, is the way in which governments, particularly in the United Kingdom, have been trying to devise preventative measures that are coercive and yet avoid the safeguards established for the criminal justice paradigm. Three principal examples of this expansion of the preventative state will be outlined here.

First, the British Government has developed the control order as a means of restraining persons suspected of involvement in terrorist activity. It is a civil order, under the Prevention of Terrorism Act 2005, and was designed to impose severe *restrictions* on liberty without amounting to a *deprivation* of liberty.[28] Thus, the Government accepts that the Convention prevents the indefinite detention of persons without trial, since that amounts to a deprivation of liberty under Art 5 that is not saved by any of the exceptions therein.[29] Instead, the control order is intended to restrict the liberty of persons without trial by confining them to a particular place for up to 14 hours per day, forbidding them to use the telephone, the internet, etc. The purported rationale for these restrictions is public protection: the Government states that it does not wish to prosecute these individuals because this might require disclosure of the working practices and identities of secret service personnel, and so their liberty is restricted in this way.[30]

Second, recent years have seen the creation of numerous preventative orders which are classified as civil in nature and which may impose wide-ranging restrictions on the conduct of those subject to them. The best-known example is the anti-social behaviour order, or ASBO. It may be made by magistrates sitting in their civil jurisdiction, on complaints from the police or the local authority, so long as the court is satisfied that the person has caused harassment, alarm or distress to others and that an ASBO is necessary for the prevention of further such acts. The ASBO lasts for a minimum of 2 years, and may include various prohibitions. An important point in the present context is that the ASBO was devised in order to avoid the safeguards applicable under the criminal justice model. Thus, the fact that the right of confrontation is one of the special rights applicable in criminal cases was regarded as a strong reason to use the civil courts, where the hearsay rule would not apply to prevent third parties from narrating what they had been told about the disturbances

[28] In fact the legislation provides for 'derogating' and 'non-derogating' control orders, but those details are not essential to the present discussion. See further L Zedner, 'Preventative Justice or Pre-Punishment? The Case of Control Orders' (2007) 59 *Current Legal Problems* 174.

[29] As established by the House of Lords in *A v Secretary of State for the Home Department* [2004] UKHL 56.

[30] For those who are not British nationals, deportation is often not an option, since it might return them to a country where they would face torture and that would be contrary to human rights: *Soering v United Kingdom* (1989) 11 EHRR 439.

caused by the defendant.[31] In practice, most ASBOs are now made by the criminal courts after conviction, but the same principles apply to them. In more recent years they have been joined by a plethora of other preventative orders, including travel restriction orders, football banning orders, sexual offences prevention orders, and so forth.[32] The latest addition is a serious crime prevention order, applicable to anyone with a conviction for a serious offence who has 'conducted himself in a way that was likely to facilitate the commission by himself or another person of a serious offence'.[33] Again, the essence of the order is to prohibit the person from doing certain things, going to certain places, and so forth. All of these orders place restrictions, often substantial restrictions, on the general liberty of the persons subjected to them. The justifications are a mixture of alleged concrete danger (evidence suggesting that this individual presents a danger) and abstract risk (given a certain behavioural history), and the enhancement of security and public safety is claimed to legitimate the coercion involved.[34] In effect, as we shall see in the next paragraph, they create a personal criminal code for each individual subjected to them.

Another aspect of the same group of preventative orders is that they are a carefully designed hybrid. The order itself is classified by English law as civil. However, any breach of the terms of the order (without reasonable excuse) constitutes a criminal offence with a maximum penalty of 5 years' imprisonment. Some may say that this is simply an extension of the jurisdiction for contempt of court—that where a court makes an order, it is a contempt for the person subject to it to disobey. However, there is a significant difference of degree here, which amounts to a qualitative distinction. Preventative orders are widely used; they typically include many or far-reaching prohibitions; and the maximum penalty is much higher than the 2-year maximum for contempt of court. What the Government has tried to do is to devise a system whereby the civil order and the criminal offence are regarded as separate: the criminal proceedings for breach of the order do indeed attract all the Convention safeguards (but there is little to decide, since it is virtually a strict liability offence), whereas the earlier proceedings, in which the court devises and imposes the prohibitions that

[31] Among the many writings on ASBOs, see E Burney, 'Talking Tough, Acting Coy—What Happened to the Anti-social Behaviour Order?' (2002) 41 *Howard Journal of Criminal Justice* 469; A Ashworth, 'Social Control and "Anti-Social Behaviour": the Subversion of Human Rights?' (2004) 120 *LQR* 263 and S Macdonald, 'A Suicidal Woman, Roaming Pigs and a Noisy Trampolinist: Refining the ASBO's Definition of Anti-social Behaviour' (2006) 69 *MLR* 183.

[32] For a collection and general discussion, see A Ashworth, *Sentencing and Criminal Justice* (Cambridge, Cambridge University Press, 4th edn, 2005) 335–40.

[33] See further Lucia Zedner, this volume, ch 3.

[34] S Krasmann, 'The Enemy on the Border: Critique of a Programme in favour of a Preventative State' (2007) 9 *Punishment and Society* 301, 310.

form the basis of the criminal offence, are represented as civil in nature and as falling outside the criminal justice model and its safeguards. In effect, therefore, the civil court (when imposing an ASBO) stipulates conditions that become, effectively, a personal criminal code for the individual, with up to 5 years' imprisonment for any infringement. If this seems disproportionate, what is the normative framework that enables one to make this point?

V. NORMATIVE FRAMEWORKS FOR PREVENTATIVE JUSTICE

Just as section III opened with a re-assertion of the need for a criminal justice system, with criminal law and sentencing among its components, so this section opens with a re-assertion of the good of security. Protection of a particular citizen from, say, domestic violence or harassment is not only an important value for preventative measures to realise but also safeguarded by human rights. In such cases and more broadly, however, recognition of the value of security should not be taken to suggest that it is always an unqualified good, or that everything that is brought within that concept by its proponents deserves a welcome.[35] The point is rather that there is wide recognition that one of the basic conditions for satisfactory human flourishing is a certain level of security, in terms of freedom from attack and from accidental harm to one's vital interests. Assuring this security is a task that requires co-ordination and regulation on a large scale (as with other public goods such as clean air, utilities and transport), and is therefore properly regarded as an obligation of the state. Indeed, Ian Loader and Neil Walker go on to argue that 'our capacity to reach some level of common understanding and recognition of the terms of our collective security is itself a contributory factor to that collective security'.[36]

Although we may take it that the state has this obligation, this is not to suggest that it should have a free hand in pursuing policies to improve security. In particular, the method through which such policies are pursued should not lead us to overlook the rights that are at stake. Public health approaches to protection from certain sources of 'risk' are being developed,[37] but insofar as they involve elements of coercion they must be scrutinised. Similarly, tackling 'risk' through community treatment rather than detention may be a desirable step, but it does not remove the need to

[35] See further S Bottomley and S Bronitt, *Law in Context* (Annandale, NSW, Federation Press, 3rd edn, 2006) ch 14.

[36] I Loader and N Walker, *Civilizing Security* (Cambridge: Cambridge University Press, 2007) 164–5.

[37] See H Kemshall and J Wood, 'Beyond Public Protection: an Examination of Community Protection and Public Health Approaches to High-Risk Offenders' (2007) 7 *Criminology and Criminal Justice* 203.

examine the justifications for the compulsion involved.[38] These examples demonstrate the importance of the task of exploring what constraints on the state's pursuit of this end should be recognised, and we begin here by looking to the European Convention on Human Rights. Attention should be focused on the Convention's various anti-subversion devices, as developed by the Strasbourg Court under the concept of 'autonomous meaning'. This concept has been developed to ensure that certain key terms in the Convention have a meaning that corresponds to the substance of that which is being regulated, a meaning assigned by the Court, rather than allowing a particular country to apply its own label or meaning.[39] Thus, for example, it is not conclusive that the United Kingdom's legislature has enacted a regime for control orders that designates them as restrictions on liberty (as distinct from deprivations of liberty). The question under the Convention is whether, in substance, the regime amounts to a deprivation of liberty. The English courts have had to decide this question and, applying the leading Strasbourg decision in *Guzzardi v Italy* (which established that the concept of deprivation of liberty has an autonomous meaning),[40] the Court of Appeal has held that the restrictions imposed by a particular control order (involving home confinement for 18 hours per day, restrictions on contact with others during the remaining 6 hours, and a ban on telephone and internet use) did amount to a deprivation of liberty, and therefore violated Art 5.[41] This demonstrates how an anti-subversion device under the Convention operates: if the substance of a measure is held to fall within the concept of deprivation of liberty in Art 5, then that measure is only permissible insofar as it complies with the requirements and safeguards of that Article. Since the Government's whole purpose was to avoid those safeguards, control orders need to be made in such a way as not to amount to a deprivation of liberty—notably, by reducing the number of hours per day of home confinement.[42]

Another term with an autonomous meaning is 'criminal charge': wherever a person is 'charged with a criminal offence', all the additional safeguards listed in Art 6(2) and (3), together with certain implied rights, must be

[38] See M Donnelly, 'The Role of Rights Discourse in Theorising Compulsory Treatment Orders' Paper delivered at the *Public Health and Human Rights* Conference, Prato, Italy, 7–9 June 2007 (m.donnelly@ucc.ie) on compulsory treatment orders in the mental health setting, and also H Kemshall and J Wood, 'Beyond Public Protection: an Examination of Community Protection and Public Health Approaches to High-Risk Offenders' (2007) 7 *Criminology and Criminal Justice* 203 on the 'community protection model'.

[39] For further analysis of the 'autonomous meaning' doctrine, see Emmerson, Ashworth and Macdonald, above n 20, at 87–8.

[40] (1980) 3 EHRR 333.

[41] *Secretary of State for the Home Department v JJ* [2006] EWCA Civ 1141.

[42] Thus the particular control order was reduced to 14 hours per day of home confinement, and it remains to be decided whether this is a deprivation or merely a restriction on liberty. For critical analysis, see Zedner, above n 28.

respected in those proceedings. The various preventative orders discussed in section IV above were designed in order to ensure that these safeguards do not apply. The criminal proceedings that may be taken in the event of breach of the terms of the preventative order are presented as separate from the civil proceedings in which the preventative order was made. This argument was successful in the House of Lords,[43] although their Lordships felt it necessary to inject an element of compromise by holding that the standard of proof required in the civil proceedings was higher than normal, and probably equivalent to the 'proof beyond reasonable doubt' required in criminal proceedings. This decision is expected to be reviewed by the Strasbourg Court, looking at whether the civil proceedings which impose the prohibitions that are subsequently the focus of the criminal proceedings should themselves be held to be criminal in substance.

There may also be the question whether a preventative order is a 'penalty', within the meaning of Art 7. If it is, then it may not be imposed retrospectively, and there are certainty requirements too. The term 'penalty' has been given an autonomous meaning by the Strasbourg Court, looking to the effect of the measure (is it punitive in impact?) rather than to the purpose alone. Thus a confiscation order made upon an offender is a penalty, because of its potential severity (imprisonment in default) and the relevance of the offender's culpability, whereas the notification requirements for sex offenders do not amount to a penalty because they are less severe, clearly preventative in purpose, and enforceable only by a separate prosecution and not merely by default provisions.[44] The question is where particular types of preventative orders, such as the control order, the ASBO or the foreign travel order, lie on what appears to be a spectrum. Some will argue that they are clearly preventative in purpose, and need to be enforced by separate proceedings for breach, and so are not penalties. Others will contend that the most important feature is the potentially severe punishment (up to 5 years' imprisonment) that attends any breach, and that this demonstrates that the whole process is (at least partly) penal in nature and not merely preventative. What is interesting, however, is that if a preventative order such as an ASBO is held not to be a penalty, it falls outside that part of human rights law applicable to criminal proceedings and is limited only by more general rights such as the right to respect for private life (Art 8 of the European Convention). Thus, it would be quite permissible to impose a preventative order retrospectively, in response to conduct before the legislation creating the order came into force, because there is no principle of human rights law to suggest otherwise. Similarly, if a preventative order

[43] *R (on application of McCann) v Crown Court at Manchester; Clingham v Kensington and Chelsea RLBC* [2003] 1 AC 787.

[44] The two leading cases are *Welch v United Kingdom* (1995) 20 EHRR 247 and *Ibbotson v United Kingdom* (1999) 27 EHRR CD 332.

is held to impose a restriction of liberty but not a deprivation of liberty, it appears that none of the safeguards in Art 5 would apply to it. Apart from the right to a fair hearing under Art 6(1), these preventative measures appear to fall into a jurisprudential black hole. Can a framework of principles be constructed for such measures?

Turning away from human rights law towards broader liberal principles, on what basis could it be justifiable for the state to take coercive power over an individual who has not committed a criminal offence? John Stuart Mill famously dealt with the general issue of principle thus:

> The purpose of this essay is to assert one very simple principle, as entitled to govern absolutely the dealings of society with the individual in the way of compulsion and control ... That principle is, that the sole end for which mankind are warranted, individually or collectively, in interfering with the liberty of action of any of their number, is self-protection. That the only purpose for which power can be rightfully exercised over any member of a civilized community, against his will, is to prevent harm to others. His own good, either physical or moral, is not a sufficient warrant ... The only part of the conduct of any one, for which he is amenable to society, is that which concerns others.[45]

It is the third sentence of this passage that is the most widely quoted, in the context of criminal offences created because the conduct is thought to be immoral (rather than because it causes harm to others). Our primary interest here lies in the second sentence, where the self-protection of mankind is advanced as the sole purpose of coercive powers over individuals. This principle might be thought broad enough to encompass the dangers of terrorism, apprehension of which led the British Government to devise control orders for suspected terrorists. Before that line of reasoning is pursued, it may be noted that Mill returned, later in his essay *On Liberty*, to the question of 'how far liberty may legitimately be invaded for the prevention of crime, or of accident'. Mill regarded the preventative function of government as 'undisputed' but also as:

> far more liable to be abused, to the prejudice of liberty, than the punitory function; for there is hardly any part of the legitimate freedom of action of a human being which would not admit of being represented, and fairly too, as increasing the facilities for some form or other of delinquency.[46]

He goes on to argue, not only that it is therefore proper (and necessary) to criminalise and prevent attempts at crime, before they have caused harm, but also that it is right to label poisonous preparations and medicines so as to alert people to the danger in them. But that second example crosses the

[45] JS Mill, *On Liberty* (Oxford, Oxford World's Classics edn, 1991, first pub 1859) 13–14.
[46] Mill, above n 45, at 106.

line between harm to others and harm to self, which is why Mill proposes only labelling and not a major restriction on the sale of poisons. He does, however, accept that there is a good argument that 'sanitary precautions, or arrangements to protect workpeople employed in dangerous occupations, should be enforced on employers'. Mill depicts this as a form of limitation on free trade; yet he still approves it ('in principle undeniable'), and evidently thinks it unnecessary to offer further justifications for such coercion, in the same way as he thought it unnecessary to elaborate on the preventative function of government.

If we follow Mill and others in accepting that governments have a function of preventing harm within their jurisdiction, how far beyond the creation of criminal offences can this go? Here we return to the European Convention on Human Rights, and to the Strasbourg Court's recognition that states have positive duties to take reasonable measures to protect the lives, physical security and sexual integrity of those within their boundaries.[47] The Court's jurisprudence recognises the preventative duty of the state, while accepting that it is not absolute and only goes so far as to *require* the creation and enforcement of laws against certain types of harmful conduct. This preventative function is also apparent in one of the exceptions to Art 5: thus, as already mentioned, Art 5(1)(e) creates an exception to the right to liberty that covers 'the lawful detention of persons for the prevention of the spreading of infectious diseases, of persons of unsound mind, alcoholics or drug addicts or vagrants'. This list has a rather dated appearance, and many would object at least to the presence of 'vagrants' on it. Our interest, however, lies in the way in which the Strasbourg Court has developed restrictions on the exercise of this coercive power.

In *Witold Litwa v Poland*[48] the Court considered the purpose of Art 5(1)(e) and held that the link between all the categories of persons there listed is 'that they may be deprived of their liberty either in order to be given medical treatment or because of considerations dictated by social policy, or on both medical and social grounds'. In this case the applicant had been deprived of liberty for 6 hours on the ground that he was an alcoholic, and the Court decided that the term 'alcoholic' should be construed to mean anyone 'whose conduct and behaviour under the influence of alcohol pose a threat to public order or themselves', and does not require a medical diagnosis of alcoholism. However, the Court went on to conclude that the Polish

[47] Among the leading judgments are *Osman v UK* (1999) 29 EHRR 245 (right to life), *A v UK* (1999) 27 EHRR 611 (right not to be subjected to inhuman or degrading treatment) and *X and Y v Netherlands* (1986) 8 EHRR 235 (right to respect for private life, through protection of sexual integrity). See generally A Mowbray, *The Development of Positive Obligations under the European Convention on Human Rights by the European Court of Human Rights* (Oxford, Hart Publishing, 2004); Emmerson, Ashworth and Macdonald, above n 20, ch 18; and Leslie Sebba, this volume, ch 4.

[48] (2001) 33 EHRR 1267.

authorities had breached Art 5 because they should have used less restrictive methods of responding to the applicant's condition, and deprivation of liberty for 6 hours was unjustified. In *Enhorn v Sweden*[49] the applicant had the HIV virus and had transmitted it to another man. The Swedish medical authorities placed him under conditions as to his behaviour, and when he failed to observe those conditions they sought and obtained an order that he be kept in compulsory isolation in a hospital. This order was renewed over a period of 5 years, although the applicant absconded several times and was in fact detained for about 18 months. He argued that his Art 5 right to liberty had been unjustifiably infringed. The Court held that the essential criteria for exception (e) to Art 5(1) are:

> whether the spreading of the infectious disease is dangerous for public health or safety, and whether detention of the person infected is the last resort in order to prevent the spreading of the disease, because less severe measures have been considered and found to be insufficient to safeguard the public interest. When these criteria are no longer fulfilled, the basis for the deprivation of liberty ceases to exist.[50]

The Court went on to hold that Art 5 had been violated, because 'the compulsory isolation of the applicant was not a last resort' and, since his liberty was at stake, greater attention should have been paid to less restrictive means of protection.

The importance of these two Strasbourg judgments is that they approach the difficult task of devising appropriate limits on liberty by a procedural route, requiring consideration to be given to certain criteria. Three familiar Strasbourg principles are put to work here—the principle of necessity, that it must be clear that the restrictions are necessary to prevent the harm; the principle of subsidiary, that less intrusive measures must have been considered and adjudged to be insufficient; and the principle of proportionality, that the measures taken must not be out of proportion to the danger apprehended. It is easy to deride this kind of Strasbourg approach: it is merely procedural, and does not attempt to grapple with the substance (what kind of harm?; what degree of risk?); and it relies on broad and malleable concepts that leave room for variable interpretations. On the other hand, this approach led to findings of a violation in both the leading cases, so there are some grounds for believing that the criteria will be applied fairly strictly. This approach suggests that deprivation of liberty may be justifiable *in extremis* and as a last resort, when nothing less will provide adequate public protection. Its strength would be increased by insisting on

[49] (2005) 41 EHRR 643.
[50] (2005) 41 EHRR 643 at [44].

high standards of evidence on all issues of fact or prediction raised in a particular case.[51]

What implications does this have for the use of coercive measures less than deprivation of liberty? The British Government's response to the Court of Appeal's quashing of the particular control order was to reduce the hours of home confinement from 18 to 14 per day, in the hope of avoiding classification as a 'deprivation of liberty'. This, if upheld, still imposes considerable restrictions on liberty. The result, under the Convention, would be that the control order would leave the safeguards of Art 5 and migrate to Art 8, where it would raise questions about the degree of interference with the subject's right to respect for private life. Article 8 confers a qualified right, less powerful than that in Art 5, and interference with the right may be justified as 'necessary in a democratic society' in the 'interests of public safety', 'for the prevention of disorder or crime' or 'for the protection of the rights and freedoms of others'. These are much wider concepts than those applicable to the exceptions to Art 5, although the Strasbourg Court has insisted that the interference with a person's Art 8 rights must not be disproportionate to the danger that he is proved to present to public safety or the freedoms of others.

In relation to deprivations of liberty, the Floud Committee argued that a person predicted to be dangerous could justifiably be detained if he or she had already been found (by conviction or insanity verdict) to have committed a dangerous act. The principle on which they based this conclusion was that of the just redistribution of risk: each of us is presumed free of harmful intentions and therefore cannot justifiably be deprived of liberty on the basis that someone thinks we are dangerous; but, as soon as it is proved that we have done a dangerous act, that presumption disappears and it is fair to redistribute the risk of further harm by incarcerating the dangerous person rather than exposing others to the danger.[52] This reasoning gives insufficient weight to the rights of the offender not to be punished more than is proportionate to the crime committed, and not to be detained on suspicion of future danger. Certainly the Floud position was premised on the existence of a satisfactory level of predictive accuracy, but the question is whether the critics would rule out any form of protective custody for dangerous people. Bottoms and Brownsword adapt Dworkin's rights theory so as to argue that protective custody could only be justified in a much narrower category of cases, where a person is thought to present a 'vivid danger' of serious harm to others.[53] They contend that the defendant's

[51] For arguments along these lines, see M Dubber, *The Police Power: Patriarchy and the Foundations of American Government* (New York, Columbia University Press, 2005).

[52] J Floud and W Young, *Dangerousness and Criminal Justice* (London, Heinemann, 1981).

[53] AE Bottoms and R Brownsword, 'The Dangerousness Debate after the Floud Report' (1982) 22 *British Journal of Criminology* 229.

right not to be punished more than proportionately may be defeated by the potential victim's competing right not to be seriously injured, in circumstances where there is a high risk of a serious attack ('vivid danger'). However, this analysis assumes that the law enforcement duties of the state are transformed into rights that individuals hold against the state, which is doubtful. An alternative and stronger approach would be to rely on Dworkin's other ground for exceptions: that rights can only be overridden when the cost to society of not doing so would be so great that it could be held 'to justify whatever assault on dignity or equality might be involved'.[54] This would still need to be drawn tightly, so as to require convincing evidence of a significant likelihood of a very serious harm occurring, and even then there are grounds for regarding any such scheme as inherently problematic.[55]

The arguments just considered were directed at *deprivations* of liberty for significant periods of time, on the basis of future danger. Would they be any more persuasive if it were sought to justify *restrictions* on liberty? Mere restrictions might be thought to require less strong justifications, even though the difference from a deprivation is merely one of degree, as we have seen. Any version of the control order is likely to involve considerable restrictions on movement and on contact with others. Any steps towards justifying such restrictions must surely be premised on (a) a reliable prediction of a high probability of significant danger to others, and (b) a judgement that no lesser form of restriction would be adequate to reduce the danger presented by the individual to an acceptable level. Yet these criteria are pregnant with uncertainties and judgements of degree. How reliable must the predictions be? How high should the probability of harm be? How serious should the predicted harm be? How high a degree of risk is acceptable, to the extent of allowing less extensive restrictions out of respect for the subject's rights? Posing these questions shows the limitations of the argument so far. It is difficult to set meaningful limits on the use of protective measures, and there is inevitably a political element in such judgements. However, it must be remembered that there is an individual who is being subjected to such restrictions, and that some respect has to be shown for that individual's rights.

What about other preventative orders? Here, there is a particular aspect which needs to be dealt with first. For persons convicted of a wide range of sexual offences a 'notification requirement' is automatically imposed by the Sexual Offences Act 2003. As mentioned earlier, it has been held that the statutory notification requirements (formerly known as sex offender registration) do not amount to a penalty, and are not incompatible with

[54] R Dworkin, *Taking Rights Seriously* (London, Duckworth, 1977) 200.
[55] A von Hirsch and A Ashworth, *Proportionate Sentencing* (Oxford, Oxford University Press, 2005) 50–61.

Art 8.[56] However, the requirements do make demands and do authorise the police to check up on people subject to them. The particular aspect relevant here is that they are imposed on every offender falling within a given class (conviction of particular offences), and that what might be a proportionate interference with one offender's private life may be disproportionate to the wrongdoing or potential harmfulness of another offender—notably, one who was convicted of importing child pornography despite his belief that the subject-matter was adult pornography rather than child pornography.[57]

The Court of Appeal has held that automatic notification requirements are necessary to protect the public, without engaging with the argument that the least intrusive form of protection in each case should be adopted. In other words, the restrictive criteria adopted by the Strasbourg Court in the quarantine case of *Enhorn v Sweden*[58] were not even explored here, when in principle they should have been.

Automatic requirements are rare in English law, and so we should now turn to more general questions of justifying preventative orders. It may be possible to draw a distinction between those orders designed to protect an individual citizen from harm, such as non-molestation orders under the Family Law Act 1996 or restraining orders under the Protection from Harassment Act 1997, and other preventative orders designed to reduce a general risk of misconduct, such as foreign travel orders, control orders and sexual offences prevention orders. The reason for this distinction might be that in the former category a particular citizen is known to be the potential victim, whereas in the latter category the risk is diffuse and unspecific. However, one might argue, *per contra,* that if the evidence on which the prediction of misconduct is based is equally robust in the two types of case, the known identity of the potential victim should not be regarded as a distinguishing feature.

Important as it is to secure protection for victims of domestic violence, it is no less important to secure protection for other citizens who are merely travellers on the London Underground, spectators at football matches, or whatever. However, one difference between the former and the latter is that the former are aware of the threat; it can therefore be argued that the existence of a protective order reduces the anxiety and torment that the particular citizen may feel, and in that respect enhances the right to respect for private life. It is unlikely that the enhancement of general feelings of security that might arise from the imposition of a violent offender order, foreign travel order or even a sexual offence prevention order will be of the same magnitude. However, it is still not clear that the distinction corresponds to

[56] *Ibbotson v United Kingdom* (1999) 27 EHRR CD 332; *Adamson v United Kingdom* (1999) 28 EHRR CD 209.

[57] *Forbes v Secretary of State for the Home Department* [2006] EWCA Civ 962.

[58] (2005) 41 EHRR 643, discussed above.

different types of order: one might argue that some ASBOs are aimed to protect a particular family or group of neighbours, whereas other ASBOs are aimed at general crime reduction by someone who behaves anti-socially towards those who travel on a certain type of transport, live in a particular part of town, etc. In other words, the two ends of the spectrum (individual protection/general crime reduction) are distinguishable, but there are many orders with mixed elements.

If we focus on the various forms of ASBOs, there can be little doubt that many of the conditions commonly included in them—not to enter a certain building or part of a town; not to gather with more than two other people; not to travel on particular forms of transport—interfere with a person's right to respect for private life. There are cases in which prohibitions have been struck down for uncertainty or overbreadth,[59] but we must focus here on cases where one or more clear prohibitions have been imposed. The legislation requires a finding that the subject has acted in a manner that caused or was likely to cause harassment, alarm or distress, and also a finding that an ASBO is necessary to protect people from further anti-social acts by the subject. It is established also that any order must be proportionate to the risk to be guarded against (ie to the further acts which it is reasonable to anticipate he might commit).[60] The proportionality requirement here relates not to the acts already done by the defendant, but to the magnitude of the harms in prospect and to the probability that the defendant will cause such harms.[61] Thus, even if many ASBO prohibitions are held to be compatible with Art 8, as necessary for the 'prevention of disorder' or for the 'protection of the rights and freedoms of others', this should not be allowed to foreclose further enquiry. The fact is that these orders are made under civil procedure and do significantly restrict the liberty of those subject to them. A principled enquiry into their justification must therefore be grounded in (a) a reliable prediction of a high probability of the risk of harassment, alarm or distress to others; (b) a judgment that no lesser form of restriction would be adequate to reduce the risk presented by the individual to an acceptable level; and (c) a judgment that the restriction is not disproportionate to the harm to be averted.[62] These are the terms in which we discussed the detention of 'dangerous' people earlier. Insofar as a preventative order imposes significant restrictions on the liberty of the person subjected to it, these three heads of justification for coercive state intervention must be satisfied; and, to be sure, they are more likely to be satisfied where

[59] See *McGrath* [2005] EWCA Crim 353; *Boness and Bebington* [2005] EWCA Crim 239.

[60] *Boness and Bebington* [2005] EWCA Crim 239 at [37].

[61] For elaboration, see A von Hirsch and M Wasik, 'Civil Disqualifications attending Conviction: a Suggested Conceptual Framework' (1997) 56 *CLJ* 599, 612–15.

[62] Requirement (c) is added because, otherwise, a preventative order might be justifiable in order to stop a young boy firing a water pistol at his neighbours every time he sees them: is such a legal prohibition really proportionate to the anticipated harm?

there is a distinct risk of (further) violence or abuse than if the risk is one of low-level disorder or incivility.

VI. CONCLUSIONS

The purpose of the discussions in section V above was to explore normative frameworks for preventative justice. It was argued that we should recognise a positive obligation on the state to create conditions of adequate security: the quantum must remain obscure, since absolute security is hardly possible (and arguably oppressive) and anarchy would be intolerable. Protection from harm, particularly where it is aimed at an individual, should be taken seriously; yet Mill's warning that the state's preventative function is liable to abuse should not be neglected, since, as he observed, it is possible to regard almost any form of human conduct as a potential threat to some value or interest.

A brief discussion of the justifications for depriving people of their liberty in order to prevent harm to others suggests that this power should be reserved for extreme situations. Adapting Dworkin's rights theory, it may be argued that such power should only be used in circumstances where the cost to society of not taking action would be not merely incremental but substantial, and sufficient to justify the loss of the right and all that this would mean. A proper evidential basis for predictions must be required, even if the degree of probability may be lower for serious harms than for mere incivilities. Even if deprivation of liberty were justifiable in such circumstances—quarantine, and the detention of allegedly dangerous offenders were given as examples—it should be used only if absolutely necessary; if no lesser measure would provide adequate protection; and if the measures taken were proportionate to the harm sought to be prevented.

These are tentative and controversial propositions, which undoubtedly require further argument. There are at least two other questions for discussion. One is the extent to which the same or similar restraining principles—the high cost of not overriding the individual's right to liberty, and the principles of necessity and proportionality—should apply to preventative measures that only restrain liberty, rather than depriving the subject of liberty. Even if, *ceteris paribus*, it is less difficult to justify a restriction on liberty than a deprivation of it, most of the preventative orders interfere with one or more rights of the individual and this requires supporting reasons. The second question concerns the procedural protections that should attend a preventative measure designed to restrict liberty. It seems as though, in European human rights law, the classification of a measure as preventative rather than a penalty or criminal charge means that it can be imposed without granting any special procedural rights to the accused (as in criminal cases), and even that it can be imposed retrospectively (in respect of conduct taking place before the relevant legislative provision came into force). This is the jurisprudential black hole, to which reference was made earlier. Indeed, Lucia Zedner has argued that human rights protections may even have the effect of undermining liberty, insofar as they encourage governments to think that if they manage to construct preventative orders which do not breach human rights standards, the measures are beyond reproach.[63]

The problem is that documents such as the European Convention on Human Rights impose hardly any constraints on these preventative measures, save the general restrictions on interference with Art 8 and other qualified rights. It was established in section IV above that measures such as control orders, ASBOs and sexual offences prevention orders, impose considerable restrictions on the liberty of the individuals subjected to them, after a civil process that contains few of the safeguards mandated for criminal proceedings. In section V it was argued that preventative orders should only be made as extreme or exceptional measures, in view of the restrictions they impose, and some suggestions about appropriate constraining principles were advanced. Further enquiry is needed in order to develop and refine such principles.

[63] Zedner, above n 28.

6

The Theory of Vulnerable Autonomy and the Legitimacy of Civil Preventative Orders

PETER RAMSAY*

I. INTRODUCTION

CIVIL PREVENTATIVE ORDERS (CPOs) encompass a wide range of binding legal orders.[1] The most prominent examples are the anti-social behaviour order (ASBO) and the terrorism control order, the legal flagships of the Government's self-proclaimed tough stance on the twin threats of local disorder and global terrorism. While no two examples of the CPO are identical in form,[2] they all share several features:

— they are granted in civil proceedings, or administratively with some judicial supervision;
— they are granted on satisfaction of broad and vaguely defined conduct;
— their terms may be any prohibition (or mandatory term in some cases) deemed necessary to prevent future instances of the broad and vaguely defined conduct on which they are grounded;
— breach of any of their terms is a criminal offence of strict liability.

Although the CPO is of recent origin, it does have precursors.[3] What is novel in the new group is the breadth of the conduct which may give rise

* A Doctoral Award from the Arts and Humanities Research Council provided financial support during the writing of this chapter. My thanks to Nicola Lacey, Alan Norrie, Suke Wolton and Lucia Zedner for their comments on earlier drafts of this chapter.

[1] The term is Stephen Shute's, see S Shute, 'New Civil Preventative Orders: Sexual Offences Prevention Orders; Foreign Travel Orders; Risk of Sexual Harm Orders (The Sexual Offences Act 2003, part 4) (United Kingdom)' [2004] *Crim LR* 417.

[2] I will explicitly deal here only with the ASBO, the control order and the risk of sexual harm order. Other CPOs include the sexual offences prevention order; sex offender order; foreign travel order; football banning order; the interim ASBO, parenting order, individual support order and the proposed serious crime prevention order.

[3] The most closely related legal instrument in form is the Statutory Nuisance Abatement Notice, provided by s 79 of the Environmental Protection Act 1990 (UK). This is a power

to an order, and which the order may prohibit, by comparison with the narrow grounds and scope of earlier orders. The CPOs have not been well received among criminal law theorists.

The normative critique of the CPO has been given its most systematic statement to date by Andrew Simester and Andrew von Hirsch.[4] The particular importance of their work is that it integrates together a number of critical themes, covering the whole range of the substantive, procedural and political-constitutional aspects of the new legal instruments.[5] Simester and von Hirsch detail these criticisms of the CPO through an analysis of the ASBO, and they are unsparing. I will consider their particular criticisms later on, but it is their conclusion that forms my starting point. They compare the ASBO unfavourably with the CPO's precursors, which they term 'ancillary civil prohibitions' (ACPs),[6] and conclude that:

> The ASBO is not sustainable as a legitimate ACP, because of the wide ambit of the kinds of conduct that may trigger issuance of an order, and because of the broad range of conduct that may be prohibited by the order itself.[7]

It is this conclusion that I want to scrutinise in this chapter. For it is striking that the severe criticism of these measures, put forward by criminal law theorists of the stature of Simester and von Hirsch, cuts almost no political ice. The 'appropriate' use of the ASBO is supported by all the major political parties, and despite initial controversy surrounding the control order, when the power came up for renewal 12 months later, a mere 13 MPs turned up to debate it, and it was renewed without a vote.[8]

Such controversy as surrounds the ASBO and the control order concerns the question of whether or not they 'work', which is to say have any impact

of local authorities to impose penal orders dating back into the 19th century. An important functional precursor is the bind over to keep the peace or be of good behaviour. I have elsewhere compared the ASBO with the ancient bind over to be of good behaviour: see P Ramsay, 'Vulnerability, Sovereignty and Police Power in the ASBO' in M Dubber and M Valverde (eds), *Police and the Liberal State* (Stanford, Stanford University Press, forthcoming). For a discussion of various disqualifications attendant on conviction, see A von Hirsch and M Wasik, 'Civil Disqualifications Attending Conviction' (1997) 56 *CLJ* 599.

[4] A Simester and A von Hirsch, 'Regulating Offensive Conduct Through Two-Step Prohibitions' in A von Hirsch and A Simester (eds), *Incivilities* (Oxford, Hart Publishing, 2006).

[5] Some of these themes have been pursued in detail by other writers. See, in particular on fair trial, S Macdonald, 'The Nature of the ASBO—*R (McCann & Others) v Crown Court at Manchester*' (2003) 66 *MLR* 630; on fair trial and proportionality, A Ashworth, 'Social Control and "Anti-Social Behaviour": The Subversion of Human Rights?' (2004) 120 *LQR* 263; on proportionality, S Macdonald, 'The Principle of Composite Sentencing: Its Centrality to, and Implications for, the ASBO' (2006) *Crim LR* 791; on wrongfulness of conduct criminalised and on generality, P Ramsay, 'What Is Anti-Social Behaviour?' [2004] *Crim LR* 908.

[6] Simester and von Hirsch, above n 4. They also use the term 'Two-Step Prohibition Order' rather than 'civil preventative order'. None of these terms has any legal status.

[7] Simester and von Hirsch, above n 4, at 190.

[8] HC Deb col 1516 (15 Feb 2006).

on the experience of 'anti-social behaviour' or 'terrorism'. But the existence of the power to impose ASBOs and control orders, and to punish individuals for breach of them, is not controversial among mainstream politicians,[9] the judiciary,[10] the police and local authorities[11] and it is supported by a large majority of the public.[12] The powers in CPOs are controversial among some campaigning groups,[13] youth justice professionals, criminologists and criminal law theorists.

The gap between the normative conclusions of academic experts on criminal justice and the positive conditions of the political order is hardly unique to the CPO.[14] But the gap does need explaining and normative theory cannot do this. The purely normative approach tells us what the CPO is not—it is not 'good' criminal law from the standpoint of the theory's liberal norms. But in itself normative theory cannot tell us what the CPO is. Indeed there is a tendency to assume that, since the CPO is a violation of sound liberal norms, it must represent nothing more than unprincipled political opportunism. The flipside of normative theory's condemnation is an explanation in terms of 'penal populism', in which government marginalises criminal justice expertise in favour of a punitive playing to the fears and insecurities of the electoral gallery.[15] But, at the very least, this explanation fails to explain why some 'populist' policies are judicially endorsed (anti-social behaviour policy, for example), but others are not (the denial of welfare benefits to asylum-seekers, for example).[16] And this is because this approach fails to investigate in any depth the content of the underlying beliefs that these 'populist' measures do in reality draw on.

[9] At the time of writing, the first signs of a possible change of policy are emerging, at least in respect of the ASBO. Ed Balls, the Minister for Children in the new Government of Gordon Brown, has declared that while ASBOs remain 'necessary', their use against young people indicates a wider failure of policy: see *Daily Mirror* (London 27 July 2007).

[10] *R (McCann and Others) v Crown Court at Manchester and Another* [2003] 1 AC 787. There has been some judicial sniping at the control order procedure, some aspects of which were ruled a breach of Art 6 ECHR by Sullivan J in the Divisional Court, but the decision was overturned by the Court of Appeal: see *Secretary of State for the Home Department v MB* (2006) EWCA Civ Div 1140. For a more detailed discussion, see Lucia Zedner, this volume, ch 3.

[11] Use of the ASBO, however, varies widely between local authority areas. For a breakdown see <http://www.crimereduction.gov.uk/asbos/asbos2.htm>.

[12] A MORI opinion poll in 2005 showed 82% support for the ASBO (although only 37% claimed to know more than a little about them, and only 39% thought them effective in stopping ASB): see <http://www.ipsos.mori.com/polls/2005/asbo-top.shtml>.

[13] See especially ASBO Concern: <www.asboconcern.org.uk>; Liberty: <www.liberty-human-rights.org.uk/7-asbos/index.shtml>; Statewatch: <http://www.statewatch.ord/asbo/ASBOwatch.html>.

[14] See A Ashworth, 'Is the Criminal Law a Lost Cause? (2000) 116 *LQR* 225.

[15] On ASBOs, see, for example, E Burney, *Making People Behave: Anti-Social Behaviour, Politics and Policy* (Cullompton, Willan, 2005) 17.

[16] The higher courts have fought a running battle with the executive on this issue for more than a decade: see S Wolton, 'Immigration Policy and the Crisis of "British Values"' (2006) 10(4) *Citizenship Studies* 453. For a recent engagement, see *R (Limbuela) v Secretary of State for the Home Department* [2006] 1 AC 396.

I want here to take a different approach to the question of legitimacy from that taken by Simester and von Hirsch. Instead of their broadly 'philosophical' approach to legitimacy, in which the CPO is evaluated against predetermined liberal norms, I seek to apply David Beetham's 'social-scientific conception of legitimacy',[17] which is a judgment of the measure's 'legitimacy in context, assessed against the relevant norms, principles and criteria of consent pertaining in the given society'.[18] The 'philosophical' approach to the legitimacy of the CPOs begins with a set of normative criteria laid down in advance of the investigation of the measures themselves, and criticises the CPOs from that standpoint. By contrast, I will set out from the substantive law of the CPO. I will seek first to elucidate the character of the substantive demands on citizens made by the CPO—specifically, I will argue that the CPO places a liability on those who consistently fail to reassure others. I will then show how these demands institutionalise the protection of a norm postulated in some very influential contemporary political theories—specifically, I will argue that the CPO institutionalises a norm of 'vulnerable autonomy', a norm that is fundamental to the theories which Nikolas Rose has characterised as 'advanced liberal', that is, the Third Way, communitarianism and neo-liberalism.

My argument is that there is a framework of belief behind the legal structure of the CPO, one that is sufficiently widely shared for these orders to resonate with the concerns of wider society, appear legitimate in political life and enjoy political immunity from the criticisms of liberal normative theory (at least for the present). None of this is intended as an argument that Simester's and von Hirsch's criticisms are without any substantive value. On the contrary, it is precisely the importance, even urgency, of at least some of their criticisms that leads me to reconstruct the ASBO's claim to legitimacy. My reason for taking this approach is the belief that criticism which omits to place a governmental power in its actual legitimating context, but merely argues that the power fails to meet the requirements of predetermined normative criteria, will at best miss its target and lack practical consequences.[19] I will, therefore, return at the end of the chapter to consider Simester and von Hirsch's detailed criticisms in the light of what we have discovered about the CPOs 'legitimacy in context', and specifically the extent to which their criticisms engage with the beliefs underlying the CPO or just talk past them.

In reconstructing the theory of vulnerable autonomy, I am therefore *not* trying to engage in the 'philosophical' style of normative theory familiar in the study of the substantive criminal law. I am not attempting to elaborate a

[17] D Beetham, *The Legitimation of Power* (Basingstoke, Macmillan, 1991) 37.

[18] Beetham, above n 17, at 38. This is not to be confused with Max Weber's social-scientific concept of legitimacy, which precisely overlooks this objective judgement about prevailing norms: see Beetham, above n 17, at 8–15.

[19] See also R Barker, *Legitimating Identities* (Cambridge, Cambridge University Press, 2001) 23.

watertight normative justification of these orders in the philosophical sense. My aim here is only to show that in the political world beyond academic criminal law theory, an influential normative argument for the CPO already exists, and serves to legitimise this form of penal obligation in practice. The theory of vulnerable autonomy which I identify, and the justification of the CPO which that theory provides, may turn out to be more or less well founded. But their strengths and weaknesses cannot be assessed unless the character of the argument is first identified. Here I am taking that first step by trying to draw a draft map of the territory that I think we are in.

The chapter proceeds by first explaining the substantive content of three different CPOs: the ASBO, the terrorism control order and the risk of sexual harm order. My aim is to demonstrate that although these novel legal instruments are each applicable in different factual circumstances, they nevertheless share a common substantive content—a liability for a failure to reassure. I then look at how this liability and the policy arguments put forward in favour of it construct the ordinary citizen as intrinsically vulnerable and in need of reassurance.[20] After that I turn to an important source of this construction by identifying the protection of 'vulnerable autonomy' as a norm at the heart of the three political theories with a preponderant influence in contemporary politics in the UK. Finally, having identified this normative structure institutionalised in the CPO, I return to the detail points of Simester and von Hirsch's criticisms to indicate the extent to which the theory of vulnerable autonomy has an 'answer' to them.

II. CONTROLLING THE FAILURE TO REASSURE

There are many differences between the CPOs, but I will here analyse in turn the substantive law of three of them—the ASBO, the terrorism control order and the risk of sexual harm order—to indicate the substantive content which they share.

A. Anti-Social Behaviour Order (ASBO)

Section 1(1) of the Crime and Disorder Act 1998 (UK) gives the grounds for imposing an ASBO as follows:

> (a) that the person has acted ... in an anti-social manner, that is to say, in a manner that caused or was likely to cause harassment, alarm or distress to one or more persons not of the same household as himself; and

[20] I will only consider policy in relation to the ASBO and the control order in this section. The little-used RSHO is included only for formal comparative purposes. I will not consider the wider context of vulnerability to sexual harm.

(b) that such an order is necessary to protect relevant persons from further anti-social acts by him.'[21]

At its broadest, s 1(1)(a) requires that the defendant has done something which a court is certain would, more likely than not, cause (or be *likely* to cause) harassment, alarm or distress to someone present in the circumstances in which the conduct occurred.[22] The assessment of the necessity of an order in s 1(1)(b) is a discretionary evaluation not subject to proof as such,[23] and more specifically a risk assessment of the clinical type.[24] An order is very likely to be necessary wherever the court finds a propensity or disposition to repeat the conduct; in the absence of such a disposition it is unlikely to be necessary.[25] What is therefore controlled by the ASBO is the manifest disposition to cause harassment, alarm or distress, which is to say a manifest disposition of indifference or hostility to others' feelings. What creates liability to an ASBO is anything which manifests a lack of respect for others' feelings.

Where the court is satisfied that the s 1(1) grounds are made out then the terms of an ASBO may include any 'prohibitions ... necessary for the purpose of protecting persons ... from further anti-social acts by the defendant'.[26] The terms of an order may therefore prohibit conduct which would not be a criminal offence when committed by anyone other than the specific defendant. These obligations—restrictions on the defendant's movements, association, possession and consumption of objects, use of language and so on—by virtue of their specificity and individual tailoring, construct the person subject to them as representing a specific threat of further 'harassment, alarm or distress'. But can we be any more precise about the character of these feelings experienced (or likely to be experienced) by the victim and, therefore, of the threat the defendant poses?

Harassment, alarm and distress are each unpleasant feelings, and there is no objective limitation on the sensitivity of those who might be caused any of these feelings by the defendant, apart from the authority's discretion to bring an application.[27] One consequence of this breadth of definition is

[21] Crime and Disorder Act 1998 (UK), s 1(1), as amended by Police Reform Act 2002 (UK), s 61(1), (2).

[22] See *Chief Constable of Lancashire v Potter* [2003] 42 *Law Society Gazette* 31, (2003) All ER (D) 199 (Oct).

[23] *R (McCann and Others) v Crown Court at Manchester and Another* [2003] 1 AC 787, 812.

[24] See Ramsay, above n 5, at 915.

[25] Ramsay, above n 5, at 915. See also *R v Jones and Others* [2006] All ER (D) 97 (Sep) CA.

[26] Crime and Disorder Act 1998 (UK), s 1(6), as amended by Police Reform Act 2002 (UK), s 61(1), (7).

[27] An ASBO application may be made by the police, a local authority or a registered social landlord. The ASBO is also available to a criminal court on conviction of an offender, sometimes referred to as a 'CrASBO' (Crime and Disorder Act 1998 (UK), s 1C). This does not alter

that there has been a tendency to assume that conduct which causes these feelings can be equated with behaviour which in fact offends people.[28] And in practice many ASBO's appear to prohibit the merely offensive.[29] But, while there is an overlap between the two categories, this identification of anti-social behaviour (ASB) with offensiveness is not satisfactory, for two reasons.

First, the category 'harassment, alarm or distress' plainly includes conduct which causes another person to be afraid. But, as Douglas Husak observes, there must be some doubt as to the plausibility of claiming that a person is offended by that which causes them to experience fear.[30] However 'harassment, alarm or distress' can no more be equated with fear than it can with offence. There is no need to prove fear in order to prove harassment, alarm or distress since less grave feelings than fear will be sufficient.[31] One plausible reaction to what appears to be a lumping together of fear and offence is to conclude that 'harassment, alarm or distress' is simply a vague, catch-all category. But the second reason for doubting the identification with offensiveness is supplied by the structure of s 1 just outlined. This structure suggests that there may nevertheless be a common feature to the conduct s 1(1)(a) describes.

We saw above that it is the manifesting of a disposition of indifference or hostility, a lack of respect for others' feelings, that unifies the conduct which attracts liability to an ASBO. The behaviour which manifests this attitude may take the form of conduct which causes annoyance, offence, anxiety, shock, fear or any other feeling covered by the phrase 'harassment, alarm or distress'. Liability to an ASBO turns not only on the likely or proven effects of conduct which caused harassment, alarm or distress, but also on an assessment of the threat that the disposition made manifest in the conduct represents to the quality of the defendant's relationships with others

the analysis here. The grounds for imposition are the same, and are usually provided, at least in part, by the facts of the criminal offence proved. The terms of a CrASBO will very likely specifically prohibit future criminal offending, but then so may any ASBO in so far as the prohibited conduct is also a criminal offence. The reason for its prohibition in an ASBO is not the wrong criminalised by the freestanding offence, but the harassment, alarm or distress the conduct is likely to cause (see *R v Braxton (No 2)* [2005] 1 Cr App R (S) 36, [3]; *R v Lamb* [2005] All ER (D) 132 (Nov); *R v Stevens* [2006] 2 Cr App R (S) 453 CA).

[28] See, for example, RA Duff and SE Marshall, 'How Offensive Can You Get?' and E Burney, 'No Spitting: Regulation of Offensive Behaviour in England and Wales' in von Hirsch and Simester (eds), above n 4.

[29] ASBOs have prohibited people from singing in their houses, answering the front door dressed only in underwear, feeding pigeons, slamming doors too loudly, urinating in public, and so on: see <http://www.statewatch.org/asbo/ASBOwatch.html>.

[30] See D Husak, 'Disgust: Metaphysical and Empirical Speculations' in von Hirsch and Simester (eds), above n 4.

[31] For the purposes of ss 4 and 5 of the Public Order Act 1986 (UK), 'harassment, alarm or distress' has been explicitly held not to require the causing of fear: *Chambers and Edwards v DPP* [1995] *Crim LR* 896.

in the future, a threat which the prohibitions in the ASBO are intended to regulate. These grounds of liability share a common element with Peter Birks' account of the common law tort of harassment, an account which offers a more specific concept of the wrong of harassment.[32]

In the course of his argument that the English common law recognises a tort of harassment, Birks describes the concept of harassment as it appears in both the common law and in its equivalent form in the Roman law of *iniuria*. Birks argues that such a tort protects 'the right to one's fair share of respect' from the 'hubris', the insolent presumption of the tortfeasor.[33] Moreover, for Birks at the heart of this tort lies a belittlement of the victim which

> has two aspects, immediate and prospective, in that it infringes the protected interest and threatens the victim's future entitlement. That is belittlement is both an immediate wrong and, in that a person belittled is thereby in danger of being perceived as a person of less consequence, *an exposure to future wrongs*. Self-esteem and public esteem ... are simultaneously in issue.[34]

This gets to the heart of the concept of anti-social behaviour too. Birks' tort is narrower than anti-social behaviour. It requires an intentional harassment, which manifests contempt.[35] Section 1(1) of the Crime and Disorder Act 1998 (UK) by contrast has no requirement to prove intent. Rather, the ASBO defendant need only manifest indifference to the particular feelings of the other (although active contempt is certainly also included), and those feelings might be 'alarm or distress' rather than 'harassment'.[36] Whether or not the others are offended, anxious or afraid when they suffer 'harassment, alarm or distress', it is the indifference or contempt of the defendant that is likely to cause them to experience 'an exposure to future wrongs'. The key to anti-social behaviour, as defined in s 1(1) of the Crime and Disorder Act 1998 (UK), is that at the very least, the defendant's disrespect consists of failing to show concern for others' needs and concerns; that, whether through the contempt or indifference it manifests, the conduct *fails to reassure* others with respect to the security of their interests in the future.

The breadth of the definition of this omission, and the absence of any 'objective' standard of sensitivity of its 'victim', is such that the conduct which it will include in some cases may, to an external observer, appear to

[32] P Birks, *Harassment and Hubris: The Right to an Equality of Respect* (1997) xxxii *Irish Jurist* 1.

[33] Birks, above n 32, at 13.

[34] *Ibid.*

[35] Birks, above n 32, at 17.

[36] The addition of the words 'alarm or distress' seems to be required where unintentional conduct is to be included since the ordinary meaning of 'harass' seems to imply deliberate action at least in some degree.

be merely offensive to its victim. But it is neither offensiveness as such, nor the causing of fear as such, that makes sense of the grounds for imposing an ASBO. It is the failure to reassure others about their future security that provides a more exact account of the particular disrespect for others' feelings which establishes the liability—for it includes causing specific fears of particular threats but also feelings more inchoate than that, which are nevertheless not reducible to mere offence. The breadth of these grounds also suggests that they are more significant for providing the criterion of a risk or threat assessment than they are for providing the definition of a wrong in the manner of Birks' narrower tort, although as we shall later see the failure to reassure can be understood as a wrong. This is consistent with the House of Lords' proposition that the ASBO is not a penalty,[37] and with the Court of Appeal's dicta suggesting that the wrong which does attract a penalty is the failure to take that official assessment of threat seriously by continuing to manifest the risk in breach of the ASBO.[38]

This interpretation of the anti-social behaviour that is defined in the grounds of the ASBO power is consistent with the terms of s 1(1) and has three particular merits over simple offensiveness. First, it identifies a category in which offensive and fear-causing conduct are not arbitrarily combined. Second, it can account for the interpretation of s 1 offered by the higher courts. Third, it suggests that it is not the offensiveness as such of the conduct which causes 'harassment, alarm or distress' that is the problem, even where the conduct concerned is offensive, but rather the underlying threat to others' sense of security. And, as we shall shortly see, it is these questions of exposure to future wrong and reassurance, and not offensiveness as such, that are central to the policy rationale for the ASBO.

The ASBO can be summarised as a power to prohibit conduct which fails to reassure others, where a court believes the defendant has manifested a disposition to disrespect others' subjective security needs.

B. Control Order

The liability for a failure to reassure is more straightforward in the case of the control order, even though at first sight it seems to be focused on preventing conduct amounting to the most serious criminal wrongs rather than that which merely fails to reassure. There are two types of control order—one which involves a derogation from Art 5 ECHR and one which does not—and they have slightly different procedures.[39] Derogating control

[37] See *R (McCann and Others) v Crown Court at Manchester and Another* [2003] 1 AC 787.
[38] See, for example, *R v Braxton (No 2)* [2005] 1 Cr App R (S) 36, [17].
[39] See Prevention of Terrorism Act 2005 (UK), ss 1–4.

orders are on their face emergency powers, and I will focus here on the non-derogating orders only.

The grounds for imposing a non-derogating control order are found in s 2(1) of the Prevention of Terrorism Act 2005 which allows the Home Secretary to place individuals under specific criminal law obligations where he or she

> (a) has reasonable grounds for suspecting that the individual is or has been involved in terrorism-related activity; and (b) considers that it is necessary, for purposes connected with protecting members of the public from a risk of terrorism, to make a control order imposing obligations on that individual.

The grounds therefore constitute a risk assessment of the clinical type in which the Home Secretary evaluates the individual concerned to represent a 'risk of terrorism', with the result that that individual's future behaviour may be controlled.[40]

If a person is to avoid the reasonable suspicion of the Home Secretary then they will need to take care not to do that which might create reasonable suspicion, they will need to ensure that they do not fail to reassure the Home Secretary. The double negative indicates the subtlety of the liability created by the CPO. Liability to a control order does not impose a positive duty requiring citizens actively to reassure the Home Secretary; rather it gives citizens notice that, if they wish to avoid liability, they need to think about what will not reassure the Home Secretary, and will therefore create suspicion, and act accordingly.

Failure to reassure the Home Secretary results in an order which may impose 'any obligations that the Secretary of State or (as the case may be) the court considers necessary for purposes connected with preventing or restricting involvement by that individual in terrorism-related activity'.[41] Breach of this order is a criminal offence.[42] These obligations, particular to the defendant, may prohibit or mandate conduct and they will certainly include prohibiting and restricting the conduct that gave rise to suspicion, that failed to reassure in the first place. By imposing controls on their movements, activity, association, and susceptibility to official surveillance which are specific to the controlled individual, these obligations construct the individual who has failed to reassure as a specific threat—a potential 'terrorist'.[43] The purpose of the legislation may be to prevent serious criminal

[40] *Secretary of State for the Home Department v MB* (2006) EWCA Civ Div 1140, [57].

[41] Prevention of Terrorism Act 2005 (UK), s 1(3).

[42] Prevention of Terrorism Act 2005 (UK), s 9.

[43] 'The PTA seeks to achieve this object by empowering the Secretary of State to impose control orders on those suspected of *being terrorists*': *Secretary of State for the Home Department v MB* (2006) EWCA Civ Div 1140, [6] (emphasis added).

wrongs, it is aimed at the 'threat' of terrorism, but that threat is controlled by means of individualised penal obligations prohibiting activity which fails to reassure.

C. Risk of Sexual Harm Order (RSHO)

An RSHO can be granted by a magistrates' court where it is satisfied that the defendant has on at least two occasions engaged with a child in a very widely defined range of conduct which is related in some way to sexual activity or 'sexual communication' with a child,[44] so that, as a result, 'there is reasonable cause to believe that it is necessary for such an order to be made'.[45] Again, the procedure amounts to a risk assessment of the clinical type.

Like the ASBO, the conduct which lays the ground for the order[46] includes conduct that would be a criminal offence in any case and conduct which would not. What links these two different groups into a single set of grounds for imposition of the order is that they all lend sufficient credibility to the judgment that the defendant represents a risk of sexual harm to children so that a prohibitory order is necessary to protect against that risk.

The terms of the RSHO itself may prohibit *any* conduct, prohibition of which is necessary to protecting children under 16 generally or any particular child under 16 from harm from the defendant.[47] Many acts prohibited under the terms of the RSHO will in fact create a risk of sexual harm and might also be inchoate or complete sexual offences. But, since there need only be reasonable cause to believe that the order is necessary, there is no requirement that the prohibited acts in fact create any risk, only that they create reasonable cause to believe that there is a risk. Such acts are those which in the case of the particular defendant fail to reassure the public that he is not creating a risk of sexual harm even when he is not in fact doing so. The findings which led to the granting of the order are the basis of the failure of this conduct to reassure—they construct the person subject to them as a specific threat of sexual harm to children.

The reassurance aspect of these grounds for the order is reinforced when the precise definition of sexual activity and sexual communication for the purposes of s123 are taken into account. An activity or communication is sexual if a reasonable person would in all the circumstances, but regardless of any person's purpose, consider it to be sexual.[48] This means that activity

44 Sexual Offences Act 2003 (UK), s 123(1)(a).
45 Sexual Offences Act 2003 (UK), s 123(1)(b).
46 Set out in detail in Sexual Offences Act 2003 (UK), s 123(3).
47 Sexual Offences Act 2003 (UK), s 123(6).
48 Sexual Offences Act 2003 (UK), ss 124(5) and (7).

which is in fact sexually motivated but which a reasonable observer would not perceive to be does not create grounds for an order and vice versa.[49] What is manifest to the reasonable observer, not actual sexual motive, is the substantive key to liability.[50]

The rationale is preventative in that the inchoate criminal liability under the terms of the order may be much more extensive than in the ordinary criminal law. But again the conduct concerned is defined as that which represents a risk of the harm in the minds of the magistrates. In other words the magistrates harbour a reasonable suspicion that the defendant will cause sexual harm to children in the future. The defendant is liable to the order and the order is necessary because his conduct fails to reassure the magistrates that he represents no threat.

III. CONSTRUCTING THE ORDINARY CITIZEN AS VULNERABLE

Liability for a failure to reassure someone in authority about your future conduct is a legal burden akin to a presumption of guilt. It reverses the onus of proof in respect not of accusations about the past, but of fears about the future.[51] That criminal justice experts should find themselves politically isolated in their condemnation of such sweeping measures is testament to the political effectiveness of the Government's justification of them. So what is this justification?

In a newspaper exchange with a critic of criminal justice policy, Prime Minister Tony Blair admitted that 'we have disturbed the normal legal process with the anti-social behaviour laws', and he went on to explain why this was necessary:

> If the practical effect of the law is that people live in fear because the offender is unafraid of the legal process then, in the name of civil liberties, we are allowing the vulnerable, the decent, the people who show respect and expect it back, to have their essential liberties trampled on.[52]

The Prime Minister's comment echoes the view of Lord Hutton in the House of Lords who observed in *McCann,* the leading case on ASBOs, that in respect of ASB, the community is 'represented by weak and vulnerable people who claim they are victims of anti-social behaviour which

[49] R Card, *Sexual Offences: The New Law* (Bristol, Jordan, 2004) 239–40.

[50] Although it should be noted that this is a longstanding feature of the offence of sexual assault in England and Wales: see *R v Court* [1989] AC 28.

[51] This is closely related to the idea of the 'preemptive' turn in criminal justice discussed in L Zedner, 'Preventive Justice of Pre-Punishment? The Case of Control Orders' (2006) *Current Legal Problems*; and Lucia Zedner, this volume, ch 3.

[52] T Blair, *Observer* (London 23rd April 2006) 835.

violates their rights'.[53] For Blair the decent are vulnerable; for Hutton LJ the vulnerable represent the community.[54]

When the Prime Minister and House of Lords refer to 'vulnerability', they mean vulnerability as it is subjectively experienced rather than vulnerability as an objective estimation of any threat. In *McCann* Lord Steyn clearly encompasses this subjective sense of vulnerability to others' potential criminal behaviour when, adopting the words of one of his earlier judgements, he observed that: 'The aim of the criminal law is not punishment for its own sake but to permit everyone to go about their daily lives without *fear* of harm to person or property.'[55] Similarly Home Office anti-social behaviour policy is oriented to the subjective problem of fear of crime. The White Paper *Respect and Responsibility*, which preceded the Anti-Social Behaviour Act 2003, is explicit that although actual crime reported in victim surveys and recorded by the police has fallen in recent years:

> [T]he fear of crime has not fallen to the same extent. And it is fear of crime—rather than actually being a victim—that can so often limit people's lives, making them feel afraid of going out or even afraid in their own homes … .[56]

Where the ordinary decent citizen is understood to be defined in some sense by their subjective vulnerability to others' potential for criminal aggression against them, the attempt to control fear of crime through measures which prohibit behaviour defined by its failure to reassure others starts to make normative sense. As the Home Office suggests in *Respect and Responsibility*, the intrinsically vulnerable citizen needs reassurance before they will be willing to go about their normal lives, and the 'right to be free from harassment, alarm or distress' which is asserted by the Home Secretary in the foreword to that document is the consequence.[57] It is this construction of the ordinary, decent citizen as vulnerable that is institutionalised in the substantive law of the ASBO.

The same construction can be found in the policy underlying the control order. It is perhaps unnecessary to point out that contemporary counter-terrorism policy is driven by the conviction that the UK and its citizens face a uniquely dangerous threat in the form of Islamist radicals. In recommending the control order to Parliament the Home Secretary emphasise both the vulnerability of citizens to the subjects of control orders, in

[53] *Ibid.*

[54] On the connection of respectability and vulnerability in the official policy, see also P Squires and D Stephen, *Rougher Justice: Anti-Social Behaviour and Young People* (Cullompton, Willan, 2005) 10.

[55] *R (McCann and Others) v Crown Court at Manchester and Another* [2003] 1 AC 787, 805 (emphasis added).

[56] Home Office, *Respect and Responsibility* (London, HMSO, 2003) 13.

[57] Home Office, above n 56, Ministerial Foreword.

particular, and to Islamist violence in general. In relation to the former he observed that:

> These orders are for those dangerous individuals whom we cannot prosecute or deport, but whom we cannot allow to go on their way unchecked because of the seriousness of the risk that they pose to *everybody else* in the country.[58]

Alert to the question of why control orders were necessary in 2005 when they had not been in the quarter of a century of struggle against the Irish Republican Army, Charles Clarke made the familiar claim that '9/11 changed things'. Specifically, he asserted that Islamist militants—in their philosophical nihilism, lack of restraint, willingness to murder through suicide, ambition and sophistication, and global reach—represented a threat which is qualitatively more serious than that which was posed by the IRA. Whether or not this construction of a historically unprecedented threat is either accurate in some objective sense or strategically prudent is not the point here.[59] For present purposes we should note that the political justification of the control order is the historically unprecedented threat from terrorism that government *believes* all its citizens are confronted by.

The ASBO and control order are premised on the subjective vulnerability of citizens in respect of everyday incivilities and of extraordinary political violence. This explains why those orders impose a liability for failure to reassure, since the subjectively vulnerable are in need of reassurance. The judicial endorsement of the vulnerability of the ordinary citizen suggests that this construction is no mere eccentricity of New Labour's notorious spin machine. In fact the vulnerability of the ordinary citizen's autonomy is a fundamental assumption of contemporary political life, found in the most influential of political theories to which we now turn.

IV. THEORIES OF VULNERABLE AUTONOMY

The basic normative proposition of the theory of vulnerable autonomy has been set out by Joel Anderson and Axel Honneth.[60] They argue that self-respect, self-esteem and self-trust are preconditions of autonomy. Possession of these qualities arises from an intersubjective process of mutual recognition of each other's worth. Anderson and Honneth describe these preconditions

[58] HC Deb col 339 (23 February 2005) (emphasis added).

[59] The UK Government's claim in this respect was most controversially contested by Lord Hoffmann in a trenchant dissenting judgment in the Belmarsh case which led to the control order legislation (see *A v SSHD* [2005] 2 WLR 87, 135).

[60] J Anderson and A Honneth, 'Autonomy, Vulnerability, Recognition and Justice' in J Christman and J Anderson (eds), *Autonomy and the Challenges to Liberalism: New Essays* (Cambridge, Cambridge University Press, 2005).

as 'more or less fragile achievements, and their vulnerability to various forms of injury, violation, and denigration makes it a central matter of justice that the social contexts within which they emerge be protected'.[61] Their detailed discussion is limited to the active denigration of other people, but in summing up their theory they observe that:

> autonomy turns out to have as a condition of its possibility, a supportive recognitional infrastructure. Because agents are largely dependent on this recognitional infrastructure for their autonomy, they are subject to autonomy-related vulnerabilities: harms to and neglect of these relations of recognition jeopardise individuals' autonomy.[62]

This is useful as an explicit general statement of the theory of vulnerable autonomy. However I want to argue that the same basic construction can be found implicitly at the core of three theories which have long had the most powerful influence in British political life, and which have been tentatively characterised as 'advanced liberalism'.[63] These are the Third Way, communitarianism and neo-liberalism. The discussion of these theories that follows may seem to some readers to return to some already well-covered ground. My reason for doing so is to demonstrate that the vulnerability of autonomy is not a contingent feature of these theories but fundamental to them, and, therefore, that the concept of vulnerable autonomy is deeply rooted in theories with an influence right across the political mainstream. The focus is on these theories precisely because of their acknowledged political influence. Communitarian and republican political theories have been influential in normative theories of punishment in recent years.[64] The present analysis may well resonate with aspects of these normative penal theories. But the penal theories are not investigated here because our concern is with the question of legitimacy in a social-scientific perspective as opposed to a purely normative one.

A. The Third Way

Anthony Giddens argues that '[f]reedom from the fear of crime is a major citizenship right'.[65] This right is necessary to protect the recognitional infrastructure which lies at the core of his Third Way theory where it serves as the solution to the problem of 'social cohesion'.

[61] Anderson and Honneth, above n 60, at 137.
[62] Anderson and Honneth, above n 60, at 145.
[63] N Rose, *Powers of Freedom* (Cambridge, Cambridge University Press, 1999).
[64] See, for example, RA Duff, *Punishment, Communication and Community* (Oxford, Oxford University Press, 2001); J Braithwaite and P Pettit, *Not Just Deserts: A Republican Theory of Criminal Justice* (Oxford, Clarendon, 1990).
[65] A Giddens, *Where Now for New Labour?* (Cambridge, Polity, 2002) 17.

The Third Way sets out from the proposition that contemporary society is characterised by a new individualism in which self-fulfilment is the central object of people's lives.[66] In his earlier work, Giddens gives an account of the subjects of self-fulfilment who provide this starting point for The Third Way. He develops the idea that at root 'The self is a reflexive project .... We are not what we are, but what we make of ourselves'.[67] And the point of this reflexive project is self-actualisation: the discovery and positing of our authentic self through developing a reflexive self-knowledge of 'the various phases of the lifespan'.[68] For Giddens this 'moral thread of self-actualisation is one of *authenticity* ... based on "being true to oneself".'[69] And he points out the problem of 'social cohesion' that is posed by this literally self-centred ethics in which 'the only significant connecting thread is the life trajectory as such'.[70] The authentic self is one who successfully creates 'a personal belief system by means of which the individual acknowledges that "his first loyalty is to himself"'.[71] However the same self-actualisation concept that gives rise to this problem of self-centredness also supplies a potential solution in self-fulfilment.

The process of self-actualisation, of 'finding oneself', requires, as one of its moments, 'achieving fulfilment', and 'fulfilment is in some part a moral phenomenon, because it means fostering a sense that one is "good", a "worthy person" ... '.[72] And to foster this sense of self-esteem requires in turn the co-operation of others. For Giddens, a precondition of fostering self-esteem is the maintenance of what he calls 'ontological security' which is the 'protective cocoon which all normal individuals carry around with them as the means whereby they are able to get on with the affairs of day-to-day life'.[73] This protective cocoon is made up of the everyday conventions of interaction between human beings which establish a 'basic trust' and thereby permit the 'bracketing' out of all the myriad dangers and threats to which the individual would otherwise perceive that they are constantly potentially exposed. Without this basic trust, individuals would be beset with an enervating 'existential anxiety' in which the elaboration of any 'self-identity', let alone actually achieving authentic self-knowledge, would be impossible.

Conventional civility is thus not merely one aspect of fostering the self-esteem of self and others, but a condition of being able to maintain a secure sense of self in the first place. In this way the theory of the reflexive

[66] A Giddens, *The Third Way* (Cambridge, Polity, 1998) 37.
[67] A Giddens, *Modernity and Self-Identity* (Cambridge, Polity, 1991) 75.
[68] Giddens, above n 67, at 75.
[69] Giddens, above n 67, at 76–7.
[70] Giddens, above n 67, at 80.
[71] *Ibid.*
[72] Giddens, above n 67, at 79.
[73] Giddens, above n 67, at 40.

self establishes the interdependence of the autonomy of the self and the behaviour of others.

Giddens' ethics derive from the view that a precondition of a stable knowable sense of self is the ontological security supplied by the everyday rituals of civility. Ontological security implies ontological *vulnerability*. In this 'therapeutic individualism', self-realisation is always vulnerable to the hostility or indifference of others, the authentic self to be realised is a 'vulnerable self'.[74] This assumption of the ontological vulnerability of individual autonomy is an essential component of Giddens' therapeutic concept. The reflexive project of the autonomous self takes place in the shadow of its essential vulnerability.

Giddens draws out the political conclusions of this theory of the self by concluding that the autonomy of each individual is dependent on the lifestyle choices of others, entailing a new 'life politics' or politics of lifestyle.[75] In The Third Way this idea is developed into the political proposition that the welfare state should be reconceived as a 'positive welfare society', in which welfare is understood as a psychic rather than an economic concept.[76] A positive welfare society is concerned to ensure social cohesion, which is to say cohesion between the different and diverse conditions of the psychic welfare of its self-fulfilling subjects.[77] If their own psychic welfare is to be guaranteed, individuals acquire a duty to consider others' psychic needs.[78] Indeed, a whole new balance between rights and responsibilities is required, which is summed up by Giddens in the slogan 'No rights without responsibilities'.[79] The responsibility not to cause each other to fear crime is a key example of these responsibilities, and for that reason freedom from fear of crime is a basic citizenship right for Giddens.

Giddens' account of 'therapeutic individualism' as such is not especially distinctive.[80] But the way he poses the problems of social cohesion and 'ontological security' that 'therapeutic individualism' entails has been influential.[81]

[74] The contemporary influence of the idea of the vulnerable self in therapeutic discourse is discussed in F Furedi, *Therapy Culture: Cultivating Vulnerability in an Uncertain Age* (London, Routledge, 2003). Bryan Turner finds a philosophical source of the idea in Martin Heidegger's work: see B Turner, 'Forgetfulness and Frailty: Otherness and Rights in Contemporary Social Theory' in C Rojek and B Turner (eds), *The Politics of Jean-Francois Lyotard: Justice and Political Theory* (London, Routledge, 1998).

[75] Giddens, above n 67, at 214.

[76] Giddens, above n 66, at 117.

[77] Giddens, above n 66, at 44.

[78] Giddens, above n 66, at 37.

[79] Giddens, above n 66, at 65.

[80] See N Rose, *Governing the Soul* (London, Routledge, 1990).

[81] The influence is not only on New Labour policy makers. See, for example, J Young, *The Exclusive Society* (London, Sage, 1999); I Loader and N Walker, *Civilising Security* (Cambridge, Cambridge University Press, 2007) 166; Squires and Stephens also briefly consider ontological security in relation to ASB, above n 54, at 187.

For Giddens this problem gives rise to a 'moral dilemma' which he summarises as the question of how 'to remoralise social life without falling prey to prejudice'.[82] Traditional moralities will no longer produce social cohesion for they will often conflict with the reflexive project of the self. His solution lies in duties of mutual regard for each other's self-esteem. This dilemma of remoralising social life without recourse to oppressively conservative traditions is the same problem with which 'liberal communitarian' Amitai Etzioni has grappled.

B. Communitarianism

In responding to criticism that communitarianism is open to a highly conservative interpretation of moral order,[83] Etzioni has expounded a 'new golden rule' which he formulates as 'Respect and uphold society's moral order as you would have society respect and uphold your autonomy'.[84] The autonomy that, for Etzioni, can be well balanced with moral order is 'socially constructed' or 'socially secured' autonomy.[85] Etzioni is explicit that this 'socially secured' autonomy is a more upbeat formulation of Michael Sandel's conception of autonomy as the 'encumbered self'.[86]

For communitarians, choices are autonomous if they reflect the identity of the chooser as a moral person, if they are truly choices which that self has commanded. For communitarians the identity of the self has no existence prior to the moral and relational context in which that self makes his or her choices. The individual is intersubjectively constituted in the prior moral bonds between people.[87] As a consequence, individual choices are not autonomous, even where they appear to be unconstrained, unless they pay attention to the requirements of those moral bonds. Insofar as the choices of market actors are merely utility-maximising they are grounded only in the particular desires which an individual feels, his or her immediate preferences; they represent 'purely preferential choice'. For Sandel, the satisfaction of these preferences is not itself an autonomous act. On the contrary: '"Purely preferential choice" is thoroughly heteronomous.'[88] Autonomous choices are not those which seek to satisfy 'an arbitrary collection of desires accidentally embodied in some particular human being'. Rather, autonomous

[82] Giddens, above n 67, at 231.
[83] See, for example, N Lacey and E Fraser, 'Communitarianism' (1994)14(2) *Politics* 75, 79.
[84] A Etzioni, *The New Golden Rule: Community and Morality in a Democratic Society* (New York, Basic Books, 1996) xviii.
[85] Etzioni, above n 84, at 257.
[86] Etzioni, above n 84, at 23.
[87] C Taylor, 'Atomism' in S Avineri and A De-Shalit (eds), *Communitarianism and Individualism* (Oxford, Oxford University Press, 1993).
[88] M Sandel, *Liberalism and the Limits of Justice* (Cambridge, Cambridge University Press, 1982) 165.

choices are those which reach beyond spontaneous utility to satisfy 'a set of desires *ordered* in a certain way, arranged in a hierarchy of relative worth or essential connection with the identity of the agent'.[89] Preferences which are not evaluated as being in accordance with the values inherent in the communal bonds which constitute the individual's identity are preferences which do not reflect the identity of the person who holds them, they are not therefore autonomous.

Since the causing of fear is corrosive of the communal bonds which constitute the individual's identity, the individual who manifests a settled disposition of practical indifference to others' fears and anxieties can be understood as refusing moral autonomy. From the standpoint of this 'socially secured' autonomy, there is nothing lost in restraining and preventing choices which arise from such a disposition. On the contrary, autonomy can only be socially constructed by maintaining an intersubjective field which inhibits such choices. Where such conditions are lacking, the duty to avoid causing the fear (or, indeed, giving other lesser forms of offence), which undermines those conditions, will need to be legally enforced.[90] The 'heteronomy' of 'purely preferential choice' is nothing other than the inherent vulnerability of choice to external determination. Etzioni's account of 'socially secured autonomy' spells this out in less philosophical language:

> People are socially constituted and continually penetrated by culture, by social and moral influences, and by one another. ... the choices made by individuals are not free from cultural and social factors. To remove, on libertarian grounds, limits set by the public, far from enhancing autonomy, merely leaves individuals subject to all the other influences, which reach them *not as information or environmental factors they can analyse and cope with,* but as invisible messages of which they are unaware and that sway them in nonrational ways.[91]

For Etzioni, freedom of choice unlimited by some public regulation can only diminish autonomy, because without consciously and politically constructed limits, the individual is subject to the spontaneous operation of factors they can neither understand nor control. Left to their own devices and without the moral order of community, people cannot 'cope', and are forced by social and market pressures to act in 'nonrational ways', in other words, to make 'purely preferential choices'. They will therefore never be able to enjoy the self-command enjoyed by autonomous people who understand themselves for the people that they are, as members of their community.

89 Sandel, above n 88, at 167.

90 W Galston, 'Social Mores Are Not Enough' in A Etzioni, A Volmert and E Rothschild (eds), *The Communitarian Reader* (Lanham Maryland, Rowman & Littlefield, 2004) 92. Moreover, the prior duty to avoid causing these anxieties can be very wide ranging and failure to reassure may justify very intrusive official coercion (see, for example, A Etzioni, 'Rights and Responsibilities 2001' in Etzioni, Volmert and Rothschildat 196).

91 Etzioni, above n 84, at 21 (emphasis added).

To resolve Giddens' dilemma, and ensure that the local community does not impose a particular and oppressive moral tradition on its members, Etzioni proposes a 'pluralism with unity' in which the law would adopt a 'two-layered approach'.[92] The values affirmed by any particular community, which the individual would presumptively have to respect, would themselves be 'additionally accountable' to 'society-wide values' which are typically regarded as constitutional in some form or other.[93] It is interesting that, as we shall see, Etzioni's solution is directly reflected in the legal structure of the ASBO.[94] The philosophical success or coherence of this solution is not the issue here. The key point is that for communitarianism, individual autonomy is vulnerable to heteronomous determination in the form of the purely preferential choices of both self and others. The protection of autonomy requires respect for the moral order of communal obligation that maintains the intersubjective field in which self-command may be achieved. Where discussion of The Third Way focused our attention on the denial of autonomy to the victim of such choices, our discussion of communitarianism allows us also to see the lack of autonomy of the perpetrator, the person who causes fear and anxiety. Etzioni's formulation of the self as vulnerable in the face of market relations which are beyond comprehension is particularly intriguing because the same assumption is fundamental to the social theory of FA Hayek, the inspiration of neo-liberalism.

C. Neo-liberalism

Hayek is especially significant because his thinking was a direct influence on Britain's Conservative Governments of the 1980s and 1990s, and the broader 'neo-liberalism' which he inspired, with its preference for the provision of all kinds of public services by means of market mechanisms rather than those of state bureaucracy, has become a more or less consensus position of mainstream politics. The claim that Hayek's theory lends any sort of support to the kind of discretionary and reactive coercive decision-making characteristic of the CPO may seem perverse, given his avowed commitment to the rule of generally formulated laws.[95] But, as we shall see, a norm of vulnerable autonomy is axiomatic in his social theory. Its axiomatic position is buried by Hayek's own theoretical efforts to compensate for its effects. Unearthing it requires us, against the grain of discussions of neo-liberalism, to understand that although Hayek was a champion of free

[92] Etzioni, above n 84, at 226.
[93] Etzioni, above n 84, at 224–5.
[94] See text at n 112.
[95] See F Hayek, *Law, Legislation and Liberty: A New Statement of the Liberal Principles of Justice and Political Economy* (Chicago, University of Chicago Press, 1973–79).

market individualism, his case for it was nevertheless a relative one, and that this entails a particular vision of the subject of market relations.

Hayek was careful not to make the claim advanced by many neo-classical economists that free markets necessarily make the optimum use of society's resources. He only claimed that they are less imperfect than the alternatives, and particularly the socialist alternative.[96] For Hayek, socialism was an irrational revolt against the 'impersonal forces' of the market because it 'fails to comprehend that the coordination of the multifarious individual efforts in a complex society must take account of facts that no individual can completely survey.'[97] The true position, Hayek thought, was that:

> A complex civilisation like ours is necessarily based on the individual adjusting himself to changes whose cause and nature he cannot understand: why he should have more or less, why he should have to move to another occupation, why some things he wants should become more difficult to get than others, will always be connected with such a multitude of circumstances that no single mind will be able to grasp them … .[98]

For Hayek, the consequences of socialism's hubristic revolt against the necessarily decentralised decision-making process of the market would not be more freedom but less because:

> the only alternative to submission to the impersonal and seemingly irrational forces of the market is submission to the equally uncontrollable and therefore arbitrary power of other men.[99]

In this respect, Hayek's theory is strikingly paradoxical. The free market had generated a 'Great Society' of unparalleled wealth, and of freedom from the arbitrary despotism of other people. But it had done so only through submission to the impersonal forces of the market. Any attempt to gain control of those impersonal forces could undermine independence from other people's arbitrary power. Hayek was conscious of the tension intrinsic to the experience of a freedom founded on submission. And he was explicit that it was only through religious faith and tradition that these tensions could be managed:

> It does not matter whether men in the past did submit [to market forces] from beliefs which some now regard as superstitious: from a religious spirit of humility, or an exaggerated respect for the crude teachings of the early economists. The crucial point is that it is infinitely more difficult rationally to comprehend

[96] A Gamble, *Hayek: The Iron Cage of Liberty* (Cambridge, Polity, 1996) 69.
[97] F Hayek, *The Road to Serfdom* (London, Routledge, 1944) 152.
[98] Hayek, above n 97, at 151.
[99] Hayek, above n 97, at 152.

> the necessity of submitting to forces whose operation we cannot follow in detail, than to do so out of the humble awe which religion, or even the respect for the doctrines of economics, did inspire.[100]

Writing in the 1940s, Hayek's reference to 'exaggerated respect' for the doctrines of the early economists tacitly recognises the crisis of neoclassical economics in the wake of the Depression of the 1930s and the rise of Keynesianism with its promotion of the macroeconomic role of the state. In the face of the decline of neo-classical economics as a rationale for the free market, the authority of tradition was critical. As Hayek would later write: 'all progress must be based on tradition'.[101]

Hayek argues that social cohesion under the market relies on traditional institutions and beliefs,[102] but offers little in the way of a systematic connection between the market and traditional beliefs. Hayek recognised that the free market could not be made to be 'good in the sense that it will behave morally'.[103] He regarded it as neither innate nor designed, but a system which 'we have tumbled into'.[104] In his last work, he notes the historical connection between monotheistic religions and the values of capitalism but adds that this 'does not of course mean that there is any intrinsic connection between religion as such and such values'.[105] In Hayek's theory, the necessity of tradition and religion is external to the market's knowledge-coordinating function. Given the contingency of this relation, the notion that the secure enjoyment of the individual freedoms of the Great Society depends on traditional religious faith carries with it a necessary implication, one which is given more explicit treatment by The Third Way and communitarianism. The experience of an individual who is *not* securely embedded in traditional values or religious faith (or, presumably, is not 'irrationally' rebelling against market forces) will be an experience of vulnerability 'to changes whose cause and nature he cannot understand'.

Once the theoretically contingent presence of tradition or religion in the individual's life is eliminated, the individual subject conceived of by Hayek's theory turns out to be intrinsically vulnerable to the depredations of the

[100] Hayek, above n 97, at 152. Hayek omits to mention one circumstance in which an individual, even in the absence of religious belief, might find it relatively easy 'rationally to comprehend the necessity of submitting to forces whose operation we cannot follow in detail'. That circumstance is the knowledge that the individual concerned possesses sufficient property to protect him or herself against the unfathomable changes wrought by the market. This ideological omission is significant, for it assumes that vulnerability to others' choices is a universal characteristic of the subjects of market society.

[101] Hayek, above n 95, vol 1, at 167.

[102] P O'Malley, 'Volatile and Contradictory Punishment' (1999) 3 *Theoretical Criminology* 175, 188.

[103] Hayek, above n 95, vol 1, at 33.

[104] Hayek, above n 95, vol 1, at 164.

[105] F Hayek, *The Fatal Conceit: The Errors of Socialism,* (London, Routledge, 1988) 137.

market's impersonal forces. Neo-liberalism, once denuded of its contingent ethical moorings in traditional religion, loses any distinctive moral grounds for the duties of citizenship,[106] and is left with only the unmediated experience of vulnerability to the unknowable, uncontrollable and insecure market-place. It is this experience to which the ethics of Giddens' 'life politics', or of Etzioni's New Golden Rule respond, generating what Rose terms an 'ethico-politics', a politics of behaviour.[107] These are the politics that underpin the right of the community to live free from 'harassment' or 'distress' or from 'terror', and the power of the magistrates court or the Home Secretary to control behaviour that does not reassure.

In important respects the three theories considered here are quite different in their concerns, emphases and priorities. These differences nuance the way each theory conceives of the vulnerability of the individual subject. Nevertheless each of these influential theories contains the assumption that the individual's autonomy is intrinsically vulnerable to the spontaneous self-interested preferences of others. And it is this vulnerability which lays the normative basis for liability to the CPOs, the liability to have behaviour which fails to reassure controlled by a preventative order.

V. NORMATIVE CRIMINAL LAW THEORY VERSUS THE THEORY OF VULNERABLE AUTONOMY

The central position of the norm of vulnerable autonomy in contemporary political and social theory suggests that the political invocation of the discourse of vulnerability represents something more than merely cynical fear-mongering or a manipulative governmental technique deploying the contingently fashionable discourse of therapy.[108] Insofar as these theories form the basis of shared social beliefs they provide a legitimating context

[106] See also R Sullivan, 'The Schizophrenic State: Neoliberal Criminal Justice' in K Stenson and R Sullivan, *Crime, Risk and Justice* (Cullompton, Willan, 2001) 44.

[107] Rose, above n 63, at 170.

[108] The significance of vulnerability in these political theories has been overlooked by perceptive commentators on both the theories and the therapeutic discourse of vulnerability. In his review of Third Way politics, Nikolas Rose dismisses Giddens' contribution to political theory as 'the addition of a certain therapeutic individualism', and takes no further interest in this aspect of Giddens' theory, overlooking the way in which it supplies, in security/vulnerability, a unifying element between those 'advanced liberal' theories which are the object of Rose's own seminal critique (see N Rose, 'Community, Citizenship, and the Third Way' (2000) 43 *The American Behavioural Scientist* 1395). Frank Furedi, on the other hand, is acute to the governmentalisation of the therapeutic outlook—what he calls the 'cultivation of vulnerability': F Furedi, *Politics of Fear* (London, Continuum, 2005) 141. However, Furedi overlooks the role of political theory in this process. He too dismisses the Third Way's theoretical contribution, suggesting that it 'means very little' and that its politics are mere 'verbiage' (p 6), ignoring the axiomatic position in the Third Way (and in wider contemporary theory) of the concept of the vulnerable self, the influence of which he seeks to criticise.

for the substantive law of the CPO which institutionalises the protection of this norm.

We can now look at Simester and von Hirsch's claim that the CPO is not legitimate in this new light. The CPO institutionalises in penal obligations the normative structure of the 'advanced liberal' theories of 'vulnerable autonomy'. From the perspective of the theory of vulnerable autonomy some at least of the features of the CPO which Simester and von Hirsch regard as weaknesses reappear as its strengths. Let's look in turn at their objections and how the theory of vulnerable autonomy responds to them.

A. The CPO Criminalises Conduct That is Not a Wrong

Simester and von Hirsch object that the broad and vague definitions of the conduct that can be controlled by CPOs may criminalise conduct that is not wrong in the sense of 'satisfying a properly defined Harm Principle or Offence Principle'.[109] But from the standpoint of vulnerable autonomy, it is wrong to fail to reassure each other and/or the relevant authorities that we do not represent a threat. Without reassurance ordinary vulnerable citizens will be inhibited from going about their lawful business. Not to reassure in this view is wrong because it does harm to the 'relations of recognition', to the intersubjective field in which citizens' vulnerable autonomy is constituted.[110]

Simester and von Hirsch use the example of the potential distress caused to racists by interracial couples to note that in relation to the ASBO this may mean that we all have to be aware of every objectionable prejudice of our neighbours lest we offend them.[111] But this is why so much official discretion is built into these legal measures. Since some subjective anxieties will not be reasonably founded, the authorities and the courts are empowered to make political judgements over what behaviour is reasonable, what is reasonably suspicious, when orders are necessary and so on.[112] What is adjudged to be consistent with public policy will avoid liability,[113] but the presumption has shifted towards controlling behaviour which creates anxiety, and that is a consequence of the perceived need to protect the 'recognitional infrastructure' of 'vulnerable autonomy'.

[109] Simester and von Hirsch, above n 4, at 173–4.

[110] Although, as we have seen, the ASBO does not treat the conduct on the footing of a wrong to be punished but as a threat to be controlled, see text at n 37.

[111] Simester and von Hirsch, above n 4, at 185.

[112] Note that this structure replicates Etzioni's 'pluralism with unity' solution to the dilemma of 'remoralising society without prejudice', in which a person's indifference to local mores and sensibilities will only be legally controlled if it is also violates 'society-wide' values. See text at n 94.

[113] See Ramsay, above n 5, at 918.

The lack of attention to the theories of 'advanced liberalism' creates a particular difficulty for Simester and von Hirsch's critique on this point. They argue that the ASBO, which typically limits access to public space for those subject to one, 'raises problems of identity and self-definition'.[114] This is because 'for most of us, our lives involve, and are in part defined by, the interaction and relationships we have with other members of our society' and denying access to public space will tend to 'undermine [the defendant's] participation in the society itself; and, ultimately, to undermine D's identity as a human being'.[115] But this is to invoke precisely the 'recognitional infrastructure', as it exists in public space, which provides the normative basis of the requirement that citizens not fail to reassure each other. Simester and von Hirsch object that the ASBO criminalises conduct in a way that goes further than any Harm or Offence Principle can justify. But it is not clear why they claim this, given that they appear to accept the intersubjective constitution of identity, which, in the theories of vulnerable autonomy implies the possibility of harm to the intersubjective field. They may have reasons as to why the Harm Principle does not recognise damage to the intersubjective field as a wrong (despite their agreement that it is in this field that individual's identities are constituted), but they don't state them.

B. The Absence of a Culpability Requirement

Simester and von Hirsch object that the CPO lacks a culpability requirement both in the grounds of liability to an order and the offence of breach of an order. However, the absence of cognitive *mens rea* (ie intention or recklessness) at both stages does not mean that the CPO contains no element of culpability. The key to this is to grasp the element of positive obligation in the CPO. If the wrong is the failure to reassure, where a reasonable person would, or so as to create a reasonable suspicion in the mind of an official, then the failure amounts to a form of negligence. Furthermore, where a person has committed the wrong of failing to reassure, the authority imposing the order is nevertheless required to consider the necessity of the order. An order will not be necessary unless there is sufficient evidence to suggest that the failure to reassure is the consequence of some settled disposition to ignore or to prey upon the vulnerability of others. A person who exhibits such a disposition, and consistently fails to do what the reasonable person would do, such that the order is necessary, is a person who (in the communitarian idiom) fails to assess his or her actions in the light of the intersubjective constitution of his or her own autonomy, or (in Giddens' idiom) fails to fulfil

114 Simester and von Hirsch, above n 4, at 183.
115 *Ibid.*

the responsibilities which are the constitutive basis of his or her rights. In other words, a preventative order will be *necessary* only against a person who fails this test of moral autonomy.

This prior finding of a failure of moral autonomy is the reason that no *mens rea* is required in the criminal offence of breach of a CPO. An order is imposed where this failure has occurred, and the order will consist of highly specific and individualised prohibitions. These specific prohibitions are communicated to the defendant, who is put on notice of the consequences of failure to provide that continued reassurance. These terms construct the person subject to them as a specific threat, *as opposed to* a formally autonomous subject presumed capable of freely adjusting his or her conduct to the general criminal law.[116] This construction of the subject of a CPO as a mere threat is given in the very existence of the *actus reus* of the offence of breach of a CPO. A *mens rea* requirement in the offence of breach would be morally nugatory, whatever its practical benefits to defendants.

C. Punishment is Not Proportional to the Seriousness of the Conduct

Simester and von Hirsch object that an order might impose a 10-year-long ASBO on conduct which if prosecuted as a criminal offence would carry at most a few months in prison or a fine. But understood as a means to protect vulnerable autonomy the order is not a punishment for the wrong of a harmful or offensive interference with another individual's protected interests, as a conventional criminal punishment might be. By specifically prohibiting the failure to reassure, the order is intended to prevent wrongs to the intersubjective field in which the vulnerable autonomy, and the security, of citizens are constituted.[117] What is necessary in an order is what is proportional to those preventative and incapacitatory demands.[118] This does not dispose of the argument that the effect of a CPO is penal whatever its intention, but from the standpoint of vulnerable autonomy this coercion is imposed on a person who has been differentiated from other citizens on the grounds of a dispositional lack of moral autonomy. In such a context proportionality will become of a question of their dangerousness and the requirements of incapacitation.[119]

[116] On this distinctive characteristic of criminal law, see HLA Hart, *The Concept of Law* (Clarendon, Oxford, 1997) 39.

[117] Anderson and Honneth, above n 60, at 138–9, argue that the autonomy-protecting rights (and the violations of them) are properties of this field and not of the individuals within it; see also Barbara Hudson on the community as moral being in contemporary criminal justice policy: B Hudson, *Justice in the Risk Society* (London, Sage, 2003) 82.

[118] For discussions of the issues involved, see Andrew Ashworth, this volume, ch 5, and Lucia Zedner, this volume, ch 3.

[119] Such a position seems to be emerging in the sentencing law for breach of ASBO: see *R v Anthony* [2006] I Cr App R (S) 74.

A further objection is that punishing a defendant for breach of an order may involve punishment for conduct that is not in itself wrong but merely in defiance of the order: 'The scheme becomes, in Hegel's terms, a stick raised to a dog.'[120] But we have seen above how the imposition of a CPO is precisely premised on the defendant's lack of moral autonomy and his or her reconstruction as a threat to the recognitional infrastructure of autonomy.[121]

D. The Grounds for Liability for a CPO Do Not Give Citizens Fair Warning

The objection is that the vagueness and imprecision of the grounds for imposing an order make it difficult to know in advance what behaviour will render a citizen liable to one. This matters because, as Simester and von Hirsch put it, 'knowing where we stand augments the ability of citizens to live autonomous lives'.[122] But if by 'autonomy' is meant 'vulnerable autonomy', then knowing where we stand so as to augment our ability to live autonomous lives requires reassurance by others, and enforcing that reassurance is the purpose of the CPO.

Simester and von Hirsch continue that 'the possibility of being guided by the state's rules is foundational to our capacity as individuals to make decisions'.[123] There may be an argument that it is possible to be guided by the CPO's requirements: citizens can make any decisions they like, as long as they make sure that their neighbours' sense of security is not threatened by any conduct that might be adjudged unreasonable, that they have not given the Home Secretary grounds for reasonable suspicion of involvement in 'terrorism-related activity' and that they haven't engaged in conduct with children that a reasonable observer would regard as sexual. Public policy will give them a guide as to what is reasonable. Citizens now have to make their decisions in this precautionary context. If they fail to be aware of precaution's requirements, or make the wrong decisions, then the highly specific terms of the order to which they become liable will offer them some stern guidance as to what to avoid in future.

On the other hand it may be that it is ultimately impossible to be sure that you have acted cautiously enough in the face of the uncertainties involved and that the problem of insecurity is therefore created by the

120 Simester and von Hirsch, above n 4, at 189.

121 Where breach of an ASBO itself causes no ASB, the Court of Appeal has ruled that custodial sentences should be avoided or, where they cannot be avoided, they should be kept to the minimum necessary to uphold the authority of the court: *R v Lamb* [2005] All ER (D) 132 (Nov).

122 Simester and von Hirsch, above n 4, at 187.

123 *Ibid.*

law rather than solved by it. But normative criticism of the CPO needs to recognise that it is the operation of the 'precautionary principle' in criminal justice that is its target.[124]

E. The Civil Application Procedure for an Order Prevents a Fair Trial

The central objection in relation to the ASBO is to the admissibility of hearsay, the evidence of professional witnesses, and the absence of any necessity for a confrontation between the complainant and the defendant (or the defendant's representative), given the serious consequences that an order may have on the life of the defendant.[125] However, since substantively the liability is based on protection of vulnerable autonomy, it would be self-defeating to demand of the ordinary vulnerable citizen that they give evidence against the person who fails to reassure them.[126] Their subjective vulnerability to the defendant's failure to reassure will in many cases prevent them from giving evidence in open court in practice, they will be too afraid. This treatment of the rights of defendant and of victims as a zero-sum game is the necessary counterpart of the precautionary logic of the substantive law of vulnerable autonomy, under which all citizens have a legal responsibility in respect of each other's (in)security, fulfilment of which is prior to their rights, procedural and substantive.[127]

F. CPO Prohibitions are Not Generally Formulated

Simester and von Hirsch object that generally formulated criminal laws treat people as equal before the law, while the CPO 'abandons reciprocity in favour of burdening individual targets'.[128] But, once again, in the normative structure of vulnerable autonomy 'there are no rights without responsibilities', and what this means (if it means anything beyond a tautology) is that failure to fulfil responsibilities justifies a reduction in rights. The protection of vulnerable autonomy requires that citizens do not fail in their responsibility to reassure, and where there is a failure to reassure, a risk assessment may be necessary, and where a dispositional failure of moral autonomy is found, a preventative order may be imposed.

[124] This point has been recognised by criminal justice writers, see Lucia Zedner, this volume, ch 3; Squires and Stephen, above n 54, at 202–7.

[125] The procedural objections to the control order are much more far reaching and require separate treatment: see Zedner, above n 51.

[126] See *R (McCann and Others) v Crown Court at Manchester and Another* [2003] 1 AC 787, 814.

[127] For an expanded exposition of the point, see Ramsay, above n 5, at 924.

[128] Simester and von Hirsch, above n 4, at 181.

The purpose of the CPO is not the liberal criminal law's purpose of punishing the invasion of the protected interests of autonomous individual subjects, a purpose which takes form in the equal protection of general laws. The purpose of the CPO is to protect 'advanced' liberalism's intersubjective 'recognitional infrastructure' of vulnerable autonomy. It therefore takes the form of risk assessment, and the deliberately discriminatory distribution of penal obligations and civil rights.

G. Criminal Prohibitions Should Only be Laid Down by Representative Authority

This is Simester and von Hirsch's most fundamental objection. CPOs contain criminal prohibitions laid down by magistrates' courts or executive functionaries rather than 'a legislative body such as parliament'.[129] As Simester and von Hirsch observe 'this raises a separation of powers issue'.[130] The ASBO in particular collapses the legislative, adjudicative and executive functions into the person of the magistrate.[131] Under the CPO powers, citizens can no longer even in theory be said to be both author and addressee, subject and object, of the penal obligations, since the scope of their liability to penal coercion can be decided at the discretion of an official rather than by their elected representatives. For Parliament to abandon the monopoly on the distribution of the civil rights of citizens to executive functionaries, or judicial functionaries exercising an executive function, is incompatible with representative government.[132]

Insofar as the protection of vulnerable autonomy requires a risk assessment and the individualised distribution of civil rights (on the grounds of failure to fulfil prior responsibilities), then it does appear to require this violation of the conditions of representative authority. The deliberation upon and adoption of individualised criminal prohibitions is in its nature not a legislative or adjudicative function. Since it must be based on a risk-assessment, it is an executive function, whoever carries it out.[133]

The broader position of the theories of vulnerable autonomy on representative government cannot be pursued here. For the purposes of this

[129] Simester and von Hirsch, above n 4, at 180.

[130] *Ibid.*

[131] See Ramsay, above n 5, at 920.

[132] Of course, officials in the criminal justice system have long enjoyed discretionary powers in practice which may in some circumstances result in a deliberately discriminatory distribution of civil rights. But this is different from being granted a discretion which explicitly requires such a formally unequal distribution. This latter discretion is not entirely unprecedented. As Simester and von Hirsch (above n 4) note, regulatory powers are frequently delegated to specialised agencies. What is new is the scope of the CPOs, and their impact on civil rights beyond the right to property and beyond the regulation of circumscribed areas of social activity.

[133] See Ramsay, above n 5.

chapter it is enough to note that contemporary government appears to be staking its claims to legitimacy in the security context on something other than *representative* democracy. This suggests a new direction for criminal law theory which has tended to proceed either as a branch of liberal moral philosophy or as a critical perspective on this liberal philosophy. An explicit understanding of criminal justice in the terms of political theory and the norms of democracy is comparatively underdeveloped.[134] This is to reassert Nicola Lacey's point that 'the democratic legitimation ... of the whole range of practices involved in criminalisation, is the most pressing normative and practical question facing the contemporary criminal process'.[135]

VI. CONCLUSION

One reason that the civil preventative order enjoys its practical political legitimacy in the present is that it institutionalises the protection of vulnerable autonomy, a concept which is axiomatic to political outlooks which have enjoyed a widespread influence in recent years.

The analysis of the normative claim to protect vulnerable autonomy might make a useful contribution to the broader perspective of theorising criminalisation.[136] That contribution is specific to the present moment of a return of authoritarianism in criminal legislation,[137] and the possible emergence of a new paradigm in the criminal law.[138] By virtue of the conceptual connection between vulnerable autonomy and ontological security, vulnerability may have some potential to integrate the explanatory and instrumental concerns which have dominated criminological and policy-oriented discussions of the 'security society',[139] with the normative concerns of criminal law theory.[140]

The 'social-scientific' analysis of the CPO's legitimacy in itself does nothing to answer the purely normative criticisms of liberal criminal law theory. It rather sets out what might be called the 'contested validity claim' of the

[134] N Lacey, 'Criminal Justice and Democracies: Inclusionary and Exclusionary Dynamics in the Institutional Structure of Late Modern Societies' draft paper for Workshop on Democratic Criminal Justice, Warsaw (October 2006) and given at London Criminal Law and Social Theory Group seminar (December 2006).

[135] N Lacey, 'Contingency and Criminalisation' in I Loveland (ed), *Frontiers of Criminality* (London, Sweet & Maxwell, 1995).

[136] See also Leslie Sebba, this volume, ch 4.

[137] See Alan Norrie, this volume, ch 2.

[138] See Andrew Ashworth, this volume, ch 5.

[139] See L Zedner, *Criminal Justice* (Oxford, Oxford University Press, 2004).

[140] See L Zedner, 'Policing Before and After the Police' (2006) 46 *British Journal of Criminology* 78, 92.

political order of which the CPO is an aspect.[141] By understanding the character of that claim we can gain a better understanding of what is at stake, and clear the ground for contesting its validity in its own terms. The analysis presented here suggests that the theory of vulnerable autonomy has little interest in the value or purpose of fair warning, formal equality before the criminal law and the legal prerequisites of representative government generally. It is on this ground that the CPO may itself prove particularly vulnerable to critique since, to put the point mildly, it is questionable whether the endeavour to eliminate insecurity by eroding these aspects of democratic citizenship will prove to be coherent.[142]

[141] The term is borrowed from J Habermas, *Communication and the Evolution of Society* (London, Heinemann, 1979) 178.

[142] I argue elsewhere, in the different terms of police power and sovereignty, that the ASBO's invocation of the intrinsic vulnerability of citizens is paradoxical. See Ramsay, above n 3.

7

Expanding the Boundaries of Inchoate Crimes The Growing Reliance on Preparatory Offences

BERNADETTE McSHERRY

I. INTRODUCTION

THE TRADITIONAL INCHOATE offences of attempts, conspiracy and incitement have attracted much scholarly debate concerning the prosecution and punishment of those who have intended, but not caused, harm. Preparatory offences extend the boundaries of the criminal law beyond the traditional inchoate offences, but have not attracted as much attention.[1] The enactment of preparatory terrorism offences in response to the terrorist attacks that occurred in the United States on 11 September 2001, Bali on 12 October 2002, Madrid on 11 March 2004 and London on 7 July 2005 indicate the time is ripe to explore some of the issues raised by the increasing reliance on such offences.

Seventeen days after the terrorism attacks in the United States, the United Nations Security Council adopted Resolution 1373 which imposes on all Member States a series of obligations relating to international terrorism.[2] The obligations are not made in relation to a particular situation, but are general in nature, leading one commentator to label it a 'piece of legislation'.[3] The Resolution includes a provision declaring that all states shall ensure that the financing, planning, *preparation* or

[1] For literature on preparatory offences, see BB Levenbook, 'Prohibiting Attempts and Preparations' (1980) 49(1) *University of Missouri-Kansas City Law Review* 41; D Bein, 'Preparatory Offences' (1993) 27 *Israel Law Review* 185; D Ohana, 'Responding to Acts Preparatory to the Commission of a Crime: Criminalization or Prevention?' (2006) Summer/Fall *Criminal Justice Ethics* 23; D Ohana, 'Desert and Punishment for Acts Preparatory to the Commission of a Crime' (2007) 20(1) *Canadian Journal of Law and Jurisprudence* 1.

[2] The resolution was adopted under chapter VII of the United Nations Charter: <http://daccessdds.un.org/doc/UNDOC/GEN/NO1/557/43/PDF/NO155743.pdf?OpenElement>.

[3] P Szasz, 'The Security Council Starts Legislating' (2002) 96 *American Journal of International Law* 901.

perpetration of terrorist acts be 'established as serious criminal offences in domestic laws ... and that the punishment duly reflects the seriousness of such terrorist acts'.[4]

Offences of preparing or facilitating terrorist acts have subsequently found their way into various domestic statutes. For example, s 5(1) of the Terrorism Act 2006 (UK) sets out that a person commits an offence if he or she engages in conduct in preparation for giving effect to an intention to commit acts of terrorism or assist another to commit such acts. In Australia, s 101.6(1) of the Criminal Code (Cth) states that '[a] person commits an offence if the person does any act in preparation for, or planning, a terrorist act'. The penalty for these offences in the United Kingdom and Australia is life imprisonment.[5] In Canada, the relevant provision states that a person 'who knowingly facilitates a terrorist activity is guilty of an indictable offence and liable to imprisonment for a term not exceeding fourteen years'.[6]

The law has traditionally criminalised the assistance or encouragement of criminal activity through the extension of criminal responsibility to accessorial liability. However, accessorial liability is derivative in the sense that the prosecution must prove that the offence was committed (or at least attempted) by the perpetrator. In contrast, the preparatory terrorism offences may be proved in the absence of a terrorist act[7] or where the preparatory conduct is not related to a *specific* terrorist act.[8]

The United Kingdom and Australian statutes also criminalise the possession of undefined items related to terrorism. Section 16(2) of the Terrorism Act 2000 (UK) makes it an offence for a person to possess money *or other property* where the person 'intends that it be used, or has reasonable cause to suspect that it may be used, for the purposes of terrorism'. Section 101.4 of the Criminal Code (Cth) criminalises the possession of 'a thing' that is 'connected with preparation for, the engagement of a person in, or assistance in a terrorist act'. Section 101.5(1) of the *Criminal Code* (Cth) also criminalises collecting or making documents connected with a terrorist act.

Possession offences are certainly not new. The possession of illicit drugs, weapons and articles for use in a burglary or theft has long been a matter for the criminal law.[9] But are such offences justifiable? George P Fletcher objects

[4] Security Council Resolution 1373 (2001), § 2(e).

[5] Terrorism Act 2006 (UK), s 5(3); Criminal Code (Cth), s 101.6(1).

[6] Criminal Code (Can), s 83.19(1).

[7] Criminal Code (Cth), s 101.6(2)(a); Criminal Code (Can), s 83.19(2)(c).

[8] Terrorism Act 2006 (UK), s 5(2); Criminal Code (Cth), s 101.6(2)(b); Criminal Code (Can), s 83.19(2)(b).

[9] See, for example: Misuse of Drugs Act 1971 (UK), s 5(2); Prevention of Crime Act 1953 (UK), s 1; Theft Act 1968 (UK), s 25; Controlled Drugs and Substances Act 1996 (Can), s 4(1); Criminal Code (Can), ss 88(1), 89(1), 90(1), 91(1), 92(1), 93(1), 94(1), 95(1), 351 and

to possession offences because 'they sweep too wide ... encompass[ing] cases where there is no potential social harm'.[10] Similarly, Andrew Ashworth argues that possession offences extend the boundaries of criminal law beyond the law of attempt and can be questioned on the basis that they 'criminalize people at a point too remote from the ultimate harm'.[11]

On the other hand, Frederick Schauer and Richard Zeckhauser argue that what they term 'evidentiary offences' can be justified on the basis of crime prevention and that they are 'less abhorrent to justice than numerous courts even to the present day have believed and more properly part of the regulatory repertoire than many people have appreciated'.[12]

Drawing on the Australian case of *R v Lodhi,*[13] this chapter examines whether preparatory offences (including those of possession) can be defined adequately, whether their criminalisation can be justified using traditional justifications for inchoate offences, and what punishment should apply to such offences.

II. THE CASE OF FAHEEM KHALID LODHI

Faheem Khalid Lodhi was the first person convicted under Australia's preparatory terrorism offences. The members of the jury deliberated for 5 days and at one stage reported that they were unlikely to reach a verdict. They were directed to continue deliberations. On 19 June 2006, the jury found Lodhi guilty of three out of four charges relating to the preparation of a terrorist act in Sydney, Australia.

352; Drugs of Dependence Act 1989 (ACT), ss 169(1) and 171(1); Crimes Act 1900 (ACT), s 380(1); Drugs Misuse and Trafficking Act 1985 (NSW), s 10(1); Crimes Act 1900 (NSW), ss 33B and 114(1)(a) and (b); Summary Offences Act 1988 (NSW), s 27D; Misuse of Drugs Act 1990 (NT), s 9(1); Criminal Code (NT), s 215; Weapons Control Act (NT), ss 6(e), 7 and 8(1); Summary Offences Act (NT), s 57(1)(e); Drugs Misuse Act 1986 (Qld), ss 9, 9A(1), 10(1), 10A(1) and 10B(1); Criminal Code (Qld), s 425; Vagrants, Gaming and Other Offences Act 1931 (Qld), ss 4(1)(h)(i), 4(1)(i) and 4(1)(g)(ii); Controlled Substances Act 1984 (SA), s 31(1); Summary Offences Act 1953 (SA), s 15; Misuse of Drugs Act 2001 (Tas), ss 23–25; Criminal Code Act 1924 (Tas), s 248; Police Offences Act 1935 (Tas), s 7(3); Drugs, Poisons and Controlled Substances Act 1981 (Vic), s 73(1); Control of Weapons Act 1990 (Vic), ss 5(1)(e), 6(1) and 7(1); Summary Offences Act 1966 (Vic), s 49D; Misuse of Drugs Act 1981 (WA), s 6(2); and Criminal Code (WA), s 407.

10 GP Fletcher, *Basic Concepts of Criminal Law* (New York, Oxford University Press, 1998) 180.

11 A Ashworth, *Principles of Criminal Law*, (Oxford, Oxford University Press, 5th edn, 2005) 109. See also: M Dubber, 'The Possession Paradigm: The Special Part and the Police Power Model of the Criminal Process' in RA Duff and SP Green (eds), Defining Crimes (Oxford, Oxford University Press, 2005).

12 F Schauer and R Zeckhauser, 'Regulation by Generalization' (2007) 1 *Regulation & Governance* 68, 82.

13 *R v Lodhi* [2006] NSWSC 691, unreported, Sentence, 23 August 2006, Whealy J. At the time of writing, an appeal has been lodged to the New South Wales Court of Criminal Appeal against Lodhi's conviction and sentence.

Lodhi, who was 36 at the time of his conviction, was born in Sialkot in the Punjab region of Pakistan and trained as an architect at Lahore University before emigrating to Australia in 1998. His brother, a teacher, and his uncle, an electrician, live in Sydney, but the rest of his family remain in Pakistan.

Lodhi was originally charged with two counts under s 101.4(1) of the Criminal Code (Cth) of possessing 'a thing' connected with 'preparation for, the engagement of a person in, or assistance in a terrorist act', with knowledge of that connection. He was found not guilty on one of the charges but was convicted of the other charge, which related to 15 pages in Lodhi's handwriting in Urdu script that had been seized from his work station at an architect's firm. This material included information about how to make various kinds of explosives, a hand grenade and a 'rime pencil' (a timing device for explosives) and the use of urea nitrate and potassium chlorate as explosives. This information was described by the judge as 'not particularly sophisticated or scientific'.[14]

Lodhi gave evidence that he had seen the information on a computer when he was studying some subjects at the University of Sydney in order to be registered as an architect in Australia. He had written down the information and had kept it in his possession, but had forgotten about it.

Lodhi was also charged under s 101.5(1) of collecting documents (two maps of the Sydney electricity supply system) connected with the preparation of a terrorist act. The prosecution's evidence was that Lodhi went to Energy Supply in Pitt Street Sydney where he told an employee that he was starting a business and wanted to place a wall map in his office. He was asked to fill out a form with his name, address and company name. He wrote down the name M Rasul and that he was a partner in the firm Rasul Electrics. He also wrote down a false post office box address and telephone number.

Lodhi gave evidence that the maps were in no way connected with any preparation for a terrorist act, but that he wanted them for a business of an electrical nature he was proposing to establish. He said that the name Rasul was part of the name he proposed for the electrical company and that the address and phone number were simply errors.

The most serious charge, under s 101.6(1), was that of doing an act in preparation for, or planning, a terrorist act. The evidence led under this section was that around 10 October 2003, Lodhi sought information concerning the availability of materials capable of being used for the manufacture of explosives or incendiary devices. Lodhi exchanged faxes with an employee of Deltrex Chemicals, stating that he was going to set up a detergent business and giving a list of chemicals that he wanted. He had created

14 *R v Lodhi*, above n 13, at [24].

a fax sheet in the name of a non-existent business entitled 'Eagle Flyers', but used the fax machine at his work to send the document. Deltrex Chemicals sent a price list including prices for minimum quantities of urea and nitric acid—the components for a urea nitrate homemade bomb.

This faxed list did not go straight to Lodhi, but found its way to his superior at the architects firm where he was employed. She asked Lodhi what the document had to do with his work. He said that this related to a family business venture and he had used the fax at work because his own fax had broken down. At trial, Lodhi gave the same explanation, stating that he had been contemplating setting up a business venture exporting certain chemicals from Australia to Pakistan.

The three acts—purchasing maps, possessing information concerning explosives and obtaining a price list for chemicals—seem a long way away from committing a terrorist act and could be portrayed as innocuous if viewed independently. The prosecution relied on circumstantial evidence to build up a picture of Lodhi as a key player in a plot to bomb part of Sydney's Electrical Supply System 'to advance the cause of violent jihad'.[15]

Lodhi's charges arose as a result of investigations by the Australian Federal Police and the Australian Intelligence Security Organisation into the activities of a French citizen, Willie Brigitte, after these organisations received a message from French intelligence officers that Brigitte could be involved in planning a terrorist attack in Sydney. Brigitte allegedly trained at the Lashkar-e-Taiba paramilitary training camp in Pakistan in late 2001. The group, Lashkar-e-Taiba is a radical Sunni Islamic group based in Pakistan which was proscribed as a terrorist organisation by the Australian Government in 2003.[16]

Sajid Mir, the alleged organiser of Lashkar-e-Taiba's overseas operations, reportedly acted as the link between Brigitte and Lodhi, asking the latter to look after Brigitte when he arrived in Australia in mid-May 2003.

Brigitte was detained by the Department of Immigration in October 2003 and quickly deported from Australia for breaching the terms of his tourist visa. On arrival back in France, he was arrested and subsequently charged with 'associating with criminals in relation to a terrorist enterprise'. He was tried and convicted in Paris in February 2007 and, on 15 March 2007, was sentenced to 9 years' imprisonment with a 6-year non-parole period.[17] Sajid Mir was convicted of the same charge in absentia and sentenced to 10 years' imprisonment with a non-parole period of 6 years and 8 months.[18] Brigitte's conviction is currently under appeal.

[15] *R v Lodhi*, above n 13, at [33].

[16] By the Criminal Code Amendment (Hamas and Lashkar-e-Tayyiba) Act 2003 (Cth).

[17] P Wilson, 'French Sentence Brigitte to 9 Years' *The Australian* 16 March 2007, <http://www.theaustralian.news.com.au/printpage/0,5942,21391422,00.html>.

[18] Wilson, above n 17.

At his trial, Lodhi admitted assisting Brigitte, but said that he did this as a courtesy to a stranger traveling in a new country at the behest of a mutual friend. Brigitte was not called to give evidence in Lodhi's trial. The judge, in sentencing Lodhi, said that he was satisfied that 'Sajid was endeavouring to co-ordinate a liaison between the offender and Willie Brigitte in Sydney so that, in general terms, the prospect of terrorist actions in Australia could be explored'.[19]

Lodhi's trial in many ways provided a test case for the terrorism offences that were introduced into the Criminal Code (Cth) in 2002.[20] Numerous applications to the trial judge sought rulings as to the admissibility of certain evidence, the constitutional validity and scope of national security protective orders as well as the elements of offences relating to the preparation of a terrorist act. The next section explores this latter issue.

III. DEFINING THE ELEMENTS OF PREPARATORY OFFENCES

Lodhi's case highlights the difficulties in delineating the physical and fault elements in the Australian preparatory terrorism offences, primarily because of a lack of clarity in drafting. The preparatory terrorism offences were drafted in a short time frame without full consideration of the pre-existing sections setting out general principles of criminal responsibility in chapter 2 of the Criminal Code. Simon Bronitt and Miriam Gani explore this 'General Part' of the Criminal Code in detail in this volume, chapter eleven.

The Australian legislation that introduced the new terrorism offences into the Criminal Code was part of a package designed to increase security through the expansion of investigation and enforcement procedures and powers to seize assets that was introduced into the Commonwealth Parliament in March 2002. The Senate Legal and Constitutional Legislation Committee received over 431 submissions in the 6 weeks it had been given to report on the relevant Bills. The Committee made a number of recommendations, including that the proposed absolute liability offences of providing or receiving training, possessing things and collecting or making documents likely to facilitate terrorist acts be altered to include fault elements of recklessness and knowledge.[21] An amended version of the legislation subsequently came into force on 6 July 2002.

[19] *R v Lodhi*, above n 13, at [10].

[20] The Security Legislation Amendment (Terrorism) Bill [No 2] 2002 (Cth) inserted Divs 101, 102 and 103 into pt 5.3 of the Criminal Code (Cth). The Bill was assented to on 5 July 2002 and came into force on 6 July 2002.

[21] Senate Legal and Constitutional Legislation Committee, Parliament of Australia, Consideration of Legislation Referred to the Committee: Security Legislation Amendment (Terrorism) Bill 2002 [No 2]; Suppression of the Financing of Terrorism Bill 2002; Criminal Code Amendment (Suppression of Terrorist Bombings) Bill 2002; Border Security Legislation Amendment Bill 2002; Telecommunications Interception Legislation Amendment Bill 2002.

This legislative package contained many complex provisions and the compressed timeframe for its consideration rendered a thorough analysis of how these new crimes reflected the general principles enshrined in chapter 2 of the existing Criminal Code impossible. As a result, the terrorism offences in many instances do not adequately reflect the general principles previously enacted in the Criminal Code and give rise to uncertainty as to the requisite physical and fault elements.

The preparatory offences with which Lodhi was charged do not specify a fault element in relation to the physical elements of possession, collecting or making documents and preparing or planning a terrorist act. This is in contrast to Division 102 offences dealing with directing, recruiting and training a terrorist organisation,[22] which clearly attach the fault element of intention to the physical elements.

Section 5.6(1) of the Criminal Code states that '[i]f the law creating the offence does not specify a fault element for a physical element that consists only of conduct, intention is the fault element for that physical element'. This was followed by the trial judge, Whealy J, in importing an intention to possess a 'thing' into s 101.4 in one of the rulings in Lodhi's case.[23] This fault element is no different to that for most conduct crimes. Intention also carries over to collecting or making a document under s 101.5 and doing 'any act' under s 101.6.[24] It is important to note that intention here is confined to the relevant conduct and does not extend or relate to *why* the conduct is being carried out, that is, the conduct's connection to the preparation of a terrorist act. Section 5.2(1) of the Criminal Code states that a 'person has intention with respect to conduct if he or she means to engage in that conduct'.

Ian Leader-Elliott has pointed out that '[t]he legislature would be expected to displace most of the applications of s 5.6 by specific provisions dealing with fault'.[25] Why a fault element was not specified in relation to the physical act in these offences is unclear, but perhaps can be explained by the haste to enact offences relating to terrorism. Simon Bronitt and Miriam Gani's chapter on criminal codes in the 21st century in this volume also suggests that clarity in codification may become lost in the bureaucratic process of drafting offences in response to urgent political demands.[26] They point out that the drafting of the terrorism offences in general suggested an 'alarming willingness' on the part of the Government to depart from the presumptions at the core of the principles section in the Criminal Code.

The drafting of the preparatory terrorism offences has also led to confusion about the further fault elements that need to be proved. For example,

22 Criminal Code (Cth), ss 102.2–102.7.

23 *R v Lodhi* [2006] NSWSC 584, unreported, 14 February 2006 (Whealy J).

24 *R v Lodhi*, above n 23, at [86].

25 I Leader-Elliott, *The Commonwealth Criminal Code, A Guide for Practitioners* (Attorney-General's Department and Australian Institute of Judicial Administration, 2002) 93.

26 This volume, ch 11.

Whealy J in Lodhi's case changed his mind about the necessary fault elements for the offence of possession of a 'thing' connected to a terrorist act. In a ruling made on 23 December 2005,[27] Whealy J stated in relation to s 101.4 of the Criminal Code that the act of possession must have been done in preparation for an action that is intended to cause serious physical harm to a person, in causing a person's death or causing serious damage to property.[28] In a subsequent ruling on 14 February 2006, he stated that this was 'not accurate' and that the prosecution did not have to prove this element.[29]

Whealy J delineated the elements that need to be proved beyond reasonable doubt for the possession offence in the following way:[30]

> (1) The accused **intended** to possess the 'thing' (intention read in by virtue of section 5.6(1));
> (2) The **possession** of the thing is connected with preparation for, the engagement of a person in, or assistance in a terrorist act; and
> (3) The accused **knows** of the connection between the document and the preparation of the terrorist act.

In the 14 February ruling, Whealy J held that it was not necessary to prove that the accused has the fault element set out in s 100.1 which defines a 'terrorist act'.[31] That is, the prosecution need not prove that the preparatory conduct was done with the intention of advancing a political, religious or ideological cause and that it was done with the intention of coercing, or influencing by intimidation, a State, Territory of Commonwealth government or intimidating the public or a section of the public. The reasoning behind this was that the accused may not have any personal interest in carrying out the terrorist act. Whealy J stated that the accused 'might, for example, simply be a paid mercenary. He might simply be doing a favour for a friend or repaying a debt'.[32]

In *Faheem Khalid Lodhi v The Queen*,[33] the New South Wales Court of Criminal Appeal upheld this latter point, Spigelman CJ stating that there was no need to prove the accused him or herself had 'the intention that the act advances a particular cause or is done with the requisite purpose of coercion or intimidation'.[34]

[27] *R v Lodhi* [2005] NSWSC 1377, unreported, 23 December 2005 (Whealy J).
[28] *R v Lodhi*, above n 23, at [84].
[29] *R v Lodhi*, above n 23, at [85].
[30] *R v Lodhi*, above n 23, at [77]–[88].
[31] *R v Lodhi*, above n 23, at [103].
[32] *R v Lodhi*, above n 23, at [88].
[33] *R v Lodhi* [2006] NSWCCA 121, unreported, 13 April 2006 (Spigelman CJ, McClellan CJ at CL and Sully J).
[34] *R v Lodhi*, above n 33, at [90].

But what then of the 'knowledge' requirement as the link between the preparatory conduct and the terrorist act? Here, again, problems arose with interpretation.

Sections 101.4 and 101.5 of the Criminal Code (Cth) specify the fault element of 'knowledge' in relation to the connection between the conduct and the preparation of the terrorist act. Whealy J held that pursuant to s 5(3) of the Criminal Code (Cth), knowledge means awareness of a 'circumstance' in which the conduct occurs, that is, the preparation for a terrorist act exists or will exist in the ordinary course of events.[35] There was no need to prove that Lodhi himself intended to prepare for either a particular or general terrorist act.

What, then, amounts to an awareness of the preparation for a terrorist act? In the 23 December 2005 ruling,[36] Whealy J stated:

> In my opinion, an offence will have been committed by a person acting in a preliminary way in preparation for a terrorist act even where no final decision has been made ... as to the ultimate target.[37]

Thus there need not be an awareness of a target, but simply that some *type* of terrorist act is being prepared. This is consistent with the approach to aiding and abetting in *R v Bainbridge*,[38] where the accused need only have knowledge of the type of offence contemplated by the principal offender, a principle which is now also reflected in the Criminal Code (Cth).[39]

In 2005, the Australian Government passed legislation inserting provisions into the Criminal Code (Cth) setting out that a person commits any of the preparatory offences even where the thing, document or act (as the case may be) is not referable to a specific terrorist act or is referable to more than one terrorist act.[40] A subsequent Act inserted a new s 106.3 into the Code, setting out that the 2005 amendments apply to offences committed before the commencement of s 106.3 (which came into force after a proclamation by the Governor-General) on 16 February 2006.[41] The prosecution argued before the New South Wales Court of Criminal Appeal that the 2005 amendments applied retrospectively to Lodhi's trial. The Court held that the amendments were not applicable to criminal proceedings that had already been instituted.

Despite reading down the retrospective scope of the 2005 amendments, the Court followed Whealy J's original approach that the prosecution need

35 *R v Lodhi*, above n 23, at [82].
36 *R v Lodhi*, above n 27.
37 *R v Lodhi*, above n 27, at [52].
38 [1960] 1 QB 129.
39 Criminal Code (Cth), s 11.2(3)(a).
40 Criminal Code (Cth), ss 101.2(3)(b) and (c); 101.5(3)(b) and (c); 101.6(2)(b) and (c), inserted by the Anti-Terrorism Act 2005 (Cth).
41 See Item 22 of sch 1 to the Anti-Terrorism Act (No 2) 2005 (Cth).

not prove an awareness of a *specific* terrorist act. This was on the basis that the offences themselves refer to 'a' terrorist act rather than 'the' terrorist act.[42]

Compare this approach to that of Rutherford J's interpretation of 'knowledge' in *R v Khawaja*.[43] In that case, Rutherford J of the Ontario Supreme Court of Justice considered the fault element for the Canadian offence of knowingly facilitating a terrorist activity.[44] This offence is qualified by s 83.19(2) of the Criminal Code (Can) which states that a terrorist activity is facilitated whether or not 'the facilitator knows that a particular terrorist activity is facilitated' or whether or not 'any particular terrorist activity was foreseen or planned at the time it was facilitated' or whether or not 'any terrorist activity was actually carried out'.

Rutherford J held that the prosecution must prove knowledge by the accused of his or her contribution to a terrorist group *and* that it was such a group *and* an intention to aid or facilitate the group's terrorist activity.[45] He regarded the qualifications set out in s 83.19(2) as showing there was no need to prove knowledge of specific details such as the manner in which the terrorist activity would be carried out. However, he construed the word 'knowledge' broadly in line with the need to maintain a high degree of subjective fault as an element of serious offences. He relied on an article by Kent Roach[46] setting out what the fault element of this section should be, in addition to Fuerst J's comments in *R v Lindsay*[47] concerning principles of statutory interpretation to reach this conclusion.

Rutherford's extra fault requirement of an intention to aid a terrorist act is what is missing from the Australian provisions. The unusual drafting of the Australian possession offence highlights the difficulties with not having a fault element of intention relating to the preparation of a terrorist act as part of the offence itself.

In the 14 February 2006 ruling, Whealy J said his analysis of the elements of the possession offence was 'identical' to the offence of collection or making a document connected with a terrorist act.[48] This would mean the elements are:

[42] *R v Lodhi*, above n 33, at [63].

[43] *R v Khawaja* [2004] OJ No 845, unreported, 24 October 2006, Ontario Superior Court of Justice (Rutherford J).

[44] Criminal Code (Can), s 83.19(1).

[45] *R v Khawaja*, above n 43, at [38].

[46] K Roach, 'The New Terrorism Offences in Canadian Criminal Law' in D Daubney, W Deisman, D Jutras, E Mendes and P Molinari (eds), *Terrorism, Law & Democracy: How is Canada Changing Following September 11*? (Montreal, Les Editions Themis, 2002) 135–6.

[47] *R v Khawaja*, above n 43, at [38]–[42].

[48] *R v Lodhi*, above n 23, at [86].

(1) The accused intended to collect or make a document (intention read in by virtue of s 5.6(1));
(2) The document is connected with preparation for, the engagement of a person in, or assistance in a terrorist act; and
(3) The accused knows of the connection between the document and the preparation of the terrorist act (s 101.5(1)(c)).

Andrew Lynch and George Williams state that the 'open-ended drafting' of this particular provision means that a person who downloads from the internet a document containing instructions as to how to make a bomb would be liable if he or she knows that a document containing such information may very well be connected to the preparation of a terrorist act.[49] Lynch and Williams point out that the missing requirement is for the accused to collect or make the document '*with the intention* of using it to assist in the preparation of a terrorist act'.[50]

Compare this, for example, with s 71A of the Drugs, Poisons and Controlled Substances Act 1981 (Vic) which states:

> A person who ... possesses a substance, material, document containing instructions relating to the preparation, cultivation or manufacture of a drug of dependence or equipment *with the intention of using the substance, material, document or equipment for the purpose of trafficking in a drug of dependence* is guilty of an indictable offence (emphasis added).

This section exemplifies how an extra fault element of intention could be drafted. Instead of following this pattern, s 101.5(5) states that an accused will not be liable 'if the collection or making of the document was not intended to facilitate preparation for, the engagement of a person in, or assistance in a terrorist act'. A note to this section sets out that the accused bears the evidential burden in this regard. This is unusual both as a method of drafting and in terms of its practical implications. The end effect is that by not having an intention of using the document to facilitate the preparation of a terrorist act as an element of the offence, prosecutorial agencies have been given a wide latitude to charge people, bring them to trial and then place the burden on them to raise evidence showing there was no intention to facilitate the preparation of a terrorist act.

To complicate matters further, recklessness as a fault element for the offence of doing any act in preparation for, or planning, a terrorist act has been accepted by the New South Wales Court of Criminal Appeal.[51] The Court upheld a preliminary assessment in this regard by Whealy J made in

[49] A Lynch and G Williams, *What Price Security? Taking Stock of Australia's Anti-Terror Laws* (Sydney, University of New South Wales Press Ltd, 2006) 20.
[50] Lynch and Williams, above n 49.
[51] *R v Lodhi*, above n 33.

the 14 February ruling. Whealy J stated that it was not necessary for him to set out the elements of the possession and preparation offences as the propositions as to their construction had not been fully argued.[52] He did, however, express a preliminary view that while there was no fault element specified in relation to s 101.6(1), the fault element for doing any act in preparation for, or planning, a terrorist act would be intention (presumably by virtue of s 5.1). However, he also went on to state that 'the fault element in relation to the second physical element would be recklessness (s 5.6)'.[53]

The 'second physical element' is unclear. Whealy J may be referring here to recklessness as to a 'circumstance' in which the conduct occurs, that is, recklessness as to a terrorist act existing in the ordinary course of events.

Section 5.4(1) states that a person is reckless with respect to a circumstance if 'he or she is aware of a substantial risk that the circumstance exists or will exist' and, 'having regard to the circumstances known to him or her, it is unjustifiable to take the risk'. This seems to imply the second fault element is an awareness of a substantial risk that a terrorist act will exist and it is unjustifiable to take that risk.

In *Faheem Khalid Lodhi v The Queen*,[54] Spigelman CJ agreed with Whealy J's preliminary assessment that the fault element in relation to doing any act in preparation for a terrorist offence was 'recklessness by force of s 5.6(2) of the *Criminal Code*' and ordered that the count against Lodhi be amended in this regard.[55]

Recklessness as a fault element does not apply to the United Kingdom or Canadian provisions. Section 5(1) of the Terrorism Act 2006 (UK) states that a person commits an offence if he or she engages in conduct in preparation for giving effect to *an intention* to commit acts of terrorism or assist another to commit such acts. Justice Rutherford's emphasis on subjective fault in *Khawaja's* case led to his interpretation of a requirement that there be an intention to aid terrorist activity.[56]

Lodhi's case highlights multiple problems with the drafting of the Australian provisions which has led to confusion as to the exact nature of the physical and fault elements of each offence. In the New South Wales Court of Criminal Appeal decision, Spigelman CJ stated:

> Preparatory acts are not often made into criminal offences. The particular nature of terrorism has resulted in a special, and in may ways unique, legislative regime. It was, in my opinion, the clear intention of Parliament to create offences where an offender has not decided precisely what he or she intends to do. A policy judgment has been made that the prevention of terrorism requires criminal responsibility

[52] *R v Lodhi*, above n 23, at [86].
[53] *R v Lodhi*, above n 23, at [86].
[54] *R v Lodhi*, above n 33.
[55] *R v Lodhi*, above n 33, at [91].
[56] *R v Khawaja*, above n 43, at [38].

> to arise at an earlier stage than is usually the case for other kinds of criminal conduct, e.g. well before an agreement has been reached for a conspiracy charge. The courts must respect that legislative policy.[57]

While it may not be for judges to question legislative policy, the next section considers whether traditional justifications for inchoate crimes can be used to justify this 'unique legislative regime'. It will be argued that the subjectivist approach to criminalisation may be relevant in justifying such offences, but only if the prosecution proves an intention to commit a terrorist act on top of the preparatory conduct.

IV. SHOULD PREPARATORY OFFENCES BE CRIMINALISED?

The three main inchoate offences—attempt, conspiracy and incitement—are treated as substantive crimes in themselves, separate from the completed offences at which they are aimed. In general, the common thread among these crimes is that there can be a conviction even though the substantive offence that was intended is not completed and no apparent harm is caused. In Australia, at the federal level, the offence of attempting to commit a crime is set out in s 11.1 of the Criminal Code. Section 11.1(2) requires that for the accused to be found guilty, 'the person's conduct must be *more than merely preparatory* to the commission of the offence' (emphasis added). The law in Canada and Australia followed the formulation in the Criminal Attempts Act 1981 (UK) which requires that liability for attempts is limited to conduct beyond preparation.[58] In comparison, the United States' Model Penal Code requires the performance of an act 'constituting a *substantial step* in the course of the conduct planned to culminate in the commission of the crime'[59] provided it is 'strongly corroborative'[60] of the accused's criminal purpose.

The traditional justifications for inchoate crimes are difficult to apply to preparatory offences. This section outlines how the subjectivist approach to attempted crimes might carry over to preparatory offences, but only if there is a clear intention to carry out the substantive crime. It is, however, probably more appropriate to see preparatory offences as a separate species of offences existing outside the general justifications for inchoate offences and developing in an ad hoc manner in response to policy concerns.

In his work, *Criminal Attempts,* Antony Duff sets out 'objectivist' and 'subjectivist' conceptions of criminal law and uses the law of attempts to

[57] *R v Lodhi*, above n 33, at [66].
[58] Criminal Attempts Act 1981 (UK), s 1; Criminal Code RSC, ch 46, (1985), s 24.
[59] Model Penal Code, § 5.01(1)(c) (1962).
[60] Model Penal Code, § 5.01(2) (1962).

defend an objectivist approach to criminal responsibility.[61] According to Duff, subjectivists argue that actions should be identified in terms of their 'subjective' dimension: that is, 'by the intentions and beliefs with which [the accused] acted, or by the attitudes or dispositions which [the accused's] action revealed'.[62] Blame should be ascribed on the basis of an individual's intention as harmful consequences are strictly matters outside the control of the individual. Blame should depend on individual choices made and not just on luck or chance. Since subjective intention is the cornerstone of liability, it does not matter if the offence is incomplete (or impossible). A person should be held liable for inchoate offences, and also for preparatory offences, even where the acts are physically (or even legally) impossible.

Objectivists, on the other hand, argue that subjective intention in relation to inchoate crimes should not be 'the *sole* ground of liability',[63] but that

> objective aspects are also relevant: what I am properly held liable for, what can properly be ascribed to me, is my action as it actually impinges on the world—as it actually engages with the material world, and with the social world of rational thought and deliberation.[64]

Consequences thus have a role to play in determining questions of moral and legal blame even where the accused has no control over them.

It is difficult to apply this objectivist approach to preparatory terrorism offences given that such acts as purchasing maps, possessing information concerning explosives and obtaining a price list for chemicals are quite different from pointing a gun at someone, pressing the trigger and missing (in terms of proximity to the harm caused or likely to be caused). Each of the former acts could be considered objectively 'innocent'. In relation to preparatory offences, the minimum conduct necessary to constitute a criminal act is 'any act', a requirement which comes close to what Duff terms a 'first act' test of liability in the law of attempts. This is in contrast to the traditional position of the common law in relation to attempts which required the accused to do the last act, depending on him or herself, towards the commission of the offence before liability would be made out.[65] Duff criticises such a 'first act' test as far too broad:

> The community has an interest in the early detection and capture of intending criminals: but a respect for individual freedom generates three countervailing considerations, which argue for a much narrower law of attempts.[66]

[61] RA Duff, *Criminal Attempts* (Oxford, Oxford University Press, 1996).
[62] Duff, above n 61, at 192.
[63] Duff, above n 61, at 193.
[64] Duff, above n 61, at 237.
[65] S Bronitt and B McSherry, *Principles of Criminal Law* (Sydney, Thomson Lawbook Co, 2nd edn, 2005) 405–6.
[66] Duff, above n 61, at 36–7.

These countervailing considerations include the risk that a 'first act' test would:

(1) convict those who would have voluntarily desisted from proceeding further;
(2) lead to 'intrusive and oppressive police investigation in the search for evidence of the requisite criminal purpose'[67]; and
(3) not treat individuals as autonomous agents capable of deciding to abandon their criminal enterprises.

Barbara Baum Levenbook has dismissed such concerns in supporting the development of specific preparation statutes.[68] She argues that

> because attempt laws have not markedly encouraged intrusive police practices and citizen meddlesomeness, there is reason to doubt that preparation laws will.[69]

Levenbook further states that any claim of voluntary desistance can be taken into account in sentencing and, providing that there is uniform enforcement of such laws, 'preparations to commit morally serious crimes ought to be outlawed as are attempts'.[70]

Ultimately it is a question of policy as to whether 'first acts' should be criminalised. The subjectivist conception of criminal law has perhaps more to say as to what the elements of preparatory offences should be.

In *Whybrow*,[71] Lord Goddard CJ stated in relation to attempted crimes that 'the intent becomes the principal ingredient of the crime'. It must be shown that the accused intended to cause the substantive offence and had the requisite knowledge of facts and circumstances. In relation to conspiracy, in *Gerakiteys v The Queen*[72] the High Court echoed this approach in holding that the prosecution must prove an intention, shared by all the parties, to commit *the* unlawful act (not just *any* unlawful act) that has been agreed upon.[73]

Accessorial liability also requires a high standard of subjective fault. The majority of the High Court in *Giorgianni v The Queen*[74] set out the requirement for the prosecution to prove that the accused had an intention to assist or encourage the crime based on actual knowledge of the essential matters. Recklessness is not sufficient:

[67] Duff, above n 61, at 37. See also: A Ashworth, 'Criminal Attempts and the Role of Resulting Harm Under the Code, and in the Common Law' (1988) 19 *Rutgers Law Journal* 725, 750–1.

[68] Levenbook, above n 1, at 41.

[69] Levenbook, above n 1, at 60.

[70] Levenbook, above n 1, at 63.

[71] (1951) 25 Cr App R 141, 147.

[72] (1984) 153 CLR 317.

[73] This fault element has found its way into the Criminal Code (Cth), s 11.5(2)(b); the Criminal Code (ACT), s 48(2)(b); and the Crimes Act 1958 (Vic), s 321(2).

[74] (1985) 156 CLR 473.

> There are ... offences in which it is not possible to speak of recklessness as constituting sufficient intent. Attempt is one and conspiracy is another. And we think the offences of aiding and abetting and counselling and procuring are others. Those offences require intentional participation in a crime by lending assistance or encouragement.[75]

On this reasoning, preparatory and planning offences should also require a high subjective fault element.

If preparatory offences required proof of an intention to commit the substantive offence, then a subjectivist account might justify criminalisation. If it is proved that a person has taken steps towards the commission of the substantive offence, with an intention to commit the offence, then it could be argued that such a person has 'manifested sufficient non-self-restraint so as to deserve punishment'.[76]

Such an argument could be used to justify criminalising engaging in conduct 'in preparation for giving effect to an intention to commit acts of terrorism' as is the case in the United Kingdom. However, this argument does not fit comfortably with the Australian preparatory terrorism offences where, as discussed in the previous section, recklessness has crept in as a fault element and there is no requirement that there be an intention to carry out the substantive offence of a terrorist act.

The subjectivist approach also fails as a justification for offences of possession (or collection) where an intention to commit the substantive offence need not be proved. The common law has traditionally been wary of imposing criminal liability on the basis of possession alone. It has been held that an indictment charging a person for mere possession of articles that may have criminal uses does not charge 'an act' and therefore is bad at common law.[77]

Yet statutory offences sometimes criminalise possession without the necessity of proving intention. This is particularly the case in relation to small quantities of illicit drugs[78] and indeed some possession offences place

[75] (1985) 156 CLR 473 at 506. This approach has been criticised as too restrictive: B Fisse, *Howard's Criminal Law* (Sydney, Law Book Company, 5th edn, 1990) 336; B Fisse, 'Proceeds of Crime Act' (1989) 13 *Criminal Law Journal* 5, 12. Subsequently, s 11.2(3) of the Criminal Code (Cth) was drafted to include recklessness as a fault element for accessorial liability. The doctrine of common purpose in Australia also broadens the fault element for accessorial liability in imposing secondary liability for foreseen but unintended offences committed by other participants who are also participating in the original criminal agreement: *McAuliffe and McAuliffe v The Queen* (1995) 183 CLR 108; *Clayton v The Queen; Hartwick v The Queen; Hartwick v The Queen* (2006) 231 ALR 500.

[76] Ashworth, above n 67, at 736.

[77] G Williams, *Criminal Law: The General Part* (London, Stevens and Sons, 2nd edn, 1961) 8.

[78] Drugs of Dependence Act 1989 (ACT), s 171(1); Drugs Misuse and Trafficking Act 1985 (NSW), s 10(1); Misuse of Drugs Act 1990 (NT), s 9(1); Drugs Misuse Act 1986 (Qld), s 9; Controlled Substances Act 1984 (SA), s 31; Misuse of Drugs Act 2001 (Tas), s 25; Drugs, Poisons and Controlled Substances Act 1981 (Vic), s 73; Misuse of Drugs Act 1981 (WA), s 6(2).

the legal burden on the accused to establish that the illicit drugs are not in his or her possession.[79]

Subjectivist and objectivist conceptions of the criminal law are thus of little help in justifying the Australian preparatory terrorism offences.

Another approach to attempting to classify such offences is to view them as a species of 'status' or situational offences. While the principle of legality, or—as it is more traditionally known—the rule of law, requires that there should be no punishment without law (*nulla poena sine lege*) and that this punishment should be for criminal conduct rather than for criminal types,[80] democratic governments have long justified the detention and punishment of individuals possessing certain characteristics.

During the 19th century, 'status' offences existed to deal with vagrants, prostitutes, drunks and habitual criminals.[81] During the 20th century, there was a move towards a social welfare or medical model, and away from the criminal model, to deal with 'drunk and disorderly' individuals, and a range of civil powers of detention were available.[82] Different 'undesirable' groups have been targeted at different times. For example, Simon Bronitt contends that the current legislative responses to detaining suspected terrorists are neither novel nor extraordinary.[83] He points out that the Bushranging Act 1830 (NSW)[84] empowered the arrest of suspected bushrangers on the basis that they could not establish their identity, and required suspects to prove that they were not engaged in illegal activities. Similarly, Alex Steel refers to the existence of 'razor gangs' in New South Wales in the 1920s as leading to the introduction of a general crime of consorting with criminals or prostitutes.[85]

It may be that the preparatory terrorism offences simply reflect a trend toward detaining people for who they are, rather than what they do. There are status elements to a range of offences including membership of a

[79] See, for example, s 5 of the Drugs, Poisons and Controlled Substances Act 1981 (Vic), which states:

> Without restricting the meaning of the word 'possession', any substance shall be deemed for the purposes of this Act to be in the possession of a person so long as it is upon any land or premises occupied by him or is used, enjoyed or controlled by him in any place whatsoever, unless the person satisfies the court to the contrary.

[80] F Allen, *The Habits of Legality: Criminal Justice and the Rule of Law* (Oxford, Oxford University Press, 1996) 15.

[81] M Finnane, *Police and Government: Histories of Policing in Australia* (Melbourne, Oxford University Press, 1994) ch 1.

[82] Bronitt and McSherry, above n 65, at 749.

[83] S Bronitt, 'Australia's Legal Response to Terrorism: Neither Novel nor Extraordinary?' Paper presented at the Castan Centre for Human Rights Law, *Human Rights 2003: The Year in Review Conference*, Melbourne, 4 December 2003.

[84] Bushranging Act 1830 (NSW) 11 Geo 4 No 10.

[85] A Steel, 'Consorting in New South Wales: Substantive Offence or Police Power?' (2003) 26(3) *University of New South Wales Law Review* 567.

terrorist organisation and associating with members. For example, s 102.8 of the Criminal Code (Cth) makes it an offence punishable by three years imprisonment to meet or communicate with those involved in a terrorist organisation on two or more occasions. The physical element of meeting or communicating is innocuous enough; it is the *status* of the person (as a member of a terrorist organisation) with whom the accused associates that criminalises this conduct.[86]

Terrorists are sometimes referred to by judges as the worst type of offender. For example, in *Thomas v Mowbray*,[87] Callinan J referred to 'groups of zealots' associated with Al-Qa'ida as 'making common cause of hatred, against communities posing no threat to them' and as showing 'a willingness and capacity to use whatever weapons they can obtain, and to inflict casualties upon many innocent persons and property, both private and public'. Justice Callinan was also keen to point out that modern-day terrorism has no historical counterpart:

> Populations today are both more numerous and more concentrated. They, and property both personal and public, are more vulnerable. Modern weapons, and not just horrific ones as nuclear bombs, germs and chemicals, are more efficient and destructive than ever before. The means of international travel and communication are more readily open to exploitation by terrorists than in the past ... The scale and almost inestimable capacity of accessible, modern, destructive technology to cause harm, render attempts to draw analogies with historical atrocities, as grave and frightening to their contemporary targets as they may have been, unconvincing.[88]

The view that terrorists are the worst kind of offender and that modern day terrorism is somehow 'extraordinary' certainly helps to explain the rush to create new offences and powers of detention. This view may also reflect the precautionary approach to 'known unknowns' explored by Lucia Zedner in this volume, chapter three, as well as the theory of 'vulnerable autonomy' which Peter Ramsay argues in this volume, chapter six, helps explain the rise of civil preventative orders. Yet, preparatory terrorism offences refer to engaging in conduct or doing any act; they do not refer to a 'state of being'.[89] They differ from older status offences that, for example, punish being drunk or disorderly or being an habitual criminal. It is not 'being a terrorist' that is the subject of the offence, but some sort of conduct that may indicate a propensity for harm.

[86] B McSherry, 'Terrorism Offences in the Criminal Code: Broadening the Boundaries of Australian Criminal Laws' (2004) 27(2) *University of New South Wales Law Journal* 354, 364ff.

[87] (2007) 237 ALR 194, 341.

[88] *Thomas v Mowbray*, above n 87, at 342.

[89] The one exception to this seems to be the criminalisation of membership of a terrorist organisation: Criminal Code (Cth), s 102.3.

Perhaps the most practical approach is to view preparatory terrorism offences as a separate species of offences beyond that of attempts, conspiracy or incitement and different from status or situational offences. Such an approach may be explained by the rise of what Markus Dubber terms the 'Police Power Model' of the criminal process.[90] In 1968, Herbert Packer outlined two models for the criminal process: the Due Process Model, which emphasises procedural protections such as the presumption of innocence, and the Crime Control Model, which focuses on the suppression of crime rather than the rights of the accused.[91] Dubber suggests these two models have now given way to the Police Power Model, which focuses on the protection of the authority of the state rather than the protection of individual rights.[92] Dubber argues that this model enables the existence of offences of possession which do not 'fit' with the general principles relating to inchoate offences, rather they are a '*miniature code* unto themselves'.[93] In Dubber's view, possession 'is not conduct, but evidence of future or past conduct.'[94] This is also the case with preparatory terrorism offences. The acts of collecting maps, possessing handwritten notes on dangerous items, or asking for a price list of chemicals are all criminalised on the basis that they indicate a propensity to carry out future harm. This echoes Bentham's notion of 'presumed offences' which criminalise conduct that, although not wrong in itself, infers that those engaged in it are doing something else that is in fact wrong.[95]

According to Dubber, the common theme among possession offences (and by extension, preparatory offences) is that of dangerousness.[96] He states:

> Possession is criminalized if it poses a threat, and more precisely, under the Police Power Model of the criminal process, a threat to the authority of the state. Possessor and possessed are considered as a threat unit. The threat can either emanate from the possessor or from the possessed. Some objects are so dangerous that their *being possessed* is presumptively criminal. And some individuals are so dangerous that their *possessing* is presumptively criminal.[97]

Since collecting maps, possessing handwritten notes on explosives and asking for a price list of chemicals are not dangerous acts in themselves, on Dubber's reading, preparatory terrorism offences must be aimed at the dangerous

[90] Dubber, above n 11.

[91] HL Packer, *The Limits of the Criminal Sanction* (Stanford CA, Stanford University Press, 1968).

[92] Dubber, above n 11, at 93.

[93] Dubber, above n 11, at 115.

[94] Dubber, above n 11, at 103.

[95] J Bentham, 'Principles of the Penal Code' in E Dumont (ed), Charles Milner Atkinson (tr), *Bentham's Theory of Legislation* (London, H Milford, 1914) 271. Bentham's work is discussed by Schauer and Zeckhauser, above n 12, at 69ff.

[96] Dubber, above n 11, at 113.

[97] Dubber, above n 11, at 113–4.

individual. They are designed to punish individuals who have a presumed propensity to commit future crimes rather than criminal conduct.

Ashworth states:

> Assuming that D has done a sufficient preliminary act and that it can be established that he [or she] intended to commit the substantive offence, this may be accepted as sufficient evidence of a dangerous disposition and it supplies a good reason for intervening so as to prevent the consummation of the attempt.[98]

Douglas Husak argues that it is profoundly unjust to criminalise such an act which *indicates* wrongful conduct rather than being wrongful in itself.[99] But even if it were just, is a 'dangerous disposition' sufficiently evidenced by purchasing maps, possessing information concerning explosives and obtaining a price list for chemicals, particularly if taken separately? Does the act of buying maps show a disposition to cause the prohibited harm of a terrorist act? The inference of such a disposition from this act alone is insupportable. This evidentiary problem brings the argument back full circle to the necessity of proving an intention to commit the substantive offence.

Preparatory offences can really only be justified on the basis of police intervention to prevent future harm occurring, but this should be based on inferences as to the likelihood of effectively preventing the wrongful conduct. Frederick Schauer and Richard Zeckhauser point out that 'mild' forms of regulation by generalisation may be justified in turning on probabilistic inferences, but 'it may be unacceptable for such probabilistic generalizations to provide the basis for imprisoning or fining people who might be wholly innocent'.[100]

In Dubber's view, possession offences

> reflect an approach to criminal law that emphasizes crime control over just punishment, application over definition, results over rules, and ultimately the protection of state authority over the prevention and vindication of personal harm.[101]

The same must be said of preparatory offences.

V. THE PUNISHMENT FOR PREPARATORY OFFENCES

If Dubber's approach is correct and preparatory offences indicate that the Police Power Model is now the paradigm model of criminal process, indicating

[98] Ashworth, above n 67, at 737.

[99] DN Husak, 'Reasonable Risk Creation and Overinclusive Legislation' (1998) 1 *Buffalo Criminal Law Review* 599; DN Husak, 'Guns and Drugs: Case Studies on the Principled Limits of the Criminal Sanction' (2004) 23 *Law and Philosophy* 437.

[100] Schauer and Zeckhauser, above n 12, at 75.

[101] Dubber, above n 11, at 117.

such offences are here to stay, what should the punishment be for such offences? The penalty for the United Kingdom and Australian preparatory offences is life imprisonment.[102] In Canada, facilitating a terrorist activity is punishable by imprisonment for a term not exceeding 14 years.[103]

Whealy J sentenced Faheem Lodhi to imprisonment for 20 years for doing an act in preparation for a terrorist act and for 10 years each for the possession and collection offences, the sentences to be served concurrently. The normal range for a non-parole period for Commonwealth offences is 60–66 per cent of the total sentence.[104] However, Item 1B of sch 1 to the Anti-Terrorism Act 2004 (Cth) introduced a new provision, s 19AG, into the Crimes Act 1914 (Cth), making it mandatory for the sentencing judge in terrorism related trials to fix the single non-parole period at a percentage of at least three-quarters of the sentence. This meant that Whealy J was obliged to fix a non-parole period of at least 15 years. The prosecution did not argue for a non-parole period greater than 75 per cent of the aggregate of the sentences, so that 15 years applied.[105]

Twenty years' imprisonment with a minimum non-parole period of 15 years for purchasing maps, possessing information concerning explosives and obtaining a price list for chemicals seems an inordinate amount of time when compared with the average sentence for offences that result in death such as murder. For example, the Sentencing Advisory Council of Victoria found that between 1998/99 and 2003/04, the average imprisonment length for murder was 18.1 years, with a non-parole period of 14.3 years.[106] The average imprisonment length for manslaughter for the same time period was 6.3 years, with an average non-parole period of 4.1 years.[107]

The other point to note is *the nature* of the punishment. Lodhi has been classified as an 'AA' risk to national security—the highest risk classification available. This means that since 22 April 2004, when Lodhi was received into custody, he has been segregated from other prisoners. In sentencing Lodhi, Whealy J pointed out that this in reality means that Lodhi has been placed in solitary confinement.[108] He is allowed to exercise in a small exercise yard outside his cell for between 90 minutes and 3 hours a day and if for any reason he is moved to another part of the prison complex, he is required to wear an orange set of overalls and he is shackled on such occasions.

Lodhi is constantly monitored and videoed and his cell is searched daily. He is secured in his cell at 3.30 pm each day. Visits from his family are

[102] Terrorism Act 2006 (UK), s 5(3); Criminal Code (Cth), s 101.6(1).

[103] Criminal Code (Can), s 83.19(1).

[104] *R v Bernier* (1998) 102 A Crim R 44.

[105] *R v Lodhi*, above n 13, at [105]–[112].

[106] Sentencing Advisory Council, *Sentencing Snapshot No 4: Sentencing Trends for Murder in Victoria* (September 2005) 2.

[107] *Ibid.*

[108] *R v Lodhi*, above n 13, at [79].

videoed and must take place within the earshot of a Corrective Services officer. All telephone calls are recorded, other than calls to his lawyer, and all of his mail is read. He is not allowed access to a computer and he is not permitted to speak to an Official Visitor.

Whealy J, in passing sentence, stated that he was prepared to make some allowance 'for the strict conditions in which [Lodhi] has been confined up to the time of trial'[109] and for the conditions which would be imposed after sentence.[110] He also recommended to the prison authorities

> that they ought not lose sight of the need to consider the re-classification of the offender at a relatively early stage during his prison term.[111]

Lodhi's sentence and the conditions under which he must serve it are very difficult to justify in the light of his conduct when compared with the sentences for substantive offences where harm has occurred. While the long-term effects of segregation in prisons on mentally healthy individuals are not known, mental health professionals working in American 'supermax' prisons have observed prisoners 'who do not have preexisting serious mental disorders develop irritability, anxiety, and other dysphoric symptoms when housed in these units for long periods of time'.[112]

In *R v Roche*,[113] McKechnie J stated that terrorism offences are 'abnormal' crimes that require 'consideration of a range of penalties which do not necessarily correlate with normal, though grave, crimes'. Similarly, in *R v Demirian*,[114] in considering the appropriate sentence for a conviction for conspiracy to bomb the Turkish consulate in Melbourne, McGarvie and O'Bryan JJ made the following remarks:

> The type of activity engaged in by the applicant and others is rare in this country but terrorist acts are commonplace in the country from whence the applicant emigrated to Australia. Unless courts in this country are vigilant in imposing condign sentences for such conduct evil-minded persons might seek to emulate this conduct ... When a crime of such notoriety and heinousness is committed in the name of a political cause this Court is not required to fix a minimum term. The political nature of the offence and its seriousness render the fixing of such a term inappropriate. A sentence imposed in these circumstances should be exceptional to mark the seriousness with which the crime is viewed and therefore no minimum term should be fixed.

[109] *R v Lodhi*, above n 13, at [83].

[110] *R v Lodhi*, above n 13, at [88].

[111] *Ibid*.

[112] J Metzner and J Dvoskin, 'An Overview of Correctional Psychiatry' (2006) 29(3) *Psychiatric Clinics of North America* 761, 765.

[113] *R v Roche* [2005] WASCA 4, unreported, Supreme Court of Western Australia, 14 January 2005 (McKechnie J at [119]).

[114] *R v Demirian* [1989] VR 128 (McGarvie and O'Bryan JJ at 131–2).

On this reasoning, the principle of proportionality in sentencing which provides that the type and extent of the punishment should be proportionate to the gravity of the harm and the degree of the offender's responsibility becomes obsolete. Yet, despite the rhetoric in Demirian's case, it is interesting to note that the sentence for conspiracy was 10 years' imprisonment. The term and nature of Lodhi's punishment for preparation is in excess of this sentence for an inchoate crime.

Andrew Ashworth's work on the punishment of attempted crimes is relevant in assessing whether proportionality should still be taken into account in sentencing individuals for preparatory terrorism offences. In exploring what punishment is justifiable, Ashworth divides attempts into 'incomplete attempts' as opposed to 'complete attempts', the latter being where the accused has done all the steps he or she set out to do, but has failed to produce the intended result.[115] Incomplete attempts cover the situation of where the accused has only performed some of the acts intended, but has either desisted or been prevented from going further. This definition of incomplete attempts can be viewed as related to preparatory offences.

Ashworth looks at the justifications for punishing incomplete attempts and finds them wanting. Harm-based retribution does not 'work' as the accused has not caused any harm, unless the latter is defined very broadly to include some form of fear in others. However, causing fear is not one of the elements of incomplete attempts or the preparatory terrorism offences.

Ashworth has further pointed out that both consequentialist and retributive theories of punishment may offer concessions for incomplete attempts in the sense of 'the more remote from the complete crime, the more lenient the punishment'.[116] For consequentialists such as Jeremy Bentham, this is to enable 'the possibility of repentance or a prudent stopping short'.[117] For retributivist theorists, 'each step of an attempt betokens greater wickedness and therefore deserves greater punishment'.[118] As Lewis posits, complete attempts (what Lewis terms 'wholehearted' attempts) are worse than incomplete attempts because they involve 'more careful planning, more precautions against failure, more effort, more persistence, and perhaps repeated tries'.[119]

If incomplete attempts should be punished more leniently than complete attempts, it follows that preparatory offences should also be treated more leniently to give an incentive to abandon the substantive offence rather

[115] Ashworth, above n 67, at 725.

[116] Ashworth, above n 67, at 739.

[117] J Bentham, *Theory of Legislation*, C Ogden (ed) (London, Routledge & Kegan Paul Ltd, 1931) 427.

[118] Ashworth, above n 67, at 740.

[119] D Lewis, 'The Punishment that Leaves Something to Chance' (1980) 18 *Philosophy and Public Affairs* 53, 56.

than carry it out. Ohana goes even further in arguing against criminal punishment in favour of civil preventative measures:

> [I]n most cases of preparation, the culpability of the actor and the threat posed by his [or her] conduct to the legal interest concerned are not sufficiently intense to justify criminal punishment—even upon proof of a firm intention.[120]

Serving at least 15 years in prison under exceptionally harsh conditions for preparatory conduct, particularly where no intention to commit a terrorist offence need be proved, is insupportable.

VI. CONCLUSION

The conviction and sentence of Faheem Khalid Lodhi for preparatory terrorism offences have raised a number of issues as to the scope, elements of and punishment for such offences.

Preparatory offences extend the boundaries of criminal law beyond the law of inchoate crimes and can be questioned on the basis that they are based on inferences as to the dangerous disposition of the accused. The subjectivist approach to attempted crimes might be used to justify preparatory offences, but only if there is a clear intention to carry out the substantive crime. The Australian offences, at least, cannot be justified on this basis. It has been pointed out, however, that it is probably more appropriate to see preparatory offences as a separate species of offences that have developed in an ad hoc manner in response to policy concerns.

Given that the United Nations Security Council's Resolution 1373 requires Member States to criminalise the preparation of terrorist acts, it would be naïve to think that preparatory terrorism offences, or indeed preparatory offences in general will disappear. The punishment for such preparatory acts, however, must be questioned. In this regard, Whealy J's comments in sentencing Lodhi are particularly apt:

> [I]t seems to me that, no matter how much we deplore and disapprove of a particular offender, no matter how repulsive we may find his or her actions, we sacrifice our essential decency if we fail to treat him or her as a fellow human being.[121]

Keeping a person in solitary confinement for up to 15 years for preparatory conduct can certainly be viewed as sacrificing decency for the sake of being seen to be tough on terrorism.

120 Ohana, 'Responding to Acts' above n 1, at 24.
121 *R v Lodhi*, above n 13, at [86].

8

Social Science and Criminal Law Reform

Beyond Mere Opinion Polling and Penal Populism

MARK NOLAN*

I. INTRODUCTION

THIS CHAPTER EXPLORES the strengths and weaknesses of using empirical social science to guide criminal law reform debates. It is argued that using sound social science well will greatly assist decisions made about regulating and criminalising deviance, *especially* in the most difficult cases. The difficult cases discussed here include those where attempts are made to regulate extreme deviance such as sexual offending, political violence or terrorism, and crime in small, rural communities. Such regulatory decisions attract much public debate including expressions of urgency based on fears about unregulated deviance and fears about 'new' forms of criminal behaviour. Many chapters in this volume discuss how legal theory and criminal doctrine are used to justify regulatory choices. However, the aim of this chapter is to extend the analysis of influences upon regulatory choices to the data provided to law reformers by social scientists. The chapter describes both useful and less useful examples of how regulatory choices may be shaped by social science.

Examples of 'good' evidence-based law reform can be contrasted to examples where 'mere opinion polling' methodologies are used to measure public sentiment rather unscientifically and via quite abstract questioning that is devoid of important contextualising stimuli. Such empiricism is often atheoretical or based upon impoverished meta-theories of social attitudes and intergroup relations. Problematic empiricism is often also flawed in

* This research was funded by an Australian Research Council grant *Terrorism and the Non-State Actor After September 11: The Role of Law in the Search for Security* (DP0451473 awarded for 2004–2007): <http://law.anu.edu.au/terrorismlaw/>.

terms of the statistical methodologies employed to describe and evaluate the attitudinal trends surveyed. It is feared that the use of such 'mere opinion polling' in law reform debates facilitates penal populism.

The examples of social science discussed in this chapter include the surveying of issues relevant to debates about counter-terrorism law, criminal justice in rural areas, and the continuing detention of serious sex offenders following the expiration of their sentences. Examples of problematic 'mere opinion polling' are drawn from the work of social scientists as well as media organisations. Examples of better social scientific approaches that move beyond mere opinion polling are highlighted. These better approaches adopt more subtle and more sensitive research methodologies that can assist law reformers more as well as maintaining the reputation of social science in general.

II. THE SOCIAL SCIENTIST AND REFORM RESPONSIBILITY

The empirical social scientist, whether they be, say, a sociologist, criminologist, political scientist or social psychologist, bears significant responsibility as a participant in law reform debates. Use of dubious empirical methodologies must be avoided when the social scientist becomes a public intellectual attempting to service demand for the provision of empirical data.

However, it is important to note that there are a number of ways that a social scientist can contribute to criminal law reform debates. The role of the social scientist in such debates is not limited to being the *generator* of the empirical data. In addition to being the generator of empirical research, an important role for the social scientist is that of *science translator*: providing an accessible overview of a body of empirical literature relevant to a law reform debate. Psychologists, for example, who perform this role as interveners in United States Supreme Court cases are referred to as authors of *science translation amicus curiae briefs*.[1]

A recent Australian example of a science translation report is the literature review provided to the Sentencing Advisory Council of Victoria by criminologist Karen Gelb in January 2007.[2] This report appears instrumental in influencing a majority of the Council to recommend against the introduction of post-sentence, continuing detention orders for high-risk serious sex offenders. The Victorian law reform debate followed similar debates in the Australian Capital Territory which were informed by science translation

[1] MJ Saks, 'Improving APA Science Translation Amicus Briefs' (1993) 17 *Law and Human Behavior* 235.

[2] K Gelb, *Recidivism of Sex Offenders*, Research Paper (Melbourne, Sentencing Advisory Council of Victoria, 2007): <http://www.sentencingcouncil.vic.gov.au/wps/wcm/connect/Sentencing+Council/resources/file/eba90307f6f1f0f/Recidivism_Sex_Offenders_Research_Paper.pdf>.

reports of the empirical literature,[3] and the debates which resulted in the introduction of such legislative schemes in Queensland,[4] Western Australia[5] and New South Wales.[6] The constitutional validity of the Queensland scheme of preventative detention of sex offenders was upheld by a majority of the High Court of Australia even though a dissenting judgment by Justice Kirby made brief reference to some scholarly views on the unreliability of predicting the risk of recidivism for serious sex offenders.[7]

The Victorian proposal would allow, as in other states, the detention of offenders beyond the expiration of sentences; detention arguably justified by the risk of recidivism and the dangerousness of offenders post-release. As in other Australian states,[8] introducing such preventative detention orders in Victoria would be in addition to existing regimes of extended supervision orders for serious sex offenders post-release.[9] The impact of the Gelb report illustrates the importance of evidence-based discussion in such a controversial area of criminal law reform that divides both lay and expert legal commentators alike.

Empirical social scientists, as science translators as well as science generators, can best assist law reformers if they avoid facilitating penal populism. The remainder of this chapter focuses on the choices made by science generators who survey penal attitudes and community views on law reform initiatives. Social scientists avoid facilitating penal populism if their methodologies move beyond mere opinion polling: the simplistic measurement of general attitudes in response to uncontextualised 'distal stimuli'. A better approach is to rely on sensitive methodologies that measure social attitudes in response to contextualised and 'proximal stimuli', especially where the measurement of those attitudes is made in rich stimuli contexts reflecting the real attitudinal and social dilemmas relevant to a particular socio–legal problem.

Social scientists as public intellectuals should also be prepared to admit that many empirical questions posed by law reformers cannot be answered by some empirical methodologies such as simplistic measurements of general attitudes via abstract and uncontextualised questionnaire items. It is irresponsible of the social scientist to suggest that such data sets can answer all empirical questions. A professional social scientist should avoid encouraging penal populism in law reform debates for many

[3] D Biles, *Report Prepared for the ACT Government on Sentence and Release Option for High-Risk Sexual Offenders* (Canberra: ACT Department of Justice and Community Safety, 2005): <http://www.jcs.act.gov.au/eLibrary/OtherReports/Biles%20Report.pdf>.

[4] Dangerous Prisoners (Sexual Offenders) Act 2003 (Qld).

[5] Dangerous Sexual Offenders Act 2006 (WA).

[6] Crimes (Serious Sexual Offenders) Act 2006 (NSW).

[7] *Fardon v Attorney-General (Qld)* (2004) 223 CLR 575 (Kirby J at 623).

[8] For example, Crimes (Serious Sexual Offenders) Act 2006 (NSW), pt 2.

[9] Serious Sex Offenders Monitoring Act 2005 (Vic).

reasons, including the risk of diminishing the legitimacy of applied social science in the eyes of law reformers who may bypass social science as a controversial irrelevancy. Evidence-based law reform would then give way to a political process that is even less informed by systematic research and the review of existing empirical literatures. That result would endanger much interdisciplinary scholarship as well as the future of evidence-based law reform. It is an outcome to be avoided by any social scientist who enters a law reform debate. It is an outcome that can only be avoided by acknowledging the responsibility of the social scientist in a law reform debate *and* by adjusting the methodologies and reporting of social scientific research accordingly.

III. PENAL POPULISM

Both scholarly and media-sponsored use of 'mere opinion polling' has the potential to fuel penal populism. The definition of penal populism used here is that provided by Roberts, Stalans, Indermaur and Hough:

> [T]here are three essential elements to our definition of penal populism. Populist penal policies arise from one or more of the following:
>
> an excessive concern with the attractiveness of policies to the electorate;
> an intentional or negligent disregard for evidence of the effects of various criminal justice policies; [and]
> a tendency to make simplistic assumptions about the nature of public opinion, based upon inappropriate methods.
>
> Penal populism can therefore be contrasted with a more positive form of responsiveness to public attitudes, in which penal policies are developed that are consistent with (a) a careful reading of *informed* public opinion [emphasis added in original], (b) the results of systematic criminal justice research, and (c) well-established, consensual principles of sentencing, such as proportionality and restraint with respect to the use of imprisonment.[10]

These authors are not anti-social science. They do not believe that law reform should be done in a vacuum. Instead, these commentators endorse the view that law reform should follow consultation with the wider community. They claim that there is nothing wrong with 'attending to the informed views of the public [as that is] not the cause of the [penal populism] problem'.[11]

Importantly, they emphasise that public opinion polling or other social surveying must be conducted with an *informed* group of respondents and

[10] JV Roberts, LJ Stalans, D Indermaur, and M Hough, *Penal Populism and Public Opinion: Lessons From Five Countries* (Oxford, Oxford University Press, 2003) 8.
[11] Roberts, Stalans, Indermaur and Hough, above n 10, at 8.

designed consistently with sophisticated assumptions about the nature of social attitudes. Respondents to social surveys of criminal justice attitudes should be presented with stimuli and response items drafted to operate as truly informative *proximal* stimuli. This is explored further below.

Roberts, Stalans, Indermaur and Hough highlight the superficiality of many attempts to measure public opinion:

> Even when a more systematic approach to sounding the views of the community is taken, opinion can be canvassed in a superficial way. Our view is that penal populism involves the frequent misreading of public opinion with respect to crime and crime control strategies ... we argue that it is essential to listen to the views of a properly informed public. This consultation must be thorough and involves more than simply a question on a public opinion survey.[12]

Of course, sometimes providing 'questions on surveys' is the only feasible methodology to use for a particular project. However, in section IV, I endeavour to elaborate how methodological weaknesses can creep into and contaminate such research, facilitating penal populism. In doing so, I extend the fears held by Roberts, Stalans, Indermaur and Hough regarding uninformed polling and non-systematic research by identifying examples of mere opinion polling that demonstrate one or all of the following problems: distal attitude measurement, impoverished statistical analysis, impoverished meta-theory about social attitudes, and the co-option of survey participants. These weaknesses describe a form of data generation I have labelled with the pejorative 'mere opinion polling'.

IV. MERE OPINION POLLING

A. Distal Attitude Measurement

'Distal attitude measurement' is a term used here to describe the measurement of attitudes via responses to generalised and uncontextualised questionnaire items. It is the measurement of attitudes formed in response to a distal stimulus. For example, respondents could be asked to rate on a five-point Likert scale the extent to which they agreed with a list of statements (noting that some of these are reverse scored to prevent response biases). The following items are drawn from the work of Eric Lambert[13]:

> Terrorism is one of the most serious problems facing our society today.
> Terrorists deserve the same legal rights as everyone else.

[12] Roberts, Stalans, Indermaur and Hough, above n 10, at 8.

[13] EG Lambert, 'Views of Women and Men on Terrorism and the Punishment of Terrorists: A Preliminary Study among Midwestern College Students' (2003) 16(3) *Criminal Justice Studies* 217, 224–5.

Torturing captured terrorists for information is not acceptable.
I am willing to give up some freedoms to be safer from future terrorist attacks.
I have little fear about potential attacks by terrorists.
We need to make terrorists pay for their crimes.

Many, if not all, of these items are examples of what I would call distal stimuli or (over)generalised attitude items. There has been little effort to contextualise the use of the term 'terrorist' in these items and there is a lack of detail surrounding the target offending.

Criticising the nature of such stimulus items is important in light of the aims of the research undertaken. Lambert attempted to show, with a Mid-Western United States college sample, that differences existed between the penal ideologies of men and women.[14] He further investigated if any pattern of gender differences in penal ideology changed when the target of the attitude was someone suspected or convicted of terrorism.

In another paper co-written with other researchers, Lambert uses a similar methodology to investigate racial differences in penal ideology expressed about 'terrorists' by white and non-white US college students.[15] However, it can be queried whether the methodologies used are appropriate to the stated task of exposing penal ideology. It could be argued that the methodologies employed here produce results that in fact fuel penal populism.

In the gender differences study, participants rated their agreement with 11 statements about crime, punishment and the death penalty, then rated the 15 items relevant to terrorism, some of which are listed above.[16] Most of these 26 items were devoid of a contextualising scenario other than the minimal context provided within the text of a handful of the items. To be fair, at least four of the 25 items (two from the crime, punishment and death penalty response set and two from the punishment of terrorists response set) were better designed to include contextualising statements, and may have functioned more as proximal stimuli than other items used. Examples of items used in such studies that could be called proximal items are:

I will become angry if those responsible for the September 11, 2001 attacks are not sentenced to death.

Terrorists connected with the September 11, 2001, attacks should not be allowed to appeal their sentences, even if they are sentenced to death.[17]

[14] Lambert, above n 13.

[15] EG Lambert, LA Ventura, DE Hall, A Clarke, OO Elechi, DN Baker and M Jenkins, 'United We stand? Differences Between White and Non-white College Students in Their Views on Terrorism and Punishment of Terrorists' (2003) 1 *Journal of Ethnicity in Criminal Justice* 91.

[16] Lambert, above n 13.

[17] Lambert, above n 13, at 225.

Having praised the contextualisation of these items, it should be noted that the first two items in the list still ask participants very general questions about 'a crime' which detracts from the overall proximal nature of the stimulus item.

Lambert concluded, after analysing the ratings of his (distal) stimulus items, that men were more punitive towards (non-terrorism) offenders, though that gender gap narrowed when participants were asked about rights and punishments of terror suspects.[18] These data about attitudes towards terrorists suggested that women appeared more punitive than men in terms of being 'willing to give up freedoms to be safer from future terrorist attacks' and thinking that 'we need to make terrorists pay for their crimes'. These gender differences are explained in terms of another observed gender difference, that women in this sample feared potential terrorist attacks more than men; a conclusion drawn here despite the fact that causal modelling (for example regression modelling) was not conducted by the researcher. Despite the result that men as a group feared potential terrorist attacks less than women, men still appeared to be more willing to allow the United States Government 'to assassinate suspected terrorists in other countries'.

B. Problem of Impoverished Statistical Analysis

Avoiding statistical analyses able to model the claimed causal relationship weakens analyses in attitude measurement studies. In examples of poor survey analysis and reporting, tables of percentages or frequencies appear alongside graphs that can misrepresent non-significant differences and catch the attention of and impress the untrained eye. Differences between *descriptive statistics* (such as percentages, frequencies and mean responses) may often be asserted without detection of these differences via *inferential* statistical tests (for example t-tests, ANOVA, correlation, regression analyses). Such impoverished analyses are not sound social scientific practice. Even though Lambert, for example, used t-tests to detect significant differences between means,[19] it is unclear whether he used appropriately corrected t-tests (for example applying a Bonferroni correction) to minimise the false-positive rate when using multiple, separate t-tests over 26 items.

The problem of impoverished statistical analysis and reporting of attitudinal data prevails in the newspaper reporting of law and order opinion polling. Rarely are these sometimes impressively large opinion poll data sets subjected to sensitive inferential statistical testing that data sets of this size can sustain. Instead tables and graphs are often used to explain results at the level of descriptive statistics only. Arguably, when results as those

[18] Lambert, above n 13.
[19] *Ibid.*

in Figure 8.1 are clear enough at the level of descriptive statistics (here, percentages on pie charts), then inferential statistics may add little value, even if these tests are well explained by reporters who can translate the statistical jargon.

In addition to this example of counterterrorism opinion polling from an Australian newspaper polling agency (AC Nielsen) is the example of polls such as *The Terrorism Index 2007*.[20] The Second Bi-annual, Nonpartisan Survey of American Foreign Policy Experts from the Center for American Progress and Foreign Policy[21] presents simple bar graphs to represent what their panel of non-partisan foreign policy experts[22] opined about a very

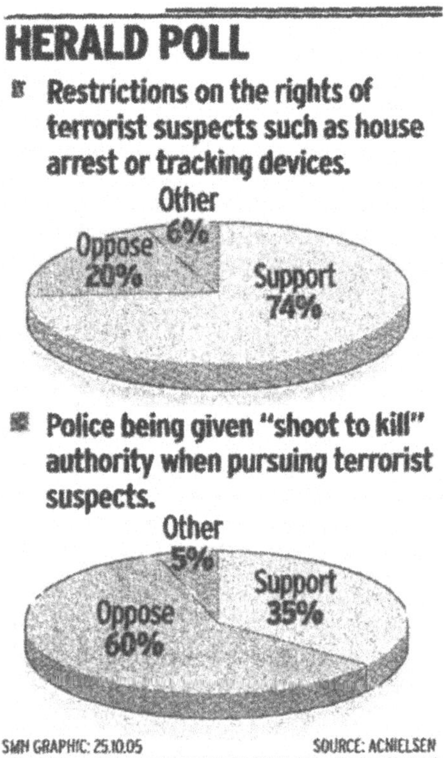

Figure 8.1: AC Nielsen Newspoll, The Sydney Morning Herald (25 October 2005).

20 <http://www.americanprogress.org/issues/2007/02/pdf/terrorism_index.pdf>.

21 <http://www.americanprogress.org/issues/2007/02/terrorism_index.html>.

22 *The Terrorism Index* Report, fn 22, suggests that: 'Eighty percent of the experts [surveyed] have served in the US Government—more than half in the executive branch, 26 percent in the military, and 18 percent in the intelligence community' (2).

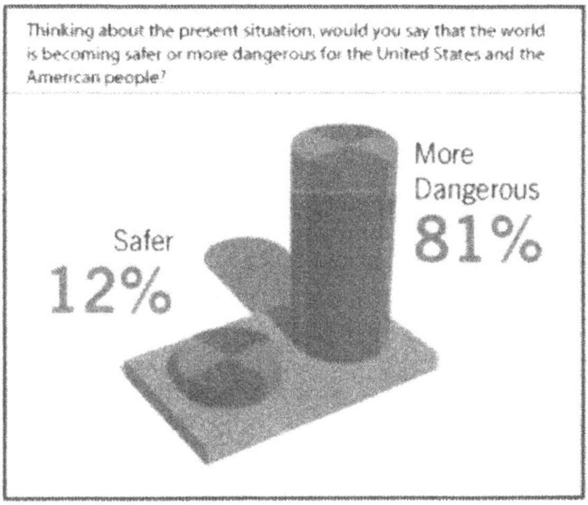

Figure 8.2: Extract from The Terrorism Index, Center for American Progress and Foreign Policy, 13 February 2007.

general question: 'Thinking about the present situation, would you say the world is becoming safer or more dangerous for the United States and the American People?'. (See Figure 8.2.)

The Terrorism Index, as a document that reports poll data, is a good example of how descriptive statistics (as percentages) are reported *without the use of inferential statistics of any form*. These simplistic comparisons are made between expert views and the views of the public on issues such as: 'Is the United States safer, about as safe, or less safe from terrorist attacks than before Sept. 11 2001?' Results on this further question are presented in the report as shown in Table 8.1[23]:

Table 8.1

	Safer	Same	Less Safe
Experts	12%	7%	81%
Public	43%	32%	25%

Even though these data patterns may be clear, the use of forced-choice questions and descriptive statistics is sadly typical of the level of sophistication of both design and data analysis commonly employed in mere opinion polls. Worse still may be the role played by the media organisation that deliberately provokes and recruits survey participants via 'co-opticons'.

[23] <http://www.americanprogress.org/issues/2007/02/terrorism_index.html> 8.

C. The Co-opticon

Mere opinion polling should not be used to guide law reform decisions in preference to using the results of well-designed, sensitive, social scientific data collection and analysis. This is especially so if that opinion poll data is collected in a way that 'co-opts' the respondent into voicing an opinion to a media provider in an atmosphere conducive to penal populism. As proximal and contextualised as the add-on poll alongside a news story may appear, the entire methodology is neither an adequate nor ethical example of social scientific practice, especially in terms of how participants are recruited.

Pamela Schulz has suggested in her discourse analysis of media messages about confidence in courts,[24] that media generally could be conceived in Foucauldian terms as a Benthamite 'panopticon'.[25] Media organisations are keen to make visible the faults within the justice system and keen to shape that system via technologies of social control aimed at, say, lenient judges or misbehaving police officers. However Schulz argues that in addition to this role of the media as panopticon, the media now use 'co-opticons' such as the 'Have Your Say' poll as a way of further involving their audience in news reporting.

Schulz provides an example where the readers of the *Adelaide Advertiser* were presented with a full-page questionnaire to complete on 13 January 2007.[26] Here the co-opticon is masquerading as an exercise in objective social scientific surveying, though mass circulation of such a survey tool is easily exploited by the penal populist. In the 2007 *Adelaide Advertiser* survey, some examples of the forced-choice ('yes', 'no', 'don't know') questions asked included:

> Should the identity of under-age offenders convicted of serious crimes remain suppressed?
> Do you think police use speed cameras too often for revenue raising?
> Should suspected firebugs be fitted with electronic wristlets to help monitor their movements?
> Do you support an immediate six-month licence disqualification for people who record a blood alcohol content of 0.08–0.149 and one year disqualification for 0.15 or more?
> Should suspected firebugs be subject to curfews on hot nights.[27]

[24] P Schulz, 'Rougher Than Usual Media Treatment: The Media, Politics and the Judiciary, a Discourse Analysis of Disrespect and Direction'. Paper presented to Confidence in the Courts Conference, 9–11 February, 2007, National Museum of Australia, <http://law.anu.edu.au/nissl/courts.htm> and <http://law.anu.edu.au/nissl/Schulz.pdf>.

[25] M Foucault, *Discipline and Punish: The Birth of the Prison* (London, Allen Lane, 1977) 125.

[26] <http://www.news.com.au/adelaidenow/pdf/finaljustice.pdf>: for other examples of regular 'co-opticons' in the form of blogs, see <http://blogs.smh.com.au/newsblog/> and in the form of polls see <http://www.news.com.au/dailytelegraph/yoursay>.

[27] <http://www.news.com.au/adelaidenow/pdf/finaljustice.pdf>.

Even though some of these questions provide context and some features of proximal stimuli, the epitome of a distal stimulus item, possibly presented to an uninformed participant, is the following question from the 2007 *Adelaide Advertiser* co-opticon: 'In general, do you think prisons rehabilitate offenders?'.[28]

Many media organisations do not even invest time and resources in distributing and analysing multi-item questionnaires such as the 2007 *Adelaide Advertiser*'s 'State of Justice' survey described above. Instead, media often invite their readers, listeners and viewers to contribute to quick (and nasty!) online polls. For example, on 29 May 2007, online readers of the 'Your Say' section of the *Daily Telegraph*[29] (an Australian tabloid newspaper), were asked the now familiar 'yes'/'no' style of forced-choice question common to mere opinion polls:

> Yes—Water is a serious problem. Cheats deserve punishment. OR
> No—While it's [water is] a serious issue, it's worse being a dobber.

These exemplify loaded and leading questions. The dynamic, online, reader/viewer/listener poll has many faults in addition to the poor question design outlined above. Chief amongst these faults are concerns over the lack of representativeness of these participant samples. This form of biased sampling via co-option relies on self-selected participation and may rarely be representative. Recruitment via co-opticon is quite impoverished methodologically when compared with the methodologies used by newspaper-sponsored, large-sample, cross-sectional, representative sampling techniques common to, say Morgan–Gallup-style polls as used in Australia. Co-opticons make even the less professional public opinion polls appear like exercises in advanced social science.

Such co-opticons may not expose non-intuitive findings and may not always lead to new insights into the attitude formation process. Instead, those people with strongly formed attitudes respond to invitations to express their views as answers to simple forced-choice questions that are then published as percentages in one of a plethora of 'Have Your Say Polls' results tables.

In section V, I explain how methodological strategies can be used to move beyond a mere opinion polling approach.

V. MOVING BEYOND MERE OPINION POLLING

One way to avoid penal populism and measure *informed* public opinion via systematic (criminal justice) research, as desired by Roberts, Stalans,

[28] Ibid.
[29] <http://www.news.com.au/dailytelegraph/yoursay>.

Indermaur and Hough,[30] is to focus on proximal attitude measurement rather than distal attitude measurement alone. Another strategy is to employ survey and experimental designs that are consistent with an appropriate meta-theory about the construction of social attitudes. Such a meta-theory would be based on the idea that the construction and articulation of a social attitude takes place in dynamic, intergroup contexts, connected to the history of law reform movements and social action. The balance of this chapter gives some examples of research that, arguably, achieve such aims.

A. Proximal Attitude Measurement

In 2005, researchers at the Australian National University (ANU) conducted an empirical, experimental study of social attitudes towards counter-terrorism law. These data were collected in the week in which the Council of Australian Governments (COAG) had a Special Meeting on Counter-Terrorism (on 27 September 2005) to decide how to enact a regime of control orders and preventative detention orders. The detailed results of that study are published elsewhere.[31] What is important for the present argument is that I distinguish the empirical approach taken in the ANU study to the methodological approach of Lambert and various co-opticons appearing in the media.

It would have been possible to ask the sample of 124 university students quite general questions about their fear of politically motivated crime and which of a set of investigatory and regulatory powers they endorsed. However, a richer approach was taken. Participants read proximal stimuli describing a food-tampering incident. Two independent variables (perpetrator motive and crime description by the police) were manipulated in a 2 x 2 between-participants, fully-factorial experiment: 2 (perpetrator motive: Jihadist, anti-corporate) x 2 (crime description by the police). This meant that different (proximal) stimuli were presented to each of four groups of participants and responses were compared between these experimental conditions.

In all of the four experimental conditions, participants read about a food-tampering incident in which the politically motivated food tampering affected a hamburger chain's food supplies, leading to the destruction of all unsold raw materials as a preventative measure. This experimental vignette, presented via written stimulus materials, stated that the hamburger chain

[30] Roberts, Stalans, Indermaur and Hough, above n 10.

[31] MA Nolan, 'Lay Perceptions of Terrorist Acts and Counter-terrorism Responses: Role of Motive, Offence Construal, Siege Mentality and Human Rights' in M Gani and P Mathew (eds), *Fresh Perspectives on the "War on Terror"* (Canberra, ANU ePress, 2008) 85–107.

had encouraged their customers with symptoms such as stomach cramps, nausea, vomiting and fainting to seek medical advice. The vignette continued to describe a situation in which hospital casualty wards and doctors' clinics were experiencing high demand and lengthy waiting times, leading to the establishment of incident-specific emergency medical hotlines.

In the 'Jihadist' motive conditions, an anonymous threat was made to the owners of the hamburger chain, suggesting that the company should not trust the safety of their food supplies as 'action has been taken so that infidels will be stopped in the name of Allah'. In the 'anti-corporate' experimental conditions, the anonymous threat explained the motive of the food tamperers as being to encourage customers to 'stop trusting the lies of multinational corporations who control our diets'. In addition to this operationalisation of the independent variable of perpetrator motive, the construal of the incident provided in a police statement was also expressed in one of two ways. In the 'exceptional crime' conditions the incident was explained by police to be an example of a new form of exceptional terrorism offending:

> This is a clear example of how the world has changed since 9/11. We must face this threat of terrorism head on and not bow to the terrorists responsible for these attacks. These actions are unjustified and deserve the full force of Australia's counter-terrorism law and policies in order to bring those responsible to justice. We have diverted all available resources to the investigation of these incidents and are working with counter-terrorism agencies to swiftly identify the culprits. Our investigation of this incident and our willingness to prosecute these terrorist acts will be evident to all.

In the 'standard crime' conditions, the differing proximal stimulus used was a police statement as follows:

> This is a clear example of how inappropriate political protest can endanger lives. From time to time we as a society have to manage such criminal acts in the best way we know how, according to long-standing norms of our criminal justice system. These actions are unjustified and deserve the full force of the criminal law in order to bring those responsible to justice. We will deploy the standard share of available resources proportionate to such events to swiftly identify the culprits. Our investigation of this incident and our willingness to prosecute these criminal acts must be evident to all.

One significant result from this designed experiment is of potential importance to understanding jury behaviour in criminal trials involving the prosecution of alleged terrorist act offences in Australia. Participants in this study were clearly not in favour of expanding a range of investigatory and regulatory powers if that expansion would be at odds with civil and political rights.

However, even these participants displayed significant differences in the perceived blameworthiness of each of these stated perpetrator motives. In particular, participants rated the 'Jihadist' motive for food tampering as more blameworthy than the 'anti-corporate' motive for the food tampering.[32] This was despite the fact that the majority of participants in this study did not seem to identify with these perpetrators as freedom fighters, since 68.9 per cent of the entire sample[33] described the food-tampering as a terrorist act. Such a result, obtained in the rich empirical milieu of a designed social psychological experiment using proximal stimulus materials, is intriguing. Such trends may affect liability judgments made by juries who must consider if the 'intention of advancing a political, religious or ideological cause'[34] can be proved beyond a reasonable doubt.

For the purposes of the current methodological argument developed in this chapter, other features of the proximal stimuli used in this study are noteworthy. Participants were asked to rate the extent to which they endorsed the use of each of 16 counter-terrorism measures *in response to the food-tampering incident presented.* Some of these measures were lawful at the time of the study, but some were being fiercely debated at the COAG meeting that week with much associated media discussion. Some powers presented in the study have subsequently been legislated into force. Participants were informed in the questionnaire, as they rated their support for such powers, whether the power was already given to investigative officers in some or all Australian jurisdictions, or whether the power to be rated was a proposed extension of existing powers. This was done to further inform participants about the nature of the counter-terrorism powers about which they were offering opinions.[35]

In addition to that example of informing the participants, both quantitative and qualitative data were collected and analysed. Quantitative data (ratings made on seven-point Likert scales) was analysed using the appropriate and protected inferential tests. A 2 x 2 between-participants ANOVA analysis was employed to detect statistically-significant mean differences. This statistical approach, and the use of open-ended response formats, compares favourably to the often misrepresentative nature of using graphs or figures to simply report percentage results from forced-choice question formats.

[32] $F(1,117) = 5.94$, $p < .05$, $\eta^2 = .05$; question asked was 'Rate the extent to which you agree (1 = strongly disagree, 4 = no opinion, 7 = strongly agree) that the motive you described above as held by the perpetrator(s) of the food-tampering incident is the most important factor in judging the blameworthiness of the act'.

[33] Jihadist conditions: 71.7%, anti-corporate conditions: 66.7%.

[34] Criminal Code (Cth), s 101.1(1), definition of a 'terrorist act'.

[35] It is interesting to note that this sample of participants, with no differences across conditions, did not support the measures (combined measure: $\alpha = 87$, entire sample: mean = 3.00 ($sd = .97$), on 7 point Likert scale anchored as 1 = strongly disagree, 4 = no opinion and 7 = strongly agree; no significant main effects or interaction on a 2 x 2 ANOVA.

B. An Appropriate Meta-theory of Social Attitudes

Methodologies employed by social scientists and pollsters reflect their underlying meta-theory about what social attitudes are and how social attitudes are constructed and expressed. If a mere opinion polling approach is used, a researcher endorses a simplistic meta-theory of attitudes, attitude construction and attitude expression. Opinion pollsters are asserting implicitly that generalised questionnaire items are sensitive ways to measure social attitudes. These social scientists seem to be assuming that social attitudes are fixed value statements that are immutable and impervious to the social context within which particular alleged crimes and the consequences of particular legal responses to those crimes are discussed. Believing that social beliefs about crime are rather asocial value statements retrieved from memory as needed, is an impoverished view of the dynamism of public opinion formation and the construction of lay responses to the legal regulation. Using methodologies that imply inappropriate meta-theories about attitudes is especially problematic when attempts are made to measure attitudes about crimes as complex as terrorist acts and terrorist organisation offences.

In the brief descriptions of the two projects below, I suggest that the methodologies employed are subtle enough to expose non-intuitive results. I suggest that underlying the methodologies of both of the following studies conducted in Australia are two qualities. First, there is a desire to extend well beyond mere opinion polling in the measurement of social attitudes. Second, social attitudes are conceptualised and measured in response to proximal stimuli as salient social constructions shaped by intergroup comparisons and historical understandings.

i. Human Rights Attitude Studies

In 2003, I conducted a suite of five studies investigating lay perceptions of human rights law and the political efficacy of using human rights arguments.[36] These studies used detailed proximal stimuli regarding social issues, most of which were salient political debates in Australia at the time of data collection. The issues investigated in each study were: potential violations of privacy rights due to use of neighbourhood CCTV security cameras (Study 1); civil and political rights of indigenous Australians under mandatory sentencing schemes (Study 2); privacy rights of students in comparison with public servants (Study 3); refugee rights (Study 4); and reproductive rights of lesbians

[36] M Nolan, 'Construals of Human Rights Law: Protecting Subgroups As Well As Individual Humans' (PhD thesis Australian National University 2003) <http://thesis.anu.edu.au/public/adt-ANU20050324.155005/index.html>; see also M Nolan and P Oakes, 'Human Rights Concepts in Australian Political Debate' in TD Campbell, J Goldsworthy and A Stone (eds), *Protecting Human Rights: Instruments and Institutions* (Oxford, Oxford University Press, 2003).

and single women in comparison with married women and women in de facto relationships (Study 5). Participants in these studies evaluated the appropriateness of appealing to human rights arguments as responses to perceived injustice sometimes presented in the context of law reform debates (Studies 2, 4 and 5). The meta-theory of social attitudes used in this work is consistent with a social identity theory approach to intergroup relations and the dynamic construction of ingroup and outgroup stereotypes and attitudes.[37]

Study 5 was conducted during robust public and parliamentary debate over the Federal Government's plans to amend the Sex Discrimination Act 1984 (Cth). The amendments would have allowed discrimination on the ground of marital status (in particular, discrimination against single women and lesbians) in the field of providing artificial reproductive technologies. The particular non-intuitive result produced by the methodology employed in Study 5 was that the majority of women's rights activists surveyed did not wish to use human rights arguments that simply promoted their identities and interests as lesbians and single women. Instead, in response to proximal stimuli (a mock speech to political allies *and* political opponents), the women's rights advocates preferred campaigning using inclusive privacy rights and rights to health, rather than sexuality rights and reproductive rights per se. If simplistic distal stimuli were used here in an attempt to merely poll the opinion of women's rights advocates in the abstract, I doubt that such subtle political strategies would have been revealed. The precise way in which the intergroup context (the persuasion and political mobilisation of historical allies and opponents) constrained responses would have been more difficult to detect via responses to distal stimuli.

ii. Rural Attitudes Towards Crime

In 2006, Hogg and Carrington documented the results of field interviews of professionals and community members in six New South Wales towns in rural Australia.[38] Rather than simply using a co-opticon published in the local newspapers, the research team took 40 field trips over 230 dedicated research days in which they conducted 210 semi-structured interviews with a cross-section of members from each rural population.[39]

[37] H Tajfel and JC Turner, 'An Integrative Theory of Intergroup Conflict' in WG Austin and S Worchel (eds), *The Social Psychology of Intergroup Relations* (Monterey, CA, Brooks/Cole, 1979); JC Turner and K Reynolds, 'The Social Identity Perspective in Intergroup Relations: Theories, Themes and Controversies' in RJ Brown and S Gaertner (eds), *Blackwell Handbook of Social Psychology: Intergroup Processes* (Oxford, Blackwell, 2001); JC Turner, MA Hogg, PJ Oakes, S Reicher and M Wetherell, *Rediscovering the Social Group* (Oxford, Basil Blackwell, 1987).

[38] R Hogg and K Carrington, *Policing the Rural Crisis* (Annandale, The Federation Press, 2006).

[39] Hogg and Carrington, above n 38, at 201.

The researchers present an objective snapshot of offending rates in the rural areas studied by reanalysing crime rate data from the New South Wales Bureau of Crime Statistics and Research (BOCSAR) and disaggregating those data by Local Government Area and population size. This provided the researchers with a realistic and objective picture of offence prevalence by specific rural area over a range of offence types including violent crimes, property crimes, drug crimes, public order offences, crimes against justice and driving crimes.[40]

This systematic approach to (re-)describing available crime rate data then helped researchers contextualise interview questions where they aimed to expose penal attitudes held by a cross-section of the local rural communities. Many resultant opinions were ripe for exploitation by the penal populist as they were often greatly at odds with crime rate data. It is doubtful whether the insights reported in this work could have been produced if a mere opinion polling approach was used by these researchers. Mere opinion polling may help describe attitudes held about offending and offenders. It may help expose the attitudes held consistent with the identity-based perspective of the members of the study communities. However, that was not the sole aim of the research.

For example, it was intriguing for these researchers to analyse the subjective perceptions of rural community members especially when the researchers knew that participants believed (erroneously) that public order crimes or property offences committed by indigenous Australians posed the greatest threat to law and order. Hogg and Carrington's systematic approach allows an understanding of *both* the nature of reported public opinion *and* the comparison of that public opinion with the crime rate data analysed by community group and population size.

Hogg and Carrington observed that the rate of public order offending *is* higher in rural communities than in the cities.[41] However, even greater is the over-representation of driving offences and violent crimes when compared to offence rates in urban centres. Moving beyond mere opinion polling here, and exploiting the power of systematic triangulation,[42] allowed the researchers to compare the measured public opinion to objective prevalence rate data for specific rural communities. Such comparisons are surely the form of systematic criminological research that Roberts, Stalans, Indermaur and Hough would endorse.[43] Hogg and Carrington's approach first exposes public opinion but, secondly, also allows those attitudinal trends to be analysed and contextualised in ways most relevant to the local law reform debates in these rural areas. When less appropriate and more populist methodologies

[40] Hogg and Carrington, above n 38, at 66–78.
[41] Hogg and Carrington, above n 38, at 69.
[42] Hogg and Carrington, above n 38, at 201.
[43] Roberts, Stalans, Indermaur and Hough, above n 10.

are used, it may be too easy to represent the Australian rural law and order 'crisis' as a 'crisis' of public order or property offending alone. Such a populist view is presented in many news headlines in rural communities.[44]

The comparisons of subjective beliefs to objective crime trends demonstrated that the real challenges in rural communities may lie in regulating driving offences, gun use, family violence, violence between the genders, and violence within *both* indigenous and non-indigenous rural communities.

The sociological reasons why public opinion is so inconsistent with objective criminological data are relevant questions for law reformers. The nuanced answers to these questions shift debate beyond the more populist agenda of simply documenting and responding to subjective public opinion alone. As Hogg and Carrington argue, public outrage and statements describing the Australian rural law and order 'crisis' will mislead law reformers if that law and order crisis is defined by concerns over property and public order offending per se.[45] Why that erroneous perception occurs is the most relevant sociological question to ask about attitudes and attitude formation in these communities.

VI. CONCLUSION

Much of the mere opinion polling described in this chapter fuels penal populism as defined by Roberts, Stalans, Indermaur and Hough.[46] It is imperative that social scientists contribute to debates about regulating deviance and criminal law reform by avoiding penal populism. This can be done by avoiding:

— methodologies employing distal stimuli only;
— statistically-inappropriate analyses and misleading data presentation; and
— data analysis that utilises only descriptive instead of descriptive and inferential statistical techniques.

Mere opinion polling should be exposed as a socially dangerous methodology that sometimes masquerades as systematic measurement of informed public opinion and the context-dependent expression of socially constructed attitudes. Mere opinion polling uses an inadequate meta-theory of social attitudes to fan the flames of populist hysteria and, in turn, discredits social science in the eyes of law reformers.

[44] A Green, 'Crime War' in *The Macleay Argus*, (11 May 2007) 1 and 5.
[45] Hogg and Carrington, above n 38, at 117; 188–92.
[46] Roberts, Stalans, Indermaur and Hough, above n 10.

Part IV

The Scope and Justification of Sexual Offences

9

Criminal Law and Private Spaces
Regulating Homosexual Acts in Singapore

KUMARALINGAM AMIRTHALINGAM

I. INTRODUCTION

THE NORMALLY STAID landscape of socio-political and legal discourse in Singapore witnessed an upheaval toward the end of 2006 after the possibility of decriminalisation of homosexual acts was flagged as part of broader criminal law reform.[1] The issue engendered an open political debate based on ideology and rights, not often seen, or encouraged, in Singapore. It was also reflective of some of the broader themes affecting criminal law in various parts of the world, as criminal law is increasingly used as a political tool to regulate and penalise behaviour that is deemed deviant or anti-social. It brought to the fore the dangers of politicising the criminal law, with the consequent risk of discrimination against particular minority groups in the community. The debate also polarised society in Singapore, and at a broader level was characterised by an '*anti*-rights discourse deployed by *conservative* social forces'[2] on the one hand, and a pro-rights discourse deployed by liberal social forces on the other.[3]

This chapter examines the debate in Singapore and argues that decriminalisation is warranted on legal, social and political grounds. The first part sets out the legal background and social context of the debate before briefly outlining the arguments made against decriminalisation. The second part analyses the legitimacy of the existing law criminalising homosexual acts from two perspectives: constitutional law and criminal law.[4] The chapter does not aim to critique existing constitutional and criminal law theories and doctrine; rather, it aims to ensure that these theories and doctrines are fully engaged in the

[1] S Lum, 'Law on "Unnatural" Sex Acts to be Repealed', *Straits Times* (9 November 2006).

[2] D Herman, '(Il)legitimate Minorities: The American Christian Right's Anti-Gay-Rights Discourse' (1996) 23 *Journal of Law and Society* 346, 347.

[3] It has also revived the debate on the role of religion in secular democracies. See, Mooi Hung Chua, 'Is there a Place for God in Public Morals Debate?' *Straits Times* (18 May 2007).

[4] See, DAJ Richards, *Sex, Drugs, Death, and the Law: An Essay on Human Rights and Overcriminalization* (New Jersey, Rowman & Littlefield, 1982).

discourse on homosexual acts and the criminal law. The third part examines some of the factual and empirical claims used to justify criminalisation.

II. HOMOSEXUAL ACTS AND THE CRIMINAL LAW IN SINGAPORE

It may be helpful to briefly set out the background and context of the criminal law of homosexual acts in Singapore.[5] The two key provisions in the Penal Code relevant to homosexual acts are ss 377 and 377A, which respectively criminalise carnal intercourse against the order of nature with any man, woman or animal;[6] and gross indecency between males. In addition, homosexual behaviour is sometimes prosecuted under the Penal Code, s 354 (outrage of modesty)[7] and the Miscellaneous Offences (Public Order and Nuisance) Act, s 19 (loitering or soliciting in public places for immoral purposes).[8] For convenience, ss 377 and 377A are set out in full below:

> **Unnatural offences**
> 377—Whoever voluntarily has carnal intercourse against the order of nature with any man, woman or animals, shall be punished with imprisonment for life, or with imprisonment for a term which may extend to 10 years, and shall also be liable to fine.
>
> **Explanation**
> Penetration is sufficient to constitute the carnal intercourse necessary to the offence described in this section.
>
> **Outrages on decency**
> **377A**—Any male person who, in public or private, commits, or abets the commission of, or procures or attempts to procure the commission by any male person of, any act of gross indecency with another male person, shall be punished with imprisonment for a term which may extend to 2 years.

[5] For further reading, see LJ Chua, 'Saying No: Sections 377 and 377A of the Penal Code' [2003] *Singapore Journal of Legal Studies* 209; JL Tsien-Ta, 'Equal Protection and Sexual Orientation' (1995) 16 *Singapore Law Review* 228; D Chan, 'Oral Sex—A Case of Criminality or Morality? (2004, September) *Singapore Law Gazette* 15.

[6] Carnal intercourse against the order of nature is not defined in the Singapore Penal Code. The Malaysian Penal Code s 377A, by an amendment in 1989, defined it as the insertion of the penis into the anus or mouth of another person. Indian and Singaporean cases suggest that it should include anal and oral sex. For an analysis of the jurisprudence on the *actus reus* of s 377, see Chua above n 5, at 217–21.

[7] Penal Code, s 354—Whoever assaults or uses criminal force to any person, intending to outrage or knowing it to be likely that he will thereby outrage the modesty of that person, shall be punished with imprisonment for a term which may extend to 2 years, or with fine, or with caning, or with any two of such punishments.

[8] Miscellaneous Offences (Public Order and Nuisance) Act, s 19—Every person who in any public road or public place persistently loiters or solicits for the purpose of prostitution or for any other immoral purpose shall be guilty of an offence and shall be liable on conviction to a fine not exceeding $1,000 and, in the case of a second or subsequent conviction, to a fine not exceeding $2,000 or to imprisonment for a term not exceeding 6 months or to both.

These provisions were introduced in various British colonies by way of codification: the British enacted criminal codes in many of their colonies, beginning with the Indian Penal Code. The Indian Penal Code was enacted in 1861 and the Penal Code of the Straits Settlements (later to be split into the Malaysian Penal Code and the Singapore Penal Code) was enacted in 1871. Section 377A was introduced into the Straits Settlements Code in 1938, and was based on s 11 of the Criminal Law Amendment Act 1885.[9] Following the Wolfenden Report,[10] England and Wales decriminalised consensual homosexual acts in 1967,[11] with Scotland and Ireland following suit in 1980 and 1982 respectively,[12] leaving British colonies to live with this legacy.[13] That criminalisation of homosexual acts in the colonies is a British legacy is underscored by the fact that Indonesia, the world's largest Muslim country and former Dutch colony, does not have state laws criminalising homosexual acts, even though Islam prohibits homosexuality.

A. Official Policy and Public Attitude

There has been a marked shift in official policy and public attitudes towards homosexuality in Singapore over the last three decades.[14] The 1980s saw a relatively liberal period when gay bars and entertainment venues were established. The latter part of this period also coincided with global publicity of the AIDS virus, which was associated with homosexuality. This AIDS theme is a recurring one in this chapter, largely because it is the strongest 'fear factor' raised by opponents of decriminalisation. The fear of AIDS led to greater scrutiny of homosexual behaviour, and in the early 1990s, there were several

[9] The history of this law in England shows that it was introduced without proper debate under the umbrella of parliamentary reforms to protect women and girls in the context of the suppression of prostitution and related vice. See FB Smith, 'Labouchere's Amendment to the Criminal Law Amendment Bill' in WR Dynes and S Donaldson (eds), *Homosexuality, Discrimination, Criminology and the Law* (New York, Garland Publishing Inc, 1992) 537.

[10] England and Wales, *Report of the Committee on Homosexual Offences and Prostitution* (London, Home Office and Scottish Home Department, 1957).

[11] Sexual Offences Act 1967 (UK).

[12] Criminal Justice (Scotland) Act 1980; Homosexual Offences (Northern Ireland) Order 1982. The Irish legislation was introducing after a successful human rights challenge: *Dudgeon v United Kingdom* (1981) 4 EHRR 149.

[13] Several leading Indian public figures, including intellectuals, artists and activists, in an open letter to the Indian Government called for the repeal of s 377 of the Indian Penal Code on human rights grounds, stating 'That is why we, concerned Indian citizens and people of Indian origin, support the overturning of Section 377 of the Indian Penal Code, a colonial-era law dating to 1861, which punitively criminalizes romantic love and private, consensual sexual acts between adults of the same sex.' The full text of the letter and its signatories are available online: <http://www.openletter377.com/>.

[14] See RHK Heng, 'Tiptoe Out of the Closet: The Before and After of the Increasingly Visible Gay Community in Singapore' (2001) 40 *Journal of Homosexuality* 81.

police operations targeted at gay men.[15] Prosecutions were generally brought under the Miscellaneous Offences (Public Order and Nuisance) Act, s19, or the Penal Code, s 354, which included caning as one of its punishments.

From the latter part of the 1990s onwards, there was a discernible shift in official policy and rhetoric, demonstrating greater tolerance of gay and lesbian people. As Singapore's economy opened up to creative industry, attraction of gay and lesbian professionals and the 'pink dollar' became more important. The Government entered the 21st century with a more liberal attitude, allowing gay and lesbian themed events and a buzzing night life aimed at the gay and lesbian market. Singapore's first Prime Minister (now Minister Mentor), Mr Lee Kuan Yew, during an interview with CNN International in 1998, responding to a question by a gay Singaporean on the future of gay people in Singapore, stated that while social acceptability of homosexuality was something he had no control over, as far as the Government was concerned, its policy was not to actively prosecute homosexuals.[16] In 2003, Singapore's second Prime Minister (now Senior Minister), Mr Goh Chok Tong, in an interview with *Time* magazine, stated that the Government had been employing gay people in public service and no longer discriminated against them.[17] Two years later, the incumbent Prime Minister, Mr Lee Hsein Loong added to this trend, stating that he agreed with Senior Minister Goh Chok Tong's statement that gay people 'are people like you and me'.[18]

Towards the end of 2006, the Government proposed reforms to the Penal Code and the question of decriminalising homosexual acts resurfaced. At the end of March 2007, the Law Society of Singapore in its report to the Government on the proposed amendments to the Penal Code threw down the gauntlet when it categorically stated:

> The majority of Council considered that the retention of section 377A in its present form cannot be justified. This does not entail any view that homosexuality is morally acceptable, but follows instead from the separation of law and morals and the philosophy that the criminal law's proper function is to protect others from harm by punishing harmful conduct. Private consensual homosexual conduct between adults does not cause harm recognisable by the criminal law. Thus, regardless of one's personal view of the morality or otherwise of such conduct, it should not be made a criminal offence.[19]

[15] Police officers, posing as gay men, would go to areas known for gay cruising and entrap gay men by pretending to be interested in sexual activity. See media reports: '12 Men Nabbed in Anti-gay Operation at Tanjong Rhu' *The Straits Times* (23 November 1993); 'Three Men Molested Undercover Policemen' *Straits Times* (3 July 1991); 'Seven Men Fined $500 each for Soliciting in Public' *Straits Times* (10 April 1990).

[16] *Sunday Times* (London 13 December 1998).

[17] DC Price, 'It's In to be Out' *TIME*, 10 August 2003: <http://www.time.com/time/magazine/article/0,9171,474512,00.html>. The interview itself took place on 5 February 2003.

[18] PS Huei, 'Fear homosexuals? No, "Govt sensitive to others too"' *Straits Times* (7 October 2005).

[19] See extract of the report in *Law Gazette* (Singapore: Law Society of Singapore, May 2007) 11.

Three weeks after the Law Society's report, Minister Mentor Lee Kuan Yee opened the proverbial Pandora's box by alluding to the eventuality of decriminalisation.

> You take this business of homosexuality. It raises tempers all over the world, and even in America. If in fact it is true—and I have asked doctors this—that you are genetically born a homosexual because that's the nature of the genetic random transmission of genes, you can't help it. *So why should we criminalise it?* But there's such a strong inhibition in all societies—Christianity, Islam, even the Hindu, Chinese societies, and we are now confronted with a persisting aberration. But is it an aberration? It's a genetic variation. So what do we do? I think we pragmatically adjust, carry our people. Don't upset them and suddenly upset their sense of propriety and right and wrong. But at the same time let's not go around like the moral police do in Malaysia, barging into people's rooms and say 'khalwat'. That's not our business. *So you have to take a practical, pragmatic approach to what I see is an inevitable force of time and circumstance* (emphasis added).[20]

This statement triggered an unprecedented public debate in the media as proponents and opponents of change expressed their views, sometimes with considerable vitriol. What has caused panic amongst those supporting the status quo is the Government's recognition that for pragmatic reasons decriminalisation of homosexual acts may be the way to go, and in Singapore politics, pragmatism has generally led the way.

B. The Proposed Reform

One of the proposals in the Penal Code Amendment Bill is to repeal the existing s 377 and replace it with a new s 377, which would deal with the sexual penetration of corpses. Under the proposals, the offence of bestiality in the present s 377 would be moved to a new s 377B and s 377A would be retained, which would leave an unfortunate legislative structure placing homosexual acts between the crimes of necrophilia and bestiality. The purpose of this proposed restructuring is to decriminalise anal and oral sex between consenting heterosexuals, as there has been considerable general public disquiet at the criminalisation of such acts.[21] The complete disjunct between s 377 and contemporary sexual mores was embarrassingly highlighted

[20] This statement was made in response to a question during a meeting with the youth wing of the governing People's Action Party. See Z Hussain, 'Homosexuality: Govt Not Moral Police but it's Mindful of People's Concerns', *Straits Times* (23 April 2007).

[21] In November 2003, a man was sentenced to jail for having oral sex with a young girl: *Annis bin Abdullah v PP* [2003] SGDC 290. In January 2004, following a series of letters and op-ed pieces in the press, lambasting the decision and the archaic law, it was announced that Parliament was considering repealing s 377 of the Penal Code. The letters and comments are archived online at the Yawning Bread website: <http://www.yawningbread.org/arch_2004/yax-348.htm>.

in a decision where a judge, in trying to acknowledge social realities without totally ignoring s 377, held that oral sex between consenting adults would not be a crime only if it were a prelude to natural intercourse![22]

It is interesting that the Bill itself did not propose dealing with s 377A. Rather, the shifting attitudes in Singapore, recent court decisions, public debate, and significantly, the Law Society's support for decriminalisation, have all put s 377A on the reform agenda. Before proceeding further, a brief observation is necessary about the interplay between s 377 and s 377A and why they should be considered together in any proposed reform. The history of s 377 and s 377A shows that the two provisions, while enacted separately, are not independent of each other and in fact are complementary elements of a framework designed to deal with certain forms of sexual conduct. The 'unnatural offences' in s 377 were limited to the more serious offences of penetration of the anus or mouth, while s 377A criminalised less serious acts of 'gross indecency' between males that fell outside s 377.[23]

Practical problems arise when s 377 is repealed, but s 377A is retained: based on ordinary principles of statutory interpretation it can be argued that s 377A does not include the acts in s 377, namely, anal and oral sex.[24] This raises the possibility that anal and oral sex between consenting males may be left unregulated under the reform proposals. Based on established principles of legality and the maxim *nulla crimen sine lege*, it is arguably impermissible to reinterpret s 377A to include what was not originally there, as this would result in the judicial creation, or extension, of a crime, contrary to the apparent intention of Parliament.[25] If such an interpretation of s 377A were attempted, it may be necessary to reconcile this with Art 11 of the Singapore Constitution, which enshrines the principle of legality in criminal matters.[26]

[22] *PP v Tan Kuan Meng* [1996] SGHC 16 (unreported decision, Lai Kew Chai J, CC No 62 of 1994 (HC), 30 January 1996); *PP v Kwan Kwong Weng* [1997] 1 SLR 697.

[23] This was made clear during the enactment of s 377A in 1938: 'The reason for the addition [of s 377A], as stated in the Proceedings of the Legislative Council of the Straits Settlements in 1938 was to "[make] punishable acts of gross indecency between male persons which do not amount to an unnatural offence within the meaning of section 377 of the Code."' See Tsen-Ta, above n 5, quoting from the Straits Settlements Legislative Council Proceeding of 25 April 1938.

[24] Tsen-Ta, above n 5.

[25] There is old authority, now largely discredited, for the proposition that courts may create common law offences to criminalise public disorder/morality offences: *Shaw v DPP* [1962] AC 220; *Knuller (Publishing & Printing Promotions) Ltd v DPP* [1973] AC 435. However, these authorities are irrelevant to Singapore, which has a Penal Code. The High Court of Australia has reaffirmed that courts 'are no longer able to create criminal offences': *R v Rogerson* (1992) 174 CLR 268 at 305 (McHugh J).

[26] Art 11(1) provides: 'No person shall be punished for an act or omission which was not punishable by law when it was done or made, and no person shall suffer greater punishment for an offence than was prescribed by law at the time it was committed.' In the case of *PP v Manogaran s/o R Ramu* [1997] 1 SLR 22, the court held that its overruling of a former authority on the interpretation of a particular provision relating to a drug offence had the result of

III. TESTING THE LEGITIMACY OF S 377A

This part of the chapter examines whether s 377A should be retained, based on an analysis of constitutional law and criminal law. In undertaking this analysis, the relevant factual and empirical arguments will be examined; as has been shown in the context of other criminal law debates, it is critical that the analysis be firmly grounded in the existing realities.[27]

A. Constitutional Law

The primary function of a written Constitution in democratic states, as part of the principle of constitutionalism, is to protect its citizens from arbitrary exercise of power by the Executive.[28] Constitutions do this mainly by prescribing the powers that the different arms of Government may legitimately exercise, and in some instances, by providing a chapter guaranteeing certain fundamental rights and liberties of its citizens. The relevance of constitutional law to criminalisation is readily apparent: the Legislature cannot enact or retain a criminal law that violates its Constitution and the Executive cannot enforce a law in a manner that offends the Constitution. There have been several successful constitutional challenges to laws criminalising homosexual acts around the world, including in the European Court of Human Rights,[29] the United Nations Human Rights Committee,[30] the United States Supreme Court,[31] the South African Constitutional

extending the law. Therefore, the court held that its decision could only have prospective effect to avoid violating Art 11. Yong Pung How CJ stated: 'In our opinion, where Art 11(1) and the ***nullum*** principle are brought into operation, the courts are precluded from retrospectively reversing a previous interpretation of a criminal statutory provision where the new interpretation creates criminal liability for the first time, and where it would operate to the prejudice of an accused. The same prohibition against retrospective overruling must apply equally where the new interpretation represents a reversal of the law as previously interpreted and effectively extends criminal liability.' (at 36).

27 Ashworth has made this point in the context of the drugs debate: A Ashworth, *Principles of Criminal Law* (Oxford, Oxford University Press, 5th edn, 2006) 53–4.

28 The written constitution is part of the bigger idea of constitutionalism, which includes the written text, constitutional conventions and political tradition. The United Kingdom, for example, has no written constitution but clearly embraces the idea of constitutionalism. See AW Bradley and KD Ewing, *Constitutional and Administrative Law* (Harlow, Pearson Education Ltd, 13th edn, 2003) ch 2.

29 *Dudgeon v United Kingdom* (1982) 4 EHHR 149; *Norris v Republic of Ireland* (1991) 13 EHRR 186; *Modinos v Cyprus* (1993) 259 ECHR (ser A) 1; *L & V v Austria* [2003] ECHR 20.

30 *Toonen v Australia* Communication Number 488/1992 (31 March 1994) UN Human Rights Committee Document No CCR/C/50/D/488/1992.

31 *Lawrence v Texas* 539 US 558 (2003). A majority of five judges overruled *Bowers v Hardwick* 478 US 186 (1986). A sixth judge (O'Connor J, who was a member of the *Bower's* majority) concurred with the majority but refused to overrule *Bowers*. Three judges dissented in *Lawrence*.

Court[32] and the Hong Kong Court of Appeal.[33] Many other legislatures have removed such offences without legal challenge in order to comply with basic human rights and constitutional obligations.

The Singapore Constitution has a chapter on Fundamental Liberties which guarantees certain rights, including protection of life and liberty (Art 9), protection of equality (Art 12) and protection of the freedom of speech, assembly and association (Art 14). As with many other constitutions, it does not have an express right to privacy, unlike the European Convention on Human Rights (Art 8) or the South African Constitution (s 14). Nevertheless, it may be argued that this right to privacy, or at least, interest in privacy, has been tacitly recognised by Singapore courts and legislators.[34] Most of the constitutional challenges to homosexual laws have been on the grounds of violation of the protected rights of equality and/or privacy.

There may be a difference between a constitutional challenge on the basis of equality and one on the basis of privacy. A successful equality challenge is viewed as empowering, as it means that the individual's interest is vindicated: the individual is equal to his or her peers and has equal protection of the law. A privacy challenge on the other hand may be viewed as a concession, as it means that the individual's interest is merely tolerated: outside the protected zone of privacy, the individual remains vulnerable, unlike his or her peers. To borrow an expression from the doctrine of promissory estoppel in equity, equality can act both as a sword and a shield, whereas privacy acts mainly as a shield. There is considerable literature on whether there is a difference between equality and privacy arguments, especially with respect to civil rights of gay and lesbian people.[35] This chapter focuses on the much narrower question of decriminalisation and takes the view that the issue of gay and lesbian civil rights is a separate matter that should not be confused with the altogether different question of criminalisation, especially when minority or vulnerable groups are targeted.[36]

[32] *National Coalition for Gay and Lesbian Equality and another v Minister of Justice and Others* (1999) 1 SA 6.

[33] *Leung TC Williams Roy v Secretary for Justice* [2006] HKCA 106. Note that Hong Kong decriminalised homosexual acts in 1992. This case concerned equality in terms of the age of consent. See also *Secretary for Justice v Yau Yuk Lung Zigo & Lee Kam Chuen* [2007] HKCFA 49 on equality for sexual acts in public.

[34] See text at nn 68–71.

[35] See, for example, LC Backer, 'Exposing the Perversions of Toleration: The Decriminalisation of Private Sexual Conduct, the Model Penal Code, and the Oxymoron of Liberal Toleration' (1993) 45 *Florida Law Review* 755; S Bedi, 'Repudiating Morals Legislation: Rendering the Constitutional Right to Privacy Obsolete' (2005–2006) 53 *Cleveland Law Review* 447; S Katyal, 'Sexuality and Sovereignty: The Global Limits and Possibilities of Lawrence' (2006) 14 *William and Mary Bill of Rights Law Journal* 1429. JH Wilkinson III, 'Gay Rights and American Constitutionalism: What's a Constitution For?' (2006) 56 *Duke Law Journal* 544.

[36] Anti-gay groups maintain that decriminalisation is merely the top of a slippery slope which leads inevitably to gay marriages and other civil rights claims. While history shows that there is a natural progression from decriminalisation to recognition of civil rights, this type of

B. The Equality Argument

Article 12 of the Singapore Constitution contains the equal protection clause which provides:

> (1) All persons are equal before the law and entitled to the equal protection of the law.
> (2) Except as expressly authorised by this Constitution, there shall be no discrimination against citizens of Singapore on the ground only of religion, race, descent or place of birth in any law or in the appointment to any office or employment under a public authority or in the administration of any law relating to the acquisition, holding or disposition of property or the establishing or carrying on of any trade, business, profession, vocation or employment.

The test that is widely used by courts in common law jurisdictions to determine whether there has been a violation of the equal protection clause is the rational review test.[37] Under this test, the court merely considers whether there is a rational nexus between the challenged law and the legislative object; it does not scrutinise the legislative object itself or the means of achieving that object. Further, the burden of proving unconstitutionality lies with the person alleging a violation of the equality clause. By any measure, the rational review test is a minimalist approach to judicial review under the equal protection clause, and dissatisfaction with it has led to more substantive review tests being developed in various jurisdictions.

Regardless of the current jurisprudence on the appropriate test, for purposes of analysis, the minimalist, rational review test will be applied to assess the constitutionality of s 377A. The leading authority in Singapore on Art 12 and the rational review test is *PP v Taw Cheng Kong*.[38] In essence, this test has three elements, listed below as a series of sequential questions:

- Is the discriminatory classification based on an intelligible differentia which distinguishes persons that are grouped together from others left out of the group?
- Does the differentia have a rational relation to the object sought to be achieved by the law in question?
- Is the object of the legislation legal?

'slippery slope' argument is nevertheless unconvincing. See, generally, R Wintemute, 'Same-Sex Marriage: When Will it Reach Utah?' (2006) 20 *Brigham Young University Journal of Public Law* 527. Paradoxically, the 'slippery slope' argument concedes that the issue at hand is not objectionable, which is why the focus is shifted to future potentialities. See F Schauer, 'Slippery Slopes' (1985–86) 99 *Harvard Law Review* 361.

[37] *New York City Transit Authority v Beazer* 440 US 568 (1979) (US); *Budhan Choudhry v State of Bihar* [1955] AIR SC 191 (India); *Datuk Haji bin Harun Idris v PP* [1977] 2 MLJ 155 (Malaysia); *Ong Ah Chuan v PP* [1981] 1 MLJ 64 (Privy Council, on appeal from Singapore).

[38] [1998] 2 SLR 410.

C. Intelligible Differentia

Section 377A is targeted at homosexual men performing acts of gross indecency whether in public or private. In light of the repeal of s 377, it is unclear what forms the basis of classification. It is not a classification based on *sexual orientation*, as s 377A includes homosexual men but excludes homosexual women. It is not a classification based on *gender* because it includes homosexual men but excludes heterosexual men. It is not a classification based on *the act* because oral and anal sex between homosexuals is included but oral and anal sex between heterosexuals is excluded. Therefore, the classification is not merely over- or under-inclusive, which is permissible; rather, it does not intelligibly differentiate persons that are grouped together from others left out of the group. There is additional arbitrariness in enforcement as there is no guidance on when and against whom it is to be used. The Government's policy is not to enforce it against consenting adults, but the possibility of selective enforcement raises serious questions of arbitrary effect.

The recent decisions from the South African Constitutional Court and the United States Supreme Court striking down sodomy laws provide valuable guidance.[39] In both cases, an important consideration lending weight to the equal protection violation was the fact that the laws criminalised only anal sex between men and did not extend to anal sex between men and women.[40] O'Connor J in *Lawrence* was explicit on this point:

> The statute at issue here makes sodomy a crime only if a person 'engages in deviate sexual intercourse with another individual of the same sex. ... Sodomy between opposite-sex partners, however, is not a crime in Texas. That is, Texas treats the same conduct differently based solely on the participants. ... The Texas statute makes homosexuals unequal in the eyes of the law by making particular conduct—and only that conduct—subject to criminal sanctions.[41]

[39] *National Coalition for Gay and Lesbian Equality and another v Minister of Justice and Others* (1999) 1 SA 6; *Lawrence v Texas* 539 US 558 (2003). It should be noted that the South African Constitution expressly protects sexual orientation and privacy, and therefore the South African jurisprudence may be distinguished. Nevertheless, the reasoning of the court in the *National Coalition* case went well beyond a purely textual approach and addressed the issues much more broadly in terms of the normative value of the concepts of equality and privacy.

[40] *National Coalition for Gay and Lesbian Equality and another v Minister of Justice and Others* (1999) 1 SA 6, 21 (Ackermann J), referring, with approval, to the trial judgment: 'He concluded that there was no justification for maintaining the common law crime of committing an unnatural sexual act by a man or between men, if such act would not constitute an offence if committed by a woman, between women or between a man and a woman.' *Lawrence v Texas* 539 US 558 (2003) at 588 (O'Connor J): 'I therefore concur in the Court's judgment that Texas' sodomy law banning "deviate sexual intercourse" between consenting adults of the same sex, but not between consenting adults of different sexes, is unconstitutional.'

[41] *Lawrence v Texas* 539 US 558 (2003), 581.

If Singapore repeals s 377 but retains s 377A, it will have created the very situation that was identified by some judges as one of the key factors reinforcing the finding that the sodomy laws under challenge in both the South African and the United States decisions violated equal protection.

D. Rational Relation

In order to determine whether there is a rational relation to the object sought to be achieved, one has to identify the object of the provision. The generally accepted objects of criminal law are the prevention of harm, maintenance of public order and decency and preservation of public health. It is difficult to draw a rational nexus between the criminalisation of consensual, homosexual activity between adult males in private and any of these objects. Such activity does not qualify as harmful conduct and when it takes place in private, it does not offend against public order and decency. So the question is whether criminalisation of homosexual acts preserves public health.

The empirical data shows that in some countries homosexual males constitute a disproportionate percentage of HIV/AIDS cases.[42] On that basis, it is argued that homosexual acts should be discouraged and thus criminalisation is justified. However, this ignores the reality that criminalisation in fact exacerbates the HIV/AIDS problem in the gay community. The Joint United Nations Programme on HIV/AIDS (UNAIDS) has categorically stated that 'Vulnerability to HIV infection is dramatically increased where sex between men is criminalised'.[43] Criminalisation forces homosexual behaviour underground. It means gay men have limited or no access to public health facilities, risk reduction programmes and HIV/AIDS testing.[44]

Criminalisation also inhibits individuals as well as public and private health organisations from effectively dealing with the HIV/AIDS problem, as funding is inadequate and structural and legal impediments abound. For example, providing informational material or condoms to gay men can be construed as aiding and abetting the commission of an offence. In India, AIDS workers have been harassed and jailed on the allegation of aiding and abetting homosexual acts. In Singapore, police prevented a local organisation from setting up a booth to distribute educational material and condoms at a gay public party.

The retention of s 377A, along with the Government's avowed policy of not proactively enforcing the law, is the worst case scenario in terms of

[42] UNAIDS has classified four high-risk groups: sex workers, men who have sex with men, injecting drug users and prisoners. UNAIDS *Report on the Global AIDS Epidemic* (2006) 104: <http://www.unaids.org/en/HIV_data/2006GlobalReport/default.asp>.

[43] UNAIDS, above n 42, at 112.

[44] UNAIDS estimated that only 9% of men who have sex with men received any type of HIV prevention services in 2005. See UNAIDS, above n 42.

public health. Far from having a rational relation to its object of promoting public health, it has the opposite effect.

The provision is also contrary to the object of general crime prevention. Anecdotal and empirical evidence in India shows that the existence of s 377 in the Indian Penal Code (India does not have s 377A) has in fact contributed to crimes being committed against homosexuals, as individuals, including public officials, have extorted, blackmailed and even abused homosexuals by threatening to reveal their sexual orientation to family members or the public.[45] The American Law Institute categorically recognised this risk of blackmail when it promulgated the Model Penal Code in 1955 and refrained from providing for the criminalisation of consensual homosexual activity in private.[46] Singapore too acknowledged this when Senior Minister Goh Chok Tong stated that gay men would have to disclose their sexual orientation when joining the public service so they would not be vulnerable to blackmail or extortion.[47]

E. Legal Object

The only object to which s 377A has a rational relation is the suppression of male homosexual activity on moral and religious grounds. This object is self-justificatory and has been expressly rejected as a legitimate object for the purpose of the rational review test by the United States Supreme Court[48] and the South African Constitutional Court.[49] Lest it be thought that these courts represent cultures that are alien to Singapore, the last word on this is best left to the Hong Kong Court of Appeal, an appellate court in an Asian country which shares many similarities with Singapore, from its culture to its legal system and history:

[45] S Katyal, 'Sexuality and Sovereignty: The Global Limits and Possibilities of Lawrence' (2006) 14 *William and Mary Bill of Rights Law Journal* 1429, 1453–4.

[46] See NM Goldsmith, *The Worst of Crimes: Homosexuality and the Law in Eighteenth-Century London* (Brookfield, VT, Ashgate, 1998), documenting instances of the misuse of sodomy laws to persecute and blackmail people in 18th-century England. Closer to Singapore is the prosecution of the former Deputy Prime Minister of Malaysia, Dato' Seri Anwar Ibrahim who was charged with corruption and sodomy. His convictions on sodomy charges were eventually overturned but the case highlights the dangers of retaining s 377A in the Penal Code.

[47] In an interview with *TIME* magazine on 5 February 2003. See transcript on Yawning Bread website: <http://www.yawningbread.org/apdx_2003/imp-116.htm>.

[48] *Lawrence v Texas* 539 US 558 (2003) at 583 (O'Connor J): 'Moral disapproval of this group, like a bare desire to harm a group, is an interest that is insufficient to satisfy the rational basis review under the Equal Protection Clause. ... Indeed, we have never held that moral disapproval, without any other asserted state interest, is a sufficient rationale under the Equal Protection Clause to justify a law that discriminates among groups of people.'

[49] *National Coalition for Gay and Lesbian Equality and another v Minister of Justice and Others* (1999) 1 SA 6 at 31 (Ackermann J): 'The enforcement of the private moral views of a section of the community, which are based to a large extent on nothing more than prejudice, cannot qualify as such legitimate purpose.'

> Denying persons of a minority class the right to sexual expression in the only way available to them, even if that way is denied to all, remains discriminatory when persons of a majority class are permitted the right to sexual expression in a way natural to them. During the course of submission it was described as 'disguised discrimination.' It is, I think, an apt description. It is disguised discrimination founded on a single base: sexual orientation.[50]

F. The Privacy Argument

Privacy as a right received prominence in tort law following the publication in 1890 of Warren and Brandeis' seminal article, 'The Right to Privacy'.[51] Yet, this right remains unarticulated in many constitutional guarantees and has proved to be elusive in the common law.[52] The right to privacy is of paramount importance in the context of personal intimate relationships. The leading US authority on privacy is *Griswold v Connecticut*,[53] which concerned a law that prohibited contraception. The law was held to be unconstitutional as it violated a married couple's right to privacy. Although the US Constitution does not contain an express right to privacy, the court found the right as a necessary adjunct of some of the other constitutional rights.[54] In some respects, the right to privacy may be seen as a foundational right.[55]

Griswold's right to privacy in marriage was then extended to unmarried couples,[56] and has since been extended to homosexual partners in *Lawrence v Texas*.[57] While *Griswold* clothed the right to privacy with the virtue of marriage and all its social and moral benefits,[58] *Lawrence* stripped off this

[50] *Leung TC Williams Roy v Secretary for Justice* [2006] HKCA 106 at [48].

[51] SD Warren and LD Brandeis, 'The Right to Privacy' (1890) 4 *Harvard Law Review* 193.

[52] It has recently cropped up in the House of Lords in a variety of contexts: *Douglas and another and others v Hello! Limited and Others* [2007] UKHL 21; *Secretary of State for Work and Pensions v M* [2006] UKHL 11; *R (on the application of Gillan (FC) and another (FC)) v Commissioner of Police for the Metropolis and another* [2006] UKHL 12; *Campbell v MGN Ltd* [2004] 2 AC 457; *Wainwright v Home Office* [2004] 2 AC 406; see also, in the Australian context, *Australian Broadcasting Corporation v Lenah Game Meats Pty Ltd* (2001) 208 CLR 199.

[53] 381 US 479 (1965).

[54] 381 US 479 (1965) at 484 (Douglas J): 'The foregoing cases suggest that specific guarantees in the Bill of Rights have penumbras, formed by emanations from those guarantees that help give them life and substance. ... Various guarantees create zones of privacy.'

[55] See DAJ Richards, 'Constitutional Privacy and Homosexual Love' in WR Dynes and S Donaldson (eds), *Homosexuality, Discrimination, Criminology and the Law* (New York, Garland Publishing Inc, 1992) 459. Compare R Wacks, *Law, Morality and the Private Domain* (Hong Kong, Hong Kong University Press, 2000) 254–5 who warns of the danger of privacy being over-used to protect the separate interests of liberty and autonomy.

[56] *Eisenstadt v Baird* 405 US 438 (1972).

[57] 539 US 558 (2003).

[58] *Griswold v Connecticut* 381 US 479 (1965) at 486 (Douglas J).

instrumentalist verbiage and Kennedy J, writing for the majority, zeroed in on the crucial question that is often deliberately ignored in this debate: 'The issue is whether the majority may use the power of the State to enforce [its own moral values] on the whole society through operation of the criminal law.'[59] Scalia J, in his dissent, argued that he had 'nothing against homosexuals, or any other group, promoting their agenda through normal democratic means'.[60] While the proper forum for promoting this 'agenda' may be the ballot box, the issue in *Lawrence* was not about any agenda; it was about whether the state could criminalise an act purely on the basis of the values of a moral majority and have that law apply to a minority group in society.

Lawrence, while a positive outcome for gay and lesbian people, has been criticised for being too conservative in its approach. By focusing on privacy rather than equality, some scholars and activists read *Lawrence* as being about the tolerance of the majority rather than the rights of the minority: crudely, as long as homosexuals 'stay in the closet',[61] their activities should be tolerated.[62] A more optimistic reading of *Lawrence* from a liberal perspective is that it went beyond privacy and had the effect of severely curtailing, if not prohibiting, purely morals-based legislation.[63] *Lawrence* privacy was not merely spatial privacy but a more empowering version based on individual status and protection of liberty.[64] Indeed, one commentator noted that while *Lawrence* appeared to be based on privacy, Kennedy J in fact focused on liberty,[65] stating at the outset, 'The instant case involves liberty of the person both in its spatial and in its more transcendent dimensions'.[66]

From a criminal lawyer's point of view, one can reconcile the 'status privacy'and 'spatial privacy' dichotomy on the ground that while status privacy engages constitutional law in terms of defining an individual's rights and liberties, spatial privacy engages criminal law in terms of defining the

[59] *Lawrence v Texas* 539 US 558.

[60] *Lawrence v Texas* 539 US 558, 603.

[61] The 'closet' is the metaphor for the hidden world of gay and lesbian people. As long as they remain hidden, they are tolerated. Coming out of the closet can be empowering for gay and lesbian people but threatening to moral conservatives in society. See AD Ronner, *Homophobia and the Law* (Washington, American Psychological Association, 2005) 8–9.

[62] See M Sandel, *Democracy's Discontent: America in Search of a Public Philosophy* (Cambridge, Belknap Press of Harvard University Press, 1996) for a criticism of the right to privacy on this reasoning.

[63] S Bedi, 'Repudiating Morals Legislation: Rendering the Constitutional Right to Privacy Obsolete' (2005–06) 53 *Cleveland Law Review* 447.

[64] The right to privacy can be interpreted both as a negative right (a shield) or a positive right (a sword); if the latter, then it can be used to advance one's civil rights in so far as status privacy is relevant. See AM Connelly, 'Problems of Interpretation of Article 8 of the European Convention on Human Rights' (1986) 35 *I CLQ* 567 with respect to Art 8 of the European Convention on Human Rights.

[65] See J Greene, 'Beyond Lawrence: Metaprivacy and Punishment' (2006) 115 *Yale Law Journal* 1862, 1869, noting that Kennedy J used the word liberty 'upwards of twenty-five times'.

[66] *Lawrence v Texas* 539 US 558, 562.

state's interest. One could then say that sexual *orientation* was protected by status privacy but sexual *conduct* is limited by spatial privacy. This treats homosexual and heterosexual people equally, as neither's sexual identity is diminished and public decency defines the limitations on sexual behaviour outside the bedroom.[67]

Singapore has not recognised a constitutional right to privacy, but both India and Hong Kong, with which Singapore shares very similar constitutions and constitutional traditions, have done so, thus providing the jurisprudential basis for Singapore to do likewise.[68] There is judicial dictum in Singapore implicitly recognising a right to privacy, as well as statements by legislators to similar effect. In *Malcomson Nicholas Hugh Bertram v Naresh Kumar Mehta*,[69] a landmark decision recognising a common law tort of harassment, there was reference to the right to privacy when the court held that there was a 'need to balance the plaintiffs' *right to privacy* against Mehta's right to free speech' (emphasis added).[70] During the parliamentary debate on the amendments to the Miscellaneous Offences (Public Order and Nuisance) Act to add a new offence of appearing nude in public, the then Senior Parliamentary Secretary to the Minister for Home Affairs stated, '*Although one has a right to privacy in one's home*, this should not, however, be at the expense of public decency such as nude exposure' (emphasis added).[71]

G. Criminalisation

Criminal law results in punishment, which includes deprivation of life and liberty; a criminal record, which has consequences for an individual's future civil rights and expectation (for example, employment and freedom of international travel); and moral condemnation, which results in stigmatisation and degradation of self-worth.[72] Constitutional arguments provide some external constraint on criminalisation, but courts take a conservative approach to constitutional challenge,[73] on the basis that in a democracy, the will of the people as represented by the legislature should be respected.

[67] No doubt there will be some initial reservations, and public displays of affection between homosexual couples will more likely be seen to cross the threshold of decency, but education, public discourse and social acclimatisation should eventually resolve the issue.

[68] Like the United States, India and Hong Kong have recognised the right to privacy: *Kharak Singh v Union of India* AIR 1963 SC 1295; *PUCL v Union of India* AIR 1997 SC 568; *Leung TC Williams Roy v Secretary for Justice* [2006] HKCA 106.

[69] [2001] 4 SLR 454.

[70] [2001] 4 SLR 454, [56].

[71] Singapore Parliamentary Debates, *Official Reports*, 27 February 1996, col 699.

[72] See also J Schonsheck, *On Criminalisation: An Essay in the Philosophy of the Criminal Law* (Netherlands, Kluwer Academic Publishers, 1994) 1–5.

[73] See DN Husak, 'Limitations on Criminalisation' in S Shute and AP Simester, *Criminal Law Theory: Doctrines of the General Part* (Oxford, Oxford University Press, 2002) 32–3.

If recourse to constitutional law or human rights does not provide sufficient checks on the reach of the criminal law, it is necessary for criminal law itself to have internal controls. Otherwise, we risk over-criminalisation, which is particularly invidious when it affects conduct that is essentially private and harmless to others. According to the traditional view, criminal law was anything that the legislature or courts declared to be criminal.[74] However, there is now greater recognition of the need to justify criminalisation by recourse to theoretical and philosophical arguments.[75] Arguments based on theory and philosophy provide important moral and political constraints on the ambit of criminal law[76] and, most significantly, they impose a burden on the state to justify criminalisation.

Theorising about criminalisation involves, inter alia, an endeavour to find the right balance between on the one hand, the need to prohibit conduct and punish an individual for transgression, and on the other, the need to respect the individual's autonomy and liberty. There is no general or universal theory of criminalisation. Instead, there is a continuum, the polarities of which are represented in the Hart–Devlin debate, pitting individual liberty against public morality.[77] Along this continuum are theories based on offence,[78] welfare,[79] republicanism[80] and the general part of criminal law itself.[81] This chapter focuses on the harm, offence and morality arguments, as that is how the debate on criminalisation of homosexual acts has been framed in Singapore.[82]

[74] See, for example, *Proprietary Articles Trade Association v AG (Canada)* [1931] AC 310, 324 (Lord Atkin): '[T]he domain of criminal jurisprudence can only be ascertained by examining what acts at any particular period are declared by the State to be crimes, and the only common nature they will be found to possess is that they are prohibited by the State and that those who commit them are punished.'

[75] Leading criminal law texts today generally have a section devoted to criminalisation. See A Ashworth, *Principles of Criminal Law* (Oxford, Oxford University Press, 5th edn, 2006) ch 2; S Bronitt and B McSherry, *Principles of Criminal Law* (Sydney, Law Book Co, 2nd edn, 2005) ch 1.

[76] See, especially, DN Husak, *Philosophy of Criminal Law* (New Jersey, Rowman & Littlefields, 1987).

[77] P Devlin, *The Enforcement of Morality* (London, Oxford University Press, 1965); HLA Hart, *Law, Liberty and Morality* (London, Oxford University Press, 1963).

[78] See especially, J Feinberg, *The Moral Limits of the Criminal Law (vol 2): Offence to Others* (New York, Oxford University Press, 1985).

[79] See especially, N Lacey, *State Punishment: Political Principles and Community Values* (London, Routledge, 1988).

[80] See, especially, J Braithwaite and P Pettit, *Not Just Deserts: A Republican Theory of Criminal Justice* (Oxford, Clarendon Press, 1990).

[81] DN Husak, 'Limitations on Criminalisation' in S Shute and AP Simester, *Criminal Law Theory: Doctrines of the General Part* (Oxford, Oxford University Press, 2002).

[82] It should be noted that the leading criminal law reformists of the 18th century in Europe were firmly of the view that homosexual acts should not to be criminalised. For example, Jeremy Bentham wrote an essay of several hundred pages in 1785, arguing strenuously against the criminalisation of homosexuality, even though he himself personally disapproved of homosexuality. The essay, called 'Paederasty', was never published until the late 20th century when it was discovered, edited and published in two parts. See J Crompton, 'Jeremy Bentham's Essay on 'Paederasty" Part I (1978) 3 *Journal of Homosexuality* 383–405; Pt II (1978) 4 *Journal of Homosexuality* 91–107, 392–3.

H. Prevention of Harm

The starting point is always John Stuart Mill's *On Liberty*,[83] in which Mill argued that the only justification for the state to intrude on an individual's freedom is to prevent harm to others. What is equally significant is the reason for his articulation of the principle that prevention of harm to others is the only justification for state intervention. Mill recognised that individuals have to be protected not just from the state or the tyranny of the majority, but equally importantly, from the tyranny of the moral majority:

> Like other tyrannies, the tyranny of the majority was at first, and is still vulgarly, held in dread, chiefly as operating through the acts of the public authorities. ... Protection, therefore, against the tyranny of the magistrate is not enough: there needs protection also against the tyranny of the prevailing opinion and feeling; against the tendency of society to impose, by other means than civil penalties, its own ideas and practices as rules of conduct on those who dissent from them; to fetter the development, and, if possible, prevent the formation, of any individuality not in harmony with its ways, and compel all characters to fashion themselves upon the model of its own.[84]

A literal interpretation of Mill would limit the scope of criminalisation to actual harm to others. A narrower interpretation of Mill would permit the criminalisation of conduct that does not result in direct harm, but causes indirect harm or offence to others.[85] The harm principle was highly influential in the 1957 Wolfenden Committee Report on homosexuality and prostitution. The committee, which took advice from a wide range of sources, including religious leaders and health experts, concluded that homosexual acts performed in private between consenting adults were not harmful and should not be a crime. The Singapore Law Society came to the same conclusion for the same reasons.

Proponents of criminalisation rely on an extended interpretation of the harm principle, arguing that homosexuality leads to indirect harm and/or is offensive. The indirect harm that is generally asserted by the anti-homosexuality lobby as being associated with homosexuality include HIV/AIDS, paedophilia, destruction of the family unit and the general disintegration of society. While there is a real issue with respect to HIV/AIDS, the solution, as argued earlier, does not lie in criminalising homosexual acts: decriminalisation would allow better regulation, safer sex practices and easier access to health. The spread of infectious diseases is in any event covered by other provisions in Singapore; for example, s 23 of the Infectious Diseases Act

[83] S Collini (ed), *On Liberty and Other Writings* (Cambridge, Cambridge University Press, (1989).

[84] Collini, above n 83, at 8.

[85] J Feinberg, *The Moral Limits of the Criminal Law (vol 1): Harm to Others* (New York, Oxford University Press, 1984); J Feinberg, *The Moral Limits of the Criminal Law (vol 2): Offence to Others* (New York, Oxford University Press, 1985).

(Cap 137) specifically deals with transmission of HIV/AIDS through sexual intercourse and ss 269 and 270 of the Penal Code deal with negligent or malignant spreading of disease.

With respect to the other harms, these are bald assertions without credible empirical evidence.[86] Indeed, there are many other activities with respect to which similar arguments of harm to health or family may be made, but have never been pursued. It is difficult to defend the selective application of these arguments to homosexuality. For example, there is a causal link between smoking and various serious public health risks: in short, smoking kills, yet it is not criminalised on this ground. There is empirical evidence linking gambling to harm to individuals and families: gambling destroys the family, yet the Singapore Government recently has sanctioned casinos. Common sense and empirical evidence suggest that adultery is a cause of marital problems: adultery ruins marriages, yet is not illegal.

During the abortion debate in Singapore, opponents of abortion argued that decriminalising abortion would lead to promiscuity, maternal mortality and the general decline of society. The then Minister for Health and Home Affairs rejected these arguments in very strong terms:

> As it has turned out, nearly five years of experience of the operation of the Abortion Act has proved that many of the moral and medical objections to the Bill were unfounded. For example, availability of legalised abortions has not led to the breaking down of moral standards and increased promiscuity. Neither has it led to increase in maternal mortality and morbidity for our pregnant women. ... Of course, the religious arguments against legalised abortions for obvious reasons could not then as well as now be proved or disproved. As I have stated then, to allow ourselves to be tied up with the religious arguments for and against abortions, which in any case would never result in any conclusion even if the debate went on till the cows came home, was entirely futile. The religious viewpoints must necessarily be based on one's own religious beliefs and faith as well as conscience. And these must differ from individual to individual.[87]

The indirect harm argument is clearly untenable as a basis for criminalisation of homosexual acts in Singapore. Does the offence principle provide a rational basis? Two examples illustrate how the offence principle may properly be used. In Singapore, as in many other jurisdictions, racial or religious vilification is a crime,[88] as is appearing nude in public.[89] Leaving aside for the moment the issue of what constitutes offence, in both cases there is an additional factor justifying criminalisation, that is, independent of the

[86] See text at nn 104–23 for a discussion of some of these claims.

[87] Singapore Parliamentary Debates, *Official Reports*, 6 November 1974, col 1100.

[88] The Penal Code, s 298, prohibits religious vilification. The Sedition Act, s 3, prohibits racial vilification.

[89] An example is the Miscellaneous Offences (Public Order and Nuisance) Act, s 27, which makes it an offence to appear nude in public or in private if exposed to public view.

offensiveness of the conduct there is an element of wrongdoing.[90] In the first example, the conduct is targeted at others and is intended or known to cause offence or hurt. In the second example, the act is in public or affects the public. Homosexual acts that occur in private and with consent should not be caught by the offence principle.

Even leaving aside the wrongdoing element, there is a serious question as to whether homosexual acts are sufficiently offensive. Joel Feinberg, in his influential treatise, argued that for the offence principle to be invoked, 'very real and intense offence [must be] taken predictably by virtually everyone, and the offending conduct [must have] hardly any countervailing personal or social value of its own'.[91] Homosexual acts between two consenting adults clearly have strong countervailing personal value. Do homosexual acts offend 'virtually everyone'? This is far from the case in Singapore. While there are many who find homosexuality objectionable, the trend in the last decade shows increasing acceptance of homosexuality, with a very recent survey suggesting that a majority of youths no longer find homosexuality unacceptable.[92] Thus, in Singapore, homosexual acts would not pass the Feinberg test of offensiveness to justify criminalisation.

I. Enforcement of Morals

The competing theory of criminalisation is based on Lord Devlin's reaction to the Wolfenden Report, where he argued that criminal law should be about the enforcement of morals. This is the theory on which supporters of s 377A generally rely. There are two difficulties with this theory: one, there are problems with identifying what moral norms should be legitimised by the state and enforced by way of punishment; and two, it results in arbitrariness, as not all moral wrongs are criminalised.

Looking at the first issue, it is apparent that the Penal Code, imposed by the British on their colonies, reflected Judaeo–Christian ethics, whereas the religions of the Asian colonies were mainly Hindu, Muslim, Buddhist, Taoist and Confucian, which did not necessarily share the same Victorian attitude toward homosexuality. It is significant that the United Kingdom has itself since repealed its laws criminalising consensual homosexual

[90] See, generally, AP Simester and A von Hirsch, 'Rethinking the Offense Principle' (2002) 8 *Legal Theory* 269.

[91] J Feinberg, *The Moral Limits of the Criminal Law: Offence to Others* (New York, Oxford University Press, 1985) vol 2 36.

[92] A Government survey in 2001 showed that over 80% of Singaporeans found homosexuality unacceptable. A survey by a local newspaper in early 2007 of a lower-middle-class section of society (where one would expect more conservative views to be held) showed that about 60% disapproved of homosexuality. A university survey of youths showed that more than half no longer disapproved of homosexuality. See, for analysis, 'Mediacorp's Survey on Decriminalisation' Yawning Bread: <http://www.yawningbread.org/>.

activity.[93] The imposition of one view of morality on all the people of Singapore, which is a multi-racial, multi-religious, secular democracy that respects the rights of persons of all religions as well as persons who profess no religion, is difficult to defend on normative grounds, and indeed has been rightly rejected by the Singapore Government. The then Minister for Health and Home Affairs, during the Second Reading of the Abortion Bill, in rejecting religious objections, asked: '[I]s it right in our multi-racial and multi-religious society for opponents to the liberalisation of the law on abortion to impose their moral or religious standards upon the entire community?'[94]

Had the Government not rejected such a view, questions would have to be asked as to whether Muslim criminal laws such as *khalwat*, which criminalises close proximity between a man and woman who are not married to each other, should be part of Singapore's general criminal law; otherwise there is an argument of discrimination on the ground of religion, which is specifically prohibited under Art 12 (2) of the Constitution. Furthermore, the pseudo-secular argument that homosexuality is immoral on the ground that it does not lead to procreation and is therefore not a 'basic human good' can no longer apply in Singapore given the proposal to repeal s 377.[95]

With respect to the second issue of arbitrariness, criminalising homosexual acts on the basis of moral wrong raises questions about, amongst others, Singapore's legalisation of abortion,[96] its non-criminalisation of prostitution,[97] its proposed repeal of the offence of enticement of another's wife (s 498), its approval of embryonic stem cell research, its sanctioning of casinos, as well as its laws which allow two persons originally of the same gender to marry once one of them has undergone a sexual reassignment procedure.[98] These are matters that may be viewed as morally wrong in the same religious vein that deems homosexuality morally wrong; yet these activities have been legalised. The proposed repeal of s 377 and consequent decriminalisation of anal sex between men and women is another example of selective enforcement of morals. To indiscriminately criminalise one aspect of 'unnatural sex' to target a particular group (homosexual males), while leaving other aspects of 'unnatural sex' unregulated is arbitrary.

[93] During the decriminalisation of abortion, the then Health Minister stated at the second reading of the Abortion Bill: 'First, let me give a reason why it is necessary to reform and liberalise our laws on abortion. Our laws on abortion are based on the old Indian Penal Code which in turn was derived from English law. Even the English have liberalised their laws on abortion by the passage of the United Kingdom Abortion Act of 1967 which became operative on 27th April, 1968.' Singapore Parliamentary Debates, *Official Reports*, 8 April 1969, col 861.

[94] Singapore Parliamentary Debates, *Official Reports*, 6 November 1974, col 1100.

[95] This type of natural law reasoning defending homosexual laws has been put forth by J Finnis, *Natural Law and Natural Rights* (Oxford, Clarendon Press, 1980).

[96] Termination of Pregnancy Act (Cap 324, Rev Ed 1985), s 3.

[97] Women's Charter (Cap 353, Rev Ed 1997), s 140 criminalises related offences, eg pimping, aiding etc, but not actual prostitution itself.

[98] Women's Charter, above n 97, s 12(3)(b).

It is also disingenuous to speak of enforcement of morals with respect to consensual homosexual conduct between adults in the privacy of their homes when the stated policy of the Government is *not* to enforce the law. The policy of non-enforcement of s 377A is problematic for two reasons. First, it sends conflicting signals: on the one hand, the law says that homosexual acts are wrong; on the other, the Government says that such acts will not be prosecuted if they are consensual and in private. If that is the policy of the Government then the law should be amended to exclude private, consensual homosexual activity. Second, a non-enforcement policy undermines the integrity of the Penal Code, as it suggests that there is something amiss with the law. If a law is not to be enforced, then it should not be retained. The eminent American jurist, Learned Hand J put it bluntly during the American Law Institute's deliberations on the Model Penal Code in 1955:

> Criminal law which is not enforced practically is much worse than if it was not on the books at all. I think homosexuality is a matter of morals, a matter very largely of taste, and it is not a matter that people should be put in prison about.[99]

IV. THE POLITICS OF FEAR

Bearing a title that resonates with the global war on terror, the author of a recent book, *America's War on Sex,* describes the Religious Right as the most powerful minority in the United States waging a battle against the freedom of individual choice:

> The Religious Right has masterfully portrayed itself as the voice of the sex-sober majority being oppressed by the sex-crazed minority. They demand sympathy and righteous indignation about the way 'children,' 'families,' 'tradition,' 'morals,' 'values,' and 'decency' are under attack. They have gotten the government and media to support them as defenders of America's wholesomeness—against some mythical, incredibly powerful 'them.'

The Right portrays America as under siege by a dangerous ideology, a villainous intelligence, which simply doesn't exist. The evil that the Right is battling so energetically isn't evil, and it isn't out there. It's the simple decision-making *of its own people*. And they make the same choices people around the world make whenever they have a chance.[100]

[99] Quoted in S Gilreath, *Sexual Politics: The Gay Person in America Today* (Ohio, University of Akron Press, 2006) 16.

[100] M Klein, *America's War on Sex: The Attack on Law, Lust and Liberty* (Connecticut, Praeger, 2006) 25–6.

Fear politics has become a convenient and popular tool to justify the introduction or retention of laws which encroach on fundamental rights and liberties. Left unchecked, there is a real danger that cherished freedoms and liberal values will be sacrificed at the altar of ideological rhetoric. The events of 9/11 resulted in a spate of illiberal laws being enacted in many jurisdictions with inadequate debate as to whether such laws are genuinely necessary, or at least whether the same result could have been achieved with fewer intrusions on personal liberty. Amnesty International in its 2007 report highlighted this threat to human rights and democratic freedom in an eloquent foreword:

> [F]ear destroys our shared understanding and our shared humanity. When we see others as a threat, and are ready to negotiate their human rights for our security, we are playing a zero-sum game. Human rights—those global values, universal principles and common standards that are meant to unite us—are being bartered away in the name of security ... the agenda is being driven by fear—instigated, encouraged and sustained by unprincipled leaders ...
>
> Today far too many leaders are trampling freedom and trumpeting an ever-widening range of fears: fear of being swamped by migrants; fear of 'the other' and of losing one's identity; fear of being blown up by terrorists; fear of 'rogue states' with weapons of mass destruction.[101]

A leading Canadian criminal law academic, reviewing Canada's anti-terrorism laws identified four myths, which he argued should be exposed and avoided when examining such laws.[102] The first myth is that stronger criminal laws and wider police powers are necessary to protect Canadians from the threat of terrorism; the second is that such laws should be retained on the books for preventative reasons; the third is that the authorities can be trusted to use the laws judiciously; and the fourth is that laws that survive a Charter (or constitutional) challenge are necessarily just or good laws. Parallels are evident in the debate on criminal law and homosexual acts.

Proponents of criminalisation of homosexual acts in Singapore argue that the state has the power to criminalise such acts and therefore such laws are valid. This legal argument is buttressed by a political argument based on the claim that such laws are supported by the 'core constituency'—be they the 'moral majority' or, in Singapore, the 'heartlanders.'[103] The citizenry is divided into two: the 'core,' whose interests should be protected, and 'the other', against whom protection is needed.

[101] I Khan, 'Foreword: Freedom from Fear' *Amnesty International Report 2007* 1–2: <http://thereport.amnesty.org/eng/Download-the-Report>.

[102] See D Stuart, 'Avoiding Myths and Challenging Minister of Justice Cotler to Undo the Injustices of Our Anti-Terrorism Laws' (2005) 51 *Criminal Law Quarterly* 11.

[103] The term 'heartlander' was popularised by former Prime Minister Mr Goh Chok Tong, who used it to described the lower middle class of Singapore, who live in Government-subsidised housing and generally have a local rather than global perspective on life.

Some of the arguments raised to defend the status quo include the assertion that homosexuality is not immutable and therefore homosexuals can be 'cured', and do not qualify as a class that deserves special constitutional protection. Another argument is that homosexuality is one of the main causes of the spread of HIV/AIDS and therefore homosexual acts should remain a crime. A third argument is to allege that homosexuals are deviant and more likely to be paedophiles, and therefore it is necessary to criminalise homosexual acts in order to protect children. Having depicted homosexuality as dangerous to society and homosexual people as deviant, there is a curious reassurance that gay people will not be discriminated against because the state will not be proactive in enforcement; yet, the laws must apparently remain on the books to prevent that which will not be prosecuted.

A. Immutability and Disorder

In 2000, a church in Singapore placed a large banner outside its premises, proclaiming 'Homosexuals Can Change' to promote its counselling sessions.[104] The belief was that homosexuality was not immutable and was in fact a disorder or illness that needed to be cured. This view has been rejected by all credible scientific and medical organisations. The American Psychiatric Association (APA), by a unanimous vote in 1973, removed homosexuality as a mental disorder from its list of mental disorders. Other institutions have taken a similar position, including the World Health Organization, the British Psychological Society, the Canadian Psychological Association and the Australian Psychological Society. This trend is not confined to the West, with homosexuality being removed as a mental disorder by the Japanese Society of Psychiatry and Neurology in 1995, the Chinese Psychiatric Association in 2001 and Thailand's Mental Health Department in 2002.

Despite this, proponents of anti-homosexual laws continue to argue that homosexuality is not immutable and is the result of a disorder that can be cured.[105] They argue that the APA was pressured by homosexual lobby groups to remove homosexuality as a disorder. One of the key figures in that process, Dr Robert Spitzer has gone on record to dismiss this

[104] See A Tan, 'Singapore Gays Find Tacit Acceptance, Seek Some More' *Reuters News* (1 July 2001); JW Ting, 'Boys Night Out. We're here. We're Queer. Get Used to it. Can Singapore Accept its Gay Community?' *TIME Asia* (19 March 2001).

[105] Minister Mentor Lee Kuan Yew's statement that homosexuality may actually be genetic and not a matter of choice may dampen this argument in Singapore, although the recent statement of the Minister of State for Education, Mr Lui Tuck Yew, suggests that in the minds of the believer, little has changed. Acknowledging Mr Lee Kuan Yew's statement, Mr Lui nevertheless stated that he was not convinced that homosexuality was not a medical condition and compared it with paedophilia and psychopathy. See DA Pauloderrick, '"Main Society Not Ready'; Minister Says He is 'Not Ready To Move' on Homosexuality"' *Today Newspaper* (23 May 2007).

as 'nonsense'.[106] According to him, during the 1972 APA meeting, homosexual lobby groups did disrupt the session. He had an informal discussion with one of their representatives, following which he decided to convene a symposium to consider whether homosexuality should be removed as a disorder. Eventually, in 1973, the APA by majority decided to remove homosexuality from the list of disorders. The process may have been prompted by politics, but it would be wrong to say that the decision was purely due to political pressure.

Ironically, a quarter of a century later, in 1999, a reversal of the 1972 incident occurred when a group of ex-gay Christians disrupted the APA annual meeting, lobbying for APA to reclassify homosexuality as a disorder. Again, Spitzer was intrigued and undertook a study to find out whether conversion of sexual orientation was possible. He interviewed 200 people who claimed that they had previously been homosexuals but had changed their sexual preference. The results of the study were published in 2001 and the anti-homosexual lobby has used it to argue that homosexuality can be cured.[107] However, Spitzer's study merely concluded that change in limited cases was possible and that therapy should not be banned; he did not advocate therapy to force change. On the contrary, he made this public statement after discovering how his study was being used by some:

> My study concluded with an important caveat that it should not be used to justify a denial of civil rights to homosexuals, or as support for coercive treatment ... to my horror, some of the media reported the study as an attempt to show that homosexuality is a choice, and that substantial change is possible for any homosexual who decides to make the effort. ... I suspect the vast majority of gay people would be unable to alter by much a firmly established homosexual orientation.'[108]

B. Paedophilia

Another argument is that there is a link between homosexuality and paedophilia and therefore, in order to protect children, homosexual acts ought

[106] Referred to in O Stålströ and J Nissinen, 'The Spitzer Study and the Finnish Parliament' in J Drescher and KJ Zucker (eds), *Ex-Gay Research: Analysing the Spitzer Study and its Relation to Science, Religion, Politics, and Culture* (New York, Harrington Park Press, 2006) 320, fn 20.

[107] RL Spitzer, '200 Subjects Who Claim to have Changed Their Sexual Orientation from Homosexual to Heterosexual' Preliminary Report, presented to the Annual Meeting of the American Psychiatric Association, New Orleans, 9 May 2001. See also RL Spitzer, 'Can Some Gay Men and Lesbians Change their Sexual Orientation? 200 Participants Reporting a Change from Homosexual to Heterosexual Orientation' (2003) 32(5) *Archives of Sexual Behavior* 403. This study has been widely criticised as fundamentally flawed. See generally, the collection of papers in J Drescher and KJ Zucker (eds), *Ex-Gay Research: Analysing the Spitzer Study and its Relation to Science, Religion, Politics, and Culture* (New York, Harrington Park Press, 2006).

[108] RL Spitzer, 'Psychiatry and Homosexuality' *Wall Street Journal* (23 May 2001) A26.

to be criminalised. By linking homosexuality to the sexual exploitation of children, a powerful emotive argument is presented. One of the leading supporters of the argument that homosexuals are more likely to be paedophiles is Paul Cameron, founder of the anti-gay Family Research Institute,[109] whose work has been discredited by independent experts and professional organisations.[110] Most tellingly, his expert testimony in one case was dismissed as misleading and fraudulent by the judge, who found that Cameron had distorted the data to support his anti-gay claims.[111]

According to studies, the majority of adult males who sexually abuse young boys identify themselves as heterosexuals. Empirical research suggests that the link between paedophilia and homosexuality is 'more a societal myth than a reality'.[112] In fact, a substantial number of paedophilia cases, in Singapore and abroad, involve adult males and young girls, usually within the family, or increasingly, victims picked up through internet chat sites. The American Psychological Association in an amicus curiae submission provided further empirical support for the conclusion that homosexuality and paedophilia are not necessarily linked:

> However, all available research data and clinical experience indicates that gay men are not more likely than heterosexual men to sexually abuse children. A study of children seen for sexual abuse in a one-year period at a Denver children's hospital, for example, found that less than one percent of the identified adult offenders were gay or lesbian. Of the 219 abused girls, only one instance of abuse had been attributed to a lesbian. Of the 50 abused boys, only one instance of abuse had been attributed to a gay man. In contrast, 88 percent of the offenders had documented heterosexual relationships and most were heterosexual partners

[109] Its mission statement highlights its anti-homosexual agenda: 'The Family Research Institute was founded in 1982 with one overriding mission: to generate empirical research on issues that threaten the traditional family, *particularly homosexuality*, AIDS, sexual social policy, and drug abuse.' (emphasis added). The statement is available on the Family Research Institute's website: <http://familyresearchinst.org/>.

[110] The American Sociological Association condemned Cameron's work in no uncertain terms and passed this motion at its First Council Meeting of 1986–87: 'The American Sociological Association officially and publicly states that Paul Cameron is not a sociologist, and condemns his consistent misrepresentation of sociological research. Information on this ... [is to be sent] ... to the officers of all regional and state sociological associations and to the Canadian Sociological Association with a request that they alert their members to Cameron's frequent lectures and media appearances.' See *ASA Newsletter*, Footnotes (February 1987, vol 15 at 14).

[111] *Baker v Wade* 106 FRD 526 (1985) per Buchmeyer DJ at 536: '[Cameron's] sworn statement that "homosexuals are approximately 43 times more apt to commit crimes than is the general population" is a total distortion of the Kinsey data upon which he relies—which, as is obvious to anyone who reads the report, concerns data from a non-representative sample of delinquent homosexuals (and Dr Cameron compares this group to college and non-college heterosexuals).'

[112] This was the conclusion of a Research Fellow at the Australian Institute of Family Studies, who reviewed the available empirical research. See AM Tomison, 'Update on Child Sexual Abuse' *Issues in Child Abuse Prevention,* Number 5, Summer 1995: <http://www.aifs.gov.au/nch/issues5.html>.

of a family member (77 percent of those who abused the girls and 74 percent of those who abused the boys).[113]

Strong laws are needed to protect children against abuse, sexual and otherwise. However, criminalising private, consensual homosexual activity between adult males to achieve greater protection of children is not necessary. There is a network of laws in place, or about to be introduced in Singapore, protecting children from sexual assault, abuse, molest, prostitution and child sex tourism.[114]

C. Public Health and HIV/AIDS

The fact that homosexual men, or men who have sex with men, are at a higher risk of contracting HIV/AIDS is exploited by those in favour of criminalisation. Rather than working towards managing the risk, some conservatives use it to promote their religious agenda on sexual behaviour. The fear of an increase in HIV infections amongst gay men in 2004 resulted in a reversal of a liberal trend on gay and lesbian issues in Singapore which began in 2000. The Government had previously sanctioned Singapore's first gay and lesbian party, called 'Nation' in August 2001, held to coincide with Singapore's National Day on 9 August.[115] In 2004, the Minister for Health gave a public speech, pointing out that the rate of HIV infections was rising amongst the gay male population and could lead to an epidemic.[116] Soon after that, gay parties were banned.

Action for AIDS (AFA),[117] a non-governmental organisation in Singapore, argued that while there was a rise in HIV infections amongst gay men, one reason for this was the success that AFA had in getting gay men to come forward to be tested.[118] When AIDS was first announced in the 1980s in America, it was linked to gay, white men and the early strategies to battle AIDS risked marginalising other groups who were also at risk, including 'women, people of color, and more socially marginal groups like sex workers and injection drug users'.[119] Present statistics suggest that globally

[113] *Boy Scouts of America v James Dale*, Brief of Amicus Curiae American Psychological Association in Support of Respondent in the Supreme Court of the United States, 29 March 2000.

[114] Penal Code, ss 354, 375(e); Children and Young Persons Act (Cap 38, Rev Ed 2001), s 7; Women's Charter, pt XI.

[115] The Nation parties were highly successful events, drawing large crowds of international tourists and sparking off other gay and lesbian parties.

[116] Speech available online: <http://www.moh.gov.sg/mohcorp/speeches.aspx?id=1902>.

[117] <http://www.afa.org.sg/home.asp>.

[118] See AFA's response to the Minister for Health: <http://www.afa.org.sg/news/2004/1113/111301.asp>.

[119] J Rollins, *AIDS and the Sexuality of Law: Ironic Jurisprudence* (New York, Palgrave Macmillan, 2004) 7. See also M Barnes, 'AIDS and Mr Korematsu: Minorities at Times of Crisis' in WR Dynes and S Donaldson, *Homosexuality, Discrimination, Criminology and the Law* (New York, Garland Publishing Inc,1992) 4–5.

women account for about half the HIV cases and in Sub-Saharan Africa, women between the age of 15 and 24 comprise 75 per cent of HIV cases.[120] In India, 80 per cent of HIV/AIDS transmission is through heterosexual sex, much of it spread by lorry drivers and prostitutes.[121] The first reported AIDS case in India was a female sex worker.[122] Although estimates vary, India presently has the world's largest national population of HIV/AIDS sufferers.[123] To pretend that this is merely a gay disease will result in public health policies that are deficient. The spread of HIV/AIDS is a complex matter that requires an integrated strategy; but criminalisation of homosexual activity is not part of the solution—it is part of the problem.

V. CONCLUSION

It is suggested that a constitutional challenge to s 377A in a Singapore court has a good chance of being successful. The provision violates Art 12 on the rational review test and is an unjustified intrusion into an individual's privacy. The recent decisions from Asian, African and Western jurisdictions support this conclusion. The case in Singapore is stronger because of the proposal to repeal s 377 and the Government's own stated position of not enforcing s 377A against consenting adults. This leaves s 377A as a provision that can only be used arbitrarily against homosexual men.

It has also been demonstrated that s 377A is not justified on general theories of criminalisation in a modern, secular democracy. Far from furthering public interests, s 377A does the opposite. Non-enforcement of s 377A against consenting adults means homosexual activity will be permitted; but maintaining it as a criminal offence has serious detrimental repercussions for public health, social cohesion and individual liberties. It also has severe, negative consequences on children who are discovering their sexuality, as s 377A contributes to a climate of homophobia leading to some children, at a very vulnerable stage, being exposed to increased risk of bullying, stigmatisation and violence.

Decriminalisation of private, consensual homosexual activity between adults would not mean that the Government endorsed or approved of homosexuality, just as the legalisation of abortion and gambling does not mean that the Government encourages abortions or gambling. Equally, repealing s 377A would not mean that the Government intended to, or

[120] See UNAIDS website: <http://www.unaids.org/en/Issues/Affected_communities/women.asp>.
[121] See *Frontline: The Age of AIDS*: <http://www.pbs.org/wgbh/pages/frontline/aids/atlas/world.html>.
[122] *Frontline,* above n 121.
[123] See World Health Organization, *Epidemiological Factsheets on HIV/AIDS and Sexually Transmitted Infections India* (2006): <http://www.who.int/GlobalAtlas/predefinedReports/EFS2006/EFS_PDFs/EFS2006_IN.pdf>.

would come under pressure, in the civil arena to legislate for same sex marriages or adoption rights for gay and lesbian people. These are separate issues for a democratic society to decide upon at the appropriate juncture and must be kept distinct from the altogether different issue of whether or not, in accordance with constitutional law and theories of criminalisation, the Penal Code should retain s 377A.

The subtext of the debate on homosexual acts in Singapore is the fear that decriminalisation may lead to claims for further civil rights as part of what is described the 'homosexual agenda'.[124] It is unlikely that any such agenda will prevail in Singapore, where the Government has firmly committed itself not to ideology but to pragmatism. Various senior officials who have countenanced decriminalisation have done so for pragmatic, not ideological, reasons. The arguments for criminalisation ultimately are almost exclusively based on ideology. If the Singapore Government retains s 377A and eschews pragmatism for ideology,[125] then paradoxically, this may alter the landscape of Singapore politics, with ideological lobby politics triumphing over pragmatic policy making.

[124] One cannot but pause to wonder whether the 'homosexual agenda' or the 'fundamentalist religious agenda' presents a greater threat to the peace and stability of nations, and the dignity and autonomy of individuals.

[125] Compare Thio Li-ann, 'Pragmatism and Realism do not Mean Abdication: A Critical and Empirical Inquiry into Singapore's Engagement with International Human Rights Law' (2004) 8 *SYBIL* 41, 90, referring to a statement by Singapore's foreign Affairs Minister: 'The "pragmatic realism" of Singapore eschews any "theological moralizing" over assertions of universal moral truth, in an age where "law is politics", as "we want to be effective rather than just feel virtuous."'

10

Moral Uncertainties of Rape and Murder

Problems at the Core of Criminal Law Theory

NGAIRE NAFFINE

I. THE NEED FOR MORAL CERTAINTY

THIS BOOK IS about the spread of criminal responsibility, well beyond the conventional criminal wrongs—well away from core criminal liability. It is about the proliferation of non-standard crimes which do not appear to have a clear wrong-doer nor a clear wrong. This proliferation is an acknowledged problem.[1] As Andrew Simester and Robert Sullivan observe, 'the sheer variety of conduct that has been designated a criminal wrong defies reduction to any "essential" minimum. The criminal law has been used—indeed overused—as a regulatory device, and consequently can extend to conduct that can lack any inherent moral turpitude whatsoever'.[2] Sadly, they say, '[a]s things stand, persons may be convicted of offences despite the lack of—or indeed any—culpability'.[3]

With the proliferation of criminal laws, there seems to be a new need to reaffirm the true role and terrain of criminal law—to delimit the criminal law and to insist that the proper province of criminal law is 'true crime',[4] real wrongs and real wrongdoers. There seems to be a need for greater moral certainty at the core of criminal law and criminal law theory, as criminal law itself seems to depart from central concerns and principles. My concern here is with problems that remain at the core, not at the periphery, of criminal law theory and more particularly, my concern is with what

[1] See, for example, the reflections of Douglas Husak in 'Criminal Law Theory' in M Golding and W Edmundson (eds), *The Blackwell Guide to the Philosophy of Law and Legal Theory* (Boston, Blackwell Publishing, 2005).

[2] AP Simester and GR Sullivan, *Criminal Law Theory and Doctrine* (Oxford, Hart, 2000) 3.

[3] *Ibid*, at 638.

[4] For example in *He Kaw Teh v The Queen* (1985) 157 CLR 523, the Australian High Court referred to offences which are 'truly criminal'.

might be called the 'grand theories' of criminal responsibility and their very moral certainties.

In a recent survey of criminal law theories of responsibility, Antony Duff reflects critically on 'the yearning for grand theory'. He understands the 'powerful temptation ... to search for grand unifying theories of criminal liability' but thinks that it should be resisted. Those who offer large-scale all-embracing theories of liability should realise that they cannot possibly be describing law as it really is, in its 'contingent historical complexity'.[5] Only those of 'Herculean disposition' could believe otherwise. My subject here is just those Herculean theorists who are still searching for a theory which will give moral certainty to the ascription of criminal liability. My doubt is that such certainty can be achieved.

II. THE CHARACTER OF CORE THEORY

The grand theory that interests me, because it is so influential, tends to rely on a particular model of responsibility. It entails certain understandings of a moral agent, of a moral wrong, and of a moral criminal law. At the risk of appearing excessively schematic, this model tends to invoke a moral agent who is called to account by criminal law for a true or core or pure wrong which the criminal law has with surgical precision identified and encapsulated in its substantive norms; the criminal law then obliges the accused to give a rational and moral account of himself[6] for the alleged commission of this core wrong if he is to escape liability. The idea is that one respects the very personhood of the accused by addressing him as the right sort of moral agent and calling him to account, in the right sort of way, for a true moral and criminal wrong. As Andrew Ashworth has urged, 'individuals should be respected and treated as agents capable of choosing their acts and omissions, and ... without recognising individuals as capable of independent agency they could hardly be regarded as moral persons'.[7]

A. True Agents

There appear to be two prevailing models of the legal actor as moral agent in criminal law theory of the grand variety. One is Kantian, the other

[5] RA Duff, 'Virtue, Vice, and Criminal Liability: Do We Want an Aristotelian Criminal Law?' (2002) 6 *Buffalo Criminal Law Review* 147, 154.

[6] The male pronoun will generally be employed in this chapter in recognition of the male dominance of the crime statistics. The main subject of this paper, John Gardner, uses the female pronoun when writing about crime and I will comment later on the problems with this usage.

[7] A Ashworth, *Principles of Criminal Law* (Oxford, Oxford University Press, 5th edn, 2006) 26.

Aristotelian. Briefly stated, the Kantian agent is an intelligent reasoner whose practical choices are guided by respect for the intelligent reason of others. He must treat both himself and others as reasoners, as rational subjects, not as mere means to achieve his own ends. The Aristotelian agent is also an intelligent reasoner but his practical decisions are guided by virtue, by the exercise of good character, in whatever role he finds himself.

These theories of the moral agent have different emphases but both are rationalist. They purport to offer supposedly timeless metaphysical truths of the individual moral agent derived from the insights of different strands of moral rationalist philosophy. Criminal law is thought to be well resolved when it is itself rational, in the sense that it describes a deep wrong, and speaks to this rational individual, this moral agent, in the right manner about the reasons for his alleged commission of this deep wrong, respecting his agency and his responsibility for his actions. As Duff himself expresses this understanding of true criminal law and justice: it is 'a system of communicative and redemptive punishments [which] would, ideally, respect and care for the criminal as moral agent.'[8]

B. Core Criminality

Criminal law theory, in the grand style, is thought to do its best work, its true work, at what is thought to be the core of criminal law, that is with crimes which are regarded as deep moral wrongs, 'inherent turpitudes', which attract great moral censure. Criminal law theory thus tends to focus on certain criminal wrongs: these are the most serious crimes involving deliberate harms to others, about which, it is assumed, the people of 'the civilised world' would agree[9]—they would regard the wrong as inherent. These are considered true crimes which attract great social stigma. They are sometimes referred to as '*mala in se*' because they are thought to be 'intrinsically morally wrong'. Although it is conceded that 'much of the modern criminal law involves prohibitions which are only wrong because they are illegal (*mala prohibita*)',[10] the true work of criminal law and its theory is with the true wrongs. Murder and rape are typically regarded as true or core crimes.

The idea of core crimes and of murder and rape as clear examples of core crimes is conventional criminal legal wisdom. Victor Tadros introduces his book on criminal responsibility with the assertion that 'it is central to the criminal justice system that it morally criticises defendants for their

[8] RA Duff, *Trials and Punishments* (Cambridge, Cambridge University Press, 1986) 295.

[9] The reference to the laws of 'the civilised world' comes from Joel Feinberg in *Harm to Others* (New York, Oxford University Press, 1984) 10 but is quoted and endorsed by J Gardner and S Shute in 'The Wrongness of Rape' in J Horder (ed), *Oxford Essays in Jurisprudence* (Oxford, Oxford University Press, 2000) 193.

[10] Simester and Sullivan, above n 2, at 3.

conduct. This is most obviously true', he says, 'of what we may call the *"central" offences* of the criminal law, offences such as murder, rape, theft and assault ... This is a consequence of *the very nature of those offences*'.[11] Douglas Husak assures us that 'As long as we are talking about rape, theft and murder and other cases of *core criminality*, virtually all theorists agree that punishment is justified'.[12] Andrew Ashworth declares that '[t]he operation of the criminal law requires little explanation in *clear cases*'; he then identifies intentional killing and rape as 'clear cases'.[13] Tadros explains that with conviction for such 'serious criminal offences ... symbolically the individual is marked out as worthy of public criticism, and perhaps even condemnation.'[14] (My emphases throughout.)

The crimes of rape and murder have played especially important roles in the theory of criminal responsibility. They have been treated as obvious serious natural universal moral wrongs—at least in the 'civilised' nations—as sites of natural convergence of moral and criminal wrongs.[15] They have been regarded as crimes worthy of great moral censure, condemnation and blame therefore demanding an intentional moral wrong-doer (not just an unwitting offender) who must be brought to justice and asked to give an account of his actions. In legal pedagogy, they are used as crimes which serve well to explain and defend the importance of engaging with an intentional moral agent.

C. True Criminal Law

True criminal law calls the moral agent to account for his alleged wrongdoing in the right way: it encapsulates the wrong and demands an adequate account in the right forum. The person who cannot demonstrate his moral agency when thus called to account for apparent criminal wrongdoing is an appropriate subject for the moral blame which is entailed in the assignment of criminal responsibility. As Gardner and Shute explain, 'the criminal law has a role in requiring us to reason acceptably'.[16] While, according to Duff:

> The underlying assumption here is that criminal liability should, in principle, be ascribed in accordance with moral responsibility. A defendant should be

[11] V Tadros, *Criminal Responsibility* (Oxford, Oxford University Press, 2005) 2.

[12] Husak, above n 1, at 118.

[13] Ashworth, above n 7, at 1.

[14] Tadros, above n 11, at 2.

[15] Gardner and Shute, above n 9, at 205 state this emphatically: 'rape is the central case' of the 'sheer use of a human being' and therefore 'Joel Feinberg is right to place it on the short list of wrongs' which are criminalised everywhere which is civilised. The major exemption for husbands gets no mention at this point. Perhaps we were less than civilised before the 1990s.

[16] Gardner and Shute, above n 9, at 214.

criminally liable only for conduct for which she can properly be held morally responsible or culpable; and the extent of her criminal liability (the seriousness of the offence for which she is convicted) should match the degree of her moral responsibility or culpability. That is why mens rea should be required for criminal liability, and why intention should be the most serious and legitimate kind of criminal fault.[17]

Having sketched the main features of criminal law theory, in the grand style, I now want to take a closer look at the work of one grand theorist and test his implicit claim to provide a secure theoretical foundation for the imposition of criminal responsibility.

III. A CASE STUDY OF THE OPERATION OF CRIMINAL LAW THEORY AT ITS CORE: THE WORK OF JOHN GARDNER

The particular focus of this chapter is a series of papers by leading criminal law theorist John Gardner, in which he endeavours to explain the true nature of crime and the true basis of criminal responsibility. They are 'The Gist of Excuses' (1998)[18] ('The Gist'); 'The Wrongness of Rape' (2000) (with Stephen Shute)[19] ('The Wrongness'); 'The Mark of Responsibility' (2003)[20] ('The Mark'); and 'No Provocation without Responsibility' (2004) (with Timothy Macklin)[21] ('No Provocation'). In these papers, Gardner endeavours to isolate the essential characteristics—the authentic nature—of the responsible person as moral agent and by necessary implication the true nature of the wrongdoer. He is after the true nature of the wrong and the true nature of a criminal law which is capable of putting them all together. My purpose is to question the moral certainties implicit in this central work of grand theory. The current tendency in criminal law theory is to decry the departure of criminal laws from its true centre: core crime and core criminals. But there may be little point in urging a return to the moral homeland or heartland if it does not provide a safe, secure home.

I have chosen the work of Gardner, as expounded in this series of papers, because it exemplifies criminal law theory at a high level of sophistication and operating at the core, where it is meant to do its best and most convincing work. These papers are published in some of the most prominent and authoritative places in the United Kingdom and the United States and they

[17] RA Duff, *Intention, Agency and Criminal Liability: Philosophy of Action and the Criminal Law* (Oxford, Basil Blackwell, 1990) 103.

[18] J Gardner, 'The Gist of Excuses' (1998) 1 *Buffalo Criminal Law Review* 575.

[19] Gardner and Shute, above n 9.

[20] J Gardner, 'The Mark of Responsibility', (2003) 23 *OJLS* 157.

[21] J Gardner and T Macklem, 'No Provocation without Responsibility: A Reply to Mackay and Mitchell' [2004] *Crim LR* 213.

sustain a view of crime over a number of years. Here, Gardner, like many grand theorists of the criminal law, is deeply interested in elucidating what he takes to be our true nature and matching it to real criminal law and to real criminal accused. He is therefore a metaphysical realist with solid ambitions for his theory. These are papers of considerable theoretical complexity and nuance about the supposed core wrongs of rape and murder and about the characteristics of the moral agents charged with such wrongs. This is grand theory at its best and in its heartland. It therefore provides a fitting object of critical reflection.

Gardner's papers are also useful in that they variously embrace both models of the true moral agent—the Kantian and the Aristotelian—and so they enable us to see both models at work. So although I concentrate my efforts on a small cluster of papers by one theorist, alone and in collaboration—only four papers in all—there is good reason to think that these papers can stand for a lot and tell us a great deal about the nature and limits and weaknesses of current influential criminal law theory at the core.

IV. GARDNER ON THE REAL WRONG OF MURDER AND THE ARISTOTELIAN MORAL AGENT

Three of the papers under scrutiny are about the core crime of murder and what might constitute a valid excuse to it. The wrongness of murder is taken as a given: the natural point of departure. Here the focus is on the responsible moral agent who retains her virtue after a charge of murder. With murder implicitly treated as a core wrong, the question is: how can someone retain their moral agency in reply to such a charge? In 'The Gist', 'The Mark' and 'No Provocation', Gardner develops his idea of the true responsible moral agent (though a killer) who forms a fitting subject for criminal (murder) law. Specifically, he endeavours to explain the sort of excuse to killing which would allow the accused murderer to reply to the charge and leave the court with her virtue relatively intact. Here we have the implicitly conceded worst type of crime. What and who, he wants to know, could excuse it?

In these three papers on murder, Gardner is committed to an Aristotelian view of our moral nature. He believes that the criminal excuses—and here his focus is on the partial defence of provocation—make best sense when regarded as an expression of our essential natures. Gardner tends to invoke people of surprisingly good character and typically they are virtuous women. Those who fall short of his Aristotelian ideal of the person of good character, and who incidentally poorly match his theory, tend to receive far less consideration, even though these lesser types of individuals are the more common habitués of the criminal courts.

In Aristotelian fashion, Gardner believes that someone who offers a valid excuse has demonstrated her character fitness for the part she played: she has shown the adequacy of her virtue: 'The question is whether that person lived up to expectations in the *normative* sense. Did she manifest as much resilience, or loyalty, or thoroughness, or presence of mind as a person in her situation should have manifested?'[22]

In 'The Gist', Gardner reflects on our essential Aristotelian natures. He tells us that 'whatever other roles we may have in life, we also have the distinct role of being human beings, which itself sets basic standards of character'.[23] So to perform the role of human being is to perform a role which entails certain character standards. Moreover our human role is our 'overarching role' which, Gardner concedes, raises questions about 'what it means to be human'.[24] He adds swiftly that 'this is not the place to tackle this question'[25] but effectively he has already begun to do just this. For one thing, he has explicitly aligned himself with Aristotle and his understanding of the person of character.[26] To Gardner, the human role is a moral role which must be performed according to 'proper standards of character'.[27] The human role entails a singular overarching role as well as, it would seem, a multiplicity of constituting roles. In both the singular and multiple forms of human being—the roles that comprise our lives—there are standards of character. Gardner explains that:

> There are, fundamentally, two closely related things that matter about our relationship with the life we lead, and the roles which go to make it up. The first is that we do not fail in those roles ... The second is that we are fit for those roles, that we have the qualities (the virtues, skills, and tastes, as well as the physical and mental constitution) which people in those roles should have.[28]

Gardner also refers to our fitness as 'a human being *simpliciter*',[29] that is, as a being whose human nature is universal, not relative to place or time or culture. Wherever and whenever there is a human being, this is apparently her true nature. Gardner is not claiming to know with any certainty the 'defensible standards for failure and fitness' as such a universal being.[30] He concedes that there is disagreement about this. But he has already accepted that our mere humanity constitutes us as certain types of moral beings: essentially, by our very nature, *simpliciter*. He therefore presupposes a universal human nature, unaffected by time, place and culture.[31]

[22] Gardner, above n 18, at 579.
[23] Gardner, above n 18, at 594.
[24] *Ibid.*
[25] *Ibid.*
[26] In other words, he aligns himself with Aristotle in JAK Thomson (tr), *The Nicomachean Ethics* (Harmondsworth, Middlesex, Penguin, 1955).
[27] Gardner, above n 18, at 594.
[28] Gardner, above n 18, at 586.
[29] Gardner, above n 18, at 595.
[30] *Ibid.*
[31] This presupposition would be strongly disputed by anthropologists such as Clifford Geertz. See his *Interpretation of Cultures* (New York, Basic Books, 1973).

Five years later, in 'The Mark', Gardner is willing to express with greater boldness his views on human nature. Here, Gardner tells and affirms what he calls 'the Aristotelian story' about 'why, as rational beings, we might want our wrongs and mistakes to be justified, or failing that excused'.[32] He then reflects on what it is that makes us human: he is unwilling to say that he is describing our entire human nature. But he is willing to assert that, as rational beings, it is 'part of our *nature* (in Aristotle's sense of *ergon*, purpose, destiny) to hunt for justifications and excuses as soon as we spot that we have done something wrong or mistaken—never mind what unpleasant moral or legal consequences we can or can't avoid thereby'.[33] It is part of our very *telos* to explain ourselves.

We can take from Gardner two points: one small, one large. His smaller linguistic point is perhaps that rational beings cannot, by definition, question their desire to act for reasons for as soon as they do so, they must offer a reason, thereby demonstrating both their reason and their desire to act for reasons. But his other larger metaphysical point is surely that human beings are indeed creatures of this sort; that we are rational beings by nature who wish our actions to be seen as morally defensible. And this is why we would positively want to offer decent accounts of ourselves and avoid pleas of diminished responsibility. We do not want our reason to be regarded as legally diminished; rather, we want our actions to be understood and made comprehensible.

Our nature as rational beings, for Gardner, carries the further corollary that we must want to 'excel in rationality'.[34] Moreover, 'as rational beings we cannot but want our lives to have made rational sense, to add up to a story not only of whats but of *whys*'.[35] Gardner invokes a high degree of reason in his person who acts for reasons, 'a developed ability to use reasons',[36] not just ordinary common sense and certainly not weak reasoning. In Gardner's words, 'explanation in terms of reasons is what a rational being aspires to'[37] and by nature we are rational beings. His natural human reasoners would appear also to be sophisticated language users. Thus 'to grasp our natures as human beings, we need to think of ourselves in terms of a composite speech-and-reason ability of the kind that Aristotle called *logos*'.[38]

For Gardner, the true criminal excuser is precisely not someone who is trying to duck responsibility: who says 'I couldn't help it' or 'it wasn't really me'; 'this time I behaved in a way I normally wouldn't, so please

[32] Gardner, above n 20, at 159.
[33] *Ibid.*
[34] Gardner, above n 20, at 158.
[35] *Ibid.* Emphasis in original.
[36] Gardner, above n 20, at 164.
[37] Gardner, above n 20, at 159.
[38] Gardner, above n 20, at 164.

excuse me'.[39] Rather, those who offer valid (not ersatz) excuses positively embrace responsibility for their actions and so seek to offer the court an explanation of why their behaviour was reasonable in the circumstances, thereby displaying good character within the role demanded of them, even if that role was simply that of being a sufficiently virtuous human being.

In 'The Gist', Gardner states that: 'Self-respect is an attitude which everyone ought to have if they deserve it, and which, moreover everyone ought to deserve.'[40] He is positively disparaging about what he refers to as Hobbesian defendants. These are in fact a common breed, for they are persons who simply want to get out of trouble, by whatever means, and who have little interest in giving a dignifying account of themselves.[41] (Indeed it is well known that the majority of defendants choose not to engage in reasoned defences of their conduct but opt instead to plead guilty.)

To Gardner, the criminal law should play a positive role in persuading people to conform to their metaphysical natures. This is the central thesis of 'The Mark': that it is good for our moral character, our very personhood, to be held to account. Thus Gardner assigns to criminal law an important and even noble role in recognising and reinforcing our essential (Aristotelian) natures. Because we are, by nature, in essence, rational creatures who should want to subscribe to the virtues, it is important that criminal law act upon and accentuate this noble truth about us.

In 'The Gist', 'The Mark' and 'No Provocation' Gardner sustains an interest in one very particular character who for him represents the realisation of the values and character he would like to find in all of us. This is the woman who falls victim to sustained and repulsive domestic violence, who is provoked to retaliate with fatal violence and who then goes on to argue, affectingly and effectively, the partial criminal excuse of provocation. These are Gardner's virtuous defendants who embody the Aristotelian character values. Though they are real instances of killers, they are also more importantly embodiments of an idea, a true form, of human moral agency—one which can stand for all time.

A. The Virtuous Woman

Gardner's good woman killer admirably resists the appellation of battered woman, with its suggestion of pathology, even though it might support a

[39] Indeed, he positively rejects the view that the excuses are to be explained as out-of-character defences. See discussion in V Tadros, 'The Character of Excuses' (2001) 21 *OJLS* 495 and W Wilson, 'The Structure of Criminal Defences', [2005] *Crim LR* 108.

[40] Gardner, above n 18, at 590.

[41] Such defendants are described, quite movingly, by Richard Ericson and Patricia Baranek in *The Ordering of Justice: A Study of Accused Persons as Dependants in the Criminal Process* (Toronto, University of Toronto Press, 1982).

defence of diminished responsibility. Charged with murder, this woman virtuously opts for the defence of provocation rather than the defence of diminished responsibility, though the latter might be easier to establish. This woman, we are told, wants to show that her behaviour was reasonable in the circumstances she faced, in the part she played.[42] She invites us to see why she did it and the reasons Gardner gives them are dignifying: 'she did it because she needed to save some vestige of her dignity before he destroyed it utterly' or 'she did it for the sake of the children, whom she thought would be the next target'.[43] She does not want to demean herself by arguing that her responsibility was diminished.

Gardner believes that, by using the defence of provocation, such a woman 'defends herself ... with her head held high, as a rational being. She relies not simply on her disturbed emotional condition, but on the *rational defensibility* of her disturbed emotional condition. ... She wants to give an account of herself as a fully responsible adult, sane, human being'.[44]

Although such women defendants understandably want to avoid 'consequential responsibility'—that is, the punitive consequences of a conviction for murder—they still want to assert what Gardner calls their 'basic responsibility'. That is, they want 'to assert that, in spite of all they had been through, they were fully responsible adults'.[45] Such women are invoked, almost romantically, as the heroines of criminal law; they are women with 'their heads held high' resisting the lure of diminished responsibility. They wish 'to give an intelligible account' of themselves, to answer for themselves as rational beings.[46] These virtuous women have large characters. They aspire 'to have the reason of a communicator, and the communication of a reasoner'.[47] To Gardner, the 'fundamental point is to have structured explanatory dialogues in public, in which the object of explanation is ourselves'.[48] Gardner's virtuous women have the moral character and the self-respect to do just this.

In his virtuous women, Gardner has therefore found personifications of Aristotelian good character. As Gardner explains, they are wrestling with the dreadful temptation to define themselves as battered women and so gain the benefits of a defence of diminished responsibility. But their valour prevails over discretion, over such tempting opportunism, and they decide

[42] Gardner's view that the partial excuse of provocation can be grounded in the reasonableness of the response is controversial. As William Wilson has argued: 'Provocation ... is surely a human frailty defence if ever there was one. Killing, even in justified anger, is the antithesis of reasonableness': Wilson, above n 39, at 117. See Tadros, above n 39.

[43] Gardner, above n 18, at 591.

[44] Gardner, above n 20, at 160. Emphasis in original.

[45] Gardner, above n 20, at 161.

[46] *Ibid.*

[47] Gardner, above n 20, at 163.

[48] Gardner, above n 20, at 167.

that they will go to law not as supplicants but as rational women of courage, heads high, who had good reason, indeed virtuous reason, for their actions.

Such women wish to explain and vindicate their actions. They wish to be understood in the context of their appalling circumstances and their invidious choices. The virtuous task they have set themselves is to explain the complexity of their situation, and to show the difficult relation between reason and passion in their final solution. They do this magnificently, revealing their lack of alternatives: their need to protect their children, their need to do something to stop the abusive treatment if they are to avoid the loss of all dignity. They show also that the moral agent of true Aristotelian virtue can be realised.

B. The Hunt for Platonic Forms

Gardner's good woman provides him with an invaluable illustration of his idea of moral agency and the moral law at work. But it is not essential to Gardner and to his moral approach to criminal law that his theory be realised and made flesh. Nor does it matter that most defendants may have little in common with the virtuous woman. 'For all we ... know, many defendants are people without much self-respect, who care little whether the law gives them an opportunity to engage self-respectingly with it.'[49] But they are not his concern.

For, in these papers, I suggest, Gardner is on the hunt for the true Platonic Forms of right and wrong doing. By this I mean that he is guided by a Platonic idea that there are pure wrongs and pure forms of responsible agents who must respond to accusations of wrongdoing, that is right doers.[50] Gardner strives to understand what he believes to be the true nature of the moral agent confronted with the accusation that she has committed a core criminal wrong. He seeks to define a moral essence which is enduring and can only be truly grasped by the exercise of sustained philosophical effort, 'by the power of pure thought', as Plato put it.[51] It does not depend

[49] Gardner and Macklem, above n 21, at 216.

[50] The theory of the Forms is to be found in Plato's *The Republic*: D Lee (tr), (London, Penguin, 2003) 277 where Plato also presents his Simile of the Cave: his parable on human ignorance. Here, Plato likens most of us to prisoners chained within an underground cave, obliged to acquire their knowledge of the world from their observation of mere shadows cast by real people and events behind them, which they can never directly witness. (Plato has his prisoners with their heads trained towards the wall in front of them. 'Behind them and above them a fire is burning, and between the fire and the prisoners runs a road, in front of which a curtain-wall has been built.'(279) The people walking along the road behind them only ever appear to the prisoners as cast shadows. But the prisoners foolishly believe that the shadows are the real world.)

[51] Plato, above n 50, at 277.

for its reality on empirical proofs or real instantiations. One will not *necessarily* find these moral realities in the criminal law or in the criminal justice system or the criminal courts, for these are all part of the imperfect empirical world of appearances which is shifting and changing and hence unreliable. The moral realities are part of the intelligible world, not the mere physical world of appearance, image and illusion.

Indeed, Gardner has little time for the motley crew of real defendants and their real and often motley lawyers engaged in real dealings with real criminal justice—what Plato would have termed the world of appearances. Gardner openly disparages them and is remarkably incurious about them. 'To be fair', he says, 'lawyers do often have to deal with people whose predicaments are towards the Hobbesian end of the spectrum: desperate people faced with the threat of prison or deportation or bankruptcy, destructively bitter people who have been betrayed and deserted by their spouses and partners'.[52] So be it. For this is the mere world of appearances. As a theorist of the true form of moral agency, as it should be made manifest by real moral agents in the criminal courts (whether or not it is), it is simply not his concern. From this it follows that sociological or criminological inquiry into the general nature of real criminals and real criminal laws will not necessarily prove useful.

It is this preoccupation with core crime and true moral agents, rather than real-world people and their annoying complexity, which is my particular concern. If real defendants do not live up to the theory,[53] the problem it seems is with the people, not the theory. This is a strange logic. Gardner has identified his few good women—his true moral agents. Implicitly he spurns the less than noble beings who will do anything in their power just to get off, who rationally self-maximise by minimising their responsibility. Essentially he is concerned with 'what a self-respecting defendant would prefer, never mind what the majority of defendants would prefer' in real courts of law.[54]

Anthony Duff has expressed a similar frustration with the vicissitudes of real criminals and real criminal justice by admitting that his own ideal of 'communicative justice'—in which a moral law speaks to a moral agent—'is all too easily corrupted'. He even admits that '[p]erhaps the ideal is too distant to be a human possibility: for our attempts to attain it might instead destroy it utterly'.[55] Thus does criminal law theory, in the grand style, detach itself from real people and real institutions.[56]

[52] Gardner and Macklem, above n 21, at 216.
[53] Kant was similarly vexed by the moral weaknesses of most people.
[54] Gardner and Macklem, above n 21, at 216.
[55] Duff, above n 8, at 295.
[56] For a critical appraisal of criminal law theory and its tendency to detach theory from practice, see A Norrie, '"Simulcra of Morality?" Beyond the Ideal/Actual Antimonies of Criminal Justice' in A Duff (ed), *Philosophy and the Criminal Law: Principle and Critique* (Cambridge, Cambridge University Press, 1998).

The real defendants who, far too commonly, depart from Gardner's idea and ideal appear in his work only briefly as an anonymous sea of bitter faces and are quickly dispatched. They are not his problem as a philosopher of the criminal law who is concerned to unearth the true nature of moral agency, its one true form, and who has found a woman who can do it for him. Indeed, the criminal law and its institutions deserve better than the real defendants who actually inhabit the criminal courts with their unsavoury representatives: 'For all its vulnerability to abuse by crafty and sometimes unscrupulous lawyers excessively preoccupied with getting people on or off the hook, I think we should mostly take a prouder attitude towards the legal process.'[57]

To return to Gardner's choice of the virtuous woman, there is almost a theoretical perversity about making the emblematic defendant female or trying to make the female case cover the male case (by the persistent but uncommented upon use of the female pronoun). After all, most real crime and especially most real violent crime is done by men. Somehow reality gets badly skewed, but we may not notice it because we are in the intelligible world of the Forms. Without it necessarily being spelled out, the message being conveyed is that we are safely in the realm of high (normative) theory not down in the courts, the world of appearances, where the defendants are actually mainly male and quite possibly Hobbesian and the realities of crime and justice are far messier. Moral certainty is achieved by a concerted focus on moral purity, not moral complexity or moral reality.

V. GARDNER ON THE REAL WRONG OF RAPE AND THE KANTIAN MORAL AGENT

In 'The Wrongness', Gardner (here with Stephen Shute) turns his attention to the core crime of rape and searches for its 'pure' form, again what one might call its Platonic form. He then infers from what he takes to be the real rape, the real rapist and also the real non-rapist—the person who is properly exonerated. (The real non-rapist has his moral reason still intact after the accusation of rape.) Here, Gardner largely abandons the endeavour to match real people, via real criminal laws, with real rape. Indeed 'It is no objection that the question of the wrongfulness of this rape [his pure rape] will never arise in practical deliberation'.[58]

The wrong of rape, to Gardner, is the Kantian wrong of treating another as something for one's own use, not as an end in her own right—as someone with her own ends. It is treating a moral agent as an object. The real non-rapist treats others as ends in themselves, in what Kant referred to as the 'kingdom of ends', and so adheres to the moral law of Kant.

[57] Gardner, above n 20, at 166.
[58] Gardner and Shute, above n 9, at 197.

Rape, to Gardner, is the paradigm of all wrongs because it is about the use of another's very self. It is not about the use of their body, as some feminists seem to think, for Gardner agrees with Kant that the body should not be regarded ever as a thing for use or misuse by anyone, by oneself or by another. Instead the body is the corporeal self. And it would seem that when the female body is penetrated by a penis without a prior ascertainment of whether that penis is wanted, that is the case *par excellence* of misuse of the self of another.[59]

Gardner arrives at the pure wrong of rape not by considering real defendants or real victims (as he did with murder, albeit in a highly selective fashion) or real criminal laws but by imagining himself into the wrong with the aid of Kantian reasoning. He is intent on thus finding rape's pure form—by the use of pure thought which is the Platonic philosopher's route to truth. To shed the crime of its inessentials, in order to get to the pure wrong, Gardner employs the device of the thought experiment. He then puts some surprising elements into his imagined scenario.[60] The victim of this pure rape is to be unconscious at the time and then never come to know about it. This rather startling elimination of the perspective of the victim allows Gardner to concentrate his attention on the true wrong. And the true wrong lies in the woman being treated as a sexual thing for use, not as another person, that is as a moral agent, even though she does not have to be a functional agent at the time of the rape, nor an agent who is ever cognisant of the wrong done to her.

In this experiment, the woman imagined has no knowledge of the rape at the time and no memory of it afterwards. From her point of view, it never happened. Her experience and very perception of the rape are quite incidental to the pure rape—mere epiphenomena. Rather, the essence of the crime, as we are invited to see it, lies in the inattention of the rapist to her personhood. Rape is his inattention to her as he penetrates her, not her understanding of the situation. Nor is rape intersubjective, as some have suggested: it is not about his wrongful failure to understand her or attend

[59] Why precisely it is penetration by a penis (and certainly not engulfment by a vagina) and not, say, being trodden on, say being used as a step, is not entirely clear, though Gardner says it is because the unwanted penile penetration is regarded by society as a very bad misuse of another. But both being penetrated by a penis one doesn't want and being used as a step would seem to be utter misuses of a person or a person's body. Indeed, one can think of endless examples of one person being treated by another as a thing for use—where there is no consideration of their interests and the other becomes simply an instrument of one's own needs. The real wrong of rape, to Gardner, it seems exists because that is how things are with us. This seems a thin basis for the determination of a real wrong, especially by someone looking for a true, timeless Kantian wrong. It remains unclear why it is unwanted penetrative sex which constitutes a pure misuse of another.

[60] Thought experiments, of course, encounter no problems with the improbable or even the impossible, which may be why they are so attractive to philosophers. See KV Wilkes, *Real People: Personal Identity Without Thought Experiments* (Oxford, Clarendon Press, 1988).

to her coupled with her understanding of this failure to attend. It is all about *his* wrong will. (This is an odd reading of Kant for whom the overriding of the *active* will of the moral agent—rather than misuse of the inert being—would seem to be the worst type of wrong.)

Pursuing this logic, it is not clear that the victim of the pure rape need be alive at all, as her consciousness of the wrong is immaterial to rape, purely understood.[61] Her awareness of the wrong and the harm she believes has been done to her only clouds the issue; it stops us seeing the true wrong—the pure Form—which does not depend on her view of it. It follows, it would seem, that if he believes her to be alive but fails to attend to her as a person, the wrong is done, even if she is actually dead. Gardner dismisses from the outset those feminists who lack the philosophical acumen to see that the essence of the wrong is not the experienced wrong or the harm caused to the particular victim but rather the moral deficiency of the rapist alone. And to appreciate this moral deficiency we do not need an injured or outraged victim. We need only focus on his inattention, on his impaired moral will as he has sex with her.

The problem is that as we obey these philosophical instructions and begin to imagine not only an unconscious victim, then make sure that all her memory is erased, we can just as easily move on, imaginatively, to think of the victim as corpse. This is my additional move, but the thought experiment seems to permit it. We might go further still, within the terms of the experiment, and have him commit forced sex, on line, by computer, with someone whom he believes to exist but who does not exist at all.[62] Credulity is stretched with pure rape conceived as an unexperienced wrong. We should not really need a corpse or a fantasy person to see how the experiment lacks an air of reality. Gardner himself concedes that it does not matter, for his conception, that it is unamenable to real law and to real criminal courts and so lacks empirical reality in this sense.

Many feminists would say that the unexperienced rape—which can never be expressed or explained by the victim—is simply not the wrong they are concerned about.[63] Their moral interest lies in women feeling violated and afraid and how criminal law can best respond to that violation.[64] They are not most exercised about unwitting victims whose lives remain entirely

[61] Gardner might reply that the dead are not moral agents. But, the logic of his experiment does not seem to exclude the dead.

[62] I thank Ian Leader-Elliott for suggesting this hypothetical.

[63] For an alternative conception of the wrong of rape, see N Lacey, 'Unspeakable Subjects, Impossible Rights: Sexuality, Integrity and Criminal Law' in N Lacey (ed), *Unspeakable Subjects: Feminist Essays in Legal and Social Theory* (Oxford, Hart Publishing, 1998).

[64] M Koss, 'Restoring Rape Survivors: Justice, Advocacy and a Call to Action' (2006) 1087 *Annals of the New York Academy of Sciences* 206; J Herman, 'Justice from the Victim's Perspective' (2005) 11 *Violence Against Women* 571.

unaltered by the rape and who (it would seem) do not even need to be alive to be raped or even to exist. They are not most exercised by offenders who can never, by definition, be brought to justice. Gardner's real rape—his classic core wrong—begins to take on the quality of a chimera. And one must then begin to worry about the soundness of the core of criminal law theory when it stands at such a remove from empirical reality and real social concerns (despite its very claims to realism).

Gardner's real rapist is perhaps someone a feminist can understand for he is described as a man who is inattentive to the sexual desires of the woman in question—who is not alert to what she wants. But this definition of the real rapist is hopelessly overinclusive. For how many acts of sex are there between clumsy inattentive men and women who fail to communicate effectively their lack of desire, for whatever reason? Gardner's rapist is a person of utter ordinariness engaged in an act of utter ordinariness and no criminal law that we know has countenanced such a definition in practice.

Still further, pure rapes can be fully resistant to real criminal law according to Gardner. Gardner drives this point home, that rape does not depend on the effective application of law, by insisting that not only need the victim have no awareness of the rape, but that the rapist can be killed immediately thereafter and yet the real rape remains a real rape, in the world. It remains the Platonic form of rape—the true essence of the crime regardless of its implicitly misleading empirical manifestations. Rape is therefore not a wrong produced by the criminal law (which many would say it is). It is not a wrong produced by accusers and by the presence of an accused person brought to answer the charge and by the adequacy of his reply. Nor is it a wrong produced by the perceptions of the victim—the harm she thought was done to her. It is an intrinsic wrong: a pure Kantian wrong in the sense that it entails the willed use of another (though somehow the particular significance of its penetrative nature, that which makes it the paradigm crime of use of another, is socially produced).

VI. SPREADING RESPONSIBILITY?

Douglas Husak has recently decried the poverty of criminal law theory on criminalisation by observing that when, for example, criminal law theorists 'provide accounts of defences', they 'almost certainly assume that their views will be applied to defendants who commit criminal offenses that are themselves justified'.[65] (Husak himself makes just such an assumption about the core crimes of rape and murder.) With Husak, I believe we are poorly placed to criticise the recent spread of state power and the proliferation of criminal wrongs—the central concern of this book—if we take as a given

[65] Husak, above n 1, at 118.

that there is a core set of wrongs which are naturally wrong and whose criminalisation is always justified. This leaves too much uninspected.

But once we question the natural wrongness of the core wrongs, and whether they are really doing the job they should, we begin to unsettle criminal law theory where it is meant to be most secure. For central to criminal law theory is the idea that there are certain wrongs, rape especially and also murder, which are self-evidently blameworthy and so call for, and legitimate, theories of criminal responsibility. My suggestion is that even these core wrongs may not supply a sure footing for theories of blame. Even the 'core' wrongs require us to think about how and why and whom we actually choose to and manage to criminalise.

If we focus on actual criminal legal norms and practices, rather than the deep metaphysical theory of criminal wrong and criminal responsibility, the core wrongs begin to lose their clarity and their certainty. This is especially true of the core wrong of rape, the crime that is thought by many to supply the gold standard of criminal wrongs. 'That rape is wrong, and seriously wrong at that, can scarcely be doubted', says Gardner.[66] But it can certainly be doubted, if we go by what is happening with real people and real law.

The law, the courts and therefore the community (in whose name they act) can be observed to criminalise few rapes and to permit most of them. Rape, as a matter of criminal justice practice, is not a serious wrong which leads to strong moral censure. Instead it is largely countenanced. Few offenders are brought to justice. Indeed, the rules of rape, substantive and adjectival, produce the most egregious defendant behaviour (impugning the credibility of the complainant in the most humiliating manner), are punitive to the victim, and lead to the exoneration of most, including those who are too callous and indifferent to see their wrong. (In the author's home jurisdiction of South Australia it is estimated that less than 2 per cent of rapes which come to the attention of police result in a conviction.)[67] And yet rape is treated as a core, classic, central wrong where criminal law theory is supposed to do its real work; it remains a source of extensive discussion among criminal theorists—the hothouse for the theory of criminal and moral responsibility; an assumed natural basis for the assignment of blame. The notoriously low prosecution and conviction rates for rape are simply not permitted to disturb the settled view that rape is a universally-condemned wrong which no civilised people would tolerate. That is, the theory is treated as right, and so is its moral aspiration; there just needs to be a better fit between empirical law (and perhaps the offenders) and the theory.[68]

[66] Gardner and Shute, above n 9, at 193.

[67] M Heath, 'The Law and Sexual Offences against Adults in Australia' (2005) 4 *Issues* (Australian Institute of Family Studies) 5.

[68] The reporting, prosecution and conviction rates for rape have been well documented and heavily discussed and criticised. On the Australian situation, see Victorian Law Reform Commission, *Final Report on Sexual Offences*, (Melbourne, VLRC, 2004) and Heath, above n 67. For the United Kingdom, see Home Office, *Setting the Boundaries* (London, HMSO, 2000).

Gardner, and no doubt Duff, would say that the problem here is bad law or bad procedure and yet these same theorists also keep saying that rape is a core settled agreed-upon classic wrong, at the heart of their theory. It is one of those wrongs which is 'never excusable ... never justifiable'.[69] This is a remarkable claim given the very recent immunity of all married men from prosecution for the rape of their wives.[70] Can they have it both ways? Can they say that crimes such as rape are core wrongs at the core of criminal law theory (which are universally understood to be wrong in civilised places), where the theory does its best work, and then say or imply that real criminal law and real people can be quite different but that the theory remains sound?

My point is that criminal law theory must engage with actual positive criminal laws and their actual operations if they are to serve a useful purpose. Of course, it is important to refine our concepts, to endeavour to understand more thoroughly the principal ideas which claim our attention as criminal law theorists. But these criminal concepts must have a bearing on legal realities, otherwise there is a significant danger of getting our concepts wrong. Gardner is convinced that he can find what he takes to be the deep wrong of rape by searching for its Platonic form, shorn of all epiphenomena. Perversely, this leads him to focus on precisely that form of rape which is most resistant to criminal law and which is of least practical concern to wronged women—because they do not even know that they have been wronged. It also leads him to make some surprising empirical claims which would seem to be over-generalised and unsubstantiated. Rape is not universally condemned and stigmatised, as he says it is. Rather much rape is practically tolerated and no crisis of legal authority seems to flow from the fact that most rape is not practically criminalised.

An abiding concern of feminist criminal lawyers is that rape laws, variously conceived, still do not effectively criminalise. Concerted efforts to refine the nature of the wrong of rape and to produce positive laws which will bring offenders to justice and give women greater confidence in criminal justice have met with remarkably little success. To Gardner, rarity of prosecution is not a problem for his criminal law theory. He accepts that his concept of the pure rape 'languishes at the statistical periphery' but insists that 'the question whether a certain wrong can properly be prohibited by law is a secondary question'.[71] It matters not to him that his conception of rape is 'ever so legally marginal' because it is to him 'morally central'.[72] Indeed, a common feature of the Aristotelian, the Kantian and the Platonic

[69] Gardner and Shute, above n 9, at 193.

[70] The presumptive immunity was lifted by the House of Lords in 1991: *R v R* [1991] 3 WLR 767.

[71] Gardner and Shute, above n 9, at 198.

[72] Gardner and Shute, above n 9, at 199.

aspects of Gardner's criminal law theory is its high level of abstraction. Despite important differences between these philosophies, when Gardner applies them to crime, they all involve an idealisation of the criminal, their effective removal from the rich social context of their criminality, and a degree of detachment from the specific legal norms which serve to criminalise their behaviour.[73]

But criminal law theory does not serve us well when it is preoccupied with pure rights and wrongs, with Platonic forms, which may bear little relation to actual current conventional ways of defining criminality and practically assigning (and failing to assign) blame. Nor are we well served when the focus is on moral agents who hardly typify the mass of criminal defendants (as with Gardner's virtuous woman). Criminal law theory has little purchase if it does not engage with such practical matters.

A central concern of this book is the proliferation of criminal law. It is concerned with the extension of state power and in particular with over-criminalisation and punishment. However this disturbing outward movement of the state does not occur systematically and evenly—moving from the core wrongs (which we can all agree upon) to more dubiously wrongful behaviour. The net of criminal responsibility is not always and inexorably widening from a legitimate core (where we as theorists can be sure of our principles) to a more questionable periphery. Even among the so-called 'sex offenders'—those who now seem to claim so much state attention—there are those who are subject to quite draconian and illiberal laws (the so-called paedophiles) and others who are virtually tolerated (men who rape women without obvious violence, especially within ordinary domestic relations such as marriage). It was only with great reluctance, and recently, that the courts and the legislature included husbands in the population of potential rapists.[74] Rape still has one of the largest 'dark' figures, and prosecution and conviction rates remain low. If we were bracingly honest about the core wrong of rape, we would have to say that it is not criminal in a practical sense; it is not practically condemned; in the vast majority of cases it is in effect lawful.[75] When criminal law theorists insist on the natural and universal wrongness

[73] I thank Alan Norrie for this astute observation.

[74] For example, in South Australia in the mid-1970s, the criminalisation of husbands as rapists was strenuously resisted by those who thought it represented a threat to family life. In response, the South Australian Parliament proceeded to criminalise only those husband rapists who committed aggravated rape. Non-aggravated rape remained lawful.

[75] To some feminists, rape is not, in effect, a criminal offence. As the vast majority of rapists have no real reason to fear conviction, they can rape with impunity. This creates a genuine moral dilemma for the feminist criminal lawyer who must ask herself: is it best to reveal the appalling truth about the effective legality of rape, as a stimulus to reform; or will this simply inform new rapists that they have little to fear from the law and so prove a rapist's charter? For a nice analysis of this dilemma, see M Heath, 'Lack of Conviction: A Proposal to Make Rape Illegal in South Australia', forthcoming, *Australian Feminist Law Journal*.

of certain crimes such as rape they fail to attend to these obvious, mundane and worrying realities of criminal law and criminal justice.

This is not to deny the genuine moral and intellectual difficulties of designating and defining serious crimes such as rape. But to capture the nature of these crimes, we need to attend to the actual ways that they are understood by the relevantly-affected parties. This calls for thick, not thin, social description. Rather than engage in a search for some pure and eternal essence of such crimes, it is more fruitful to consider what those who feel that they have been wronged consider that wrong to be. And that understanding of the wrong is likely to be shaped by a host of contextual factors. The wrong is not to be found outside specific social worlds; rather it is to be found within real complicated social relations which always occur in particular places, cultures and times.

Part V

Codification and the Liberal Promise

11

Criminal Codes in the 21st Century
The Paradox of the Liberal Promise

SIMON BRONITT AND MIRIAM GANI

I. INTRODUCTION

We promise according to our hopes and perform according to our fears.[1]

AUSTRALIA PROVIDES AN excellent case study for a critical examination of common law codification. It has commonly been claimed that Australia is a 'profoundly common law country'.[2] In relation to criminal law, this is only half true as the bulk of jurisdictions now work under a codified criminal law.[3] However, codification has not received much scholarly attention by criminal lawyers (at least by those from common law jurisdictions). Most Australian textbooks simply note the existence of the two distinct legal cultures, reiterating the High Court's caution that fundamental legal concepts, whether expressed in the common law or in a code, should bear the same meaning.[4] Since the Commonwealth Constitution

[1] F De La Rochefoucauld, *Reflections; or Sentences and Moral Maxims*, translated from the French editions of 1678 and 1827 by JW Willis Bund and J Hain Friswell (London, Simpson Low, Son and Marston, 1871) Maxim 38.

[2] S Stoljar (ed), *Problems of Codification* (Canberra, ANU Press, 1977) i.

[3] The federal jurisdiction and the Australian Capital Territory (formerly common law criminal jurisdictions) have adopted criminal codes based on the Model Criminal Code (see discussion below). Of the other seven jurisdictions, three have criminal codes based on a draft code developed by Sir Samuel Griffith in 1897: Criminal Code Act 1899 (Qld), Criminal Code Act 1913 (WA) (first enacted in 1902) and Criminal Code Act 1924 (Tas). The three so-called common law jurisdictions of New South Wales, South Australia and Victoria have more or less extensive criminal consolidation statutes: see Crimes Act 1900 (NSW); Criminal Law Consolidation Act 1935 (SA); Crimes Act 1958 (Vic). The Northern Territory is unique in Australia in that it is in the process of reforming its Griffith Code, the Criminal Code Act 1983 (NT), in line with principles and offences contained in the Model Criminal Code.

[4] See for example S Bronitt and B McSherry, *Principles of Criminal Law* (Sydney, Lawbook Co, 2nd edn, 2005) 71ff, noting the distinct cultures of the common law and Code jurisdictions, and the High Court's concern to promote convergence, wherever statutory language permitted, in the interpretation of common concepts such as provocation: discussing *Masciantonio v The Queen* (1995) 183 CLR 58, 66.

did not grant a general power to the Federal Parliament to enact criminal laws, federalism in Australia has promoted diversity in approaches to the criminal law, although ultimately there is a national interest in promoting its consistency.

Codification makes the common lawyer uneasy, partly because of the way the merits and demerits of case law systems have been presented by civil lawyers—code versus case law is often reduced to a 'battle of slogans, without the protagonists really joining issue over anything particularly clear or precise'.[5] Worse still, the movement toward codification is presented as the inevitable 'nail in the coffin' for the common law more generally. As Italian Professor of Criminal Law, Alberto Cadoppi concluded, the common law experiments in codification of the criminal law in the late 19th century and 20th century represent a move away from the traditional methods of the common law towards the civil law and 'as having set in train the ultimate abolition of judge-made law as an institution of the common law'.[6] As Jeremy Horder notes, the driving intellectual force behind the codification movement in part has been 'the wish to snuff out once and for all the flickering flame of judicial creativity in the field of criminal law'.[7]

Such claims provide a starting point for our research. While it is no doubt true that codification constrains the judicial role to some degree (most obviously in relation to inherent power to create new common law crimes), the liberal promise of codes and codification must be subject to close scrutiny from both an explanatory and a normative perspective.

First, though, let us consider what codification means. A definition that has been referred to in the Australian context follows:

> [A Criminal Code is a] pre-emptive, systematic, and comprehensive enactment of the whole field of law. It is pre-emptive in that it displaces all other law and its subject areas save only that which the Code excepts. It is systematic in that all of its parts, arranged in an orderly fashion and stated with a consistent terminology, form an interlocking, integrated body, revealing its own plan and containing its own methodology. It is comprehensive in that it is sufficiently inclusive and independent to enable it to be administered in accordance with its own basic policies.[8]

[5] Stoljar, above n 2, at 2.

[6] This summary of Cadoppi's research project, and his earlier work published in a leading Italian criminal law review, was offered by Justice Cullinane, Supreme Court of Queensland, in the preface accompanying A Cadoppi, 'The Zanardelli Code and Codification in the Countries of the Common Law' (2000) 7 *James Cook University Law Review* 116, 117.

[7] J Horder, 'Criminal Law' in P Cane and M Tushnet (eds), *Oxford Handbook of Legal Studies* (Oxford, Oxford University Press, 2003) 227.

[8] Matthew Goode refers to this definition, taken from a Canadian source, in his article 'Codification of the Australian Criminal Law' (1992) 16 *Criminal Law Journal* 5, 9, quoting WD Hawkland, 'Uniform Commercial Code Methodology' [1962] *University of Illinois Law Forum* 291–2. This quotation is found in G Letourneau and S Cohen, 'Codification and Law Reform: Some Lessons from the Canadian Experience' (1989) 10 *Statute Law Review* 183.

The justification for codification of the criminal law, then, has a set of fundamentally liberal ideas at its core. In England, as well as in other common law jurisdictions, codification has been presented as the vehicle for delivery of improved accessibility, consistency, comprehensibility and certainty in the criminal law.[9] In Australia, Matthew Goode, a key proponent of the Model Criminal Code (MCC), has expressed the justification for codification by reference to a similar set of liberal virtues. Codification, he says, offers the prospect of a criminal law that is 'easy to discover, easy to understand, cheap to buy and democratically made and amended'.[10] Moreover, codification is seen as a means to further other liberal values, including synthesising the due process and social protection aims of the criminal law and enabling law reform.[11] Significantly, also, codification has been identified, both in the English and Australian contexts, as performing an important constitutional role by making a 'symbolic statement about the constitutional relationship of Parliament and courts'.[12] It is seen as a liberal virtue of the codified criminal law that it be made and amended by Parliament, and not by the judiciary.[13]

How well does codification deliver on these liberal promises? Under any system of law—whether codified or not—gaps and uncertainty remain. As distinguished comparative lawyer, Samuel Stoljar, notes, poorly drafted codes may produce considerable uncertainty,[14] while the concept of leading cases (and the academic commentary they generate) can promote clarity, coherence and guiding principles far beyond the particular dispute at hand.[15] Moreover, the role of case-law and judicial creativity is not necessarily diminished under codified systems. In civil law systems, although there is

[9] These four aims were enumerated by the authors of the 1985 Draft Code for England and Wales in Codification of the Criminal Law, Law Com No 143 (1985), Introduction [14].

[10] Goode, above n 8, at 8ff. See also M Goode, 'Codification of the Criminal Law' (2004) 28 *Criminal Law Journal* 226, 229ff.

[11] ATH Smith, 'Codification of the Criminal Law Part 1: The Case for a Code' [1986] *Crim LR* 285, discussed in G De Burca and S Gardner, 'The Codification of the Criminal Law' (1990) 10 *OJLS* 559, 561.

[12] A Ashworth, 'Interpreting Criminal Statutes: A Crisis of Legality?' (1991) 107 LQR 419, 420. This rationale is also discussed by Smith, above n 11, and Goode, above n 8.

[13] Matthew Goode discusses this constitutional principle at length: Goode, above n 8.

[14] Stoljar notes that a badly drafted code would not have a liberating effect, but 'would be worse than the disease: incompetent law is much worse than muddled law': Stoljar, above n 2, at 14.

[15] Stoljar, above n 2, at 14. In the Australian context, an example of this type of landmark case is *He Kaw Teh v The Queen* (1985) 157 CLR 523. While much of the discussion concerning principles of responsibility is strictly *obiter*, the structure of the leading judgment by Brennan J, which divided his judgment into a statement of 'The General Principles', at 564ff, and then 'Application of the General Principles to s 233B(b) and (c)' at 582ff. The judgment's logical progression through the key elements of fault and strict liability has provided guidance beyond the field of drug law: Bronitt and McSherry, above n 4, at 79. Generally, see AWB Simpson, *Leading Cases in the Common Law* (Oxford, Oxford University Press, 1995) 4–7 on the 'invention' of the leading case in the 19th century and its significance to the academy and legal education.

no doctrine of binding precedent with the consequence that case-law is downgraded in legal education, cases perform a vital role, promoting consistency as illustrations of the proper application of the legal rules. Case law also provides the legal backdrop against which codification occurs. As Stoljar notes, cases operate as 'the prelude to, the preparation for, a code, just as they form the subsequent continuation of it'.[16] Both codified and uncodified systems struggle with similar issues of uncertainty and it is simply wrong to consider that these systems operate in fundamental opposition to each other, or that one is intrinsically better or worse than the other.[17]

We have noted that codification aims to shift power from the courts to the parliament. As an aspect of the liberal promise, this shift has particular significance in the context of the criminal law. For code advocates, limiting the power of the courts and judge-made law was the paramount virtue of codification (we explore this promise and Jeremy Bentham's legacy in section II below). Under a comprehensive code, judicial creativity is curbed and the role of the judge is simply to apply the law, rather than to interpret and develop it.

In the modern context, a further democratic argument for codification emerges. As the state has the responsibility to create and maintain the rules for punishment of individuals, then it is appropriate that only the elected arm of government—Parliament—be responsible for articulating those rules, the principles that will govern their application and the sanctions that will be imposed for their transgression. Andrew Ashworth views this constitutional principle of parliamentary supremacy, whereby 'the creation of offences is for Parliament alone',[18] as one of the most crucial aspects of codification.[19]

In common with other codes (and essential to their touted clarity, coherence and comprehensiveness) the Criminal Code (Cth) contains a 'General Part', which sets out the principles of criminal responsibility which apply to the range of specific offences set out in subsequent chapters. As we shall explore below, the value of and relationship between the General Part and the Special Parts containing specific offences remain contentious. Indeed, some academics argue that any attempt to hive off the General Part has little theoretical or practical value, and 'inevitably ends up presenting an impoverished picture of the 'special part', in which the latter's moral richness and diversity have been airbrushed out'.[20]

The principles contained in the General Part shape and constrain the legislature's law making role by establishing principles of responsibility and

[16] Stoljar, above n 2, at 11–12.
[17] Stoljar, above n 2, at 13.
[18] Ashworth, above n 12, at 420.
[19] Ashworth, above n 12, at 420.
[20] Horder, above n 7, at 241.

default standards as well as providing a clear framework of exceptions or derogations. Applicable to every offence, the General Part is said to operate in effect 'as a constitution for the criminal law, setting the parameters for judging all criminal conduct'.[21]

The default standards in ch 2 of the Criminal Code (Cth) tend to reflect fundamental common law principles including the presumption of innocence (where the burden of proof rests on the prosecution to prove the elements of the offence, and to rebut defences)[22] and the presumption of a subjective fault element.[23] In relation to these two fundamental principles, however, the default standard may be subject to derogation or modification, through the legislature expressly reversing the onus of proof or imposing strict or absolute liability in relation to an offence or to particular physical elements within it.

Our chapter is divided into two main parts. In section II, we explore the history, values and trends in common law codification. In section III, we examine the extent to which codes have in fact shifted power from the courts to the legislature, focusing on the latter's role in defining prospectively the jurisdictional and substantive limits of the criminal law. In particular we will look at the way in which the federal legislature in Australia has exercised its new role in two specific fields: selecting the scope of jurisdiction in respect of a particular offence, and determining whether an offence should impose strict or absolute liability. In section III, we examine whether the liberal promise of a democratically made and amended criminal law is in fact being delivered through the new approach in the Criminal Code (Cth) or whether the power shift away from the judiciary has been towards the executive rather than the legislative arm of government. Throughout, we will use terrorism offences as examples, as we assess whether legislatures can maintain fidelity to the liberal promise of codification given the politics of law and order in the post-9/11 environment.

II. HISTORY, VALUES AND TRENDS IN COMMON LAW CODIFICATION

A. Bentham's Dream: From Panopticon to Pannomion

The common law of England received into the infant Australian colonies in the late 18th century was a mish-mash of statutes and common law precedents, to be adapted (or selectively ignored) according to Blackstone's theory of settlement to suit the infant conditions of the colony. The complexity

[21] Bronitt and McSherry, above n 4, at 71ff.
[22] *Woolmington v DPP* [1935] AC 462, 481–2, reflected in Criminal Code (Cth), s 13.1.
[23] *He Kaw Teh v The Queen* (1985) 157 CLR 523, reflected in Criminal Code (Cth), s 5.6.

and pluralism of the English criminal law of the late 18th century could not be transplanted—what was transplanted was a strong judicial commitment to ensuring observance of due process and upholding the rights and freedoms of both free settlers and convicts.[24] Significantly, the 'chaos' of English law in the colonies could be ordered through the institutional writings of Blackstone, which provided a portable synopsis or academic *summa,* of legal principles, as well as relevant technical rules.

Colonies prospered and local legislatures were created with some powers to enact their own criminal laws (provided they were not repugnant with the laws of England). By the mid-19th century, the tangled mass of law became an increasing source of dissatisfaction.[25] The practical difficulties in accessing and applying common law rules made the new British colonies a fertile ground for codification and law reform more generally. The problem confronting colonial administrators and judges was two-fold—first, a large portion of the criminal law could only be found through a detailed examination of English case-law (or local precedents, which were erratically reported through the press) or reliance on authoritative scholarly works, and, second, over time, statutory accretion had overlaid the common law foundation with extensive local and Imperial statutory amendment.[26] Unsurprisingly, consolidation of the criminal law became a major preoccupation in the mid-19th century. In Australia (as in England), standing and *ad hoc* commissions were established to review portions of the criminal law with a view to reducing it to statutory form.[27] But for many, dissatisfied with this state of legal chaos, consolidation would never be enough. For some, nothing less than addressing the defects of the common law system through wholesale codification would do.

Criminal Codes are products of colonial liberal modernity—an expression of the aims of clarity, predictability and universality through law.[28]

[24] John Braithwaite has suggested that the role of procedural justice for convicts in the 18th and 19th centuries was crucial in promoting reintegration, rehabilitation and the transformation of Australia to a low crime society: J Braithwaite, 'Crime in a Convict Republic' (2001) 64 *MLR* 11.

[25] However, for the first half of the 19th century, the reform movement focused on ensuring many of the fundamental institutions of British justice such as trial by jury: see D Neal, *The Rule of Law in a Penal Colony* (Sydney, Cambridge University Press, 1991).

[26] A point noted by Griffith in his Explanatory Letter, introducing the Criminal Code.

[27] The impact of the New South Wales Law Reform Commission and the Criminal Law Commissioners in the United Kingdom on reforming criminal law and procedure are reviewed in GD Woods, *A History of Criminal Law in New South Wales: The Colonial Period 1788–1900* (Sydney, Federation Press, 2002).

[28] See M Kayman, 'A Memorial for Jeremy Bentham: Memory, Fiction, and Writing the Law' (2004) *Law and Critique* 207, 210, describing Bentham's proposals for codification as 'central to the project of modernity'. For an interesting essay exploring the role of imposed codes in colonial and post-colonial contexts, see L Sebba, 'The Creation and Evolution of Criminal Law in Colonial and Post-colonial Societies' (1999) *Crime, History and Societies* 71.

Throughout the 19th century, in common law as well as civil law countries, distinguished jurists (scholars and judges) competed to reduce the body of local customary and statutory law into a codified form. Codification gave rise to an acute form of narcissism with competing efforts among these jurists to produce the 'best model' of codification. One dominant figure stands out in the form of Jeremy Bentham, whose mission to promote codification proved ultimately to be more palatable in the colonies and Continental Europe than in England.[29]

The writings of Bentham on codification are extensive.[30] Bentham was a common law sceptic: his enthusiasm for codes stemmed from a deep distrust of unwritten customary law, not only for its inherent uncertainty, but also because it conferred power on judges to create and apply the law retrospectively. For Bentham, law meant simply positive legal rules, not customary judge-made law which Bentham notoriously described as 'dog law'.[31] In order to guide conduct, laws must be laid down in advance and knowable to all. This was undermined by the continued dominance of judge-made common law.

Bentham's model of a rational and ordered criminal law emerged as a reaction to the punitive and arbitrary nature of the criminal justice system of the previous century where the criminal law served primarily to instil legal terror in the lower orders through its draconian offences and extensive use of capital punishment. Against the backdrop of this 'Bloody Code', justice was not found in the fabric of substantive or procedural law, but rather was promoted post-conviction through sentence mitigation or executive clemency in the form of pardons or transportation.[32] Bentham argued that deterrence was the only legitimate purpose for imposing criminal punishment, and according to his theory, codification was the only way to provide a rational and ordered criminal law capable of achieving that objective.

Towards the end of his life, Bentham became obsessed with codification. In 1817, he addressed an open letter to the Americans offering to draft them

[29] Bentham's influence on civil law codification across Europe is less well known: A Cadoppi, above n 6, at 123, noting that his writing and drafts were 'points of reference which would inspire codifiers whether continental (one thinks of the Napoleonic codification itself at the beginning of the 19th century) or of the common law'.

[30] See P Scholfield and J Harris (eds), *Jeremy Bentham—Writings on Codification, Law and Education* (Oxford, Clarendon Press, 1998).

[31] Bentham viewed common law as 'dog law' because it punished individuals after the event, since 'the dog only learns after the punishment that what it has done is wrong': A Norrie, *Crime, Reason and History* (London, Butterworths, 2nd edn, 2001) 19.

[32] Norrie, above n 31, at 16–17. See further EP Thompson, *Whigs and Hunters: The Origins of the Black Act* (London, Allen Lane, 1975). In the Australian context, the extent to which transportation constituted a form of punishment or an opportunity for rehabilitation is discussed in M Finnane, *Punishment in Australian Society* (Melbourne, Oxford University Press, 1997) ch 1.

a Pannomion (or codification) of constitutional, civil and penal laws.[33] This was an offer which he had earlier made to numerous European Heads of State and their newly independent colonies, to no avail.[34] As Martin Kayman notes, the Pannomion project, which occupied his final years, aimed 'to promote through legal writing a global democratic future based on principles of utilitarian reason'.[35] Rather than representing an onset of juristic dementia, this project was consistent with Bentham's belief in the universalism inherent within the project of codification: 'The great *outlines* ... will be found to be the same for every *territory*, for every *race*, and for every *time*'.[36]

The Pannomion has been described as 'central to the project of modernity'[37] and a counterpart to Bentham's model prison—the Panopticon. Both projects shared the common objective of promoting conformity and compliance of the legal subject (whether citizen or prisoner) with rules. Rational legality favoured an approach in which offences and hence the legal power to punish must be prescribed in clear legal rules in advance, expressed in language and terms which these subjects could understand. It sought to replace the patchwork of common law (overlaid with statutory modifications) with a systematic and principled system of criminal law, combined with rational and proportionate punishments which aimed at deterrence. The resultant laws were applied rather than made by the courts, with minimal scope for discretionary interpretation or resort to legal fictions. This curbed judicial arbitrariness as well as retrospective applications of the law. Codes did not rely on the past and precedent for authority, but located their power in a philosophy of utility or utilitarianism which could guide legislative policy in any field.

Law reformers in the 19th century battled over two distinct models for the criminal law—consolidation versus codification. Many of these earlier models mentioned above were not 'true' codes in the Benthamite sense. Over the course of the 19th century, various models and approaches to codification emerged in different places and at different times. Befitting the civilian

33 Bentham was prone to legal neologism. As well as Pannomion (which did not gain currency) he is also credited with the term 'codification' and the first use of the term 'international' (coined in the context of a universal system of laws). For a discussion of the wide range of neologisms attributed to Bentham, see further <http://www.ucl.ac.uk/Bentham-Project/Faqs/Neologisms%20of%20Jeremy%20Bentham.htm>.

34 Kayman, above n 28, at 207–8, notes Bentham's offer to draft a Pannomion for the Russian Tsar, the Spanish, Portuguese and Greek liberals, and the newly independent states of Argentina and Guatemala.

35 Kayman, above n 28, at 208.

36 J Bentham, 'Legislator of the World' in Scholfield and Harris, above n 30, cited in Kayman, above n 28, at 209. This collection contains *Papers Relative to Codification and Public Instruction*, first published in 1817; *Codification Proposal, addressed to all Nations Professing Liberal Opinions*, first printed in 1822 with supplements in 1827 and 1830; and *First Lines of a Proposed Code of Law for any Nation Compleat and rationalized*: see further <http://www.ucl.ac.uk/Bentham-Project/>.

37 Kayman, above n 28, at 210.

tradition of scientific classification, Cadoppi has attempted to identify several distinct phases of codification 'models' in common law systems:

> One can say such models are: in the first place the Indian penal code, realised by Macauley; in second place the Wright draft for Jamaica; in the third place, the Field draft for New York, in the fourth place the Stephen draft for England. That the Griffith code represented a model independent of the last of these could be debatable but majority opinion seems to lean in favour of assigning the dignity of an autonomous model to the Queensland code.[38]

Although the Stephen's draft code of 1879 precluded judicial creation of new crimes, as Cadoppi notes, it did not intend to reduce the interpretive power of the courts: the code was not comprehensive, stating that it was not exhaustive of defences or excuses generally available to the accused, expressly leaving room for the development of the common law.[39] A significant exception in common law codification was the Draft Code of Criminal Law prepared by Sir Samuel Griffith, then Chief Justice of Queensland.[40] From our perspective, the Griffith Code is of most interest, not merely because of its influence on Australian criminal law, but because it is one of the most faithful and successful attempts to implement a Benthamite model for codification into law.

The 'Griffith Code', as it became known, was enacted in Queensland in 1899 and was adopted with only minor revision in many other British colonies.[41] At the time of enactment, it marked a distinct and fresh approach to codification. Building on earlier model codes (including the draft code prepared by Stephen in 1871), it also drew new inspiration from more esoteric sources including the Italian Penal Code of 1889.[42] The Griffith Code was most distinctive in its incorporation of a General Part, an innovation to which we now turn.

III. THE GENERAL PART AND CODIFYING PRINCIPLES OF RESPONSIBILITY

Codification requires that criminal laws be collected together and placed on a statutory footing. But codes also perform another function: they offer a logical structure and principled coherence through the inclusion of the General

[38] Cadoppi, above n 6, at 177 (footnotes omitted).

[39] Cadoppi, above n 6, at 127.

[40] Samuel Griffith was a Welshman, a barrister, Attorney-General of Queensland and distinguished jurist who became the first Chief Justice of the High Court of Australia.

[41] The Griffith Code was also adopted in a number of British colonies and dependencies such as Papua (1902) and New Guinea (1921), as well as a number of African colonies and Israel. On the migration of the Queensland Code, see R O'Regan, *New Essays on the Australian Criminal Codes* (Sydney, Law Book Company, 1988) 103–20 and Sebba, above n 28, at 82ff.

[42] As Cadoppi notes throughout his article, the influence of the Zanardelli Code on Griffith was profound: Cadoppi, above n 6.

Part. The General Part purports to contain all of the principles which apply generally and consistently across specific offences (which are contained in the Special Part). In this sense, the General Part performs an educative function, providing a fund of legal ideas to guide the application of the law in new situations. As criminal law theorist Michael Moore has argued:

> The criminal law thus needs some structure if its codification is to be possible and if adjudication under such codes is to be non-arbitrary. More specifically, it needs some general doctrines—doctrines applying to all types of action prohibited by a criminal code—in order to avoid an ungodly repugnancy and a woeful incompleteness.[43]

In this respect, the mapping roles of a code and its general doctrines distinguish it from a mere consolidation.[44] As Cadoppi has noted, from the Benthamite perspective:

> consolidation would never have been able to enjoy the systematic organicity of a code and in particular in the criminal law, it would never have been able to contain a general part, an indispensable instrument to guarantee a rational understanding and interpretation of the incriminatory provisions of the special part.[45]

The obsession with the General Part is a distinctive feature of late 19th-century codification. The General Part functions primarily as a legal dictionary of key concepts and guiding principles—addressed to the judicial officer and legislative drafter, rather than to the citizen at large. The construction of the General Part has been largely an academic mission, and even today, as Moore exemplifies above, the desire to define universal general principles in the criminal law may be viewed as a very distinctive academic project.

As has been noted above, ch 2 of the Criminal Code (Cth), which contains the general principles of criminal responsibility applying to the substantive offences contained in the rest of the Code (and federal offences elsewhere), constitutes the General Part of Australian federal criminal law. The principles it contains replace those of the common law and apply to all Commonwealth offences, regardless of whether they are contained in the Code itself or in other criminal statutes.[46]

It is the existence of this General Part which renders the Criminal Code (Cth) a 'pure code' of the type favoured by Bentham—and which places it

43 M Moore, *Act and Crime* (Oxford, Oxford University Press, 1993) 4.

44 Codification may be regarded as one genre of legal cartography, and theme explored by Kayman, above n 28. As Lindsay Farmer has observed, legal scholarship may be regarded as a form of legal cartography, concerned with constructing the metaphysical space in which the law is imagined and represented: L Farmer, *Criminal Law, Tradition and Legal Order* (Cambridge, Cambridge University Press, 1997) ch 1.

45 Cadoppi, above n 6, at 123.

46 Criminal Code (Cth), s 2.1.

in a unique position in Cadoppi's hierarchy of models outlined above. On the surface, the Code appears to deliver clarity and comprehensiveness and to make accessible to ordinary citizens the foundational principles of the criminal law: the physical and fault elements which constitute the lexicon of the criminal law drafter are defined in clear, plain English; defences are enumerated and explained; principles for how criminal liability will extend both to corporate entities and to inchoate offences are set out; jurisdictional options are laid out; and so on.

Moreover, the assumptions upon which the General Part of the Criminal Code (Cth) is based are generally unalarming to a common law criminal lawyer: the principles that are embodied there are familiar and, broadly speaking, do not represent a departure from established common law doctrines and concepts.[47] Concepts and definitions peculiar to the Griffith Code have largely been avoided. Indeed, some of these common law principles have been strengthened in ch 2—an example is the formulation of the presumption of subjective fault which is not only preserved but arguably enhanced.[48] Section 5.6 of the Criminal Code (Cth) has the effect of ensuring that if an offence is silent as to a fault element, then either recklessness or intention will apply in respect of each physical element making up the offence. Accordingly, default fault elements apply to each and every physical element of an offence unless an offence or element thereof is specified to be strict or absolute liability. This is discussed below.

The General Part provisions in ch 2 of the Code serve multiple purposes. They function as the building blocks of the criminal law from which elements of new offences will be selected. In addition, they (and they alone) will operate as default assumptions underlying the conceptualisation of new offences. At the trial and appeal stages, the ch 2 principles will be the chief interpretive tools (replacing principles derived from the common law) available to practitioners and the court. Ian Leader-Elliott has described the General Part in the following terms:

> The primary audience for these statements of general principle is not courts, but legislatures. If Pt 2.2 of the Criminal Code is to provide effective guidance to courts in their interpretation of legislation, it must speak first of all to those who will draft the legislation. Pt 2.2 of the Code is akin to rules of statutory

[47] That said, ch 2 is not comprehensive. Gani has noted elsewhere that there is no overt reference to the doctrine of concurrence in ch 2, though note the wording of s 3.2(b): M Gani, 'Codifying The Criminal Law: Issues of Interpretation' in S Corcoran and S Bottomley (eds), *Interpreting Statutes* (Sydney, Federation Press, 2005) 222, fn 20. Chapter 2 also fails to recognise or define the concept of ulterior intention, which is incorporated into many common criminal offences: I Leader-Elliott, 'Benthamite Reflections on Codification of the General Principles of Criminal Liability: Towards the Panopticon' (2006) 9(2) *Buffalo Criminal Law Review* 391.

[48] I Leader-Elliott, 'Elements of Liability in the Commonwealth Criminal Code' (2002) 26 *Criminal Law Journal* 28, 36, in relation to s 5.6 states 'The implications of the change effected by the Code are profound'.

> interpretation, which similarly address legislators and courts alike. Of course, the conventions and presumptions of Pt 2.2 have a deeper level of significance as well. They possess a quasi-constitutional status because they articulate principles of common law which are generally taken to embody fundamental principles of criminal justice. In practice, their most significant effect is likely to be found in the emerging conventions of legislative drafting that require close attention to the formal requirements of the general principles when new offences are drafted.[49]

Leader-Elliott's assessment is apposite in a number of respects. Chapter 2 is certainly a guide to drafters, though a complex one which needs further explanation, even to lawyers. Indeed, there are now several official guides and handbooks directed to legal practitioners as well as to parliamentary drafters on how to interpret the Code as well as how to construct offences concordant with the principles of responsibility contained in ch 2.[50] It is also, as Ian Leader-Elliott states, the primary tool of statutory interpretation for the courts (a matter upon which the Code itself is mysteriously silent).[51]

Leader-Elliott also points, perhaps inadvertently, to another aspect of codification that is at odds with the liberal promise: the bureaucratisation of the law-making process. It is undoubtedly true that codification of the criminal law provides democratically made law in the sense that it is the elected legislature rather than the unelected judiciary who make and control the development of the criminal law. In our political system, however, this criminalisation emerges as a task of government, which is both highly bureaucratic and politicised through the politics of law and order. In this context, the Criminal Law Division of the Attorney-General's Department (working to the Attorney-General and Minister for Justice and under guidelines which those Ministers provide) plays an important part. Indeed, proposed legislation dealing with criminal offences only reaches Parliament after it has been drafted in accordance with the principles

[49] Leader-Elliott, above n 48, at 31.

[50] Commonwealth Attorney-General's Department in Association with the Australian Institute of Judicial Administration, *The Commonwealth Criminal Code, A Guide for Practitioners,* March 2002; The Australian Government, A *Guide to Framing Commonwealth Offences, Civil Penalties and Enforcement Powers*, February 2004, Issued by Authority of the Minister for Justice and Customs.

[51] The subject of interpreting the Criminal Code (Cth) is comprehensively addressed in Gani, above n 47. The common law principles governing the interpretation of codes can be summarised as: a code is a piece of legislation so that legislation governing interpretation of statutes applies (in the case of the Criminal Code (Cth), the Acts Interpretation Act 1901 (Cth); the first loyalty is to the code so that interpretation must be internally consistent; common law should only be resorted to in situations where an undefined term has a special or technical meaning at common law; criminal codes should be interpreted as far as possible consistently with the other Australian jurisdictions. See the judgments of Kirby J in *R v Barlow* (1997) 188 CLR 1, *Charlie v The Queen* (1999) 199 CLR 387 and *Murray v The Queen* (2002) 189 ALR 40.

contained in ch 2.[52] While this enhances the coherence and uniformity of law making on the one hand, on the other, it means that important decisions relating to issues like jurisdiction and fault have been largely predetermined (and justified in explanatory memoranda and other documents to which parliamentarians have access). In the current political environment (and particularly in the 'age of terror'), this has often meant that these preliminary judgments about the scope of liability made at the drafting stage pass into law unchallenged. While, some would argue that it has ever been thus (representing a general defect of our parliamentary system), what distinguishes the current situation is that under a codified system, the role of the judiciary is strictly to interpret the code without the opportunity for judicial tempering of legislative excesses through the application of common law principles. It is arguable therefore, that codification of the criminal law, without the limitations arising either from a bill of rights or from principles which preserve such rights embedded in the code itself, effectively shifts power to the executive as well as to the legislature. Upon closer scrutiny, law is not 'democratically made and amended' in the way the proponents of codification would have us believe. This theme will be developed throughout this section of our chapter, with particular emphasis on the terrorism offences contained in Part 5.3 of the Criminal Code (Cth).

A. The Criminal Code (Cth), Chapter 2 and Jurisdiction

Unlike other principles contained in ch 2 of the Criminal Code (Cth), jurisdiction is an area that represents a notable departure from established common law principles. It is a basic tenet of the criminal law that '[a]ll crime is local'[53] with physical or geographic territoriality long representing a rebuttable presumption in relation to establishing jurisdiction over criminal offences at common law. This starting premise had already undergone significant judicial development in Australia and has now been further expanded by the Criminal Code (Cth). In relation to cross-border crime, the High Court decision of *Ward v The Queen*[54] in 1980 established that the 'terminatory theory' of jurisdiction (focusing on the place where the consequences or effects of conduct were felt) rather than the 'initiatory theory' (focusing on the place where the conduct was carried out) governed the conferral of jurisdiction at common law.[55] In the late 1990s, the High

[52] See below n 78 for discussion of the guidelines followed by the Attorney-General's Department.

[53] *MacLeod v Attorney-General (NSW)* [1891] AC 455, 458-459 (Halsbury LC). See, generally, Bronitt and McSherry, above n 4, at 857ff.

[54] (1980) 142 CLR 308.

[55] Bronitt and McSherry, above n 4, at 86–8.

Court further expanded its notion of criminal jurisdiction beyond the territorial connection. In *Lipohar v The Queen*[56] the majority held in relation to conspiracy to defraud that the test should be whether there was a 'real connection', 'sufficient connection' or 'real link' between the offence and the jurisdiction seeking to try it.[57]

Part 2.7 of ch 2 which deals with the principles of criminal responsibility in relation to jurisdiction was inserted into the Criminal Code (Cth) in 1999. It takes this broader view of jurisdiction developed by the courts significantly further. The Code sets out five categories of jurisdiction which can apply to Commonwealth offences, ranging from standard geographical jurisdiction through to category D extended jurisdiction. The default jurisdiction for Commonwealth offences is the standard geographical jurisdiction set out in s 14.1(2) which extends to conduct occurring wholly or partly in Australia (or on board an Australian ship or aircraft) or conduct occurring outside Australia but whose effects are felt wholly or partly in Australia (or on board an Australian ship or aircraft). For any of the extended jurisdiction provisions to apply, they must be specifically stated to operate in the provision or Act creating the offence.[58]

The other four categories of jurisdiction are increasingly broad, requiring ever more tenuous connections with Australia (citizenship or incorporation in Australia—Category A; residence in Australia—Category B). Category C extended jurisdiction is essentially universal jurisdiction with some exceptions while Category D is unambiguously so. Under s 15.4, liability will apply to Category D offences 'whether or not the conduct constituting the alleged offence occurs in Australia' and 'whether or not a result of the conduct constituting the alleged offence occurs in Australia'.

The default jurisdiction provision in the Code represents a combination of the initiatory and terminatory theories of jurisdiction. That provision may be viewed as a statutory expression of the 'real and substantial link' test from *Lipohar*. However, those categories which extend jurisdiction to Australian citizens and residents significantly expand the reach of the federal criminal law. The new computer offences inserted into the Criminal Code (Cth) by the Cybercrime Act 2001 (Cth) was one of the first areas

[56] (1999) 200 CLR 485.

[57] The tests of the majority were broadly similar though expressed in different terms: Gleeson CJ (real connection); Gaudron, Gummow and Hayne JJ (sufficient connection); Callinan J (real link). These formulations were influenced by the 'real and substantial link' test in Canadian law: *Libman* [1985] 2 SCR 178. Victoria has adopted a real and substantial link test in preference to the territorial nexus test: s 80A, Crimes Act 1958 (Vic). The Canadian test has the support of many commentators: M Goode, 'Two New Decisions on Criminal "Jurisdiction": The Appalling Durability of Common Law' (1996) 20 *Criminal Law Journal* 267, 279–80. The case has been described as a 'nail in the coffin' for territoriality: Bronitt and McSherry, above n 4, at 90.

[58] Section 14.1(1).

of law to which this new codified model for jurisdiction was applied. As we have previously noted, the application of Category C and Category D extended jurisdiction effectively represents an assertion of jurisdiction by the Australian Commonwealth over the whole world—claims which are more commonly a feature of civil rather than common law systems.[59]

At this stage, the terrorism offences in pt 5.3 of the Criminal Code (Cth) (the offences relating to terrorist acts, terrorist organisations and financing terrorism) are one of only a few Commonwealth offences that have been made subject to Category D extended jurisdiction.[60] As Bell J, the trial judge presiding over the prosecution of Izhar Ul-Haque for receiving training from a terrorist organisation commented,[61] this form of extended jurisdiction creates offences 'that may be committed by a foreigner against a foreigner in a foreign country remote geographically from, and of no particular interest to, Australia'.[62] In justifying this choice of the most extreme form of jurisdiction, the particular nature of terrorist crimes was invoked. Universal jurisdiction was 'appropriate due to the transnational nature of terrorist activities, and to ensure that a person could not escape prosecution or punishment based on a jurisdictional loophole'.[63] Similar explanations for the choice of Category A jurisdiction for cybercrime offences were also made by the then Attorney-General.[64] In reality, of course, for multiple reasons of sovereignty and international comity, in practice Australia would not assert jurisdiction of this kind except in the most unusual or extreme of cases.

Jurisdiction, then, is a vivid illustration of the failure of the liberal promise. The law governing jurisdiction in Australia has, with the exception of some statutory tinkering, largely been developed case by case by the judiciary in the context of prosecutions where an offender disputes a jurisdiction's right to prosecute. The setting out of the five different categories of jurisdiction in the Criminal Code (Cth) represents an attempt at transparent and coherent law-making. Under the Code it becomes the concern of the legislators, the supreme arm of government, to turn their mind from the beginning to the

[59] See discussion of jurisdiction in S Bronitt and M Gani, 'Shifting Boundaries of Cybercrime: From Computer Hacking to Cyberterrorism' (2003) 27 *Criminal Law Journal* 303.

[60] See Criminal Code (Cth), s 101.2, s 101.2(4), s 101.4(4), s 101.5(4), s 101.6(3), s 103.1(2), s 102.9 and s 103.3. These provisions cover each and every one of the current terrorism offences. Other offences subject to Category D extended jurisdiction include the crimes of genocide, crimes against humanity and war crimes: Ch 8, Div 268.

[61] Izhar Ul-Haque was charged under s 102.5 with receiving training from a terrorist organisation (Lashkar e Toiba) in April 2004. His trial has been delayed due to a 2006 application to the High Court in relation to the constitutionality of the legislation: see Transcript of Proceedings, *Ul-Haque v The Queen* (High Court of Australia, 4 August 2006).

[62] *R v Ul Haque* (unreported, NSW Supreme Court, 8 February 2006, Justice Bell) [32].

[63] Explanatory Memorandum, Security Legislation Amendment (Terrorism) Bill [No 2], 17.

[64] Including that 'computer crime is often perpetrated remotely from where it has effect': Second Reading, Cybercrime Bill (2001), *Hansard* (Cth), 27 June 2001 (Darryl Williams), 28641.

reach of the offences they are creating. And if no jurisdiction is nominated in the new offence, whether through legislative inadvertence or actual reliance on the default standard jurisdiction provision, offences apply where conduct occurs or its effects are felt in Australia—effectively, where there is a substantial link between the offence and Australia. However, in setting out a further range of jurisdictional options, the General Part of the Criminal Code (Cth) significantly expands the common law view of the jurisdictional reach of the criminal law. Crucially, ch 2 contains no central principles to guide the legislature's choice of jurisdictional scope in relation to a particular type of offence. This is simply left as a political and policy matter.

Whilst the legal principles relating to jurisdiction are now clearly articulated and structured, there is nothing in ch 2 that promotes the application of Categories A-D in a consistent or principled manner. What is apparent, from the Second Reading Speeches and Explanatory Memoranda accompanying the cybercrime and terrorism legislation (as well as submissions by the Attorney-General's Department to parliamentary committees scrutinising the proposed cybercrime and terrorism legislation)[65] is that determination of jurisdictional reach is made by the executive based on the *nature* of the offence and desire to assist cross-border law enforcement cooperation. Indeed, domestic political pressures to be seen to be fighting crime at the international level may be difficult to resist. The process of normalisation of extra-territoriality in the criminal law will be fostered and legitimated by the large (and increasing) number of international treaties dealing with transnational and global crime in many fields including drug laws, computer crime and terrorism. In the modern context, it seems hard to resist the inversion of the common law view of jurisdiction—since 'all crime is global' (or at least potentially cross-border) it follows that derogation from the default standard of jurisdiction may be necessary. The impetus to expanding jurisdiction is hard for legislatures to resist, though it carries an obvious danger of over-inclusiveness.[66]

B. The Criminal Code (Cth), Chapter 2 and Strict and Absolute Liability

The common law in relation to absolute and strict liability in Australia was developed through a number of significant judgments, most importantly, the High Court decision in *He Kaw Teh v The Queen*.[67] As with the principles applying to jurisdictional reach, determining whether an offence

[65] Bronitt and Gani, above n 59. See, for example, regarding the Category D jurisdiction of the terrorism offences, the following statement: broad jurisdictional reach of the offence provisions was 'appropriate due to the transnational nature of terrorist activities, and to ensure that a person could not escape prosecution or punishment based on a jurisdictional loophole': Explanatory Memorandum, Security Legislation Amendment (Terrorism) Bill [No 2] 17.

[66] Bronitt and McSherry, above n 4, at 818–21.

[67] (1985) 157 CLR 523.

is the archetypical one requiring fault (proof of *actus reus and mens rea*) or, alternatively, an offence of strict or absolute liability at common law has been an issue of statutory interpretation based on presumptions and principles developed reactively by the courts in the context of particular offences. The High Court decision of *He Kaw Teh*, particularly the leading judgment of Brennan J, sets out those presumptions and principles that will guide a court in determining into which category an offence falls. In the briefest possible terms, those principles can be summed up as follows: there is a presumption in relation to each offence that *mens rea* is required, that is a presumption of subjective fault. However, that presumption can be displaced by reference to several factors: the language of the statute, its subject matter, and the extent to which strict liability would aid enforcement (in terms of the consequences for the community and the accused).[68]

A consultant to the drafters of the Model Criminal Code upon which the Criminal Code (Cth) is based, Ian Leader-Elliot, has stated that pt 2.2 of ch 2 of the Criminal Code (Cth) owes much to Brennan J's judgment in *He Kaw Teh*.[69] It sets out in clear terms the physical and fault elements of an offence and defines concepts central to those elements,[70] including: conduct, voluntariness, omissions, intention, knowledge and recklessness.[71] Most importantly, in the context of our discussion of strict and absolute liability, ch 2 firmly embeds the common law presumption of subjective fault in s 5.6 in the Criminal Code (Cth). This section provides that, if an offence is silent as to a fault element, then either recklessness or intention will apply in respect of each physical element making up the offence.[72] For an offence or one of its elements to be of strict or absolute liability,[73] it must be specified as such. Again, s 5.6 appears to deliver the liberal values of both enhanced certainty and protection for offenders. Indeed, Ian Leader-Elliot has asserted that the 'implications of the change effected by the Code are profound. Unless the legislature says otherwise, the prosecution must

[68] See further Bronitt and McSherry, above n 4, at 857.

[69] See Leader-Elliott, above n 48, at 24.

[70] Sections 4.1 and 5.1.

[71] See ss 4.2, 4.3, 5.2, 5.4 and 5.5.

[72] Section 5.6 provides:

(1) If the law creating the offence does not specify a fault element for a physical element that consists only of conduct, intention is the fault element for that physical element.
(2) If the law creating the offence does not specify a fault element for a physical element that consists of a circumstance or a result, recklessness is the fault element for that physical element.

Under subsection 5.4(4), recklessness can be established by proving intention, knowledge or recklessness.

[73] See ss 6.2 and 6.3. What distinguishes the two is that the defence of reasonable mistake of fact defined in s 9.2 is available in relation to strict liability offences or elements. Other Code defences are available under ss 6.2 and 6.3.

prove intention or recklessness with respect to each physical element of the offence'.[74] As with the issue of jurisdiction, then, the Criminal Code (Cth) requires legislators to address the issue of fault at the initial stages of law-making. The role of the courts will be to apply ch 2 principles to their interpretation of the offences.

Issues relating to strict and absolute liability under the Criminal Code (Cth) have been the subject of scrutiny and consideration in recent years in relation to both technical and policy concerns. Given that, from 15 December 2001, ch 2 principles were to apply not just to Code offences but to *all* Commonwealth offences (located in a vast array of Commonwealth statutes),[75] an important task that was undertaken by the Attorney-General's Department was that of harmonising existing offences in order to ensure that they operated appropriately under ch 2 principles. The harmonisation process (undertaken over a number of years starting in 1997) had, as an important part of its focus, the assessment of whether an offence or element was intended to impose strict or absolute liability. Pre-existing legislation rarely specified this expressly, but rather there was a reliance on judicial interpretation and the presumptions outlined above. The harmonisation project did not look at policy issues. In fact, in the Attorney-General's Department repeatedly stated that 'harmonisation was not intended to be a fresh approach to the policy merits of fault, strict and absolute liability, but was a process to determine the original character of each offence'.[76] Subsequently, in 2001, the Senate asked the Standing Committee for the Scrutiny of Bills (which has a standing brief to scrutinise proposed legislation for its potential to trespass unduly on rights and liberties) to undertake an inquiry into and report on Commonwealth policy and practice in relation to the application of strict and absolute liability under Commonwealth legislation.[77]

The Attorney-General's Department told that Committee that it scrutinised all proposed Commonwealth legislation to ensure a consistent approach to strict and absolute liability across departments and agencies and had issued guidelines for the drafting of offences. In brief, those guidelines restated the position that Commonwealth offences should generally require proof of

[74] Leader-Elliot, above n 48, at 36.

[75] Sections 2.1 and 2.2.

[76] Leader-Elliott, above n 48, at 258.

[77] Senate Standing Committee for Scrutiny of Bills, *Application of Strict and Absolute Liability Offences in Commonwealth Legislation*, 26 June 2002 257. The terms of reference of the Committee required it to inquire and report on: the application of absolute and strict liability offences in Commonwealth legislation, with particular reference to: (a) the merit of making certain offences ones of absolute or strict liability; (b) the criteria used to characterise an offence, or an element of an offence, as appropriate for absolute or strict liability; (c) whether these criteria are applied consistently to all existing and proposed Commonwealth offences; and (d) how these criteria relate to the practice in other Australian jurisdictions, and internationally.

fault for each physical element, but that there were 'circumstances where strict or absolute liability may be appropriate'.[78] The guidelines listed types of offences or elements where strict liability had been found to be appropriate (including regulatory offences, particularly those relating to the environment or to public health and where it is difficult for the prosecution to prove a fault element because a matter is peculiarly within the knowledge of the defendant). They also stated that a strict liability offence should not be punishable by imprisonment, nor have a maximum penalty more than 60 penalty units ($6,600 for an individual and $33,000 for a body corporate). Absolute liability should apply only to elements of offences relating to jurisdiction or offences not punishable by a penalty of more than 10 penalty units. The recommendations of the Committee included endorsement of the approach to fault set out in ch 2 of the Criminal Code (Cth), in particular the default presumption of fault embodied in s 5.6.[79] While also endorsing the general policy approach of the Attorney-General's Department to strict and absolute liability (particularly the penalty and jurisdictional limits detailed above), it set out a list of further principles that should apply to the consideration of the merits of imposing strict or absolute liability in Commonwealth offences. These principles, which are regarded in the new drafting guidelines as 'more prescriptive than the Commonwealth Government's long-standing approaches'[80] to the issue, reflect what the Committee called the basic principle that 'fault liability is one of the most fundamental protections of criminal law; to exclude this protection is a serious matter'.[81] They include that 'strict liability should not be justified by reference to broad uncertain criteria such as offences being intuitively against community interests or for the public good; criteria should be more specific'.[82]

Whether a particular offence or element of an offence is strict or absolute liability is squarely an issue for consideration by the Federal legislature at the first instance. What this means in practice, of course, is that it is an issue considered by Government Departments (and relevant regulatory agencies) when legislation is at the proposal and drafting stages. Those Departments consult with the Attorney-General's Department[83] and follow drafting guidelines and principles issued by the authority of the Minister for Justice.[84] It is also the role of the Minister for Justice—a role agreed upon by Government

[78] The Senate Standing Committee listed the A-G's guidelines: Senate Standing Committee for Scrutiny of Bills, above n 77, at 259–60.

[79] Senate Standing Committee for Scrutiny of Bills, above n 77, at 283.

[80] Australian Government, above n 50, at 25.

[81] Senate Scrutiny of Bills Committee, above n 77, at 283.

[82] Senate Scrutiny of Bills Committee, above n 77, at 284.

[83] Paragraph 6.26 of the Legislation Handbook sets out the requirement that agencies involved in preparing a Bill must consult with the Attorney-General's Department about offences, penalties and certain other provisions.

[84] See Australian Government, above n 50, at 25.

Ministers—to approve offence provisions before their introduction into Parliament. It is arguable, therefore, that the determination of whether an offence or element is strict or absolute liability is not a matter so much for the Parliament but rather one for Ministers, Government Departments and the Attorney-General's Department. The decision is effectively made through the non-transparent process described above and is (as a result of a procedure agreed upon by the Executive) simply adopted by the Minister for Justice (another member of the Executive) before the Bill is introduced into Parliament. Admittedly, of course, that decision can then be accepted or rejected by the Parliament and is subject to scrutiny by parliamentary committees, though departments and agencies often subsequently prepare submissions and appear before committees to justify wider provisions and powers for their regulators. As with the issue of jurisdiction, discussed above, there are no principles embedded in ch 2, nor subordinate legislation, to ensure principled and consistent decision-making. What is in place are administrative procedures dictated by the executive arm of government.

The issue of strict and absolute liability must be contextualised within a wider regulatory perspective. A parallel development relevant to this question is the major study into regulatory and civil penalties undertaken by the Australian Law Reform Commission (ALRC). In its 2002 report, the ALRC identified a lack of coherence and of overarching principles governing the use of regulatory offences. It recommended that the distinction between criminal and non-criminal (civil) penalty law and procedure should be maintained and, in some circumstances, reinforced. The Commission concluded, in its statement of principle, that: '[p]arliament should exercise caution about extending the criminal law into regulatory areas unless the conduct being proscribed clearly merits the moral and social censure and stigma that attaches to conduct regarded as criminal.'[85] This suggests that, in relation to strict and absolute liability, Parliament should give careful consideration to achieving the desired policy or regulatory outcome through civil measures rather than criminal offences. Andrew Ashworth has advocated for a similar position in England, suggesting that the criminal law should be reserved only for serious wrongdoing (seriousness measured by harm and culpability), and the creation of a new category of civil wrong:

> A fine solution would be to create a new category of 'civil violation' or 'administrative offence', which would certainly be non-imprisonable and would normally attract a financial penalty; procedures would be simplified but would preserve minimum rights for defendants, such as access to a criminal court. Another

[85] Australian Law Reform Commission, *Principled Regulation: Civil and Administrative Penalties in Australian Federal Regulation* (ALRC Report 95, 2002), Statement of Principle, [3.110]. It also recommended that a Regulatory Contraventions Statute of general application should be enacted to cover various aspects of the law and procedure governing non-criminal contraventions of federal law in accordance with the recommendations in the Report.

> implication of the principles should be that any new criminal code for this country ought to declare the most serious offences in English law, rather than simply those traditional offences that have been the focus of textbooks over the years.[86]

Although these suggestions and the ALRC study clearly bear on the use of stricter forms of liability, the development of a 'principled' approach to regulation (and its relationship to the criminal law) remains illusive. In this sense, we agree with Ashworth that the criminal law is a 'lost cause, from the point of view of principle'.[87]

This somewhat pessimistic conclusion is certainly borne out by a review of the new terrorism offences enacted in Australia. The ambit claim of the Government when it introduced the Security Legislation Amendment (Terrorism) Bill 2002 into Parliament in March 2002 was extraordinary and demonstrated an alarming willingness to depart both from its own guidelines and from the presumptions at the core of ch 2. The proposed terrorist act offences in that Bill were drafted as absolute liability ones: this egregious departure from the presumption of subjective fault in relation to offences of such a serious nature was justified in the Explanatory Memorandum.[88] While these provisions (as proposed) did not pass into law, there are currently several terrorism offences with strict liability elements. Such provisions demonstrate the complexity which plagues many offences under the Code despite the existence of ch 2 as an interpretive tool. Section 102.5(2),[89] for example, makes it an offence to intentionally provide training to or receive

[86] A Ashworth, 'Is the Criminal Law a Lost Cause?' (2000) *LQR* 225, 255.

[87] Ashworth, above n 86, at 255.

[88] Some submissions to the Senate Legal and Constitutional Legislation Committee in relation to these proposed provisions in the Security Legislation Amendment (Terrorism) Bill 2002 [No 2] strongly criticised the original conception of these offences as absolute liability ones (with no fault or mental element): Report of the Senate Legal and Constitutional Legislation Committee, Parliament of the Commonwealth of Australia, *Consideration of Legislation Referred to the Committee: Security Legislation Amendment (Terrorism) Bill 2002 [No 2]* (2002) 35–45.

[89] The offence provision reads as follows:

> 102.5 Training a terrorist organisation or receiving training from a terrorist organisation
> (1) A person commits an offence if:
> (a) the person intentionally provides training to, or intentionally receives training from, an organisation; and
> (b) the organisation is a terrorist organisation; and
> (c) the person is reckless as to whether the organisation is a terrorist organisation.
> Penalty: Imprisonment for 25 years.
> (2) A person commits an offence if:
> (a) the person intentionally provides training to, or intentionally receives training from, an organisation; and
> (b) the organisation is a terrorist organisation that is covered by paragraph (b) of the definition of ***terrorist organisation*** in subsection 102.1(1).
> Penalty: Imprisonment for 25 years.
> (3) Subject to subsection (4), strict liability applies to paragraph (2)(b).
> (4) Subsection (2) does not apply unless the person is reckless as to the circumstance mentioned in paragraph (2)(b)

training from a terrorist organisation when that organisation is proscribed in accordance with paragraph (b) of the definition of terrorist organisation.[90] Sub-section (3) of that provision explicitly states that strict liability applies to whether the organisation is a terrorist one under paragraph (b), so that no inquiry needs to be made into whether the accused knew the organisation was proscribed. However, strict liability under s 6.1 allows the accused to raise mistake of fact as a defence under s 9.2. In addition, though, sub-s (4) includes a 'recklessness' exception. There will be no offence if the accused was not reckless as to the organisation being proscribed. The accused bears the evidential burden in relation to this matter in accordance with s 13.3. So much for the clarity of codification.

If Parliament is struggling with the principles underlying ch 2, the courts (both trial and appeal) seem to be faring no better. Despite its purported clarity, judges struggle with reconciling the operation of ch 2 with their preferred interpretation of the particular offence. This relationship between the General Part and specific offence provisions has always proved problematic for common lawyers. One distinguished High Court judge, Dixon CJ, described the General Part equivalent in the Criminal Code (Tas) as largely 'academic', containing:

> wide abstract statements of principle about criminal responsibility framed rather to satisfy the analytical conscience of an Austinian jurist than to tell a judge at a criminal trial what he ought to do.[91]

There is also a tendency to overlook, as well as downgrade, the significance of the General Part in specific contexts. One such recent example is *Crowther v Sala*[92] where the Supreme Court of Queensland heard an appeal against conviction for the federal offence of using a carriage service to menace, harass or cause offence, contained in s 474.17 of the Criminal Code (Cth):

> 474.17 Using a carriage service to menace, harass or cause offence
> (1) A person is guilty of an offence if:
> — the person uses a carriage service; and
> — the person does so in a way (whether by the method of use or the content of a communication, or both) that reasonable persons would regard as being, in all the circumstances, menacing, harassing or offensive.
> Penalty: Imprisonment for 3 years.

On its face, the provision appears to require no fault element of intention, knowledge or recklessness. Under ch 2, of course, this is clearly an offence

[90] Section 102.1(1).
[91] *Vallance v The Queen* (1961) 108 CLR 56, 61.
[92] [2007] QCA 133.

where the default provisions in s 5.6 must be considered, both in relation to using a carriage service and in relation to that use being regarded by reasonable people as menacing, harassing or offensive. What is striking is that none of the lawyers involved in the case, nor the magistrate at first instance, nor the District Court hearing the first appeal against conviction considered the operation of s 5.6 in relation to the second physical element. On appeal, the majority of the Supreme Court of Queensland quashed the accused's conviction, finding that this was in error. For the first time, on the second appeal, the issue of the application of s 5.6(2) was raised by counsel. That subsection provides that, where no fault element has been specified, recklessness applies to physical elements that are circumstances or results. McMurdo J found that the fact that a reasonable person would regard the use of the telephone as 'menacing' in s 474.17 should be characterised as a circumstance. Accordingly, since the offence provision did not expressly exclude the operation of a fault element, s 5.6(2) applied and recklessness was the required fault element attaching to the 'menacing' physical element. Applying the definition in s 5.4(1) then, what had to be proved in this case was that the applicant was at least aware of a substantial risk that a reasonable person would regard her conduct as menacing and that it was unjustifiable to take that risk. Accordingly, the majority judgment used ch 2 as the primary interpretation tool and applied it to the offence in the way it was intended.

The dissenting view of Williams JA, on the other hand, showed a distinct lack of understanding of ch 2 principles and their application to specific offences. His difficulty may be traced to a misunderstanding of the operation of s 3.1(2) and the necessity for the express exclusion of fault elements that this section requires. Rather, Williams JA found that the exclusion of fault element could be determined through 'inference from the definition of the offence' in cases where no fault element for that component of the offence was specified.[93]

The use of ch 2 of the Criminal Code (Cth) in *Crowther v Sala* reveals a number of general points. First, in accordance with s 6.2 of the Criminal Code (Cth), it is for Parliament, not the courts, to determine whether an offence or particular physical element is one of strict or absolute liability. Second, the availability of secondary material aimed at guiding legal practitioners and legislative drafters is critical to the effective implementation of a Code (significantly, there was no reliance in the Supreme Court on either the Guide for Practitioners or on the Drafting Guide).[94] Third, there is still uncertainty as to the proper approach to interpretation of the Code: McMurdo J made no reference to the principles guiding Code interpretation.

[93] [2007] QCA 133, para 26.
[94] See above n 50.

Put plainly, if experienced legal practitioners are not using ch 2 principles in arguing their cases and if judges (albeit dissenting ones) fail to understand how those basic principles apply to specific offences, then the liberal promise of clarity and coherence is simply not being delivered.

IV. FUTURE DIRECTIONS IN CODIFICATION

Although codification is a professedly liberal exercise, the paradox of codification is that the legal object—namely criminalisation—is produced within a highly politicised and fundamentally *illiberal* context. As we have demonstrated, codification is often produced in a highly bureaucratic and administrative context where the democratic processes of parliament are marginalised. The uncivil politics of law and order, structured around notions of 'commonsense' rather than liberal principle, severely strain legislative fidelity to the liberal blueprints and fundamental principles which underpin codification. In the face of clear expressions of bureaucratically constructed 'legislative intent', courts are no longer in a position to retrospectively reinstate or imply fundamental liberal principles onto the substantive law through presumptions and statutory interpretation. Once more, there is a significant divergence between the liberal rhetoric of the criminal law, and its reality. What then follows from this paradoxical insight?

Rather than dream of a 'pure' code of criminal law (in the tradition of Bentham's design for a Pannomion), an alternate model commends itself, namely, a *dialogic* model in which the provisions of the code and the principles of the common law perform complementary rather than antagonistic roles. In some systems, such as the United States and Canada, this dialogue is mediated through the key due process provisions of constitutional bills of rights. For example, the principle of 'fundamental justice' contained in s 7 of the Canadian Charter of Rights and Freedoms confers substantive not merely procedural rights, and thus has been used by the Supreme Court of Canada to invalidate offences that dispense with fault while carrying imprisonment as a possible penalty.[95] This innovation has had a profound impact on the availability of strict and absolute liability, even in cases where Parliament has expressly and unambiguously designated the crime as requiring no proof of fault. The Canadian experience provides the clearest example in a common law jurisdiction of how constitutionalising abstract

[95] Section 7 provides: 'Everyone has the right to life, liberty and security of the person and the right not to be deprived thereof except in accordance with the principles of fundamental justice': Constitutional Act 1982 (Can). The principle of fundamental justice in Canada has been used to initiate a wide-ranging review of the law of criminal responsibility: E Colvin, 'Recent Developments in Canadian Criminal Law' (1995) 19 *Criminal Law Journal* 139.

principles (such as fundamental justice, due process or fair trial) can produce significant rethinking of traditional doctrinal concepts and strengthen judicial commitment to core liberal principles of responsibility. But in jurisdictions like Australia and the United Kingdom—which lack a constitutional bill of rights—international human rights law serves only as a guide to the interpretation of criminal law. In Australia, in the absence of a federal bill of rights and with only limited human rights protection under State and Territory law,[96] the prospect of constitutionalising (along the Canadian lines) the fundamental principles of criminal law seems remote. It is more likely that Australian courts will content themselves with examining ch 2 of the Criminal Code (Cth) to interpret the specific provisions of the offence, while falling back on an examination of pre-existing common law either to fill the gaps or to corroborate their preferred interpretation! A preferable approach, consistent with the ideals behind codification, would be to clarify and determine the approach to statutory interpretation in the Code itself, a topic which has been overlooked in the Model Criminal Code.

Ultimately, Codes will never fully curtail the role of the courts. The liberal promise of clarity and universality is impossible to achieve; by default, it is *through statutory interpretation* (not simply rule application) that courts will legitimately continue to share a role with the legislature.[97] It is only proper, in a codified system, that this fundamental question of how the dialogue between courts and parliament should be conducted (and its limits) should be addressed by the Code itself, rather than left to the courts to determine over time.

Our final concluding thought is this: ch 2 (and general parts generally) should be given a real constitutional role in the criminal law by incorporating clear statements of the priority and significance attached to the fundamental principles of criminal responsibility. Under the current framework, the fundamental principles upon which our criminal law has developed can simply be derogated from in the interests of law and order, with the attendant danger that illiberal exceptions of strict and absolute liability will become the general rule. Rather than prospectively enabling such derogations, ch 2 should provide a set of normative parameters for criminalisation which, when exceeded, trigger judicial competence to review the fairness of imposing particular forms of criminal liability in particular contexts. Benthamites would likely object to such powers of review being given to the courts under ch 2. However, they should be reminded that their very inclusion in the General Part of the Code would reflect Parliament's own acceptance of the legitimacy and paramount status of these principles. In

[96] Human Rights Act 2004 (ACT); Charter of Human Rights and Responsibilities Act 2006 (Vic).

[97] A point further developed in Gani, above n 47.

common with human rights instruments, derogation from these norms would still be possible although any derogation would need to be demonstrably justifiable and proportionate—concepts which could be further elaborated in the Code itself. Only when the core principles of the criminal law are 'constitutionalised' in this manner will the liberal promise of codification in the criminal law be truly realised.

12

Faultlines Between Guilt and Punishment in Australia's Model Criminal Code

IAN LEADER-ELLIOTT

I. INTRODUCTION

As outlined by Simon Bronitt and Miriam Gani in the previous chapter, the Australian Model Criminal Code is a template for the codification of Australian criminal law. The Code has been influential as a model for law reform, though its influence has fallen short of the original hope that it would find universal acceptance in nationally consistent criminal laws.[1] The Code includes a general part in chapter 2—*General Principles of Criminal Responsibility*, which is a lineal descendant of the United States Model Penal Code.[2] That chapter was intended to provide a uniform analytic vocabulary and a set of general principles governing criminal liability for all Australian jurisdictions. That intention is unlikely to be realised in the near future. The Commonwealth adopted chapter 2 in its codification of federal criminal law and it has been adopted in the Australian Capital Territory and Northern Territory. Elsewhere in Australia diversity prevails.

[1] MR Goode, 'Constructing Criminal Law Reform and the Model Criminal Code' (2002) 26 *Criminal Law Journal* 152 provides an authoritative history of the Code project, during its early years.

[2] Model Criminal Code, ch 2—*General Principles of Criminal Responsibility*, Final Report (Canberra, Australian Government Printing Service, December 1992). Chapter 2 now exists in two slightly different forms. The original version was subjected to drafting changes, mostly minor, with the exception of the provisions dealing with intoxication, and the provisions were re-numbered when it was enacted by the Commonwealth in the Criminal Code Act 1995 (Cth). Subsequent chapters of the Model Criminal Code issued by the Model Criminal Code Officers Committee reprint the modified, Criminal Code version of ch 2, rather than the original, and refer to it as ch 2 of the 'Model Criminal Code'. In this chapter I follow their practice in references to ch 2. The Model Criminal Code is available in its entirety on the website of the Commonwealth Attorney General: <http://www.crimeprevention.gov.au/www/agd/agd.nsf/Page/Model_criminal_code>.

The substantive chapters of the Model Code have been far more generally accepted, though state and territorial uniformity or even consistency in the formulation of most of the major offences is still a distant prospect.

This chapter is concerned with the formulation of the fault elements in chapter 2 and their relationship, in particular, with the offences against the person in chapter 5 of the Model Code.[3] My argument is that an unwise choice was made from the outset, when the Model Criminal Law Officers Committee[4] [MCLOC], which presided over the formulation of the Code, chose the offences against the person as the vehicle for articulation and analysis of the fault elements. These offences, which are predominantly concerned with the imposition of punishment for causing harm to others, are not typical of the diverse range of offences in a modern criminal code. Most offences do not require proof of a resulting harm: they are crimes of conduct. In many, criminal liability depends on proof of the intention that actuated the conduct or the risks, whether taken consciously or unconsciously, associated with that conduct. As these crimes of conduct proliferate, there is an increasing need for a sophisticated and discriminating vocabulary of fault elements that will enable distinctions to be drawn between conduct that is tolerable and conduct that is appropriately punished by criminal penalties. The offences of causing harm do not require the same precision in the formulation of their fault elements. Indeed, I shall argue that very little in the way of precision is required, once an offender crosses the threshold of criminal liability.

The MCLOC took a very different view—one that it believed to be founded on high principle. The Model Code provides an elaborate code of graded offences against the person, each with its distinctive fault element. Those distinctions, I suggest, confuse factors that are more appropriate to a sentencing enquiry than they are to the determination of criminal liability. Moreover the MCLOC's concentration on these offences has obscured the role of fault elements in the great majority of Code offences, which do not require proof that the offender's conduct caused harm. I will return to the second of these contentions at the conclusion of this chapter in section VI. Most of what I have to say concerns the offences of causing harm to the person.

The Model Criminal Code offences against the person are set out below in Table 12.1, ranked in order of seriousness. They make no provision for a crime of assault. In part that appears to have been a consequence of a

[3] Model Criminal Code, ch 5—*Non-Fatal Offences Against the Person*, Report (Canberra, Australian Government Printing Service, September, 1998): <http://www.ag.gov.au/www/agd/agd.nsf/Page/Modelcriminalcode_Chapter5-OffencesAgainstthePerson>.

[4] The Committee has changed its name on several occasions since it was first formed. It was initially known as the 'Criminal Law Officers Committee'; subsequently as the 'Model Criminal Code Officers Committee' and became the 'Model Criminal Law Officers Committee' in 2007. In this chapter I refer to the Committee throughout by its current name. Its membership is drawn from senior government lawyers in each of the Australian jurisdictions and it advises the Standing Committee of Attorneys General on matters of criminal law policy. Its current references and previous reports can be found on the Commonwealth Attorney General's website, above n 2.

judgment that the common law of assault was confused and beyond redemption. The more significant reason, however, was the MCLOC's acceptance of the premise that the offences should have, as their only objective, protection from physical or mental injury.[5] In practice, the offence of assault has proved, for a variety of reasons, to be indispensable.[6] The model provisions have been adopted, with variations, by the Commonwealth, the Australian Capital Territory and South Australia. Victoria enacted similar legislation some years before the MCLOC reported.

The reformed law displaced statutory provisions derived from the Offences Against the Person Act 1861 (UK).[7] That Act, which was a consolidation of earlier offences by that splendid polymath Charles Sprengel Greaves, was adopted by each of the Australian states in the 19th century and it endured, virtually unchanged, in the south eastern states until the recent reforms.

Table 12.1: Offences Against the Person: The Model Criminal Code Version[8]

Sections	Offence Category	Penalty (basic)	Penalty (aggravated)
5.1.18	Cause harm (recklessly)	7 yrs	9 yrs
5.1.26	Recklessly endanger (serious harm)	7 yrs	9 yrs
5.1.21	Threaten to cause serious harm	7 yrs	9 yrs
5.1.17	Cause harm (intentionally)	10 yrs	13 yrs
5.1.16	Cause serious harm (negligently)	10 yrs	
5.1.20	Threaten to kill	10 yrs	13 yrs
5.1.25	Recklessly endanger (life)	10 yrs	13 yrs
5.1.15	Cause serious harm (recklessly)	15 yrs	19 yrs
5.1.14	Cause serious harm (intentionally)	20 yrs	25 yrs
	Attempt murder[9]	Life imprisonment	

[5] Model Criminal Code, above n 3, ch 5, 13.

[6] In South Australia, the initial legislative proposal for codification contained no offence of assault. It was eventually included as s 20 of the Criminal Law Consolidation Act 1935, as a consequence of the Government's failure to secure passage of an offence of causing serious harm by negligence. In Victoria, where corresponding legislation reforming the law of offences against the person contained no offence of assault, the Supreme Court held that common law assault survived the legislative codification of the offences against the person: *R v Patton* [1998] 1 VR 1.

[7] 24 & 25 Vict c.100.

[8] Table compiled from the Model Criminal Code, above n 3, ch 5, 8.

[9] The Model Criminal Code, above n 2, ch 2, s 11.1 *Attempt*, imposes the same penalty for attempt as for a completed offence. That principle has been accepted in the Australian Criminal Code. See, for example, s 115.1 *Murder of an Australian citizen or resident of Australia*. Most state and territorial jurisdictions set lower maximum penalties for attempts, as for example South Australia: Criminal Law Consolidation Act 1935, s 270A *Attempts*. The role of the law of attempt in supplementing the offences of causing harm intentionally and the offences of causing harm recklessly, adds complexity to the scheme and involves conceptual problems that will not be considered in this chapter.

I will defer analysis of the offences for the moment. An understanding of their structure requires consideration of two problems about the fault elements that the MCLOC had to solve in formulating the elements of criminal responsibility in chapter 2 of the Code. The account that follows is a brief sketch of an unexplored history of the development of Australian criminal law theory.

The first problem was the continuing tendency in Australian common law to merge the concepts of intention and recklessness. The second was the problematic role of negligence as a ground for criminal liability, particularly in the offences against the person.

The tendency to merge intention and recklessness is apparent in successive editions of Professor Colin Howard's influential text on Australian criminal law.[10] The same tendency is apparent in the influential judgments of Dixon CJ in *Vallance v The Queen*,[11] and of Brennan J in *He Kaw Teh v The Queen*.[12] These and other common law sources are reflected in the definition of intention in the immediate precursor to the Model Code, the *Review of Commonwealth Criminal Law,* which provided the basis for the MCLOC reformulation of the fault elements.[13] In the *Review*, intention was extended to include knowledge that a consequence or circumstance will probably exist or occur.[14] That is equivalent to modern definitions of recklessness. The concept of recklessness was in turn defined in the *Review* so as to extend to awareness of any risk at all, so long as the risk was unreasonable. The source of this confusion of intention and recklessness is to be found, almost exclusively, in the Australian common law of homicide and in the interpretational interstices of the old statutory offences against the person. The problem faced by the MCLOC—common to most endeavours to codify the law—was that of preserving continuity with its authoritative sources whilst achieving

[10] C Howard, *Australian Criminal Law* (Melbourne, Law Book Company, 1st edn, 1965) 314; B Fisse, *Howard's Criminal Law* (Sydney, Law Book Company, 5th edn, 1990) 488–9. In Howard's first summation, in 1965: 'recklessness emerged as an extension of responsibility for intention. ... [M]alice has been replaced by intention, intention has been broadened to include both purpose and belief, and now recklessness is largely replacing intention'. After some minor amendments to the passage in intervening editions, later editions settle on the formulation that appears in Fisse's 5th edition at 489: 'recklessness represents an extension of the concept of intention'. The progression of meaning, if it can be so described, is subtle.

[11] (1961) 108 CLR 56, 59–61. This judgment is central to the analysis of intention and recklessness in Howard, above n 10, 114, 117, 199 and 356 and succeeding editions of that text. Howard's interpretation of what Dixon CJ had to say of the meaning of 'intention' is disputable.

[12] (1985) 157 CLR 523, 568–9.

[13] *Interim Report: Principles of Criminal Responsibility and Other Matters* (Canberra, Australian Government Printing Service, 1990). The Review was conducted by a committee chaired by Sir Harry Gibbs, a former chief justice of the High Court.

[14] *Interim Report,* above n 13, at 44–45: 'It is true that foresight of probable consequences is, strictly speaking, different from intention but for the practical purpose of the criminal law they can be assimilated and the light of recent Australian cases it seems more appropriate to make the test whether the consequences are probable rather than highly probable'. Section 3F 'Definition of Degrees of Fault in the Draft Bill', in Part IX of the *Review*, is consistent with the recommendation though consequences are subsumed under 'circumstances'.

incremental reform. It will be argued that the Model Code definitions of intention and recklessness cleave too closely to their sources, both in their formulation and in the underlying assumptions about their applications.

Negligence was a problem for the Committee because of objections based on the prevailing subjectivist orthodoxy of the mid-20th century that it was an unacceptable basis for criminal liability.[15] Colin Howard provided a succinct formulation:

> It is ... not immediately obvious how a principle of criminal responsibility can be justified which concedes that D was not aware of the risk of harm that he was creating but nevertheless authorises his punishment for creating it.[16]

Negligence, in its application to the offences against the person, is regarded as an anomaly throughout Howard's text. The problem in this instance was easier for the MCLOC to resolve, for it simply required a decision whether to embrace that orthodoxy or reject it and it was duly rejected. There was, however, an additional complication. When liability for causing harm is in issue, the concept of criminal negligence is recalcitrant to definition for it must extend beyond absence of care to include liability for the consequences of wrongful acts. The problems of defining negligence are addressed briefly at the end of this chapter.

The fault elements of the Model Code are an eclectic assemblage which, in several respects, makes the worst of their sources.[17] The definition of intention was taken from the English Draft Criminal Code, with a side contribution from the Canadian Draft Criminal Code.[18] A result is said to be intended if it is *meant* to occur as a consequence of conduct or, following the lead provided by the English Draft Code, if the person is 'aware that it will occur in the ordinary course of events'.[19] The definition goes some way towards rejection of the earlier tendency to merge intention and recklessness: intention so defined extends no further than 'oblique' intention, though the MCLOC was careful to avoid that expression.

The definition of recklessness draws on the United States Model Penal Code.[20] It requires proof of awareness of a 'substantial and unjustifiable' risk that an incriminating circumstance or result might exist or occur.[21] The Committee rejected, however, the Model Penal Code requirement that recklessness involves a gross deviation from the standard of conduct of a law abiding person and set the threshold of liability far lower. In the Australian

[15] Model Criminal Code, above n 3, ch 5, at 45.
[16] Fisse, above n 10, at 496.
[17] Discussed in Model Criminal Code, above n 2, ch 2, at 27–33.
[18] *A Criminal Code for England and Wales* (Law Com 177, 1989), s 18(b).
[19] Model Criminal Code, above n 2, ch 2, s 5.2 *Intention*.
[20] Proposed Official Draft, 1962 (Philadelphia), s 2.02(2)(2).
[21] Model Criminal Code, above n 2, ch 2, s 5.4 *Recklessness*.

version, a person is reckless if a risk taken consciously was objectively 'unjustifiable'.[22] A requirement that the risk be justified is a demanding standard for risk takers. Here, too, the MCLOC believed itself to be constrained by 'established concepts', though no reference to precedent or authority was given.[23] Code offences of recklessness will have an extended application if courts adopt Professor Howard's contention that a risk may count as 'substantial' *because* it is unjustifiable.[24]

Negligence[25] was defined in terms drawn from the decision of the Victorian Supreme Court in *Nydam v The Queen*.[26] A person is negligent if his or her conduct involves a 'great falling short' of the standard of care of a reasonable person combined with such a high risk that an incriminating circumstance or result will exist or occur that the conduct merits criminal punishment for the offence in question. The potential for negligent wrongdoing to exceed reckless wrongdoing in culpability was noted by the MCLOC.[27] The fault elements of intention, knowledge, recklessness and negligence were nevertheless supposed to represent distinct and descending degrees of fault.[28]

For the most part, the MCLOC relied on cases dealing with the common law of unlawful homicide for its illustrative discussion. Statute law was neglected as a source, though it has always provided a far more extended and discriminating array of fault elements than the common law. Tensions are apparent in the MCLOC's attempts to explain the definitions in its

[22] The Victorian Supreme Court explained the distinction between the liability thresholds of absence of justification and negligence with admirable clarity in *Lucas v The Queen* [1973] VR 693, 699–701.

[23] Model Criminal Code, above n 2, ch 2, at 27. No reference is given though it seems likely that the immediate source was Fisse, *Howard's Criminal Law,* above n 10, at 489: 'To be relevant to recklessness in the criminal law a risk must be both substantial and unjustifiable.' Though Howard's discussion is based on the Model Penal Code definition, he elides the requirement that the defendant's conduct must involve a 'gross deviation from the standard conduct that a law abiding person would observe in the actor's situation'.

[24] Fisse, above n 10, at 489, 490–1: 'If a risk is unjustified, its degree of probability or substantiality need only be very slight to suffice for recklessness, no more than enough to move from the apparently impossible to the apparently possible.' The discussion confuses the question whether a risk is justified with the 'social value' of an activity in the course of which a risk is incurred. See Fisse, above n 10, at 490, fn 23: 'It is the concept of social value which accommodates the case of the driver who is aware that exceeding the speed limit is dangerous but is not guilty of murder if he kills someone.' This is clearly wrong. Whatever the social value of the activity of driving, the act of exceeding the speed limit whilst driving is unjustifiable and, on Howard's analysis, a motorist who is aware of any risk at all of causing death by speeding must be guilty of murder if death does result from that unjustifiable risk. See *R v McGrath* [1999] VSCA 197.

[25] Model Criminal Code, above n 2, ch 2, s 5.5 *Negligence*.

[26] [1977] VR 430, 444.

[27] Model Criminal Code, above n 2, ch 2, at 31.

[28] The assumption that the fault elements represent distinct degrees of fault arranged in an ascending order of culpability is apparent in the *Interim Report: Principles of Criminal Responsibility and Other Matters* (Canberra, Australian Government Printing Service, 1990) 32 and Model Criminal Code, above n 2, ch 2, at 27. Compare *Codification of the Criminal Law: A Report to the Law Commission* (Law Com Report 143, 1985) para 8.26.

commentary on the Code. Unlike the United States Model Penal Code, which includes a fault element of 'purpose', the Australian Code provides no alternative to its extended definition of intention. The commentary on the Code contradicts itself at this point. It begins with the promising assertion that legislatures have need of a fault element, described as 'true intention', that will require the prosecution to prove that a result was *meant* to occur.[29] The MCLOC argued that the necessity for precision in the formulation of statutory offences required rejection of the proposal in the *Review of Commonwealth Criminal Law* that intention should be extended to include realisation of a probable risk. That concession to ordinary usage was followed almost immediately, however, by the assertion that '"intention" to cause a result should include awareness that the result will occur in the ordinary course of events'.[30] That is to say, the Committee accepted that one must be taken to intend a result though it was *not* meant to occur.

Contradiction is also apparent between the assumption that the fault elements represent an ascending order of culpability and the Committee's concession that negligence with respect to a risk may exceed, in terms of culpability, recklessness with respect to the same risk.[31]

These fault elements were soon deployed in chapter 5 of the Model Code, which deals with fatal and non fatal offences against the person.[32] The non fatal offences against the person, set out in Table 12.1, were inspired by the scheme of offences first proposed by the English Law Commission in 1980.[33] The division of offences in the Model Code is far more elaborate, however, than anything contemplated by the Law Commission. Intentional, reckless and negligent harms are arranged in concentric circles of diminishing blameworthiness as one moves from intention at the centre to the outermost circle of negligence. The penalties for the offences are correspondingly arranged in bands of diminishing severity. The Model Code provisions are both more insistent on distinctions among the fault elements and more general in their expression of the physical elements of the offences than their English progenitors.[34] The comparative specificity

[29] Model Criminal Code, above n 2, ch 2, at 27.

[30] *Ibid.*

[31] Model Criminal Code, above n 2, ch 2, at 31.

[32] Chapter 5 of the Model Criminal Code was the subject of two reports and a discussion paper: *Non Fatal Offences Against the Person*, above n 3, *Sexual Offences Against the Person*: Report (Canberra, Australian Government Printing Service, 1999) and *Fatal Offences Against the Person*, Discussion Paper (Canberra, AGPS, 1998).

[33] *Fourteenth Report, Offences Against the Person* (Cmnd 7844, 1980). The genesis of the Australian provisions is explained in Model Criminal Code, above n 3, ch 5, at 4–6.

[34] Sections 75 and 76 of the English Draft Criminal Code distinguishes between offences of intentionally and recklessly causing injury only when the injury is 'serious': Law Commission (Law Com No 143, 1985), *Codification of the Criminal Law*. The authors of the Australian Model Criminal Code considered the distinction between intention and recklessness too fundamental to be compromised in this way: Model Criminal Code, above n 3, ch 5, at 41–3.

of the English references to 'injury' or 'serious injury' has been diluted to 'harm' and 'serious harm' in the Australian provisions and the offences of causing harm are augmented by a parallel series of offences of endangering harm.[35]

In its rejection of the subjectivist argument that negligence should not provide a ground for offences of causing harm, the MCLOC bowed to the imperatives of statutory history. With the exception of South Australia, all Australian jurisdictions impose criminal liability for serious injury caused by negligence. This is no new development. Victoria enacted the offence in 1862.[36] It was from the beginning quite general in its application and unrestricted by reference to particular relationships of duty or dangerous things or activities, though concern about railway passenger safety and negligent railway employees provided the original impetus for its enactment.[37] Two years later the offence was simply inserted among the other offences when the Victorian Parliament adopted the Offences Against the Person Act 1861 (UK).[38] In New South Wales an attempt to enact a similar offence in 1883 was flawed by grammatical solecism and defeated by ridicule.[39] It was enacted however, after revision of its terms, in 1900.[40] In the jurisdictions that adopted versions of Sir Samuel Griffith's criminal code, the provisions that imposed liability for negligently caused harms were more complex but similar in their effect.[41] In Griffith Code jurisdictions the threshold of liability for offences of causing harm was determined on the alternative grounds of negligence or conduct that could not be excused as a consequence of reasonable mistake or unforeseeable accident. South Australia remains the exception. It did not include a general offence of negligent injury when it adopted the Offences Against the Person Act 1861 (UK) in 1876 and it did not do so thereafter. The Government's recent attempt to include such an offence in the 2005 codification of offences against the person was defeated in the Legislative Council.[42]

[35] The Model Criminal Code is relatively parsimonious in its proposal for two offences of recklessly endangering death or serious harm: above n 3, ch 5, at 64–9. Section 29 of the South Australian Criminal Law Consolidation Act 1935 has separate offences of recklessly endangering serious harm and recklessly endangering harm.

[36] An Act For The Punishment Of Any Person Who Shall By His Negligence Cause Grievous Bodily Injury To Any Person 1862 (Vic).

[37] Victoria, *Parliamentary Debates*, 1861–62, vol 8, 1862, 1062, 1079, 1123, 1139–40, 1151, 1196–7, 1210, 1349.

[38] Crimes Act 1864 (Vic), s 24.

[39] G Woods, *A History of Criminal Law in New South Wales* (Sydney, Federation Press, 2002) 279–81.

[40] Crimes Act 1900 (Vic), s 54.

[41] The Northern Territory Criminal Code Act 1983 originally made provision for negligent harms in s 154. See now s 174E: Negligently causing serious harm.

[42] There are, however, specialised offences that impose liability for negligent drunkards who cause harm: Criminal Law Consolidation Act 1935 (SA), s 268(4).

In this chapter I propose a flat structure for the offences of causing harm in which negligence sets the threshold of criminal liability and there are no distinctions, so far as liability is concerned, between harms caused intentionally, recklessly or negligently.[43] The argument depends largely on the increasing importance of sentencing law in the offences against the person and the role that victims are now expected to play in the determination of the offender's sentence. It also depends on the premise, of which I have more to say later, that offenders owe obligations of explanation and apology to their victims. The initial stage of the criminal trial, when guilt is determined, offers few incentives and many disincentives to defendants to meet those obligations. During the second stage, when sentence is determined, emerging doctrinal developments in case law provide a structured set of incentives for the offender to explain, if explanation is necessary, and to apologise for the harm that has been done. It is at this point in the trial that enquiry into the offender's intentions should take place.[44]

Distinctions in terms of relative culpability can be drawn between intention, recklessness and negligence. Their significance is not sufficient, however, to justify their deployment as the formal organising principles of the Model Code offences of causing harm. When guilt is in issue, the significance of the distinctions among harms caused intentionally, recklessly and negligently rests largely on charitable assumptions about defendants' motives and their attitudes. Those charitable assumptions are buttressed by the presumption of innocence and a defendant's right to refrain from saying anything at all in answer to the charge. In that respect, the question whether harm was caused intentionally, recklessly or negligently is quite different from the question whether the defendant was the person who caused the harm or whether harm was caused at all. If those questions are of concern, their significance is unlikely to evaporate when the answers are known. It is quite possible, however, that the apparent moral significance of the differences between intentional, reckless and negligently caused harms will evaporate, more or less completely, when more is known about the offender's reasons for acting.

Two subsidiary themes will be pursued in this chapter. The first is the tendency, pervasive in the Model Code and its commentary, to perceive the primary importance of intention, recklessness and negligence as grades of culpability. Chapter 2, in its formulation of the general principles, neglects,

[43] Though the debt may not always be obvious, the argument owes much to the work of Alan Norrie, in particular to his *Punishment, Responsibility and Justice* (Oxford, Oxford University Press, 2000).

[44] See I Leader-Elliott, 'Negotiating Intentions in Trials of Guilt and Punishment' in N Naffine, R Owens and J Williams (eds), *Intention in Law and Philosophy* (Aldershot, Ashgate, 2001) 103–5 on the role of intention in offenders' claim of mitigation or palliation in sentencing hearings.

in particular, the far more important explanatory and descriptive role that intention can play in delineating Code offences. That role has a longer and more intellectually sustained history in the criminal law than the use of intention to mark a particular degree of culpability. The distinction that I have in mind between legislative recourse to intention to mark a degree of culpability and recourse to its descriptive or explanatory use in delineating offences involves no philosophical niceties: it merely reflects long established legislative usage. When the conduct of another person is the subject of enquiry, it may be explained or described in terms of his or her intended objective or the intended meaning of his or her conduct. This is the familiar, everyday sense of the concept, in which one adopts what Daniel Dennett would describe as the 'intentional stance' in order to understand what it was that another person meant to do, or what the person meant to do next.[45] The actual or potential objectives of conduct are distinguished from its side effects. When harm is done however, and culpability for causing that harm is in question, there is ample legal authority for an extension of the meaning of intention to include harms that were known to be certain[46] or, in a further extension, to harms that were known to be likely, on the ground that they are morally equivalent in terms of culpability. Intention is used in both senses in the criminal law, though the descriptive or explanatory use is of greater antiquity and continues to be more pervasive in legislation. In this chapter, that descriptive or explanatory use will be called 'ulterior intention' to distinguish it from the extended definition of intention in the Model Code.[47]

The first of these subsidiary themes will be pursued through a re-telling of the development of the statutory offences against the person.

The second of my subsidiary themes has to do with the adoption of negligence as the threshold for criminal liability in the offences against the person. The MCLOC accepted negligence unwillingly, as a ground for liability in the offences against the person. The concept is not well formulated, in part because of the fragile distinctions that the Code attempts to sustain between negligence and recklessness. The chapter concludes with a set of brief remarks on the need to rework the concept.

The implications of the argument can be quickly sketched. The non-fatal offences against the person should not differentiate among intention to

[45] D Dennett, *The Intentional Stance* (Cambridge, Mass, MIT Press, 1989).

[46] See RA Duff, *Intention, Agency and Criminal Liability* (London, Basil Blackwell, 1990) 76–82 on the distinction between 'intended' and 'intentional' harms and their equivalence, in legal blameworthiness.

[47] Ulterior intention, as the expression is used in this chapter, is an intention to engage in a course of conduct or bring about a consequence when that conduct or that consequence is not itself an element of the offence. Legislatures frequently impose criminal liability for projected conduct, or for conduct that failed of its objective, by prohibitions that make the intention with which the offender acted an element of the offence. The place of ulterior intentions in the Model Criminal Code is discussed in I Leader-Elliott, 'Benthamite Reflections on Codification of the General Principles of Criminal Liability: Towards the Panopticon' (2006) 9 *Buffalo Criminal Law Review* 391, 429–32.

cause harm, recklessness or negligence, when liability for causing harm is in issue. Attempted murder, requiring proof of an intention to kill, would remain an offence. When liability for undifferentiated harm is in question, however, negligence should be sufficient. The degree of moral condemnation appropriate to the offence would be for the court to determine when it comes to sentence the offender.

It was the example of the English Draft Code that inspired the MCLOC to adopt the offences of causing harm to the person as its vehicle for articulation of the fault elements. The familiar Anglo-centric bias of Australian law reformers probably accounts for that choice. The United States Model Penal Code would have been preferable as a source of inspiration. The fault elements are defined in the United States Code with more precision. Purpose and intention are distinguished from knowledge of consequences and recklessness and deployed with precision in formulating the offences against the person.[48]

II. ANSWERING FOR HARM: 'WHY DID YOU DO IT?'

One important thing expected of the criminal process is that it will require a person to answer for a wrong or harm that he or she has done to others. JR Lewis asserts that the 'the central core of the concept of responsibility is that I can be asked a question "Why did you do it" and be obliged to give an answer'.[49] Antony Duff, drawing on Lewis and HLA Hart,[50] makes the obligation to respond to an accusation central to his account of responsibility. If a person is responsible for a wrong or harm he or she is, he asserts, called to account for what he or she has done and obliged to explain or justify it.[51] Acceptance of blame is not sufficient if the reasons for inflicting the harm remain unexplained.

[48] See United States Model Penal Code, above n 20, § 2.02 *General Requirements of Culpability*, defining the fault elements: 'purposely', 'knowingly' and 'recklessly'. Those provisions are supplemented by § 1.13, *General Definitions.* § 1.13(12) states: '"intentionally" or "with intent" means purposely'. In Art 211 of this Code (which defines the offences of assault and reckless endangering), the fault elements of purpose, knowledge, recklessness and negligence delineate the offences. When liability for causing harm is in issue, however, it is sufficient that the defendant's conduct reaches the threshold requirement for liability: distinctions that may be drawn among purpose, knowledge, recklessness and negligence with respect to harm are relegated to the sentencing enquiry.

[49] JR Lucas, *Responsibility* (Oxford, Clarendon Press,1993) 5.

[50] HLA Hart, 'Varieties of Responsibility' (1967) 83 *LQR* 346, 363.

[51] RA Duff, *Punishment, Communication and Community* (Oxford, Oxford University Press, 2001) 180. See also J Gardner, 'The Mark of Responsibility' (2003) 23 *OJLS* 157, 171: '[o]ur basic responsibility depends not only on the conditions that obtain when we commit our wrongs and mistakes, but also on the conditions that obtain later when we are confronted with those wrongs or mistakes.' Elsewhere in the same paper [at 168] Gardner describes the trial of a criminal defendant as a 'site of intrinsic value' where defendants faced with the prospect of punishment are placed under pressure to 'give decent public accounts of themselves'.

In transferring this generalised account of responsibility to the criminal law, Duff ignores what I take to be a significant difference between Hart and Lewis on the nature of the obligation to answer an accusation. For Hart, the obligation did not extend to answering questions or providing an explanation. It was an obligation to rebut the charge or, failing that, to accept liability.[52] That is an accurate reflection of the trial process, when guilt is in issue. So far as their legal obligations are concerned, defendants are entitled to maintain an impassive silence even on the issue of guilt or innocence. When guilt is in issue there is no obligation to explain or try to justify what was done. If a defendant will not answer the charge, a not guilty plea will be entered on their behalf. There may be a cost incurred in maintaining silence, but Australian courts have taken elaborate precautions to minimise that cost and ensure that the right to silence is unfettered by adverse consequences. There is, however, no corresponding right to silence after conviction. Because it is so obvious, the proposition may sound unfamiliar. It has significant consequences, however, and I will have more to say about it towards the conclusion of this chapter. There are inducements to speech during the sentencing enquiry that can be taken as an implicit recognition in the criminal process of the moral obligation to explain why the harm was done, unless the reason is obvious, and to apologise for what was done.

The quotation from Lewis with which I began section II suggests that the obligation to answer does not arise until it is established that an individual has done something that requires an explanation. When that is a wrong to another or a harm of some kind, the question will often take the form of an accusation that invites confirmation, explanation or denial. Take, for example, the analogous situation where a person stung by a hurtful remark responds with the accusation that the hurt was inflicted intentionally. Since the thing has been done, it would be entirely inappropriate for the person who caused the hurt to respond to the accusation by saying, 'Prove it—prove that I meant to hurt you'. That would be a puzzling, off-key denial of a social obligation of responsive behaviour. If the person who made the hurtful remark does not choose to confirm the accusation and declare that the hurt was quite intentional, or compound it in some other way, the occasion calls for an explanation that will deny or deflect the accusation and, perhaps, for an apology. The criminal process, I suggest, displays the same structure, with a marked caesura between the guilt finding and sentencing stages of the trial. The obligation to provide an explanation only arises after conviction, when the time comes to determine the penalty for the offence. Many defendants who choose to contest the charge will offer their explanations earlier of course. But that is a tactical decision, not the fulfilment of

[52] Hart, above n 50, at 362–4.

an obligation. Australian law recognises no such obligation—it is, on the contrary, strenuously denied.

To be liable for an offence is to be responsible for it and, in that sense, responsibility is not a matter of degree.[53] From the legislator's point of view, however, the point at which responsibility for a wrong or harm is imposed is often a matter of degree. Conduct that prompts legislative intervention may have no sharply defined borders. When that is so, the legislature must determine the point at which liability is incurred on a continuum of socially irresponsibility, malice or harm. In a Cartesian moment, Hart once asked the legislator's question: '[H]ow closely connected with ... harm must the embodied mind or will of an individual person be to render him liable to punishment?'[54] The answer will vary, of course, according to the nature of the harm and the anticipated severity of the punishment, among other criteria. The legislator will set a threshold below which 'Cartesian' and other connections are too attenuated for the imposition of criminal liability.

Very different considerations are involved, however, when the legislator must decide whether to distinguish among offences by reference to degrees of harm, degrees of causal connection[55] or modes of culpability. The legislature may choose to paint with a broad brush and define offences inclusively, avoiding the multiplication of separate offences graded by degrees of causal connection, seriousness of harm or culpability. That is usually the case, for example, in statutory liability for injury to property rather than to persons.

In this chapter, which is concerned with the 'non-sexual' and 'non-fatal' offences against the person, I accept established Australian law that negligence marks the threshold of liability for the offences of causing harm. Once an offender crosses the negligence threshold, so as to be liable to punishment, the measure of that punishment will depend, in part, on the outcome of an enquiry into the degree of the offender's responsibility for the harm. From the legislator's point of view, the answer to the question whether to use a broad brush and leave questions about the degree of responsibility to be determined during sentencing will determine the nature of that enquiry. When liability is in issue, the accused owes no obligation to explain his or her conduct. The obligation to explain or justify that Duff identifies receives no recognition in law until the defendant is convicted. The enquiry that takes place after conviction, when sentence must be determined and the

[53] Hart, above n 50, at 355: 'to say that a man is legally responsible for some act or harm is to state that his connection with the act or harm is sufficient according to law for liability.'

[54] Hart, above n 50, at 355.

[55] On degrees of causal connection, see P Robinson, *Structure and Function in Criminal Law* (Oxford, Clarendon Press, 1997) 176–7. Compare s 14 of the Criminal Law Consolidation Act 1935 (SA), *Criminal liability for neglect where death or serious harm results from unlawful act* which imposes liability for death or injury though the causal connection is tenuous.

offender no longer enjoys the presumption of innocence, is conducted under very different rules from those that govern the preceding enquiry into guilt.

The divergent nature of these enquiries into guilt and punishment reflects the development of sentencing law over the past half-century and, over the same period, the development of an array of protections associated with the presumption of innocence when guilt in is issue. Any endeavour to codify an area of criminal law ought to be conducted with careful attention to the question whether factors constituting the criminality of the offender should be located in the initial stage of the enquiry, when guilt is in issue, or later, when sentence is determined. In practice the issue is ignored. The relationship between the elements of the offences against the person and sentencing law was not considered in 1861 in their original compendious formulation.[56] Nor was it considered by the MCLOC, when it proposed its reform and codification at the close of the 20th century. The elaborate structure of distinct offences, differentiated according to whether harm was done intentionally, recklessly or negligently, was an attempt to formulate new equivalents for the old offences. They are, in fact, far from equivalent in their allocation of penalties, but that is incidental to present concerns. The possibility that the modern relationship between the trial to determine guilt and the sentencing enquiry might require a more fundamental reconsideration of the elements that constitute the offences against the person was ignored.

In retrospect, the 1861 consolidation can been seen as a transitional form, poised between earlier offences of particularised conduct coupled with requirements of ulterior intention, and the subsequent emergence of offences of causing harm, in which the fault elements were meant to express a grade of culpability. It was, in almost every respect, an unsatisfactory foundation for a modern law of offences against the person.

III. A LITTLE HISTORY OF THE OFFENCES AGAINST THE PERSON: THE ROAD TO MORAL VACUITY AND BEYOND[57]

I take the reference to 'moral vacuity' from Jeremy Horder's defence of the Offences Against the Person Act 1861 (UK) against the Law Commission proposals for radical reform of its provisions.[58] The proposals were

[56] On this aspect of the 1861 Act, see L Radzinowicz and R Hood, 'Judicial Discretion and Sentencing Standards: Victorian Attempts to Solve a Perennial Problem' (1979) 127 *University of Pennsylvania Law Review* 1288, 1304–5.

[57] The phrase recurs as a *leitmotif* in J Horder, 'Rethinking Non-Fatal Offences Against the Person' (1994) 14 *OJLS* 335.

[58] *Legislating the Criminal Code, Offences Against the Person and General Principles* (Law Comm no 218) (Cmd 2370, 1993). The earlier history of the draft provisions, which were first proposed in 1980, is recounted in Horder, above n 57, at 336.

remarkable for their brevity and their generality. Horder argued that the Law Commissioners had sacrificed the moral particularity of the 1861 Act in pursuit of bland technicality in legal definition. He was not alone in his rediscovery of the virtues of Greaves' consolidation of the offences against the person or in his criticism of the proposed reforms.[59]

The arguments advanced by the critics are of particular interest for their attempt to derive, from close analysis of the provisions of the 1861 Act, principles that should guide Parliament in its formulation of criminal offences that involve serious moral wrongdoing.[60] In this particular instance, the principle that Horder sought to derive from the Act was a requirement of moral particularity, or 'representative labelling' in the legislative description of the offences: Parliament, he argued, 'must try to fix on a definition of the crime that captures the moral essence of the wrong in question, by reference to the best moral conception of that essence in society as it is today.'[61]

Until the recent discovery of its merits, the usual attitude to Greaves' consolidation was one of disappointment compounded by scorn. Together with the other Acts that comprised the great consolidation of 1861, it was the 'most that could be salvaged' from the failure to codify English criminal law during the first half of the 19th century.[62] Greaves himself shared that disappointment, though he took pride in what he had managed to accomplish, in the face of adversity. He was a generalist, who would almost certainly have disagreed with Horder's argument for moral particularity. Had he been given a free hand, the offences would have been far more general in form. Though they fell short of his ideals, he described the consolidation as the 'most perfect Acts that have ever been passed on the subjects to which they relate'.[63] Critics were less kind. Stephen condemned the 1861 Act as obscure in structure, cumbrous in its language and unintelligible to anyone

[59] J Gardner, 'Rationality and the Rule of Law in Offences Against the Person' (1994) 53 *CLJ* 502. See, in addition, the related papers: J Gardner and H Jung, 'Making Sense of Mens Rea: Antony Duff's Account' (1991) 11 *OJLS*559; J Horder, 'Two Histories and Four Hidden Principles of Mens Rea' (1997) 113 *LQR* 95; RA Duff, 'Criminalising Endangerment' in RA Duff and SP Green (eds), *Defining Crimes: Essays on the Special Part of the Criminal Law* (Oxford, Oxford University Press, 2005) 43.

[60] The critics' case against the Law Commission proposals display an affinity with Luc Wintgens' suggested principles of legislative coherence: 'Rationality in Legislation—Legal Theory as Legisprudence: An Introduction', in LJ Wintgens (ed), *Legisprudence: A New Theoretical Approach to Legislation* (Oxford, Hart Publishing, 2002) 37–8.

[61] Horder, above n 57, at 335. Compare J Gardner, 'On the General Part of the Criminal Law' in RA Duff (ed), *Philosophy and the Criminal Law* (Cambridge, Cambridge University Press, 1998) 208, on the 'supervisory general part' of the criminal law which includes principles to guide legislatures.

[62] KJM Smith, *Lawyers, Legislators and Theorists* (Oxford, Clarendon Press, 1998) 137.

[63] CS Greaves, *Criminal Law Consolidation and Amendment Acts of the 24th and 25th Vict with Notes and Observations* (Stevens, Sweet & Maxwell, London, 1861) lxi.

not versed in the law.[64] Andrew Ashworth described it as 'antiquated and illogical'.[65] In Australia, Colin Howard criticised the proliferation of offences and the absence of any consistent scheme in their formulation.[66] The MCLOC quoted Howard's remarks and expressed the same opinion in more scathing terms when advancing its proposals for codification.[67] Jeremy Horder's argument for moral particularity was given cursory consideration and rejected outright.[68]

For the time being, the Australian codifications mark the terminal point of a series of transformations of the offences against the person towards what Horder characterised as a state of 'moral vacuity'.[69] If that description can be applied to Law Commission proposals, the offences in the Model Criminal Code, which are more general in form, are even more starved of moral oxygen. Their abstract terminology provides very little in the way of morally informative labelling of the offences. One may accept Horder's characterisation of the new offences without, however, accepting the implied conclusion that we should have retained the old counterparts for their descriptive particularity. Rather than a progression to moral vacuity, the central emphasis on harmful consequences might be seen as a preliminary step towards relocating the particularised moral assessment of the offender's conduct in the sentencing stage of the trial. On that view, the Model Criminal Code provisions can be criticised on the ground that the reform process has not gone far enough in repudiating the 1861 Offences Against the Person Act.

The United Kingdom Parliament enacted few offences dealing with offences against the person until the beginning of the 19th century. Earlier legislation was radically restricted in its applications. The Coventry Act[70] created offences of maiming and wounding in the late 17th century, but these required proof that the offenders had lain in wait for their victim. Firearms were later singled out for legislative attention. The Waltham Blacks Act of 1722 made it a capital felony to 'wilfully and maliciously shoot at any person'.[71] In 1803, in the first of the Acts that was intended to provide a more comprehensive coverage of the offences against the

[64] JF Stephen, *History of the Criminal Law of England*, vol 3 (Burt Franklin, New York, 1883) 114–8.

[65] A Ashworth, *Principles of Criminal Law* (Oxford, Oxford University Press, 1st edn, 1991) 281. The current edition is equally critical: see *Principles of Criminal Law* (Oxford, Oxford University Press, 5th edn, 2006) 333.

[66] Howard, above n 10, at 109. The passage appears without significant alteration in Fisse, above n 10, at 136.

[67] Model Criminal Code, above n 3, ch 5, at 1–6, citing Fisse, above n 10, at 136.

[68] Fisse, above n 10, at 5, 136.

[69] Horder, above n 57, at 339ff.

[70] 22 & 23 Car II, Ch 1. An Act to Prevent Malicious Maiming and Wounding, known as the 'Coventry Act' because it was enacted as a consequence of an attack on Sir John Coventry, a member of the House of Commons.

[71] 9 Geo II, c 22.

person,[72] the offence of shooting at another was augmented by making it an offence to aim or point a loaded gun at another with intent to discharge it at them. The Act included as well, offences of stabbing or cutting another with intention to murder, rob, maim, disfigure, disable or do some other grievous bodily harm. Successive consolidations during the first half of the 19th century repeated the same pattern as new offences of ulterior intention were added to the original prohibitions against cutting, stabbing and shooting at others.

To modern eyes it may seem a remarkable feature of these early offences against the person, before Greaves' reconstruction, that they do not require proof of any determinate degree of harm and some do not require proof of any harm at all.[73] Instead they describe various forms of 'attack'[74]—by shooting, cutting, stabbing, poisoning, attempted strangling, drowning or suffocation.[75] Harm of some degree is inseparable from many of these acts but the harm is incidental. It was the form of the attack, involving the use of a gun, edged weapon, poisons, explosives or stoppage of breath, rather than any consequential harm, which might be minor or non-existent, that was the essence of the offences.[76] The reason, it seems, was that each of these offences was conceived originally as an inchoate form of murder in which the victim fortuitously survived.[77] The various intentions specified in the offences—to rob, maim, disfigure, prevent lawful arrest and so on—were each sufficient to support a conviction for murder, in case the victim died. The inchoate form of these offences—a description of a particular act, accompanied by a specified ulterior intention—had an extensive statutory history, covering a broad range of criminal conduct, dating from Elizabethan times, if not earlier.

[72] 43 Geo III, c 58.

[73] Noted by Stephen, above n 64, at 118–9. Compare Horder, above n 57, at 335, 340, 344–5, whose proposed reconstruction of the offences against the person is based on a dissection of different kinds of harm, characteristic of far earlier law, rather than on the form of the attack and its accompanying ulterior intention.

[74] On the notion of 'attack' as characteristic of these offences, compare RA Duff, 'Criminalising Endangerment' in Duff and Green, above n 59, at 135.

[75] These offences were repealed and replaced by An Act to Amend the Laws Relating to Offences Against the Person 1 Will 4 & 1 Vict c 85. Section 5 departed from the earlier pattern by making it an offence to cause grievous bodily harm, with intention to do so, by explosives, corrosive fluids or other dangerous things. The open-ended nature of the category of dangerous things probably accounts for the requirement of grievous bodily harm. Compare s 2, which made it an offence to cause, 'by any means' bodily injury dangerous to life, with intent to murder.

[76] But see *R v Griffith* (1824) 1 Car & P 298, and its accompanying notes, which indicate that some courts would not convict of the felony of cutting with intent to murder if the wound was minor and unlikely to cause death.

[77] Compare G Binder, 'The Meaning of Killing' in MD Dubber and L Farmer (eds), *Modern Histories of Crime and Punishment* (Stanford, Stanford University Press, 2007) 88–114, on similar requirements of attack in the common law of unlawful homicide during the first part of the 19th century and earlier. Binder, above n 77, at 107 writes: 'Homicide was not just a crime of "harmful consequences" but required that death be produced by a "manifestly criminal

It was not until 1829, in an Act restricted in its application to Ireland, that Parliament enacted an offence that required proof that the offender inflicted grievous bodily harm.[78] That offence was re-cast by Greaves in 1851, in legislation that applied to England, in the familiar form of the offence of unlawful and malicious wounding or infliction of grievous bodily harm.[79] The offence was incorporated, with minor alterations, in his 1861 consolidation, which also introduced the offence of causing grievous bodily harm, 'by any means whatsoever', if done with intent to maim, disfigure, disable or do some other grievous bodily harm.[80] These two offences, which made the degree of harm rather than the form of attack determinative of the offender's guilt, were significant innovations: they were the mutant forms from which the modern Australian offences of causing harm have evolved.[81] The other offences in Greaves' consolidation, with their many variations, preserved for the most part their original form as offences of ulterior intention that required proof of a particular form of attack, rather than the infliction of harm.

This exploration of the evolution of these statutory offences provides a surprising counterpoint to the orthodox, subjectivist narrative of a gradual movement away from reliance on objective criteria of guilt towards the modern concern with subdivisions of subjectivity.[82] In these statutory offences the development runs the other way. From the beginning, most of the offences required proof of ulterior intention.[83] As statute law extended its reach, in a gradual colonisation of the common law, there was a shift

act". *Killing* meant causing death by violence: by intentionally battering a person with a weapon, producing a wound or injury.'

[78] 10 Geo 4, c 34, s 29. It seems likely that the Act was particularly directed against the Irish 'chalkers' who marked their victims by slashing their faces, like the razor gangs of Sydney's Darlinghurst during the thirties. Greaves remarks that the Irish Act departed from the English model by including alterations and additional clauses 'adapted to the then existing state of crime in Ireland': above n 63, at x.

[79] Section 5, An Act for the Better Prevention of Offences 14–15 Vic, c 29. Greaves recounts the origin of the offence in 'Malicious Wounding' (1872) NS vol 1, *Law Magazine and Review: A Quarterly Review of Jurisprudence* 379; Greaves, above n 63, at xiii–xiv. See also 1 Vict c 85, s 2, which made it an offence to 'stab, cut or wound any person', or cause, 'by any means whatsoever … any bodily injury dangerous to life', with intent to commit murder.

[80] Greaves, above n 63, at xli–xlii, 31. Greaves was explicit about his objectives in his prefatory remarks. Though the room for manoeuvre was limited, he sought to generalise the statutory offences so as to reduce their length and particularity, so avoiding unwarranted acquittals and, in consequence, enlarging the sentencing powers of the courts.

[81] They were supplemented, in South Australia, by s 20(4) of the Criminal Law Consolidation Act 1935, which preserved the offence of assault causing harm. The offence, which imposes absolute liability with respect to the harm has no counterpart in the Model Criminal Code, or Commonwealth or Victorian statute law.

[82] See Robinson, above n 55.

[83] See 5 Henry IV c 5, which made it a felony to cut out the tongue or pull out the eyes of the King's subjects. The offence required proof of 'malice prepensed', which was equated in the statute with 'purposely' inflicting those harms. The Coventry Act, above n 70, ch 1, which was concerned with similar injuries, required proof of an 'intention … to maim and disfigure'.

from the original almost exclusive preoccupation with the form of the attack and its accompanying purpose, to the development of offences that would impose liability for causing harm. That reorientation of the law did not begin until the 19th century and it was far from complete by 1861, when Greaves prepared his consolidation. It is a curious consequence of the exhaustive nature of that consolidation that an evolutionary process, which produced no less than five statutory restatements of the law of offences against the person between 1803 and 1861, came to an end in that year so that the law remained frozen for more than a century thereafter.

Had he felt able to do so, Greaves would have eliminated the particularities of earlier legislation, in favour of broadly drafted offences of causing harm. That the statutory development was incomplete is obvious from a consideration of the hybrid form of his offence of unlawful and malicious wounding or causing grievous bodily harm, which combined a crime of attack—wounding—with a quite distinct prohibition against infliction of grievous bodily harm.[84] No fault element was specified, beyond the conventional requirement that the wound or the harm be inflicted unlawfully and maliciously. Unlawful and malicious wounding, as it was commonly known, was to become the subject of more than a century of unresolved judicial dithering, in the United Kingdom and Australia, over its fault elements.[85]

In most of the offences of the 1861 consolidation, the requirement of intention does not express a grade or level of culpability, as it does in modern codifications of the offences of causing harm. Liability for these offences was inchoate and the defendant's conduct attracted criminal liability only if it was animated by an intention to secure some further, specified objective.

[84] The requirement that the harm be 'inflicted' would once have required proof of an assault of some kind. Discussed by Gardner, above n 59, at 509–11. See, in particular, *R v Clarence* (1882) 22 QBD 23. That requirement has been eroded by judicial reinterpretation. For a survey of Australian cases, see *R v Lee* [2001] ACTSC 133 (21 December 2001).

[85] Horder, above n 57, recounts the English history of interpretation of the provision. See also Smith, above n 62, at 163–6. In Australia, the offence had no precise counterpart in the Griffith Code jurisdictions, though the decision of the High Court in *Vallance v The Queen* (1961) 108 CLR 5 and subsequent decisions in those jurisdictions reflect the same underlying uncertainty about fault elements in the lesser offences against the person. In Victoria, *R v Newman* [1948] VLR 61 held that unlawful and malicious wounding could be committed by negligence. That decision seems to have represented the judicial consensus of the time in Victoria. Later, however, a succession of rulings at first instance followed the staggering path mapped by English precedents. See *R v Smyth* [1963] VR 737 in which Sholl J followed *R v Cunningham* [1957] 2 QB 396 and required proof of recklessness with respect to the infliction of grievous bodily harm; *Lovett* [1975] VR 488 followed *R v Mowatt* [1968] 1 QB 421 and held that it was sufficient for guilt if the defendant realised that some physical harm, whether or not serious, might result to someone. The issue of interpretation passed without notice in *R v O'Connor* (1980) 146 CLR 64 and became moot in Victoria with the abolition of the offence by the Crimes (Amendment) Act 1985, which adopted the Law Commission proposals for reform of the offences against the person. In New South Wales, *R v Mowatt* [1968] 1 QB 421 prevails: *Pengilley v The Queen* [2006] NSW CCA 163. South Australia, prior to codification of the offences against the person,

In many of the offences, conduct and intention were closely linked so that offenders' actions were usually eloquent of their incriminating objective.[86] That was particularly likely to be the case when the offence coupled a particular form of physical attack on the person with the intention of inflicting some particular form of injury.[87] In other offences of ulterior intention, however, act and intention were more likely to part company[88] From the prosecutor's standpoint, responsibility for these offences of ulterior intention was established by adopting the 'intentional stance' and proposing an explanation of a defendant's conduct in terms of their objectives, their motives or the intended meaning of their conduct.[89] So, for example, poisoning and attempts to administer poison or stupefying drugs eventually comprised five distinct offences, depending on the intended objective of the poisoner. Proof of harm was unnecessary in most of these offences. They were differentiated by the offenders' ulterior intentions. In the language of current criminal law scholarship, intention was made to 'serve a rule articulation function' in the definition of most of the offences against the person.[90]

The course of development of the statutory offences against the person, in which causing harm played an increasingly important role, is one of slow and halting convergence with the common law of homicide, in which the harm was always central.[91] With that shift to liability based on causing harm, the role of intention was transformed from an explanatory or descriptive mode to one of supplying a standard of culpability. Though the difference is far from sharp, it is readily discernible. When legislatures imposed criminal liability for conduct accompanied by a specified ulterior intention, criminal liability requires proof of what the offender intended to do next,

required proof of recklessness with respect to the wound or the infliction of grievous bodily harm: *R v Hoskin* (1974) 9 SASR 531; *Gillan v Police* [2004] SASC 279.

[86] Compare the proliferation of modern offences of ulterior intention in which conduct that bears no obvious signs of criminality is transformed into an offence by the imputation of criminal intention: MD Dubber, 'The Possession Paradigm: The Special Part and the Police Power Model of the Criminal Process' in Duff and Green, above n 59, at 91.

[87] But see the cases where the question was whether injury was inflicted with intent to avoid apprehension or, on the other hand, to disable, maim or inflict grievous bodily harm: Cases discussed in WM Russell, *A Treatise on Crimes and Misdemeanours* (London, Saunders and Benning, ed by Greaves, CS, 3rd edn, 1843) vol 1, 734ff.

[88] The most striking and best known instance of judicial insistence on proof of the ulterior intention is *Rhenwick Williams* (1790) 1 Leach 528, in which the defendant's conviction for a statutory assault with intent to cut and tear the clothes of his victims was vacated on the ground that he intended to injure them, rather than their clothing.

[89] Dennett, above n 45, at 13–33.

[90] Robinson, above n 55, at 133–7. Compare A Halpin, *Definition in Criminal Law* (Oxford, Hart Publishing, 2004) 144–5, suggesting that intention, in this particular role, is really part of the '*actus reus*' of the offence. For a similar view, see Barwick CJ in *R v O'Connor* (1980) 146 CLR 64 at 77.

[91] Note, however, Binder, above n 77, at 107, on the gradual enlargement of unlawful homicide to become a crime of 'harmful consequences'.

as for example in the offence of pointing a gun with intent to discharge it at another. Or, in the alternative, liability was imposed for conduct that was meant to have a particular effect as, for example, in the laws against ship wreckers, which made it a capital offence to erect a 'false light ... with intent to bring any ship or vessel into danger'.[92] In these offences of inchoate liability the objectives and motives of the defendant are central: they determine the threshold of criminal liability. By contrast, when liability for harm is in issue, a requirement that the harm be caused intentionally is meant to express a particular degree of moral condemnation.

When the question is one of blame for causing harm intentionally, the common law sacrifices particularity in the attribution of intention by stretching ordinary language or redefining the concept for the purposes of the criminal law.[93] Liability is imposed for intentional harm when the defendant 'as good as intended' that harm and the jury is permitted a certain amount of 'elbow room' in determining the offender's criminal responsibility.

Jeremy Horder provides an illuminating account of intention in his discussion of its role in the definition of murder. Intention, in his account, is a 'moral beacon' or 'centre of gravity' that constrains the outward extension of liability for more attenuated forms of malice aforethought.[94] In England, knowledge that death is practically certain to result from the defendant's conduct is taken to be equivalent, in moral turpitude, to an intention to kill.[95] In most Australian jurisdictions, the beacon shines more brightly but the gravitational pull of intention is far weaker: fault elements for murder include recklessness with respect to death, which is accepted as near enough, in terms of moral turpitude, to intention to kill. In some jurisdictions, recklessness with respect to grievous bodily harm is sufficient.

That accommodating amplitude in Australian definitions of the fault elements for the offence of murder is inconsistent with the distinctions drawn in the Model Criminal Code between intention and recklessness when liability for lesser harms is in issue. Why, it may be asked, are intention and recklessness distinguished in these offences when they count as equivalents in murder? If the difference does not matter when liability for the most serious of the offences is in issue, the same disregard would be expected in the lesser offences against the person.[96]

[92] 22 Geo II, c 19.

[93] See RA Duff, above n 46. Duff's approach is discussed in Gardner and Jung, above n 59, at 563–73. Gardner and Jung refer (580) to rules that 're-fashion the concept of intention strategically, creating "artificial intentions"'. As an instance, see the Model Criminal Code, ch 2, above n 2, at 5.2 *Intention*, which extends the concept to include awareness that a result of conduct 'will occur in the ordinary course of events'.

[94] J Horder, 'Intention in the Criminal Law: A Rejoinder' (1995) 58 *MLR* 678, 687.

[95] *R v Woollin* [1998] 3 WLR 382.

[96] These offences, it may be suggested, are the practical expression in modern statute law of Jeremy Horder's principle of 'moral nomalism' or 'representative labelling': Horder, above n 57.

Before turning to a more detailed consideration of the Model Criminal Code fault elements, it is worth remarking that Horder's principle of representative labelling flourishes at the expanding peripheries of the offences against the person, where democratically responsive or populist governments respond to media and public concerns by inventing and labelling new offences of drink spiking, intentional or reckless transmission of HIV infections, genital mutilation, torture, cyberstalking, offensive or intrusive use or acquisition of digital images and so on.[97] Legislative delineation of many of these offences requires recourse to the descriptive and explanatory use of fault concepts, in particular, of intention.[98] These modern offences, in which the descriptive or explanatory role of intention is often central to their definition, have their counterparts in earlier legislation, from the 17th century on, when Parliament displaced common law with new statutory offences, that were similarly particular in the descriptive detail of the offender's conduct and intentions. The virtues of particularity are obvious enough at the outer limits of criminal liability where boundaries must be drawn with descriptive precision and the educative effects of criminal prohibitions are of primary importance. These offences are supplementary, however, to the familiar and general crimes of consequential harm.

IV. STRUCTURE AND FUNCTION OF THE FAULT ELEMENTS IN OFFENCES AGAINST THE PERSON[99]

Most criminal law scholars and reformers accept the premise that intention to cause harm is central to an understanding of the offences against the person. It is far less certain, however, what legislative consequences should flow from that premise of centrality. In the discussion that follows I will try to avoid direct engagement in the continuing debate over the grounds for drawing moral distinctions between intentional, reckless and negligent wrongdoing. The distinctions have been the subject of exhaustive analysis by others,

[97] The principles that should govern the formulation of these offences are quite different from those that are appropriate when liability for harm is in issue. In general, these are offences restricted in their application to conscious, intentional and, often, deliberate wrongdoing. Many are offences in which the harm may consist precisely in the fact that the conduct was meant to hurt, humiliate, offend or violate some expectation. See Duff, above n 46, at 111–15.

[98] See, for example, the MCLOC Discussion Paper, *Drink Spiking* (Canberra, Australian Government Printing Service, May 2006) <http://www.ag.gov.au/www/agd/agd.nsf/Page/Modelcriminalcode_Discussionpaper-DrinkSpiking-May2006>.

[99] See Robinson, above n 55. Robinson proposes a grading scheme similar to the Model Code provisions with fault elements of recklessness, knowledge and purpose: 231–5. In Robinson's version, however, the discrimination between fault elements is done during sentencing with a threshold requirement for guilt of recklessness.

in depth and sophistication that I could not hope to emulate.[100] My concern is rather with the ways in which these distinctions have been deployed in legislation that grades the offences of causing harm in a hierarchical arrangement of increasing culpability. I suggest that the means of expression available to legislatures and courts in making these distinctions are so inflexible and so insensitive to the moral responsibility of offenders that we shall do better to abandon them altogether, when liability for harm is in issue.

Table 12.2 which follows extracts the offences of causing serious harm from the more comprehensive table provided earlier. Circumstances of aggravation have been omitted.

Table 12.2: Model Criminal Code—Causing Serious Harm

Offence Category	Basic Penalty
Cause serious harm (intentionally)	20 yrs
Cause serious harm (recklessly)	15 yrs
Cause serious harm (negligently)	10 yrs

The structure is ambiguous in its implications. Maximum penalties are specified, but there is no statement of minimum or presumptive penalties.[101] Nor are minimum or presumptive penalties specified in jurisdictions that have enacted the Model Criminal Code provisions. Taken at face value, the arrangement of fault elements, harms and penalties might seem to do no more than express a legislative judgment about the maximum penalty in worst case scenarios. If that were taken to be the object of the scheme, one would expect that the distinction between intention and recklessness might not be of great significance in the generality of cases. The distinction between recklessness and negligence might similarly be of no great significance in the generality of cases where their applications intersect and overlap. The idea that the extended penalty range might only be required in exceptional cases can be illustrated by a comparison between harms inflicted intentionally and harms inflicted recklessly. Intentional wrongdoing occupies a broader moral spectrum, in terms of its potential for moral depravity, than wrongs done knowingly, recklessly or negligently. Intentional and reckless wrongdoing can be taken as morally equivalent when an offender's conduct expresses an attitude of callous indifference with respect to the infliction of injury. That is, however, the worst that can

[100] A helpful account of the debate can be found in A Halpin, *Definition in the Criminal Law* (Oxford, Hart Publishing, 2004) ch 3, 'The Unlearned Lessons of Recklessness'. See also, AP Simester, 'Why Distinguish Intention from Foresight?' in AP Simester and ATH Smith (eds), *Harm and Culpability* (Oxford, Clarendon Press, 1996) 71.

[101] Compare the more elaborate scheme proposed in Robinson, above n 55, at 231–5, in which the offences against the person are graded in sentencing bands, with upper and lower limits, according to whether harm is inflicted purposely, knowingly or recklessly.

be said of an offender who causes injury or death by recklessness since, by definition, the harm suffered by the victim forms no part of the offender's reasons for action. Worse than callous indifference, however, is the malevolence that may actuate an intentional injury, when the offender's reasons for acting exacerbate the wrong,[102] as, for example, when a child is killed or injured in order to take revenge against a parent. Understood in that way, the provision of a higher maximum penalty for intentional harms would require a higher penalty when the reasons for causing intentionally go beyond even callousness in their moral depravity.[103]

The alternative implication of the structure of offences, with their graded maximum penalties, is that it expresses a legislative judgment that, other factors being constant, intentional harms must always be punished more severely than reckless or negligent harms. If that is accepted, an offender charged with intentionally causing harm would always be entitled to a proportionate discount in the penalty if the prosecution could only prove recklessness.

These are quite distinct possibilities and nothing in the text of the Model Criminal Code provisions indicates which of these alternatives was intended. It is apparent, however, from the accompanying commentary on the provisions, that the MCLOC did mean its provisions to express a hierarchical arrangement in which intentionally causing harm is always more blameworthy than doing so recklessly and causing harm recklessly is always more blameworthy than doing so negligently, when other factors are constant.[104]

There are good reasons for rejecting those assumptions. In the first place it is apparent that other factors cannot be held constant so as to enable a comparison of fault elements in this way. That would require a far more morally sensitive and accommodating structure of defences than any code could be expected to provide.[105] Criminal liability is discontinuous. With the rare exceptions of the partial defences to murder, defences either

[102] *Knight v The Queen* [2006] NSWCCA 292. See the related point that an intentional harm is an instance of successful accomplishment of a wrong by the offender: J Gardner, 'On the General Part of the Criminal Law' in RA Duff (ed), *Philosophy and the Criminal Law* (Cambridge University Press, 1998) 205. See also, T Nagel, *The View from Nowhere* (Oxford University Press, 1986) 180–8.

[103] Compare *Baumer v The Queen* (1988) 166 CLR 51 on the effect of provisions that extend the range of penalties for an offence when a potentially aggravating factor is present. The question whether it is appropriate to use the extended range will depend on the particular circumstances of the instant case.

[104] The assumption that the fault elements represent distinct degrees of fault arranged in an ascending order of culpability is apparent in the *Interim Report: Principles of Criminal Responsibility and Other Matters*, above n 22, at 32 and Model Criminal Code, above n 2, ch 2, at 27. Compare *Codification of the Criminal Law: A Report to the Law Commission* (Law Com Report 143, 1985) para 8.26. See also, Model Criminal Code, above n 3, ch 5, 41–3.

[105] See, in particular: A Norrie, *Law and the Beautiful Soul* (London, Routledge Cavendish, 2005) 53, 62–5 on the inflexibilities of 'law's architectonic'.

exculpate or they fail. It is only after guilt is determined that degrees of responsibility can be assessed on a continuum and defences that fail during the first phase of the trial can be reconsidered during sentencing as factors that can mitigate the offender's wrongdoing.[106]

The second and more significant reason for rejecting the Model Criminal Code division of offences can be illustrated by a reconsideration of the MCLOC conclusion that intention to cause harm and realisation that harm would certainly occur are equivalent varieties of fault.

Willingness to take a risk of causing harm is certainly different from intention to cause that harm or knowledge that it was an inevitable consequence of conduct. But the moral significance of the difference depends largely, if not entirely, on the assumption that the risk taker would have desisted or changed course, if they had known that the harm would certainly occur. Similar considerations apply when the moral significance of the difference between recklessness and negligence is in question.[107] A person who fails to realise that there is a risk of causing harm to another might be expected to desist or change course if they had been aware of that risk. That is, however, a charitable assumption concerning an offender's attitudes or morality, akin to the presumption of innocence. If realisation that harm was certain would have made no difference to the offender's conduct, there may be no moral distinction worth taking between harm done intentionally, knowingly, recklessly or negligently.[108] In any particular instance where harm has been done the question whether a defendant would have behaved differently is potentially open to question. The distinctions between harms inflicted intentionally, recklessly or negligently are certainly significant, but they rest on a counterfactual assumption about the offender's response to realisation of risk.

If the analysis is accepted to this point, the implication is clear. The justification for separate offences and graded penalties, according to whether harm was caused intentionally, recklessly or negligently is speculative in the circumstances of any particular case. The distinctions that are drawn in terms of intentional, reckless and negligent infliction of harms appear to be provisional stages in the course of enquiry into an offender's moral culpability.

[106] See Robinson, above n 55, at 176–8.

[107] The argument is explored in detail in K Huigens, 'Homicide in Aretaic Terms' (2003) 6 *Buffalo Criminal Law Review* 97; A Michaels, 'Acceptance: the Missing Mental State' (1998) 71 *Southern California Law Review* 953. See also Simester, above n 100, at 71.

[108] The significance of the fact that harm was done intentionally may vary, however, according to the kind of harm that is done. Some harms are constituted, to a greater or less extent, by the fact that the thing done was intended to hurt, offend or violate some expectation. See Duff, above n 46, at 111–15. These forms of harm may be appropriately stigmatised by specialised offences that supplement the general offences of causing undifferentiated physical or mental injury.

A conclusion that harm was done recklessly rather than intentionally may be more or less significant, depending on further enquiry.

Grading offences according to whether harm was caused intentionally, recklessly or negligently pre-empts enquiries that should take place in the sentencing hearing. It makes very little sense to divide the enquiry into the relationship between fault elements and moral responsibility between the first and second phase of the trial. The first phase, when the defendant enjoys the privilege of silence, will determine the course of the enquiry that can take place if a guilty verdict is returned. A failure to prove intention or recklessness, when they are elements of an offence charged against the defendant, will preclude any further enquiry into the offender's intention to cause the harm or awareness of risk of harm during sentencing.[109]

There is another consideration that militates against grading offences by fault elements which should be mentioned briefly. The harm specified as the object of the offender's incriminating intention in offences against the person, whether it is death or some lesser harm, is always a minimal set of the factors that constitute the physical, emotional and social dimensions of that harm. Some offenders will have minimal understanding of the extent of suffering that will result from their crime. For most murder victims and their families or associates, death is a catastrophe but it is unnecessary, in a murder trial, to prove that the offender intended to cause a catastrophe of that nature or magnitude. It is sufficient to prove that the defendant's intention to kill included the minimal set of elements that mark the obvious difference between a person who is alive and a person who is dead.

Similar considerations apply in cases where injury short of death is inflicted intentionally. The moral spectrum may be even more extended here, for 'injury' is a more complex predicate than 'death'. It makes no difference, when liability is in issue, that the offender was not aware of the emotional, social or economic implications of the infliction of injury before the act was done. Nor does it matter that the act was no sooner done than regretted. Impulsive and intentional harms may be less blameworthy than calculated exposure to risk or callous indifference to consequences.

I have argued that the imperfect match between considerations that go to moral responsibility and considerations that go to the attribution of intention, recklessness and negligence militate against grading offences by reference to fault elements. The sentencing enquiry which follows a finding of guilt offers the hope or promise of a more responsive enquiry into blameworthiness.

109 *R v De Simoni* (1981) 147 CLR 383.

V. SENTENCING AS A COMMUNICATIVE RELATIONSHIP

In his study of the *lex talionis*, William Miller remarks that it is not necessary for a 'perfect revenge' that its victim be told why he is about to die; for the avenger, the payback may be all the more satisfying or perfect in its retribution if the victim 'did not know what hit him or for what'.[110] Criminal punishment, on the other hand, is necessarily articulate. In exchange for revenge, the criminal process offers the victim the promise that the offender will be sentenced to a penalty that will represent a lawful and proportionate return for the wrong or harm done to the victim. The court is bound to explain the reasons for its sentence to the offender.[111] I began section II with a quotation from JR Lucas, asserting that the core idea of responsibility is the offender's obligation to answer the question: 'Why did you do it?' In this section, I suggest that the law recognises that obligation to the extent at least of providing a set of incentives to induce offenders to engage in the sentencing enquiry as a communicative dialogue. South Australian sentencing law, which is unusual in its solicitude for victims of crime, provides an illustration of the possibilities.

The sentencing enquiry is based on the assumption that there is a communicative relationship between the offender, the court and the victim in which the offender is obliged to listen to what the court and the victim have to say and obliged to make a response. The legal incentives to listen are well established in South Australian law. The incentives to speak are less developed. They can be discerned, however, in the emerging rules of proof of factors that will aggravate or mitigate the offence. First, however, there is the obligation to listen.

Victims are permitted to address the court in written statements and orally and to provide an account of the effect that the crime has had on their lives.[112] Considerable latitude is permitted in the form of the statement that the victim will make though there are restraints against vilification of the offender and statements that directly address the question of an appropriate penalty. The offender must be present in court for sentencing and during the presentation of the victim impact statement.[113] The sentencing

[110] WI Miller, *Eye for an Eye* (Cambridge, Cambridge University Press, 2006) 151.

[111] South Australia and the Australian Capital Territory make the obligation explicit in legislation: Criminal Law Sentencing Act 1988 (SA), s 9; Crimes (Sentencing) Act 2005 (ACT), s 82. In other jurisdictions, where the obligation is not given explicit statutory recognition, requirements for explanation vary. Discussed in *Same Time, Same Crime*, Australian Law Reform Commission Report, No 103 (Canberra, ALRC, 2006) <http://www.austlii.edu.au/au/other/alrc/publications/reports/103/> at paras 13.35–13.61; 19.2–19.14.

[112] The account that follows draws on the Criminal Law Sentencing Act 1988 (SA), pt 2—*General Sentencing Provisions*.

[113] Section 9B, Criminal Law (Sentencing) Act 1988 (SA). Amending legislation, the Criminal Law (Sentencing) (Sentencing Procedure) Amendment Act 2001 (SA), was passed during legal proceedings against Peter Liddy, a paedophile, to compel offenders to be present in court, during the presentation of victim impact statements: see *R v Liddy* (2002) 81 SASR 22.

remarks of the trial judge are delivered orally and made available to the media. Bleby J provided an eloquent account of the purpose of the sentencing hearing and the pronouncement of sentence in rebuking a judge who expressed the view that the process was a waste of his time:

> The expression of victim impact statements and of a Judge's sentencing remarks are not matters which can be done effectively in a remote, clinical or impersonal way. They are important messages to a person, and are messages which that person, often not well educated, is required to hear, to understand and to face up to. That must be done in the most effective way possible, without the person being able to avoid the message. The Court will fail in its duty to that person and to those who rely on the Court to carry out its duty if it imposes possible barriers to the effective hearing and understanding of those messages.[114]

Implicit in South Australian practice is an acceptance of Antony Duff's assertion that the criminal process ought to compel the offender, so far as it can, to recognise the wrong done to the victim and to apologise for it.[115] Recognition of the wrong may be taken to include the obligation to explain why the harm was done, when explanation is necessary. When the sentencing enquiry concludes, the pronouncement of the sentence, which condemns the offence and stigmatises the offender, is itself part of the penalty for the offence. The conduct of the offender during the trial and sentencing hearing[116] will be taken into account in determining the sentence. Of course, it is possible that the offender's interests will be best served by saying nothing, for fear of revealing even more damning facts. The inducements to participate in the sentencing enquiry are, however, not insubstantial.

There will be cases in which the facts are eloquent and there is nothing to be said by the offender, beyond an apology for what was done. My concern, however, is with those cases in which an enquiry is necessary to establish what the offender did and why it was done, if the obligation to provide an explanation is to be fulfilled. There are limits, of course, to the measures that can be taken to compel explanation, an expression of remorse or an apology.[117] There is, it can be suggested, a right to recalcitrant impenitence

[114] *Leach* (2003) 38 A Crim R 281, 287; *R v Becker* [2005] SASC 186.

[115] RA Duff, *Punishment, Communication and Community* (Oxford University Press, 2001) 114.

[116] The nature and extent of the offender's responsibility for recalcitrant or hurtful conduct during the trial is bounded in ways that cannot be explored here. See *Siganto v The Queen* [1998] 194 CLR 656, 663, citing earlier authority for the proposition that 'it is impermissible to increase what is a proper sentence for an offence in order to mark the court's disapproval of the accused's having put the issue to proof or having presented a time-wasting or even scurrilous defence'.

[117] Discussed in RA Duff, *Trials and Punishments* (Cambridge University Press, 1986) 132–5 with reference to the right to silence.

in the face of an established finding of guilt. Whatever the extent or nature of that right, however, it could not justify a claim comparable to the rights that obtain before guilt is established. The right to silence is lost after a verdict of guilt and the offender is no longer entitled to the benefit of the doubt.

A succession of cases over recent years has established the rules governing fact finding in the sentencing enquiry.[118] The prosecution must establish, beyond reasonable doubt, any fact that would aggravate the offence. The offender must prove, on the balance of probabilities, any fact that would mitigate the offence. Where the facts are uncertain or disputed, the court must sentence on the known facts, however exiguous.[119] In such a case the offender is entitled to no charitable assumptions so far as mitigating factors are concerned. In circumstances where a mitigation or aggravation cannot be proved, the penalty will express the court's uncertainty about the facts, neither inclining to the lenience sought by the offender nor to the severity sought by the prosecution.

Since the sentencing enquiry is not limited by anything resembling a presumption of innocence, the benefits to the offender of maintaining silence in the face of an accusation are correspondingly diminished. If nothing more can be established, the objective circumstances of the case and the degree of harm suffered by the victim will be the primary determinants of the proportionate penalty. Prevarication or silence on the part of the offender during the sentencing hearing cannot increase the sentence beyond the proportionate limit, nor can it provide a substitute for an unproved prosecution allegation. Considerable discretion is exercised, however, within those constraints and recalcitrance will have a direct bearing on the question whether the proportionate penalty should be mitigated for remorse.[120] These are significant inducements to participate and to provide a believable explanation and apology.

It may seem a paradox of this proposal for the reconstruction of the offences against the person that it would exclude the jury, which is supposed to speak with the voice of common sense, from the fine-grained enquiry into matters of human behaviour and motivation that will follow its verdict. If one considers the role of the modern jury, however, and its

[118] *R v Olbrich* (1999) 199 CLR 270, *Weininger v The Queen* (2004) 217 CLR 198 and *R v Storey* [1998] 1 VR 359, are the doctrinal salients.

[119] *R v Olbrich* (1999) 199 CLR 270.

[120] The penalty can include, in this way, a component for 'reactive fault' that is contained by the principle of proportionate punishment for the harm done. On reactive fault in corporate sentencing law, see B Fisse and J Braithwaite, *Corporations, Crime and Accountability* (Cambridge, Cambridge University Press, 1993) 48. The extension of reactive fault to individual offenders is discussed briefly in J Braithwaite, *Restorative Justice and Responsive Regulation* (Oxford, Oxford University Press, 2002) 118–20 and P Cane, *Responsibility in Law and Morality* (Oxford, Hart Publishing, 2002) 36–9.

access to information that might provide a basis for its enquiries, it is far from clear that it is a paradox.[121] Moreover, the paradox, if it is that, is of less consequence in jurisdictions where liability for these offences is commonly settled by a plea bargain. Of more concern is the practice of the defendant and prosecutor settling on an 'agreed statement of facts' that will exclude or limit the possibility of an enquiry into the offender's intentions during sentence. That practice, in which fault elements are used as bargaining chips, is inimical to the enquiry into responsibility and the obligation to answer for wrongful harms.[122]

VI. CONCLUDING REMARKS

Two fugitive themes have accompanied my argument for relocating the enquiry into the extent of the offender's responsibility for harm in the sentencing hearing. The first has to do with the role of intention in legislative practice and the second with negligence which, in all jurisdictions except South Australia, marks the threshold of liability in the offences of causing serious harm to another.

The evolutionary process that I have sketched, in which the statutory offences against the person were transformed into offences of causing harm, akin to the common law homicides, has obscured the role of intention in both traditional and modern legislative practice. Australian common law has always tended towards an undifferentiated blend of intention, recklessness and negligence in a generic concept of 'criminal intent'.

The general part of the Model Criminal Code was a significant advance on the confusions of Australian common law in its attempt to distinguish the concepts. The fault element definitions are still, however, geared to the assumption that the distinctions are important primarily because they mark degrees or grades of culpability. The definitions, in particular the definition of intention which extends to include 'oblique intention', do not reflect the requirements of legislative practice. Statutory criminal law, which has doubled and re-doubled its bulk in recent years, requires a far more precise vocabulary of fault. Unlawful activities are increasingly distinguished from lawful activities by legislative specification of the objectives of those who

[121] It is arguable that the primary purpose of the trial, as it has developed, is to test the strength of the prosecution case: J Langbein, *The Origins of the Adversary Criminal Trial* (Oxford, Oxford University Press, 2003) ch 5. If that premise is accepted, it may be taken to provide some further persuasive grounds for locating an enquiry into the offender's intentions, beliefs and motivation in the sentencing enquiry.

[122] See *Nemer v Holloway and Others* (2003) 87 SASR 147 at 168, for a particularly striking episode in which a determined victim successfully contested a negotiated plea bargain between an offender and the Director of Public Prosecutions settling agreed facts. See also *R v AEM Snr, R v KEM, R v MM* [2002] NSWCCA 58.

engage in them. In these offences, which number in the hundreds, the intention with which the activity is pursued delineates the offence and determines the threshold of liability. These offences require a precise, nuanced and context-dependent use of the vocabulary of intention that is unnecessary in the general offences of causing harm to the person. They require, in particular, explicit recognition of the role of ulterior intention in the legislative delineation of prohibited conduct. The recent flood of legislation imposing criminal liability for offences of sedition and terrorism, for example, requires careful distinctions to be drawn between ulterior and oblique intention that are elided in the Model Criminal Code.[123] Recognition of the 'rule articulation' function of the concept of intention is absent from the Australian Criminal Code, which ignores the role that ulterior intention has played in legislative practice since the 16th century, if not earlier.

The second theme concerns the definition of negligence, which involves issues that are no less intractable but of lesser significance.

Negligence is a misnomer for the concept that marks the threshold of liability for the offences of causing harm. The Model Criminal Code adopted a common law definition of negligence as conduct that involves so high a risk and departs so far from 'the standard of care that a reasonable person would exercise in the circumstance ... that the conduct merits criminal punishment for the offence'.[124] The circularity of that definition poses obvious problems that are exacerbated by the fact that there are many serious criminal offences that set a lower threshold for liability.[125] Offences of strict liability, which include a number that are punishable with extreme severity, require less in the way of culpability than do negligence offences. Less obvious is the MCLOC's failure to perceive that the duties owed to others are not limited to taking 'reasonable care' to avoid causing harm. There is also a duty not to wrong others.[126] Antony Duff, among others, distinguishes between a 'wrongful attack' and culpable failure to avoid causing harm:

> If I wrongfully attack you, the harm that I intend figures in my reasons for acting as I do: I act thus because I believe in doing so I will harm you.... If I culpably endanger

[123] See, for example, the critical definition of 'terrorist act' in the Criminal Code (Cth), pt 5.3—Terrorism, s 100.1 which requires proof that conduct, if it is to amount to a terrorist act, was accompanied by an ulterior intention to advance certain causes, to coerce, intimidate and so on.

[124] Model Criminal Code, above n 2, ch 2, 5.5 *Negligence*. The definition was derived from the decision of the Victorian Supreme Court in *Nydam v The Queen* [1977] VR 430. In Griffith Code jurisdictions the negligence standard has traditionally been expressed as 'recklessness involving grave moral guilt deserving of punishment'. Discussed, *R v BBD* [2006] QCA 441.

[125] Compare the US Model Penal Code, s 202(2)(d), which simply insists on a 'gross deviation' from a reasonable standard.

[126] It is significant that the prevailing Australian common law definition of negligence was enunciated in *Nydam v The Queen* [1977] VR 430, which involved conduct intended to threaten that, on the defendant's account of events, resulted in unintended and unexpected death.

> you, by contrast, my reasons for acting as I do may be perfectly legitimate; what goes wrong is that I am not guided by the reason against acting thus (the reason for refraining from the action or taking precautions) that the risk of harm to you provides.[127]

There is certainly a difference between Duff's 'harmful wrongs' and 'wrongful harms', but the difference is gradual rather than sharp. Those references to wrongdoing and 'attack' obscure the reality of an unbroken continuum between active harm and culpable endangering. There are many occasions when conduct that involves an active and unwanted interference with another is acceptable, tolerable or at least excusable. There is, for example, a continuum between socially acceptable practical jokes, that require care to be taken, and conduct that shades into a wrongful or malicious attack.[128] A joke that might be accepted if it comes off is likely to be re-characterised as a wrongful attack if it misfires and unintended injury results. Violent games and dangerous, consensual sexual activity can occupy the same ambiguous territory.[129]

Another area of shaded graduation includes the many situations in which individuals are entitled to take measures involving physical interference with others, in asserting their interests or rights or the interests or rights of others. There are many ways in which the necessities of the occasion can be exceeded in self defence or rescue. Some will involve a culpable failure to take care. Others can hardly be characterised in that way, as for example when excessive force is used in self defence.[130]

There is something akin to a vocal register break in the language of legal responsibility in these cases. Liability for harms that result from failure to take precautions is incurred because the defendant failed to meet a standard of care but liability for harms that result from wrongful acts is incurred because the act can be neither excused nor justified. There is a potential discrepancy in degrees of responsibility between these alternatives

[127] RA Duff, 'Criminalising Endangerment' in Duff and Green, above n 59, at 47. Horder, in the same Duff and Green collection, 32–5, similarly distinguishes between 'active' wrongdoing and 'passive' failure to avoid causing harm. Active wrongdoing, in this sense, is an expression of the 'malice principle' proposed by Horder in an earlier paper, 'Two Histories and Four Hidden Principles of Mens Rea' (1997) 113 *LQR* 95, 96: 'the essence of malicious conduct is conduct wrongfully directed at a particular interest … of the victim.'

[128] See, for example, *R v Hodgetts and Jackson* [1990] 1 Qd R 456, in which a cruel practical joke tragically misfired and killed its victim. For an early example, see *R v Errington* (1838) 2 Lew 217.

[129] Games with guns for instance: *R v Lamb* [1967] 2 QB 981, discussed in Ashworth, above n 65, 5th edn, at 288. See also *Maurice* (1992) 61 A Crim R 30, a case of accidental death during 'blackout sex'.

[130] See, for example, *Mason v WA* (2005) 154 A Crim R 219, in which the offender, threatened by the occupants of an oncoming car, lobbed a rock through the windscreen causing the death of one of the occupants.

because one requires a *gross* departure from acceptable standards while the other imposes the more demanding standard of justification or excuse.[131] The problem has long been familiar in the law of manslaughter, in which dangerous unlawful acts and gross negligence are alternative grounds for liability and the same difficulty in expressing equivalent standards of fault is apparent. An acceptable concept of negligence would encompass the duties that are owed to others to avoid both harmful wrongs and wrongful harms. Perhaps the threshold test for liability, when liability for causing serious harm is in issue, should be one that requires, in either case, a serious or gross breach of the duty not to cause harm to the victim of the offence.

But the negligence problem is one for another day. It has no significant consequences for the general provisions of the Model Code for it is limited in its effects to offences of causing harm. Among the offences of the Model Code, offences that impose criminal liability for harmful results are a small and specialised minority. The more significant defects in the general provisions of the Code, which define the relationship between intention and recklessness, were a consequence of the mistaken idea that the offences of causing harm are of paradigmatic importance as models for legislative theory and practice.

[131] The oscillation between liability for 'wrongful harm' and 'harmful wrong' is painfully apparent in the Queensland Court of Criminal Appeal decision in *R v Hodgetts and Jackson* [1990] 1 Qd R 456. A canonical discussion of the issue can be found in P Brett, 'Manslaughter and the Motorist' (1953) 27 *Australian Law Journal* 6.

Index

www.ingramcontent.com/pod-product-compliance
Ingram Content Group UK Ltd.
Pitfield, Milton Keynes, MK11 3LW, UK
UKHW020239290926
15470UKWH00002B/632

9 781841 138893